Astrological Psychology

The Huber Method

edited by Barry Hopewell

HopeWell

Knutsford, England

Original course material for the *Diploma in Astrological Psychology* 1985-2016
First published in the UK in 2017 by HopeWell

HopeWell
130 Grove Park, Knutsford
Cheshire WA16 8QD, UK
www.hopewellpublisher.com

on behalf of the Astrological Psychology Association
www.astrologicalpsychology.org

Copyright © Astrological Psychology Association 2017

Editorial team: Barry Hopewell (lead), Ghislaine Adams, Iris Schencks, Joyce Hopewell

Cover design: Barry Hopewell
Cover images show the three charts (nodal, natal, house) of Bruno Huber

Astrological charts reproduced using Cathar software,
www.catharsoftware.com

ISBN: 978-0-9956736-0-1

Dedication

to Richard Llewellyn, original course creator

and in memory of Bruno and Louise Huber, the pioneers of astrological psychology and the Huber Method.

Acknowledgements

The APA Diploma Course and this book on which it is based were created by the co-operative efforts of many people who supported and benefited from astrological psychology.

Worthy of special mention in this multitude are the following:

Richard Llewellyn, who created the original course for the Diploma in Astrological Psychology.

Pamela Tyler, who was the catalyst for getting that process going.

Joyce Hopewell, David Kerr and Ghislaine Adams who have over many years stewarded and safeguarded the content of the course manuals and improved them to their current level of usability.

In addition to the above, the numerous other tutors who have worked with their students and the material, and improved it over the years: Alice Llewellyn, Brenda Miller, Val Burnham, Brian Vickery, Joan Swallow, Jonathan Powell, Jan Romander, Amos Siohn, Yvonne Taylor, Diana Brandt, Sira Beaumayne, Jeremy Cooper, Deborah Maw, Lola Ferrer, Maggie Lewis, Donald Millar, Wendy Oak, Sue Seymour, Nascita Williams, Nadja McDevitt, Christa Hensel, Jaki Rothery, Sue Cameron, Sue Lewis, Kathy Rogers, Iris Schencks, and Trish Crawford.

Colin Wilton, Reyn Swallow, Jane Brooks, Andy Duncan, Sara Inkster, Elly Gibbs, Linda Tinsley, Barbara Byatt, Sue Parker and many others who have done the unsung background work that made all this possible.

The many students who have gone through this life enhancing process and provided us with such positive feedback, particularly from the UK, US, Spain, Scandinavia and South Africa.

And not forgetting other Huber schools in Spain (notably Rosa Solé, Joan Solé), Switzerland (the Huber family) and Germany (notably Wolfhard König, Harald Zittlau) who have remained in contact along the way.

The whole process would not have been possible in the modern age without the development of chart software corresponding with the Huber approach - notably Cathar Software run by Juan Saba in Argentina and more recently Astrodienst (www.astro.com).

This book is the result of a long collaborative multinational learning process that has along the way validated the approach pioneered by Bruno and Louise.

With heartfelt thanks to you all.

Contents

Preface

Becoming Whole

The Huber Method of Astrological Psychology

Modern psychological understanding shows that most of us never fulfil our true potential, and we often end up in life situations that do not align with our true inner selves. Often, we are trapped in behaviour patterns learned from childhood that are never really transcended. Or we find ourselves in materialistic roles that do not fulfil our spiritual nature. Or we simply have no idea why we do things.

At its leading edge, modern science has shown that the Newtonian mechanistic universe is an illusion and all is interconnected, indirectly validating the assertions of astrologers over the ages. Indeed, astrology is alive and well to this day.

Assisted by the founder of psychosynthesis, Roberto Assagioli, Swiss astrologer/psychologists Bruno and Louise Huber researched their two subjects over many years and came up with a new system of 'astrological psychology', using astrological charts to assist in the process of psychological and spiritual growth. It encompasses our heredity, environment, spirituality and links with the cosmos. Thus are we made more whole – both within ourselves, and in our integration with the world and the universe. Their approach became known as the 'Huber Method'.

Based on the Astrological Psychology Association's long-running *Diploma Course in Astrological Psychology*, this book introduces all the main features of astrological psychology, together with a progressive set of exercises which will help you to learn more about yourself and, if you so choose, embark on the path of helping others.

Introduction

Bruno Huber described this approach to psychology through astrology as 'gilt edged', in that he could diagnose within one or two sessions psychological problems that would only become clear after many hours of psychoanalysis. Known as the **Huber Method**, this approach has also proved an invaluable personal aid to psychological and spiritual growth.

This book presents, in a single volume, a comprehensive description of the Huber Method and a systematic approach to learning it. It is based on the course for the *Diploma in Astrological Psychology*, offered to new students by the Astrological Psychology Association between 1985-2016.

You can use this book on a number of levels, and you will get out of it according to what you put in.

If you simply read the text, you will gain an appreciation of what is involved in astrological psychology, but are not likely to be much changed by the experience. This book certainly provides a valuable reference to most of the features of astrological psychology.

However, this book is more than that. It is really a working book to help you to learn about yourself, and about astrological psychology, and thus become more whole. Each major section of the book includes at the end an exercise, related to your own birth charts. Additionally, after every alternate chapter, there is a further exercise to consolidate your learning so far. If you assiduously do all these exercises, you will likely gain much insight into yourself, your history, environmental influences, motivations and so on.

You may be doing this simply for your own personal development. Many people are profoundly changed by their experience in this learning process.

You may be doing this to improve your ability to help others, add another string to your bow of counselling/consulting aids, which has been done by many professionals in this area, including psychoanalysts. In the hands of an experienced professional the birth chart can prove to be a very rapid diagnostic tool pinpointing problem areas.

In either case, this is likely to trigger changes in your life. You may at some point need to consider some sort of counselling to help you along the way, if you do not have a suitable support network around you.

We recommend that you also look at as many charts as you can, particularly family members or friends who are willing to be part of your learning process. This is likely to give you a greater insight, which will certainly be needed if you are going to work with others.

You will find a number of 'study resources' to help your studies on the website www.astrologicalpsychology.org. This includes details of any tutors willing to work alongside you in your studies, which is likely to greatly speed and add depth to your learning process.

Be aware that this is not a 'quick fix' process. The time taken to complete this process may be a number of years, as your psychological and astrological understanding begins to mature. But it does work. You are unlikely to engage in this process and emerge without having obtained great benefit, both for yourself and for those around you.

We wish you well in your studies!

What you need to know

To get the most out of working through this book you need to have a basic understanding of astrology, which you can obtain from a wide variety of sources such as books, websites and courses.

This will involve an understanding of the following:
- the basic astronomy of the solar system
- the signs of the zodiac, the planets and the houses, their relationships (illustrated in Figure 0.5) and archetypal meanings
- their relationships with the elements or temperaments fire, earth, air and water, and with the qualities cardinal, fixed and mutable (e.g. Figure 0.4)
- the concept of aspects, planetary latitude and longitude and the birth chart
- the various approaches to astrology, such as mundane, electional, medical, horary, predictive...
- the nodes of the Moon
- the variety of house systems.

The glyphs used here for planets, signs and aspects are introduced along the way. A brief illustration is in Figures 0.1-3.

Glyphs and Correspondences

Ego Planets		Tool Planets		Transpersonal Planets	
Sun	☉	Mercury	☿	Uranus	♅
Moon	☽	Venus	♀	Neptune	♆
Saturn	♄	Mars	♂	Pluto	♇
		Jupiter	♃		

ascending Moon Node = North Node ☊

Figure 0.1 Planet glyphs

Aries	♈	♎	Libra
Taurus	♉	♏	Scorpio
Gemini	♊	♐	Sagittarius
Cancer	♋	♑	Capricorn
Leo	♌	♒	Aquarius
Virgo	♍	♓	Pisces

Figure 0.2 Sign glyphs

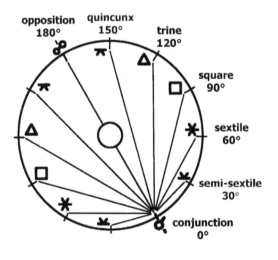

Figure 0.3 Aspect glyphs

	Cardinal	Fixed	Mutable
Fire	Aries	Leo	Sagittarius
Earth	Capricorn	Taurus	Virgo
Air	Libra	Aquarius	Gemini
Water	Cancer	Scorpio	Pisces

Figure 0.4 Sign Qualities

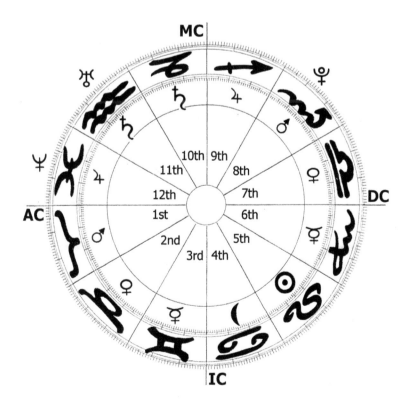

Figure 0.5 House/Sign/Planet ruler correspondences

Note
With the discovery of the outer planets, earlier sign rulers were supplanted. Their archetypal/ energy relationship remains. Sign rulers are not in themselves emphasised in astrological psychology.

4

Chapter 1. In the Beginning

This first chapter introduces a number of concepts to provide the foundation for your study of Astrological Psychology. Later chapters go into detail about particular areas, building up to a consolidation of the overall picture in chapter 8.

Contents:

1.1 Introduction

This introductory section provides you with:

- some history on the development of astrological psychology and the Huber Method, and the organisations that were involved in developing the course for the *Diploma in Astrological Psychology*, on which this book is based.

- an outline of some important features of the Huber approach to the natal chart.

Origins

The Hubers

Bruno Huber's early background includes the formal study of physics, astronomy, psychology and philosophy and it is in the latter subjects that his and Louise's interests combined after their marriage in 1953. Both had also been studying astrology for a number of years prior to this.

Whilst continuing to study the history of religions and parapsychology they began their early investigative work into astrology. During the period between 1956 and 1958 they helped with the foundation of the *Arcane School* in Geneva before going to Italy to work as assistants to Roberto Assagioli at his *Psychosynthesis Institute* in Florence. Here, for three years, they were able to intensify their astrological research because of the amount of psychological comparison data that was available. It became obvious to them that astrology and psychology were closely inter-related, and through subsequent work a clearly defined concept to translate one into the other was developed.

In 1962 Bruno and Louise moved back to Switzerland and continued to research psychological counselling through the birth chart. In 1968 they started teaching and founded the Swiss *Astrologisch-Psychologisches-Institut* (API), devoting their lives to further research and teaching. They ran seminars in many countries and trained more than 8,000 students all over the world, many of these being professional men and women engaged in medical and therapeutic fields

After Bruno Huber's untimely death in November 1999, their son, Michael, took over more responsibility for the teaching and training offered by API in Switzerland. Other training centres were soon established in Switzerland and Germany, which remains the centre of gravity of this work.

Bruno & Louise's approach became known as the Huber Method, an intensively researched, highly detailed and comprehensive way of analysing a birth chart. Their use of astrology follows traditional thinking in many respects, with the addition of innovations resulting from their understanding of modern psychology and their astrological-psychological researches. At the same time, however, it has stripped away many confusing issues which have built up over past centuries, concentrating on the most psychologically significant astrological factors.

You can learn more about the Hubers and the development of astrological psychology on the website www.astrologicalpsychology.org.

Astrological Psychology in the UK

The English-language school was conceived by astrologers Richard Llewellyn (UK) and Pamela Tyler (USA) in the summer of 1983. It had become clear that many English speaking astrologers wanted to learn more than was possible from the infrequent English language seminars the Hubers were able to include in their crowded work schedule.

Richard spent two years intensively studying the Hubers' approach and writing the original *Diploma Course* manuals which have evolved continuously since then to provide the basis for this book.

The first students were enrolled by the *Astrological Psychology Institute UK* in the spring of 1985. The course provided tuition by correspondence, along with workshop seminars which proved a valuable part of the learning process.

Astrology is seen not as an end in itself, but as the means to an end. This process aims to help you to work with a birth chart to achieve greater self-understanding and awareness as part of an ongoing process of personal growth and fulfilment. This understanding may then be used to help others.

A few years later the course was translated to Spanish, providing the basis for the *Spanish Huber School*, and into German where it was offered as an option by API.

In September 2003, API-UK reformed as a membership organisation - the *Astrological Psychology Association* (APA), which continued to offer tutored courses to new students until the end of 2016, when the decision was taken to make the materials available to everyone in this book.

Over those years 1985-2016 many hundreds of English-speaking students enrolled to train in the Huber Method.

An overview of this book

This book comprises 8 chapters, outlined briefly below. To use the book to lead your learning process into astrological psychology and yourself, you are recommended to follow the sections in numerical order, assiduously performing the exercises at the end of each section before proceeding to the next.

1. In the Beginning - seeing the birth chart from a psychological point of view.
Chapter 1 introduces psychosynthesis and the concept of the **five levels of the chart** and how these relate to Roberto Assagioli's **Egg model**.

2. The Aspect Level – Inner Motivation
Chapter 2 introduces the **aspects** between planets in the chart and how they signify inner motivation. This includes colour, shaping, cohesion and direction of the aspect structure, and an introduction to **aspect patterns**.

3. The Planet Level – Levels of Consciousness
Chapter 3 considers the **planets**, in the major categories of tool, ego and transpersonal planets, and their association with subpersonalities. This is related to **levels of consciousness**, showing how increasing conscious awareness affects the ways in which the planets function – from early impulsiveness to the wider levels of the transpersonal.

4. The House Level – Meeting the World
Chapter 4 covers the astrological **houses** and the ways in which the inner motivation of the personality seeks to find expression in the world. This includes consideration of hemispheres, quadrants, the **house intensity curve** with the important concepts of low point and stress planets, and the resolution of **polarities** that may occur across various axes.

5. Nature or Nurture?
Chapter 6 shows four ways in which conflicts of nature versus nurture may emerge from the birth chart. The **Family Model** shows relationships between the child and parents. The **House Chart** identifies environmental influences that may conflict with innate characteristics in the natal chart. Position of planets by house and sign in the natal chart may show **conflicting demands**, which may be emphasised by the system of **Dynamic Calculations**.

6. The Element of Time
Chapter 6 considers how time is reflected in the birth chart, starting with the Hubers' method of **Age Progression**, which provides a life clock of significant influences over a lifetime. This is related to other astrological techniques of **Transits** and Progressions. Finally it is considered how age progression can be used as an aid to **rectifying** an unknown birth time.

7. Personal and Transpersonal Growth
Chapter 7 discusses the process of personal development through **integration of the ego**. It looks at the important role of the **Moon Nodes** and the **Ascendant** as indicators for spiritual development. Finally, the **Moon Node Chart** is introduced as a tool to better understand our 'shadow' side and provide insight into unconscious drives.

8. Applied Astrological Psychology
Chapter 8 aims to consolidate the method of chart interpretation described in chapters 1-7. It considers the implications of working as an **astrological consultant**, and working with the **three charts** together - Natal, House and Moon Node. The final section brings it all together with **practical chart interpretation**.

Approach

The materials in this book should be accepted as guidelines. They do not profess to teach 'The Truth' since, as individuals we can only discover what this is for ourselves. The content is based on empirical research by the Hubers, supplemented by the experience of other astrological psychology practitioners.

The work carried out by the Hubers over the years enabled them to establish a form of astrological psychosynthesis – which offers an exciting alternative way of perceiving a birth chart and examining the layers of human existence, from the central core of the psyche (or Self) to the environment in which we live.

Psychosynthesis is, in part, the process of discovering, understanding and developing the many sub-personalities which make up a complete personality. These subpersonalities can be likened to a whole crowd of people living within you. Awareness of 'who' makes up the crowd, and of the relationships between them, will make it easier to learn how to make them function more effectively in our lives.

Awareness of who we are, of how we behave in the world, of what lies in the unconscious, and so on is an essential first step in making possible any growth of consciousness which will allow for a greater sense of 'wholeness' and personal fulfilment. Experience has shown that learning how to interpret your birth chart can prove to be an important step in your own process of becoming more self-aware and you may even discover that it has proved to be a turning point in your life.

Astrological psychology provides a modern, psychological approach to the analysis of a natal chart which will enable you to discern subpersonalities, unconscious motivations, temperament, and other energies symbolised in the chart. The whole personality can be more clearly understood and the paradoxes of traditional interpretation need not present a problem. With astrological psychosynthesis it is easier to grasp the relevance of the multitude of energies, and understand the ease or the difficulties that are likely to be encountered in expressing and using them in everyday life.

It is important to realise that we are all unique beings and that the **reality** of the same chart placement of, say, Venus in Scorpio in two charts will most likely be different for each of the two people concerned. For this reason you should try to avoid making rigid interpretations of a chart placement or aspect because there can be no single definition of any significator. The chart has to be viewed and understood as a picture of dynamic and developing energies, some of which may be dominant and others repressed. As you work through this book you are encouraged to become aware of the way in which these energies flow and how they might influence your life experiences.

Developing your understanding of energy flow, and how this is likely to affect attitudes and behaviour, avoids being restricted by text book definitions. Human behaviour and the reasons for it are so complex that no single text book could encompass its full range, let alone relate it to astrological symbols. The Hubers' approach is an intensively researched, highly detailed and comprehensive way of analysing a chart. There is nothing dramatically new in its concept because it follows traditional thinking in many respects. At the same time, however, it has stripped away many confusing issues which have built up over past centuries and it has combined this refined historic astrological knowledge with modern psychological knowledge.

If you are already a practising astrologer we suggest that you do not you attempt to combine existing concepts with new ones encountered in this book. It is better to make a clean break with any technique you are currently using, and introduce the Huber approach in its place. You will find it comparatively straightforward and immensely satisfying and, afterwards, you can return to any technique with which you are at present familiar, should you feel it is still relevant.

It is not possible for 40 years of knowledge and experience to be condensed into a single book or course. Learning is an ongoing experience and the book provides a broad and deep foundation upon which to build.

You will find that a theme or a statement may be repeated in different sections of the book and this will be either because of its importance or because its relevance overlaps and therefore needs to be seen in more than one context. Where repetition occurs the theme is likely to have been expressed in a different way so that you can see it from another perspective and gain a deeper understanding of its meaning.

As you work through each chapter, remember to look at your chart as being symbolic of you as a whole person. This means that you should not take any one significator in the chart, attach a 'cook-book keyword' interpretation to it and consider it out of the context of the whole. Try to develop an ability to focus on one area of your life, or on one sub-personality, and see the relevance of your assessment in the context of your overall potential and growth.

Practical Experience

Gaining practical experience through working on your own chart and the charts of people you know, and testing out the reality of the theory on which you are working, will greatly enhance your learning process. To assist this process an exercise is included at the end of each section, plus a further exercise after every two chapters to consolidate your learning so far. Your learning depends the degree of attention you give to these exercises or similar practical work.

Birth Charts

Huber charts vary in certain respects from all other astrological birth charts.

Therefore it is essential to only use charts generated by software that is capable of producing these charts. At the time of writing, such software is provided by the programs produced by Cathar Software (www.catharsoftware.com) or the web service provided by Astro-Dienst (www.astro.com). For the latest situation you can check the APA website www.astrologicalpsychology. org, for information on software, online and chart data services.

We have also included information on how to draw up a Huber chart manually. While it is possible to learn the whole system using only computer generated charts, you should be aware that in the early stages of learning interpretation it is often a valuable practice to manually draw charts. The time spent in doing this can provide the opportunity for feeling your way into and really getting to know the details of the chart.

Resources

Books

In the bibliography you will find a list of recommended books on astrology and psychology, including those by Bruno and Louise Huber.

We encourage you to read as widely as possible to put your studies into a broad perspective.

APA website

The APA website www.astrologicalpsychology.org provides a valuable information resource, and a means of keeping up to date. It currently includes:

- **study resources** which can be downloaded to assist and supplement your studies.

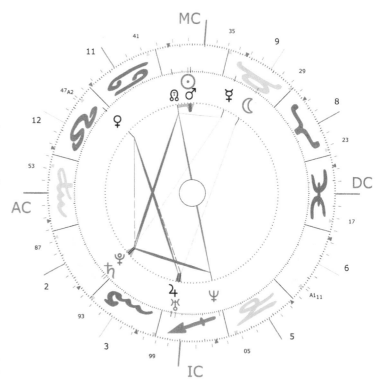

Figure 1.1.0 Chart for the Formation of API UK
Produced by MegaStar
08.06.1983, 12:30, London, UK

- **Tutor register** containing details of those offering tutoring to help you through the learning process of this book.

- **Consultants' register**, listing those offering consultation using astrological psychology. You may find it helpful to refer to one of them if you get 'stuck'.

- information on availability of **Huber software** and **chart/ data services**.

- **APA bookshop** offering recommended titles, at a discount for members.

- a **blog and Twitter feed** with news and features.

- newsletter/magazine **Conjunction** and articles not available elsewhere, available to members.

- links to related astrological/psychological websites.

Other Publications

MP3 recordings are available of lectures given at Astrological Association Conferences by Bruno and Louise Huber and a number of Huber practitioners, including Jonathan Powell, Richard Llewellyn, Val Burnham, Joyce Hopewell, Ghislaine Adams, Sue Lewis, Kathy Rogers, Marilyn Burnett. Details are on the website www.astrologicalassociation.com.

What is Astrological Psychology?

This outline was written by Bruno Huber for inclusion in his 'Astrological Glossary' and was translated from the German by Agnes Shellens.

Astrological Psychology is a branch of psychology which uses astrology as a diagnostic tool. It is primarily based on the insights of depth psychology, but also on humanistic and transpersonal psychology. In concept it is closest to Robert Assagioli's **psychosynthesis**.

Astrological Psychology starts from the concept of a living, self-regulating and inherently healthy human being and not, like most psychologies, from the standpoint of pathology. *"You are sick only for as long as you think you are"* and to find the causes for our feelings of dis-ease is a central tenet of astrological psychology.

The basic purpose of Astrological Psychology, through its teaching, advisory or therapeutic approach, is to increase our understanding and to stimulate our own thought processes. It is not to dish out ready made recipes, nor to offer easy solutions but to offer us a useful instrument for self-discovery so that we can learn to accept ourselves for what we are and what we may be, as this will enable us to live freer, happier and more creative lives.

First and foremost it offers a holistic approach to our human condition. This does not just apply to psychological concepts, as it includes our choice of astrological techniques. The methodology of Astrological Psychology has to comply with the prerequisite that all its constituent parts work together to form a coherent whole. It is a method complete in itself, but it is not closed to further developments or refinements.

Even so, it was for this very reason unavoidable that some techniques of traditional astrology had to be excluded because, although logical and valid within themselves, they did not fit into the whole picture. For example, techniques not used are those which depict man as being dependent and without free will, plus those which create a "loop" effect and thereby distort the whole picture.

Above all there are the various techniques of foretelling the future, which are largely reductionist, and usually deal with events which are perceived as happening to us from the outside. It is the state of our inner being which determines the nature of our reality, how the available energies affect us, which external events make an impression upon us and how we experience them, evaluate them and respond to

them. This reactive world in Astrological Psychology is expressed and interpreted by the Age Point and Age Progression. This is a steady progression through time which shows how we work our way through our chart and thus, in the course of a life time, experience all the various facets of our character.

The choice of techniques employed has been influenced by an important organic principle: **simplification**. Today's method of using our intellect is predominantly linear and logical, the cause and effect approach which proceeds via precise analytical steps. It has the tendency to divide a whole organism into its individual constituent parts, and thereby leads to fragmentation and over-complication, until in the end we lose sight of both means and aims. A multitude of techniques doesn't actually help us to arrive at a valid chart interpretation; in fact it only succeeds in making it more difficult.

It is often maintained in astrological thinking and teaching that an interpretation can only be valid when it has been confirmed by a variety of techniques. In Astrological Psychology we think the opposite; if we feel we have to make a number of parallel pronouncements in order to achieve clarity it simply means that we haven't sufficiently exploited the primary information at our disposal. That is why we state very clearly the basic tenets of our method; they were discussed by Ptolemy.

The following are the four fundamental tools:

1. The **aspect patterns** – all aspects are multiples of 30° – they show motivation

2. The **10 planets** and the Moon's north node – the tools at our disposal

3. The **12 signs of the zodiac** – our genetic makeup, the archetypes.

4. The **12 houses,** or fields – our conditioning, learned behaviour.

This fundamental information is utilised to the utmost advantage, in great detail and with precise definitions depending on position in one of the four major areas of the chart – the **quadrants**.

Now read on!

Astrological Roots

We begin with a few words about how the Huber approach developed and how it is different from aspects of traditional astrology, which may help you to understand something of the territory you are about to explore. Bruno and Louise Huber did not claim to have invented a new astrology. They were constantly at pains to point to their links with astrological understandings which stretch back over two thousand years.

It was Ptolemy, among others, who proposed that the earth was at the centre of the universe, and that the planets went around it. Our present-day birth charts are still drawn from this geocentric point of view, even though we now know that the Sun is the centre of our Solar system, rotating around the centre of our galaxy which in turn revolves around the centre of the still relatively unknown universe. Symbolically, the earth is still the centre of the human being's world, and the planets continue to move in relation to it. The birth chart drawn from the geocentric viewpoint has meaning for the individual in relationship to the wider universe.

Ptolemy was aware of the existence of just the seven planets visible to the naked eye, so all the astrological knowledge of that time was developed without any awareness of Uranus, Neptune and Pluto. The relationships between planets and signs expressed a symmetry and balance that is found in nature. Taking 0° Leo as the point of balance, with the Moon and Sun on either side, the planets follow round the zodiac in each direction expressing a quality of that aspect to the point of balance. See Figure 1.1.1 – also Chapter 2 which further explores colour and motivation.

A major difference between the Huber method and other approaches to chart interpretation is that only planetary relationships based on 0° and 30° are used. 30° and the number 12 are the two basic numbers of the circle from which astrology is derived. At a later stage you will find another way in which the Hubers have linked together numbers with the concept of Age Progression.

It is helpful to bear in mind that the various numbers that will be met with in the Huber approach have not arisen randomly, but on closer examination can be seen to have a deep relationship with the unfolding universe, as far as it is known. This follows the tradition of the Hermetic dictum 'As above, so below'. The microcosm is a reflection of the macrocosm.

Reference to Figure 1.1.1 shows

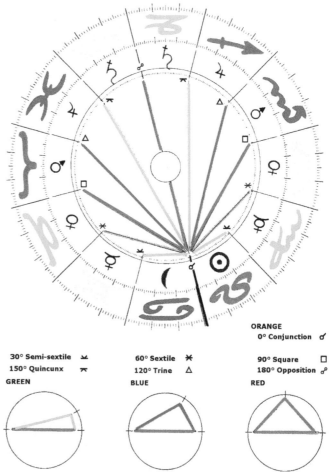

Figure 1.1.1 The Ptolemaic Arrangement of the Aspects

- Mercury, the 30° aspect, is linked with Gemini and Virgo – this is the learning aspect

- Venus, the 60° aspect, has a quality of the easy flow of talent linked with Taurus and Libra

- Mars, the 90° aspect, has the quality of tension and energy associated with Aries and Scorpio

- Jupiter, the 120° aspect, is another flowing aspect of talent linked with Sagittarius and Pisces

- the 150° aspect to Saturn, the great teacher, signifies links with Capricorn and Aquarius.

Thus it can be seen that from long ago man has perceived a balance in the astrological forces surrounding him.

Note

Figure 1.1.1 is important. It illustrates an association of energies found in the birth chart and is a foundation stone for much of what follows. You will find it helpful to study this carefully.

Psychological and Spiritual Roots

Alongside Bruno's insights, Louise brought a deep understanding of esoteric teachings and the ageless wisdom. These teachings have, in more recent times, been linked with Alice Bailey and the Arcane School, but their roots stretch back into history. In this way Louise's contribution is not something which is a new, up-to-the-minute discovery, but is rather the development of deep insights related to the nature and purpose of the individual within the framework of a cosmic viewpoint.

Initially when studying the Huber approach and applying it to your own chart, or to that of others, it is possible to leave to one side the deeper spiritual implications. As our understanding deepens, and depending upon where we are as individuals on our own path, the Huber approach offers a way into a broader concept of our place in the universe, and the purpose and direction of our present life.

Thus the strands that are woven into the Huber approach reach to incorporate insights and knowledge from more than two thousand years ago. Complementing these insights is a modern psychological approach which seeks to understand the conscious and unconscious motivating forces within the individual. Through looking at the chart, firstly as a whole, and then in more detail, themes, directions and areas of conflict emerge.

When, as a young man, Bruno listened to Roberto Assagioli lecturing in Florence, Italy, he was greatly influenced by what he heard about psychosynthesis. Many years later both Bruno and Louise were to spend some time working with Assagioli at the Psychosynthesis Institute, and from this association Bruno developed his ideas about the psychological functioning of the individual as reflected in the natal chart. Psychosynthesis suggests that the individual exists at a number of different levels, or layers, and that the divisions between these layers are permeable. Assagioli's diagram of an individual psyche is shaped like an egg and is shown in Figure 1.1.2.

- In the lower portion of the diagram is represented the **lower unconscious**, which contains much repressed and undigested material. It corresponds with what Freud termed the unconscious.

- The **middle unconscious** is an area of ourselves of which we are not consciously aware but into which we can move and retrieve memories without undue difficulty.

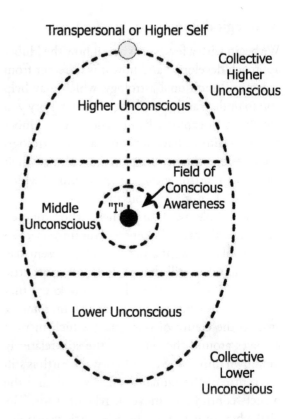

Figure 1.1.2 Assagioli's 'Egg' Model

- The **higher unconscious** is the region from which we receive our higher intuitions and inspirations – artistic, philosophical or scientific, ethical imperatives, and urges to humanitarian and heroic action. The distinction between the lower and higher unconscious is a developmental not a moralistic one. The lower unconscious merely represents the most primitive part of ourselves, the beginner in us so to speak, whereas the higher unconscious represents what we can reach in our evolution.

- The **field of consciousness awareness** is our area of everyday awareness.

- In the centre is our **personal self** or 'I'. It is both active (directing) and passive (observing)

- The **higher self** is that part of us which, whilst retaining a sense of our own individuality, lives at the level of universality, where personal plans and concerns are overshadowed by a wider vision (hence 'transpersonal').

- The Egg lies within the **collective unconscious** as described by CG Jung. There is a **lower**, as well as a **higher** collective unconscious

In the birth chart both the personal and the transpersonal self are symbolised by the circle at the centre of the chart. This self, psyche, or whatever name you wish to use to describe this unique area, has contact with the universal energies and directs them via the aspect structure to the personality represented by the planets.

Aspects of the personality, i.e. mind, body and feelings are seen reflected in the three personal, or ego, planets: Sun, Saturn and Moon. Part of the journey for the individual is the integration of the personality, as distinct from the transpersonal self, which is pure beingness, and has no need of integration.

From an astrological-psychological viewpoint, it is important to keep in mind the distinction between the self and the personality. Many astrological consultations are pitched at the level of the personality, but that is not who the person really is. It is necessary to hold in mind the broader context of the horoscope so that when you look at a chart you begin to see in the aspect structure and in the position of the planets, characteristics which exist at the level of self as well as those at the personality level, either conscious or unconscious.

Some of these characteristics we term sub-personalities – roles, masks or aspects of ourselves that we become, but which are not the true essence of who we are. Others may represent much deeper parts of ourselves with which we can connect in various ways, one of which is through astrological counselling. In time it becomes possible to identify parts of ourselves from the chart, i.e. sub-personalities, of which we may not have been aware. We begin to have a sense of our psychological make-up.

In working through this course of study you will discover how some aspects of the personality work more effectively in the external environment and how other parts represented by different planets can be ways, or tools to be used, in making contact with our inner world.

In addition to providing a means of studying the birth chart for the purpose of understanding the psychological make-up of an individual, Bruno and Louise developed a method of analysis which provides information about the environmental forces which impinge upon a person. Looking at the nature of inherited characteristics and environmental forces through the chart, some indication is obtained about the nature of the qualities which the environment is calling upon the individual to develop.

Simultaneously with this movement towards the integration of the personality is another movement or direction in the chart at a different level. This is the spiritual direction of an individual in this lifetime, as seen through the placement of the Moon's nodes, the outer planets and the higher ideals of the ascending sign.

Frequently in his teaching Bruno emphasised the need to be as clear as possible about layers and levels in the chart and not to confuse the energies at different levels, for example planets in signs are at one level, but the houses, including AC and MC function at a different level. This will be repeated and become more evident as we progress. Even within the limitations of this brief introduction, it can be seen that Bruno and Louise developed an astrological-psychological approach which seeks to combine ancient teachings, wisdom and insights with a modern transpersonal psychological understanding through the medium of the natal chart.

The Huber method of analysing a chart gives us a clue about the layers we find on our journey to the centre. It assists us in perceiving our characteristic ways of behaving in the external world, and seeing some of our underlying motivations. The analysis of the chart through this approach can be a powerful tool for self-discovery, and it is only through understanding ourselves that we can start to fulfil our potential.

This might be a good point at which to pause and reflect on your own thoughts as to how and why astrology works. In the foregoing we talked about the self being in contact with universal energies, but this is a bold statement which deserves careful consideration. Astrologers hold differing views on the subject and although many thousands of words have been written about it the simple fact remains that no-one knows the answer.

It appears to be a fact that the position of the Sun, Moon and planets relative to the time and place of birth does play a role in revealing the character and personality of an individual. With our still limited knowledge of both the self and the cosmos, we can at present only theorise as to how and why.

One theory is that there may be a direct link between the planets and earth created by some force or energy radiating from the planets. We are familiar with such things as x-rays, gamma rays, radio waves and so on but it seems probable that we are protected by the earth's atmosphere from any cosmic radiation, which might provide a foundation for our belief in astrology. Another theory on the same lines concerns the force of gravitational pull but science suggests that this would not be powerful enough from such planets as Pluto to have an influence, on its own, sufficient to form a basis for astrology working.

An alternative theory concerns rhythms. We are, of course, familiar with certain bodily functions which operate rhythmically such as the heart beating 76 times a minute, the normal respiratory rate of 22 per minute, and so on, but perhaps we may not know that every other bodily function also has a regular cycle of operation and regeneration.

And, of course, it's not just the body which operates to clearly defined rhythms, or wave patterns. Many others we take for granted, such as night and day, the tides, the seasons, natures growth cycles, bird migration and the movement of heavenly bodies. We have mass behaviour patterns, as well as social and economic events which can be measured in a rhythmic pattern of cycles.

Scientific research is establishing that everything appears to function in a definable cycle so perhaps the ancient premise that man is a microcosmic reflection of the macrocosm – that man is made in the image of god – finds a practical expression in astrology.

In looking at an individual's birth chart we are looking at a pattern of potential inherent in a moment of time, or put in another way the birth chart reflects a pattern of cosmic energy that was flowing at the moment of birth. We use the planets in our own solar system to measure this pattern and by reading them as though they were the hands of a cosmic clock and plotting their position on a birth chart we gain some idea of the universal energy flow of which we remain a part during our lifetime on earth.

The truly ancient art of astrology was a part of the ageless wisdom which taught the universal harmony of nature and the connections between all effects and causes.

Recommended Reading

You cannot learn the whole of astrological psychology from this one book alone. At each stage, we recommend appropriate complementary reading material. At this early stage you will find the following two books a valuable part of your reading:

The Cosmic Egg Timer by Joyce Hopewell & Richard Llewellyn - strongly recommended introduction to astrological psychology.

Psychosynthesis: The Elements and Beyond by Will Parfitt - a valuable introduction to psychosynthesis.

Exercise 1.1

In this section we have stressed the importance of the Ptolemaic arrangement in Figure 1.1.1. To make sure you become familiar with this, we recommend that you photocopy the blank chart form on the next page, Figure 1.1.3, or download from www.astrologicalpsychology.org, and draw in the arrangement of signs, planets, colours and aspects, etc., as they appear in the diagram.

BIRTH CHART
Huber Method
Koch Houses

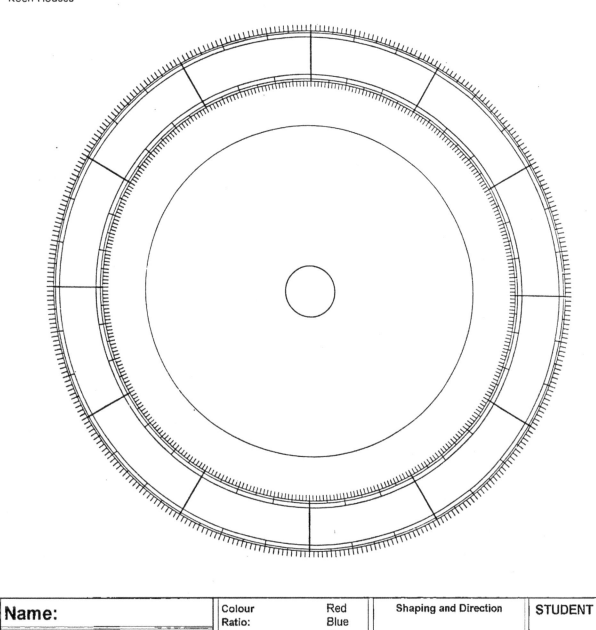

Name:				
	D	M	Y	
Birth Date				
Birth Place				
Latitude				N / S
Longitude				E / W

Time	H	M	S
Birth Time as Given			
Zone Standard E - W +			
Summer (or Double) time -			
GMT (or UT)			am / pm
GMT Date	:	:	
Local Sidereal Time at Birth			

Colour — Red
Ratio: — Blue
— Green

Stress Area Planets

Low Point Planets

Shaping and Direction

Strength of Ego Planets
Strongest:
Weakest:

STUDENT No:

Quadrant Emphasis

Aspect Patterns / Structure

Figure 1.1.3 Blank Natal Chart Form
Available as a download from Study Resources at www.astrologicalpsychology.org.

1.2 The Huber Chart

This section describes how to set up a natal chart in the unique Huber style, including:

- Features specific to the Huber chart in terms of colour, aspects and orbs.
- Guidelines for hand drawing the chart to a professional standard.

In the early years, all Huber charts were drawn by hand. Now they can be all drawn by computer, so in theory it is not strictly necessary to be able to hand draw a chart and you could skip this section. However, it will help you to understand how the chart is constructed, and the very process of hand drawing the chart gives a deeper connection with the underlying energies being revealed by the chart.

Introduction

The interpretive information given in this section is introductory and is covered in more detail in later chapters.

Bruno and Louise Huber, as psychologists and astrologers, devoted their lives to finding ways of relating the birth chart to the complexities of human motivation and behaviour. They stripped away many of the confusing notions which had developed over the years, and which tended to cloud the astrologer's understanding. They rediscovered some of the basic truths in astrology, and by uniting these with modern psychological knowledge produced a method of chart analysis which makes it easier to look at an individual as a whole person, rather than as scattered and unlinked parts.

A first and important step in this process of seeing the human being as a whole person is for the birth chart to be drawn in a manner which is visually graphic as well as reflecting the Hubers' carefully researched work. From such a chart it is easier to trace the underlying motivations which influence a person's behaviour in the outside world.

If you are an astrologer who is familiar with erecting natal charts, you will need to adapt your present technique in order to be able to use the Huber approach. If separate significators are singled out and looked at out of the context of the chart as a whole it will be difficult, if not impossible, to know whether the significator will be applicable to the individual or not. When the chart is set up in the manner described an holistic view can be obtained, which will show whether or not an individual part of that chart is relevant to the analysis.

Note that you will sometimes find the term 'radix chart' used instead of 'natal chart'.

Key features of a Huber chart

When you look at a Huber style chart , you will notice that the main differences between it and charts that you may be used to looking at are probably in respect of colour, aspects and orbs.

Colour

Colour plays an important role when first you look at a chart. It helps to establish an understanding of the nature of the energies which are a part of the pattern of the chart. The following are some simple rules to observe when drawing a birth chart.

Signs

Glyphs of the zodiac signs are coloured to portray the elements:

RED	FIRE Signs
GREEN	EARTH Signs
YELLOW	AIR Signs
BLUE	WATER Signs

Planets

The glyphs of the ego planets, Sun, Moon and Saturn, are drawn in the chart in RED, the remaining planets are drawn in black.

> **Note**
> Throughout this book the symbols used for Uranus and Pluto are ♅ and ♇ respectively. You will also occasionally see the continental glyphs ♅ and ♇ used in illustrations.

Aspects

You will already have noted that only 0° and multiples of 30° aspects are used when drawing up a Huber chart. This means that you only take account of the following aspects:

CONJUNCTION

SEMI-SEXTILE

SEXTILE

SQUARE

TRINE

QUINCUNX

OPPOSITION

Aspect lines are NOT drawn to the ascendant or midheaven.

Aspect lines **are** drawn to the Moon's north node. Before computer generated data was readily available the only node which was feasible to calculate and use was the mean node. Although the Hubers worked with this for many years they subsequently found that the true node provided greater accuracy in analysis. (There is never more than a degree or so difference between the true and mean nodes.)

Aspect lines are drawn in colour to portray motivation, as follows:

CONJUNCTION	ORANGE	0°
SEMI-SEXTILE	GREEN	30°
SEXTILE	BLUE	60°
SQUARE	RED	90°
TRINE	BLUE	120°
QUINCUNX	GREEN	150°
OPPOSITION	RED	180°

These are the **only** aspects which the Hubers use. As you progress through the book the importance of these coloured aspect lines will become apparent. At this stage concentrate on learning the following keywords which relate colour and motivation:

RED: active, eager, performance orientated (CARDINAL)

BLUE: resting, relaxed, orientated to harmony. (FIXED)

GREEN: changeable, information seeking, undecided (MUTABLE)

ORANGE: intensive contact, immediate, binding.

When aspect lines are drawn on the chart in these colours you will become aware of distinct colour combinations and patterns emerging. Aspects represent motivation which may be largely unconscious. Any obvious imbalance seen at first glance is likely to provide an important clue as to the type of person involved. This, and the psychological meaning of colour, is dealt with more fully in Chapter 2.

Orbs

Astrologers use many different orbs. The Hubers found the orbs defined in Figure 1.2.1 (next page) to work in astrological psychology. You will notice that different planets have different orbs for the **same** aspect. This can result in an aspect existing from one planet to another but **not** from the second planet back to the first. This is known as a **one-way aspect**; how to draw it on the chart is explained in "One-Way Aspects" on page 20.

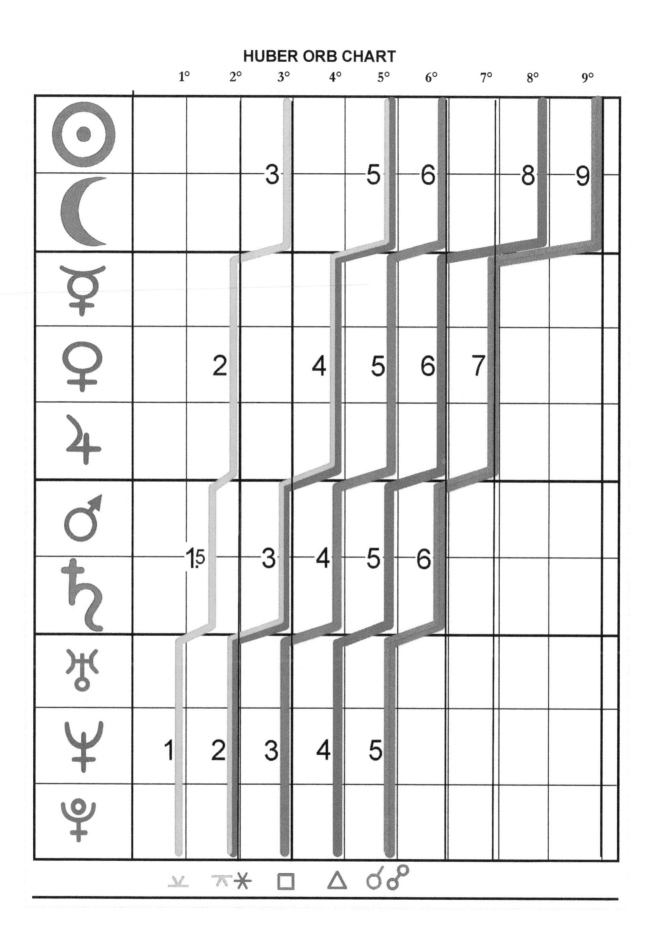

Figure 1.2.1 Huber Orb Chart

You will notice in Figure 1.2.1 that the orb of Jupiter is greater than that of Mars, even though Jupiter, astronomically, is placed further out in the solar system. When Bruno Huber was researching, Jupiter was provisionally assigned a higher orb than Mars because of its greater physical mass. This was subsequently confirmed by many years of empirical research.

One-Way Aspects

As you can see from Figure 1.2.1 the same aspect made by different planets does not necessarily have the same orb, e.g. an opposition from the Sun is 9° whereas an opposition from Pluto only encompasses an orb of 5°. Or a square from Venus has an orb of 5°, whilst the same aspect from Saturn is only 4°. What does this mean in practice?

Example 1

Let us assume that the Sun is at 20° Cancer and that Pluto is at 27° Capricorn. An orb of 7°. This means that the Sun makes an opposition aspect to Pluto but that Pluto (with an opposition orb of only 5°) does not make an opposition aspect to the Sun. How do we show this **one-way aspect**? Quite simply! Half the aspect line, from the Sun to the centre circle, is a solid red line, whilst the aspect from Pluto to the centre is a dashed line.

Figure 1.2.2

Example 2

Imagine Mercury at 10°15' Leo and Mars at 15°45' Sagittarius, a possible trine aspect, i.e. 120°. The Orb Chart shows that a trine aspect from Mercury has a 6° orb whilst from Mars the same aspect only has a 5° orb. In this example therefore, with an angle of 125°30', we have another one-way aspect. So again, this aspect is drawn on the chart with half the line (from Mercury) solid blue and the other half (from Mars) dashed.

Figure 1.2.3

Example 3

If Uranus is at 7°32' Sagittarius and the Moon is at 8°56' Taurus there is a potential quincunx (150°) aspect. The angle is 151°24'. The Orb Chart shows that Uranus has an orb of 2° for a quincunx aspect and that the Moon has an orb of 5° for the same aspect. So a full aspect exists between the two planets and would be drawn on the chart with a solid green line. If, however, Uranus had been at 6°55' Sagittarius, making an angle of 152°01', the orb would have been 2°01' and there would have only been a one-way aspect.

Figure 1.2.4

The significance of one-way aspects is covered in Chapter 2.

The Moon's North Node

The Moon's north node is always drawn in on the chart and aspects to it are noted and also drawn. Since this node is not a planet and therefore not a focus of energy it always has the same orb as the planet to which it is aspected. Therefore **no one-way aspect can exist to the north node**.

Example 1

The node at 10°01' Pisces and the Sun at 17°13' Virgo. An orb of 7°12'. An opposition aspect from the Sun exists and is drawn on the chart as a solid red line.

Figure 1.2.5

Example 2

The node still at 10°01' Pisces, but Neptune at 17°13' Virgo. The orb is still 7°12' but an opposition aspect from Neptune only has a 5° orb so **no** aspect exists.

Figure 1.2.6

Other Points to Note

Goodwill Aspects

Goodwill Aspects are those aspects which are just outside the allowable orb. In one sense these aspects are not relevant since they **are** outside of allowable orb, but it may be useful to know of them because a person may be aware of their influence. However, we recommend you do not include these 'Goodwill Aspects' in your charts.

Circle at the Centre of the Chart

This always remains an empty space. This is explained further in section 1.4.

Houses

It is essential that house cusps should be calculated using the Koch division. No other House System has been found to work satisfactorily for this approach. Reference to *The Astrological Houses* page 35 explains the reasoning behind the choice of Koch Houses. For students interested in learning more about house division, the most comprehensive work on this subject is *The Elements of House Division* by Ralph William Holden.

Drawing the Chart by Hand

Use the notes on the following page and the specimen hand drawn birth chart Figure 1.2.7 on page 24 as examples of how a Huber chart should be drawn. You can copy the blank chart form "Figure 1.1.3 Blank Natal Chart Form" on page 15, or download it from the APA website, as in "Resources" on page 9.

The principles which dictate that the chart should appear in this particular form are important, so you are recommended to follow these instructions precisely.

Chart Data

When you are learning to interpret a chart it can be an important part of the process to take the time to draw up the chart for yourself, rather than use a computer-generated chart. However, with so many computer programs available for the use of astrologers (see "Birth Charts" on page 9) it is likely that you will choose to use computer-generated data rather than take the time to calculate longitudes, aspects, etc. Data for the charts in this book was generated using MegaStar and other programs; the information contained in the data sheets is self-explanatory.

Guidelines - *Hand-Drawing a Huber Chart to a Professional Standard*

The chart is a tool.
It needs to be accurate, **clear** (easy to read), and aesthetically pleasing. The Huber approach is highly Jupiterian so the visual impact of the chart is very important.

You will need:
- A set of broad tipped felt pens in red, green, blue and yellow for sign glyphs. They should be clearly definable primary colours; some blues and greens are hard to tell apart.
- A set of medium tipped felt pens in red, green, blue, orange and yellow for aspect lines.
- Fine nibbed black and red pens for planetary glyphs, house cusps, etc.
- A 30 cm (12 inch) ruler, preferably transparent.
- A pencil and rubber (useful for marking in house cusps and planetary positions to allow a double-check before inking them in).
- Correcting tape or fluid for minuscule errors only!

House Cusps
- House cusps are drawn in black except for the AC, DC, IC and MC which are **RED**.
- Cusps need to project about 2cm from the outer edge of the chart, and be labelled with the cusp letters or number following the cusp marker.
- Remember there are 60 minutes in each degree. A house cusp at 5 degrees 55 minutes is almost 6 degrees, NOT 5 degrees (This is especially important where planets and sign cusps are very close to house cusps).
- The AC and MC only are marked with a short red line (1cm) on the inner circle.
- If the ascending degree (AC) is greater than 15 degrees, it should be above the horizon on the blank chart form, and below the horizon if less than 15 degrees.
- Balance Points are marked in **BLUE** and Low Points in **GREEN**. (These are introduced in Chapter 4, so you can ignore them for the moment.)

Sign Glyphs
These should be **clear** and **bold** (use thicker pens), spreading across the greater part of their "box". They face inwards towards the centre of the chart.

Aspects
- The felt pens used for drawing these should be fine to medium.
- One-way conjunctions should be drawn as a small orange right-angled triangle tapering to the "receiving" planet, or in yellow.
- The more exact aspects can be "thickened" as on computer generated charts. This can make for easier reading of aspect emphasis **but** it needs to be done with care!

Planet glyphs

- Planet glyphs need to be clear, firmly drawn, all the same size – 10mm approx. – and in vertical alignment. (Spend some time doodling the glyphs until they flow and become natural).

- Ego planets (Sun, Moon, Saturn) are drawn in RED, with the other planets drawn in black.

- All planet markers on the inner circle of the chart to be 1cm long, drawn in black, and using a ruler.

- Where you have a conjunction or stellium (3 or more planets conjunct), make sure the planets are drawn showing their correct order; care and a sense of design need to be exercised so that the glyphs do not have to be made too small or look too cramped.

The birth chart is, in some ways, a work of art and it symbolises the uniqueness of a single human being. It should be drawn in such a way that not only respects this but also, by its neatness and clarity, makes interpretation easier.

You will find it helpful to fill in the information boxes at the bottom of the chart form as far as possible. Include the person's name, time, date and place of birth.

Note that the appearance of a hand drawn chart differs slightly from that of the computer-generated chart.

The birth chart is a work of art symbolising the uniqueness of a single human being. It should be drawn in such a way that respects this and, by its neatness and clarity, makes interpretation easier.

Exercise 1.2.2

1. Using a copy of the blank chart form in Figure 1.1.3 on page 15, draw your chart in the Huber style as accurately as you can. Fill in the data boxes as far as you are able.

2. Compare the result with the sample hand-drawn chart in Figure 1.2.7 (next page), and with your own chart generated by computer software. Satisfy yourself that your drawn chart is correct and professional looking.

3. Make a note of and reflect on any particular features of your chart that have been revealed to you through this process, or any that you may not have noticed before.

Recommended reading

The Astrological Houses – the following chapters:

- Introduction

- Psychological Significance of the Horoscope: pages 21/24

- The Astrological Concept of Man; pages 25/27

- Technical Specification of the Houses.

LifeClock – Appendix 'An Introduction to Astrological Psychology'

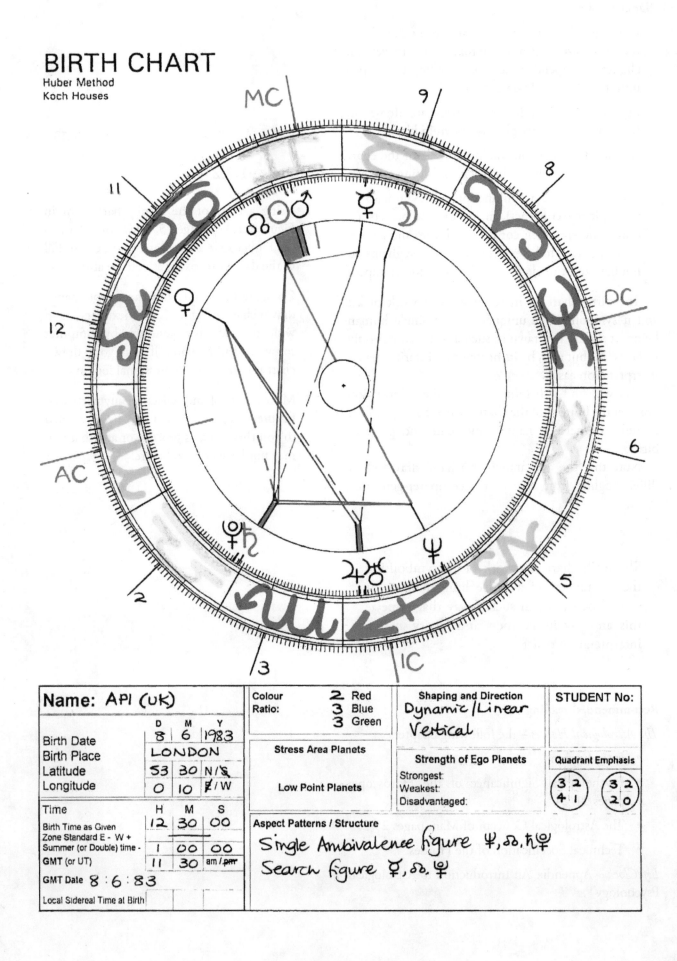

Figure 1.2.7 Sample Hand-Drawn Natal Chart

1.3 Astrology and Psychology

In this section we look at the relationship between astrology and psychology:

- Roberto Assagioli's psychosynthesis provides an appropriate model of the personality that we can relate to the birth chart.

- The concept of sub-personalities is introduced and related to planetary energies in the chart and the psychological growth of the individual.

Whilst astrology has existed for thousands of years it is only during the second half of the 20th Century that its value as a serious psychological tool began to be recognised. At the start of your exploration into astrological psychology, you might like to ask yourself some very basic questions about your reasons for deciding to discover and learn more about this particular approach to chart interpretation. For instance:

1. What is the purpose of astrology?'

2. Why am I studying astrology?

3. What do I imagine I can do with astrology when I've learned it?

4. If I imagine astrology has answers, what are the questions I'm asking?

and so on.

You may have read articles in astrological journals and wondered why so many of them set out to prove something with hindsight. Have you then wondered why, in a general sense, there seems to be no reliable way of using astrology with foresight. And even if this was possible, would that be a valid purpose for astrology, and in the extreme might we not find ourselves in conflict with the laws of nature, or even of the divine? Making predictions can be self-fulfilling and therefore potentially damaging because the way in which, for instance, the influence of transits will be experienced will depend to a great extent on the point that an individual has reached in their own personal evolution. And yet, if someone is in a crisis might it not be helpful to be able to say "It's OK, it won't last for ever." Well, it might be helpful, but perhaps the real answer to this is "No, not usually", because a crisis is so often only the surface manifestation of a much deeper problem which needs to be addressed.

Astrology can be used in working with people – individually and in groups. In astrological psychology it is not an end in itself but a means to an end – the objective being to help someone to achieve greater self-awareness. This provides an opportunity for them to make creative changes in their life and become more whole.

This vision of wholeness was inspired by Roberto Assagioli and absorbed by Bruno and Louise during the years in which they worked with him at his Psychosynthesis Institute in Florence. It was at this time that they were developing their own psychological approach to astrology and chart interpretation.

For whatever reason astrology does hold a fascination for many people. For some there is a genuine desire to use it to understand themselves better, and maybe there is a feeling that astrology might help them with this. But what does 'understand themselves better' really mean, and what can we do with this understanding if we get it?

There is a delightful little story which throws some light on this, which was published in the Wrekin Trust's newsletter *Pegasus*. It was called "Autobiography of a seeker" and it goes like this:

I walk down the street, there is a deep hole in the pavement. I fall in. I am lost. I am helpless. It isn't my fault, it takes for ever to find a way out.

I walk down the same street, there is a deep hole in the pavement. I pretend I don't see it. I fall in . . . . again. I can't believe I'm in this place again. But it isn't my fault. It still takes a long time to get out.

I walk down the same street, there is a deep hole in the pavement. I see it there. I fall in . . . .it's a habit . . . . but my eyes are open. I know where I am. It's my fault. I get out immediately.

I walk down the same street, there is a deep hole in the pavement, I walk round it.

Finally, I walk down a different street . . . .

Only with awareness can we change **taught** and, less easily, **inherited** patterns of behaviour and lead a more fulfilling and joyful life. But there's more to it than that!

It does seem that in each of us there is a niggling desire to search for something which we do not understand because it's not in our consciousness. And Jung pointed out that anything which is not in our conscious mind might just as well not exist. However, from time to time this 'niggle' breaks the surface and we do become aware of a sense of dissatisfaction, and we may or may not choose to do something about this. Roberto Assagioli, suggested that in all human beings there is an inherent urge to seek and find a connection with the Divine, or with the source of everything. Perhaps the niggle could be related to the grain of sand in an oyster – which may eventually become a pearl.

If the concept of a spiritual dimension to life is unfamiliar to you, this will obviously pose yet another question, like "What on earth is this talking about?" Well, this section puts forward some ideas which might help you to answer the question "What is the purpose of astrology?"

Before continuing please be aware that nothing written in this section is 'The Truth'. Truth is a subjective belief based, hopefully, on learning and experience. We all have to seek and find our own truth and that may be constantly changing as Jupiter helps us to push back the boundaries of our conscious awareness. Have you ever read a book about a subject and not been able to get into it at all? And yet a year later you can pick up the same book and have another look at it – and suddenly it does make sense. Something has happened in the meantime to expand your consciousness so that you are viewing the book from the perspective of a changed 'You'.

Models of the Personality

Let us start by seeking a reason for learning astrology and seeing where the birth chart fits into this process. As already mentioned the Hubers' approach is one application of astrology that can be used as a tool to create greater self-awareness and, hopefully, help someone to achieve a sense of wholeness.

The diagram in Figure 1.3.1 confirms what you probably already know – that each of us is the product of a number of different influences – all of which we hope to find reflected somewhere in the birth chart. It is probably no surprise that it is not always easy to see the reality of a human life in a birth chart because it does not have all the answers. For instance by looking at a chart it is possible to gain some idea about family background and environmental conditioning but, all too often, the chart cannot tell us about the pain and distress of emotional, mental or even physical abuse from a parent or any other person involved in a young child's life. We can only make intelligent speculation about how that chart came into being and what distortions it contains. And we can only find out more about these by gaining the trust of the client and gradually turning back the pages of his or her life history until we reach the first chapter.

Then hopefully we can begin to understand what has made the adult and how the chart can be used to identify conditioning from potential. But it is important to consider whether we can reach that stage purely as astrologers, or is it advisable, or even essential, that we add other strings to our bow? For instance, astrology does not tell us how to work with a client who grew up in an angry family, who associates anger with power and who has succeeded in repressing both – so that she projects these on to others and wonders why she always ends up as a victim – usually of violence.

Or the client who overcame a very deprived childhood to become a dentist with his own very successful practice. But who was so depressed when he had his first session as an astrological client that he was contemplating suicide.

Or the successful lawyer who, as a child, grew up in a family where she was allowed no boundaries and who now finds herself married to a man who is insecure and lacks self-confidence, and who has in-laws who attempt to control her to the extent that she has lost her sense of self and lives in a state of continual stress.

The point is that often people need help to untangle their lives. And usually their crises come into consciousness when major transits of planets, or aspects of the Age Point, are shining a searchlight on that area of their life – but the question remains "For what purpose?"

Imagine that it were possible to find out **everything** about an individual from their birth chart and to interpret this information in such a way as to give all the answers, the question might then arise: "What are the questions to which these answers refer?" In other words, why does the astrological consultant need to know who somebody is and why they might do certain things in particular ways?

If you have ever paid to have your chart interpreted by an astrologer did you learn anything about yourself that, on some level, you did not know already? And if so what did you do with this information? There is no doubt that a birth chart can reveal accurate information about us, and that our awareness of what we find out may not have been fully in our conscious mind – so perhaps going to an astrologer will bring into full consciousness something that was lying partly in our own personal unconscious. But how were we able to use this information?

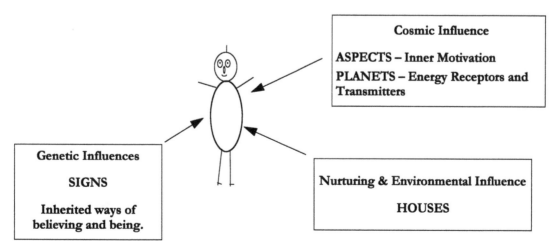

Figure 1.3.1 Personality Model 1

In the hands of an astrological consultant the birth chart can be used as a tool to reveal information relating to our genetic background; something about the inner motivation which drives us to be what we are intended to be, and finally something about the way in which our **natural process of evolving** was affected by those people who were major influences in our early years. In certain circumstances this latter factor can be of immense importance in creating behaviour which is far removed from that intended by the universe. What astrology does not tell us is how we can use this information.

For instance, in the examples mentioned it doesn't tell us how to turn back the hands of the clock, facilitate healing the wounds of childhood, help clients to develop greater self-awareness and a sense of purpose about the present and, perhaps even more important, about the future.

When we speak about our 'natural process of evolving' what does this mean? It is probable that anybody choosing to study astrology has within them, either conscious or still unconscious, a belief of some kind that as human beings we do not exist in isolation in this world. That there are other 'beings' on other levels of consciousness that can have an effect on our progress on this earthly plane. Expressed in less vague terms this would suggest that there is a divine, trans-personal source of love and will that emanates from the somewhere that we might call "The Source of Everything" or the equivalent of God, depending on spiritual beliefs. And also that there are entities that exist on other levels of consciousness who can assist us in grounding this trans-personal energy.

Anyway, if we consider the possibility that we do not exist in isolation that would bring in yet another dimension to our astrological birth chart. So this now makes our personality model look like Figure 1.3.2:

If there really is a source of everything, some kind of divine, transpersonal energy which is manifesting in us then perhaps we need to ask ourselves another question: "Why? For what purpose?" Here it is appropriate to change over to another model of the personality. At the beginning we mentioned an Italian psychiatrist by the name of Roberto Assagioli. He was a contemporary of Jung, with whom he collaborated for a while. However certain differences of opinion resulted in Assagioli conceiving a different approach in his therapeutic work which he called psycho-synthesis.

The emphasis is on the word **synthesis** as opposed to other therapeutic approaches which were more concerned with analysis – or pulling apart. Assagioli felt that we had everything within us to be able to create wholeness, or oneness with the divine source. His model of the personality, the 'Egg', was introduced in Figure 1.1.2 on page 12, which you are recommended to refer back to.

A comprehensive understanding of the concept of the 'Egg' can be obtained experientially by attending workshops on psychosynthesis, or from Pierro Ferucci's book *What We May Be*. Briefly, the model symbolises our individual 'growth' potential. In growing out of the collective lower unconscious we aim to create a balanced and integrated personality which allows us to experience and manifest the transpersonal qualities of the collective higher unconscious.

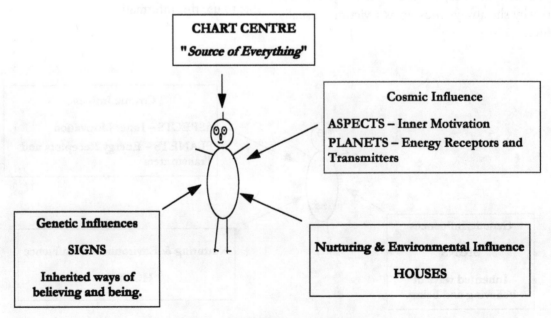

Figure 1.3.2 Personality Model 2

Relationship of Astrological and Psychological Models

Could it enlighten us if we were able to bring the astrological and psychological models together? Let us first look at the two side by side:

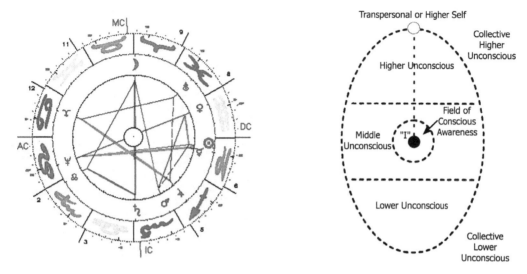

Figure 1.3.3 Astrological and psychological models

Now, if we fit the chart into the Egg model does it offer another, and perhaps deeper understanding of what a birth chart is all about?

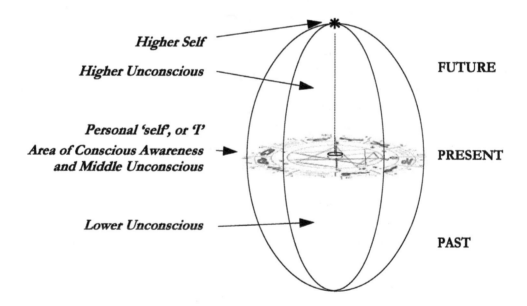

Figure 1.3.4 Combining astrological and psychological models

Relevance to Real Life

What have these models got to do with the reality of the birth chart and the reality of a human life? Why do we want to know more about our own chart or decide to visit an astrologer? Experience suggests there are two main reasons - one is a crisis situation of some kind and the other is when the grain of sand in the oyster is focussing attention on itself. This is creating a sense of something needing to change and to come into consciousness. As you probably appreciate, these two situations will often be related.

Over and over there seems to be a link between the universe speaking and a person being aware that they have reached a stage in their life when something needs to change. By 'the universe speaking' we here mean through Hubers' Age Progression and/or transits. All too often we live in our comfort zone tolerating everything within it because we know and understand it – however awful it might be. It takes courage to step outside of this self-imposed stockade and venture forth into the unknown. And yet that does need to happen before our 'growth process' can continue. Think of the leaves on a tree – in autumn they die and fall off the tree so that, when the winter is over and spring arrives, new leaves can come into existence and the tree can continue with its growth. This process of death and rebirth is just as essential for our own growth as it is for a tree.

However, for a client the concept of conscious awareness or personal growth means little or nothing. They assume that they are 'consciously aware' and they don't really need anyone to tell them about 'personal growth'. Often they are doing OK with their life, and yet there is that little niggle inside suggesting something wants to break out and see the light of day.

Without **conscious** awareness we do not change – we tend to go on living our life as though only half awake. OK, we might be very successful, make lots of money, but life can be pretty two-dimensional – work and play. For some people life can be like this – like being in a long corridor. At the end of the corridor there is the pot of gold whatever that might be. It might be winning the lottery, dreaming of a home in the sun, or finding the perfect partner. This is believed to be the one thing which will provide happiness. However, even if we reach the pot of gold we probably find that it was not really what we were looking for so perhaps we start all over again.

The point is that we can be so dedicated to the pursuit of what we believe will bring us happiness in the material world that we don't give ourselves time to pause and realise that happiness lies **inside** us. The following tale is adapted from an Eastern story which Pierro Ferrucci, a student of Assagioli, quotes in his book on psychosynthesis, *What We May Be*. It goes like this:

> *"One day the gods decided to create the universe. They created the stars, the sun, the moon. They created the sea, the mountains, the flowers, and the clouds. Then they created human beings. At the end they created the concept of happiness. At this point a problem arose: where should they hide happiness so that human beings would not find it right away? They wanted to prolong the adventure of the search.*
>
> *'Let's put happiness on top of the highest mountain', said one of the Gods. 'Certainly it would be hard to find there.'*
>
> *'Let's put it on the furthest star', said another.*
>
> *'Let's hide it in the darkest and deepest abysses.'*
>
> *'Let's hide it on the furthest side of the Moon.'*
>
> *At the end the wisest and most ancient god said: 'No, we will hide happiness inside the very heart of human beings. In this way they will look for it all over the universe, without being aware of having it inside them all the time.'"*

The adaptation lies in replacing the word truth with happiness. Perhaps the two words are not unconnected.

Hopefully, in the midst of **all** the uncertainties which each of us will experience at some stage in our lives, the universe will create an opportunity for us to come out of our shell and ask ourselves the question "What's the point of it all – why am I here?" That's the time when our search for something else begins. This can often be the time when we turn to an astrologer.

As astrologers, if we are working with clients, it is as well to be aware of what possibly underlies the presenting reason for a client coming and spending time with us. And if we are working with clients perhaps we need to ask ourselves what tools, other than astrological ones, have we equipped ourselves with in order to deal with major issues such as personal growth.

Imagine someone stuck in a long corridor, striving to reach the pot of gold, or whatever else it is that lies at the end and which they believe will bring happiness. Is it not possible that their concentration may be so intense that they don't pause long enough to notice that on either side of them there are doors? An aim of working with clients is to help them to be aware of the doors, to pause long enough to open a door and perhaps glimpse a vision of how their life might be if they were willing to break free of the ties which they experience as security.

If you were in a prison-like corridor, how would you feel if someone showed you a door to open – and through it you caught a glimpse of a beautiful landscape of green hills, woodland, flowers, and perhaps, in the distance, the sea shimmering in bright sunshine. Would you be tempted to go through? You might imagine the answer is 'Yes', but you might be surprised at the number of times that, for one reason or another it is 'No'. Saturn on that level, or even a strong emphasis in the second house, can prove to be a strong obstacle to overcome. It can be easier to live with what we know, however painful it can sometimes be, rather than take a step into the unknown. To leave our comfort zone and step into the unknown can take a great deal of courage.

Transits of Uranus and Pluto can be sure ways of catapulting us out of our stockade. As astrologers perhaps we can assist a client to be aware of what they need to let go of, so that this can be done in a planned way rather than let the universe do it in the traumatic way that can so often happen?

What's the purpose of these transits which can sometimes create such major upheavals in our lives? The suggestion made here is that it is the universe trying to wake us up, trying to make us aware of new opportunities – and this does not necessarily mean material ones. And perhaps even of the fact that we have strayed from our life path. Most of the transits which we experience in a dramatic way seem to relate to Uranus and Pluto, though perhaps also to Saturn, which at its deepest level is to do with learning. So, what's going on?

Evolution of Humanity and Transpersonal Energies

The word trans-personal (i.e. beyond the personal) provides a clue. In the same way as we can see Assagioli's Egg model as symbolising the growth of the individual, we can also see it as symbolising the growth of humanity as a whole.

Perhaps this begins to define a purpose for astrology because it gives a sense of the larger plan. Not only a

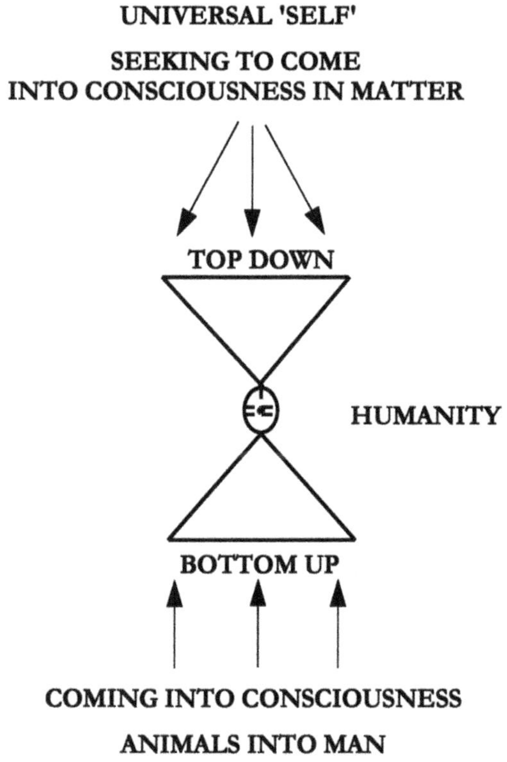

Figure 1.3.5 Evolution of Humanity

reason for us being here but **also** for doing something with our lives. Something which helps with the manifestation of these transpersonal qualities in matter and therefore with the evolution of humanity. These transpersonal qualities which originate from the source of everything, are looking for form in which to manifest. And we are that form. What are these transpersonal qualities? In case the concept is unfamiliar they include such things as joy, beauty, peace, will, freedom, wisdom, power...

When we look around the world today it may not always seem as though this process is actually happening, but then it's not always easy to see the wood for the trees when you are in the middle of the wood and have lost your way in a patch of stinging nettles.

Transits of the outer planets are encouraging us to become more aware of those areas of our life which need attention. Only with awareness can we begin to understand the need to let go of outworn patterns of behaving **and** reacting, which we probably learned as we grew up. This gives us the opportunity to make changes allowing us to function in a more positive manner, with greater clarity and creativity. These are powerful energies which can change and transform in dramatic ways.

Imagine a house, with poorly wired electrical circuits, floating a few feet above the earth, in a severe electrical storm. With no connection to the earth lightning would be striking the house and blowing apart every circuit in the house. There would be a danger of fires and all kinds of disruptions in the house. In a way this is how we experience the power of the transpersonal. When we get our own electrical circuits integrated, balanced and earthed then we can not only act as a channel for these energies for the benefit of humanity, but we can also experience their joyful qualities in every moment of our own lives.

The process of how these transpersonal energies come into being in our everyday lives is discussed in the following.

Sub-personalities

It is important to bear in mind that this is only an introduction to the concept of sub-personalities. To deepen your understanding you will probably need to read some of the psychosynthesis books in the recommended reading or bibliography, and/or look for workshops on the subject.

The above discussed the idea of using astrology as a tool, not only for personal growth but also for the growth of humanity. Let us clarify what we mean by growth . When we come into this world we are largely unconscious and do things by instinct. In the same way as a bird might instinctively know about migration within weeks of it being hatched, so we understand the need for food and nurturing for our survival. We function instinctively and without conscious understanding (from the First Quadrant of our chart). The process of growth takes us from this stage, through a gradual widening of our conscious awareness until we take control of our own lives, using **strong, skilful and good will** to implement consciously made decisions, and accepting responsibility for ourselves and our actions. At this stage we have the ability to tap into a higher wisdom and love and discover that there is also a **higher will**. If we are willing to transcend our own personal will we can allow the divine will to direct our lives for the benefit of humanity.

In practical terms how does this process take place? And how do these trans-personal energies find a home in us? The answer to the first question probably takes us back to the concept of the grain of sand in the oyster, the niggle that makes us search for a deeper meaning to our lives. The niggle that we can either respond to, or reject. If we respond to it then our search is likely to take us exploring in many different 'alternative' directions, and perhaps even into some kind of growth therapy, such as psychosynthesis. Whatever path we take the intention is to develop mindful self-awareness, to come to understand why we do certain things in the way that we do, why certain things don't work in our lives, and what we have buried in our own lower unconscious (using up potentially creative energy to keep it hidden there). We are creating a fully conscious, autonomous, integrated and balanced personality – which is also open to the energy of the Source of Everything, about which nothing can be known.

The answer to the second question lies in another of Assagioli's concepts – sub-personalities. Sub-personalities are aspects of our self which have their own self-image, their own body posture and gestures, their own feelings, ways of behaving, words and phrases they use, habits and beliefs. This constellation of elements makes up in itself a kind of miniature personality, a sub-personality. Assagioli suggested that each of us is many sub-personalities all living under one skin. At an inner, hidden, level some of these parts get on well with each other, some are in conflict. In the same way some of these parts relate well to those we meet in our outer, everyday lives whereas other parts are in conflict with the environment. So if we feel confused and stressed at times, with all our sub-personalities doing their own thing, it is not surprising.

Imagine trying to conduct an orchestra in which some of the instruments took no notice of you and played their own tune. Not a lot of fun for you or the audience! If we have unaspected planets in our natal chart we can, perhaps, become aware of their effects.

Working with sub-personalities can be enlightening when we come to look at the many paradoxes encountered when we interpret a natal chart. But it is important to remember that we **have** sub-personalities and that we **are not** our sub-personalities. Each one of us is in essence a centre of pure consciousness – not unlike the conductor of the orchestra.

When working with a birth chart it is also important to remember that, when we are in our early stages of growth, it is more than likely that some of our sub-personalities are encouraged to grow at the expense of others, depending on the needs of those responsible for our early programming. It is usually possible to spot these distortions in the birth chart. Making a client aware can often be a first step to achieving a better balance. If we can spot them in the birth chart then the supposition must be that the child creates the distortions because of its subjective view of its environment.

For instance, why is it that a child with Saturn near the AC will grow up with a fear of taking a risk? If you discuss this with the adult he or she will usually remember that the parent who looked after them was over-protective when they were small – thus creating the fear. We are born with a birth chart and we die with the chart unchanged. But of course we do change and personal growth needs to be seen in the context of the growth of humanity. After all, we are humanity!

Practical Exercise - sub-personalities

Working with sub-personalities, and associating them with both the evolving personality and the birth chart, can perhaps help you to more clearly understand the process which is taking place. One which can be helpful to students is to relate the birth chart to a garden. If this is a new concept for you, then you are invited to pause for a moment in your reading and imagine that in front of you is a circular patch of ground. Also in your imagination you see a packet of seeds, and on the front of the packet is a picture of a glorious garden in full flower. If you look inside the seed packet you can see an assorted collection of ten little black seeds. Now imagine that these seeds are sown at random around this circular patch of ground, and that at the same moment in time they germinate - and that nine months later the first little leaves burst out into the light.

If these seeds had been sown in fertile soil and had been carefully nurtured during their gestation period they would likely be healthy seedlings when they broke the surface. But think how these seedlings would be if they had been sown in rocky ground or hard clay, and that nobody had cared much for them during those nine months.

And be aware too, of the effect that further care and nurturing will have on these delicate little plants as they struggle for survival in their early weeks. Also consider the effect that their environment will have on them. And what if the gardeners decided they did not really like one or two of the seedlings and tried their best to hide them under some earth or perhaps a stone or two? Or just as damaging, if there was one particular seedling they liked above all others and they lavished all their care and attention on this one seedling, so that the others barely survived? If you think about it this is no different from what happens to each one of us. As astrological psychologists, we aim to become aware of this.

Astrologically we can enhance this analogy by attaching a basic drive to each of these seedlings. These are shown in capitals letters below, together with some of the **positive** qualities we relate to each drive:

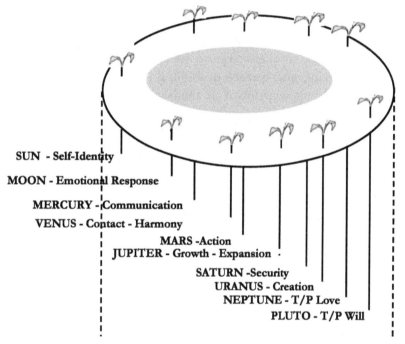

SUN - Self-Identity
MOON - Emotional Response
MERCURY - Communication
VENUS - Contact - Harmony
MARS - Action
JUPITER - Growth - Expansion
SATURN - Security
URANUS - Creation
NEPTUNE - T/P Love
PLUTO - T/P Will

Figure 1.3.6 Basic drives coming into consciousness
(expanded below)

SUN	**Will**; Individuality; Self Identity; Self-Confidence; Decision Making;
MOON	**Emotional response**; Spontaneous Inner Child; Compassionate; Sensitive;
MERCURY	**Communication**; Learning; Teaching; Questioning; Thinking; Analysing; Ideas;
VENUS	**Contact**; **Harmony**; Creativity; Balance; Female libido: Beauty; Taste: Security;
MARS	**Action**; Energy; Achieving; Skill; Courage; Strength; Purpose; Masculine Libido;
JUPITER	**Growth** - Psychological; Expansion; Judgement; Perception; Vision; Experience;
SATURN	**Security**: Reliable; Responsible; Caution; Memory; Structure; Deep Learning;
URANUS	**Creative Intelligence**: Research; Discovery; Change;
NEPTUNE	**Transpersonal Love**; Altruism; Inclusiveness;
PLUTO`	**Transpersonal Will**; Transformation; Higher purpose.

When we burst into life we don't really have any sense of consciousness. We survive by instinct but from the very start we begin to develop consciousness – an understanding of what happens when we take a certain action. New sub-personalities are developing all the while as we learn new roles in life and as our consciousness widens and widens. In the garden analogy we can see this as new leaves developing on each little plant as it grows – and each of these leaves, or sub-personalities will relate back to the basic drive which is within the seed. For instance:

Mercury will begin life with that first little cry, then go on to develop language and will gradually expand in all forms of communication from writing, to reading, to teaching, to creating web sites, and becoming part of a global village network. The possibilities for Mercury, as with all our planets is potentially unlimited.

Venus will go from the smiling and cooing stages and initial dependencies, through pleasure seeking and glamour, to achieving inner balance, developing a sense of altruism, and the appreciation of art and beauty.

Mars will go from the aggressive and selfish "Gi'me, Gi'me" stages to assertiveness, skilful achievement and action, to courage and selfless heroism.

Jupiter: from indulgence and excess through fun, wisdom and expansion of consciousness to universal wisdom

Saturn: from fear, greed, paranoia, through caution, reliability and responsibility to mentor.

Sun: from being wilful and egocentric to self-confidence, independence and selflessness

Moon: from needy, moody and emotional insecurity to childlike spontaneity, compassion, caring, and empathy, etc.

That is necessarily brief. It aims to give an idea of the immense potential for growth which exists within the natal chart. The transpersonal planets are not included here since these can be associated with the higher levels of Sun, Moon and Saturn – assuming we have managed to integrate our inner circuitry. So, for instance, when we learn to transcend our own will and the need always to be in control of our destiny, we can begin to experience the higher, liberating, transpersonal vibrations of Pluto – or the will of God.

Sub-personalities are formed when we want something. For example, when the new born baby wants to survive, (a basic instinct) he knows he wants feeding and yells to attract attention. Since the baby is probably desperate and angry he is likely to be generating sub-personalities relating to the Mars drive for action. He or she will perhaps learn that a smile brings more harmonious results so will learn to smile and so generate a Venus or Moon sub-personality. The baby, and the birth chart spring in to life. At that stage the process is all quite instinctive and without conscious awareness. As we grow older more and more sub-personalities are created, and each will be related to the basic drive associated with the seed, or the planet.

Wants and Needs
We mentioned that sub-personalities come into being because we want something, but beneath that want is always a need. We can never really satisfy a want but we can satisfy the need if we can discover what this is. For instance if someone has a craving for chocolate this is a 'want' which can only be partly satisfied by going on eating more chocolate.

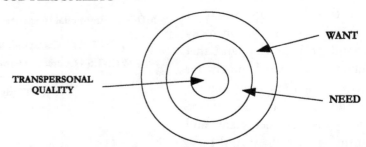

Figure 1.3.7 Wants and Needs

However if they discover that the need beneath the want is really security, or even love, then it is possible that they can find ways of changing the pattern of their life which is undermining their security or inhibiting them from experiencing love. Then that craving for chocolate will begin to diminish.

Working with sub-personalities can bring about tremendous leaps of self-understanding – and we all have many, many of them. Figure 1.3.8 shows some examples from real life:

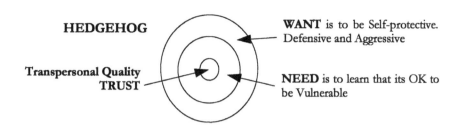

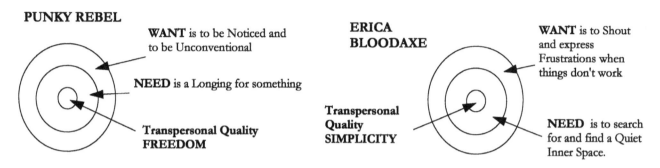

Figure 1.3.8 Example sub-personalities

It is helpful to give sub-personalities a name as we need to find ways to make them as real as possible. **Acceptance and understanding** are two essential elements of the process of working with sub-personalities so that they can transform into creative parts of the personality. Sub-personalities want to grow and transform and become a creative part of our adult life. Many are stuck in the past at the time they were created – most of us have damaged child sub-personalities which can hold us back in all kinds of ways.

Transpersonal Qualities at the Core

It is important to remember that at the core of a sub-personality lies a trans-personal quality which wants to manifest in our life – but this cannot happen until we have worked on that sub-personality and found a way, or ways, of transforming the negative aspects of this part of ourselves and integrating the positive. This is part of our own personal evolution, part of the process of allowing our own 'garden' to become as beautiful and fulfilled as the picture on the front of that seed packet. We can move beyond our normal sense of fears and insecurities and achieve a sense of wholeness from within.

What has this got to do with the evolution of humanity? Well, as we mentioned before, we are humanity so if astrology can help us to become more consciously aware, and develop a more balanced and integrated personality, then we not only achieve a greater sense of joy in our own life but we can help humanity to do the same. Since the beginning of human time the evolution of mankind has gone hand in hand with the expansion of our individual consciousness – both in scientific and humanistic

terms. Our awareness of ourselves in our relationships with one another, with the planet and with our place in the universe has gone through many changes, but always it has been expanding. We have been growing out of the collective lower unconscious towards the collective super-conscious, but a question we might ask ourselves now is whether, in the same way as we can experience a block in our individual development, humanity has encountered a collective block and, if so, are we willing to work through it?

The blocks which exist in the world to-day centre largely around intransigent attitudes towards such things as race, colour, religion, money, intellectual beliefs – even astrological beliefs, security, social class, territory, and so on. Only by breaking these down can we hope to create the same wholeness in the human race which tools such as astrological psychology aim to create in the individual. And these collective blocks exist, of course, within ourselves as individuals, so we have the power to free ourselves from them if we become sufficiently consciously aware, and if we have the will to make the necessary changes.

Whilst we can see a mirror of the way in which humanity is developing in our own development as individuals – macrocosm and microcosm – and thus can more easily understand what is needed to create positive changes in the world, it is essential to keep in mind that we cannot change other people, we can only change ourselves and in the process bring about changes around us. Having said that we can **facilitate** the **potential** for change for our clients but only they can choose to make any change. Making significant changes in life inevitably involves taking risks. As long as we resist change we almost certainly remain blind, unconsciously responding to external stimuli and thus being vulnerable to control by others, either directly or indirectly.

One of the significant aims of any growth psychology is to bring about a spiritual awareness and an understanding of the divine within each of us, through which we can find self-realisation and our own path to God.

Growth psychologies, of which astrological psychology and psychosynthesis are but two, do not seek to impose this on us as a new belief system, instead they use experiential techniques which allow this understanding to develop from within, and through personal experience.

Personal Evolution – Five Stages of Growth

When we begin working with sub-personalities we can recognise five stages which we need to embark upon in order to allow these parts of ourselves to transform.

- Recognition
- Acceptance (not Resignation)
- Understanding
- Choices
- Will

Recognition

Roberto Assagioli suggested that we are like many people living in one skin. He called these parts of us 'sub-personalities'. When we don't really know who we are and why we behave in certain ways, our sub-personalities are more likely to be reacting to people and circumstances around us in habitual ways, many of these learned in childhood when survival was the name of the game. When we begin to become aware of these many parts of ourselves and how they live life for us we also begin the process of being in control, and of living our lives in a more positive and fulfilling way.

Acceptance

When we look at ourselves in a conscious, open and honest manner we may discover certain aspects about our personality that we don't really like. It is an essential part of our growth process that we can accept, and love, all parts of ourselves. This gives them the opportunity to transform and become a creative force in our life.

Understanding

This stage develops our conscious awareness of who we are and whether the way in which we react to the environment is what we really need. Might there be other and more positive ways of using our energy, and if we changed a habitual way of reacting to life, what would happen? Stepping out of familiar ways might mean taking a risk.

Choice

When we recognise that we can be 'in the driving seat' and not a passenger, then we can also become aware that being in control means that we can make choices for ourselves. We can choose to do what feels right for us. This may sound easy, but making choices also means that we have to take responsibility for the consequences of what we choose to do. In other words, we would be in control of our own life – there would be no one else to blame for any decisions we make. But we also give ourselves freedom to do what is right for us.

Will

In order to implement the choices we make for ourselves we have to employ our will. Otherwise we can just dream about what we might do. Will is the ability to make happen what we choose to do. There are three elements of will – strong will; skilful will and good will. Strong will alone suggests power, skilful will on its own suggests manipulation and good will on its own suggests passivity. We need to ensure that we are using all three of these elements if we are to use will successfully and become a truly autonomous human being.

Finally

Assagioli suggested that we might inhibit our own psychological and spiritual development by experiencing fears about losing control of our own life, or believing that we aren't good enough. He referred to this as the 'Repression of the Sublime'. We conclude by quoting from the writings of Marianne Williamson, used in a speech by Nelson Mandela.

"Our deepest fear is not that we are inadequate,

Our deepest fear is that we are powerful beyond measure.

It is our light, not our darkness, that most frightens us.

We ask ourselves 'Who am I to be brilliant, gorgeous, talented, Fabulous? Actually, who are you not to be. You are a child of God,

Your playing small doesn't serve the world. There's nothing enlightened about shrinking so that other people won't feel insecure around you.

We are all meant to shine, as children do. We were born to manifest the Glory of God that is within us.

It is not just for some of us; it's in everyone. And as we let our own light shine, we unconsciously give other people permission to do the same.

As we're liberated from our own fear, our presence automatically liberates others."

Recommended Reading

Psychosynthesis

Psychosynthesis: The Elements and Beyond by Will Parfitt

or

What We May Be by Piero Ferrucci

Sub-personalities

Discover Your Subpersonalities: Our Inner World and the People in It, by John Rowan

or

Our Inner Actors – the Theory and Application of Subpersonality Work in Psychosynthesis, by Dr Margaret Rueffler

Exercise 1.3

1. This section poses a number of important questions relating to the reasons for learning astrology, and indeed about the purpose of astrology itself. Allow yourself time to consider your own responses to the issues these raise.

2. From your current level of understanding, are you able to identify some of your own sub-personalities?

   If so, think about how and when you use these in your day to day life.

3. Can you begin to see sub-personalities operating in those around you?

4. Do you get a sense of how becoming aware of our sub-personalities might relate to astrological psychology and the process of self development?

1.4 First Steps in Chart Interpretation

In this section we introduce some basic considerations in chart interpretation:

- The Five Levels of Human Existence and how they are reflected in the birth chart
- The use of colour in the chart and its relationship with human motivation
- The first step in chart interpretation by looking at the chart in a visual and intuitive manner.

The five levels of human existence

Chart analysis as practised by many astrologers involves looking at individual aspects, planets in signs and houses, sign rulers, house rulers and other factors, often in isolation. This makes it difficult to see which significators are relevant to the individual and which are not. To some extent this can be likened to doing a jigsaw puzzle in the dark.

The puzzle comes in a box with no picture of the completed puzzle on the outside and all you can do is tip the pieces out on to a table and try to feel how one piece fits another without being able to see what you are doing. Difficult to say the least! Now imagine doing the same puzzle in a well-lighted room and with a clear picture on the box of what you are trying to achieve.

Using the techniques of astrological psychology it is possible to view the birth chart as though it were the picture on the puzzle box (Figure 1.4.1), and so become aware of the whole human being before starting to analyse the chart in detail. The core of psychological energy at the centre of the chart is the hub of four surrounding layers, each one influencing motivation and conditioning behaviour in the outside world.

Figure 1.4.1 shows how the pieces of the puzzle fit together. Although the descriptions in this section are brief they are important because they portray, in simple terms, the skeleton of the Huber approach to astrological psychology and it is upon this that subsequent chapters will build.

The Circle in the Centre

Looking at the chart we can assume that the true essence of the human being lies in the circle at the centre of the chart. This centre has many names. Some call it soul, psyche or atman, others call it spirit, self or monad, but in reality we cannot describe and understand this essential core in satisfactory human terms. It is the source of basic spiritual, psychic energies, tuned to the universe and unique to the individual and as such we leave this circle in the middle open and do not draw aspects lines through it.

It is that part of us which is unchanging and there will be times for many when they have a sense of 'being' at a deep level, a sense of their essence which has little connection with what they are at the level of the personality.

The chart is drawn around this circle. Symbolically, when baby is born, this central core begins to beam energies in all directions and it is from this centre that child grows into his or her world, to become and to be. We may, perhaps, begin to explore and understand this core through Transpersonal Psychology – or at least be able to acknowledge its existence and see it as the door which opens us to the universe where we all belong.

See diagram in *The Astrological Houses* on page 22.

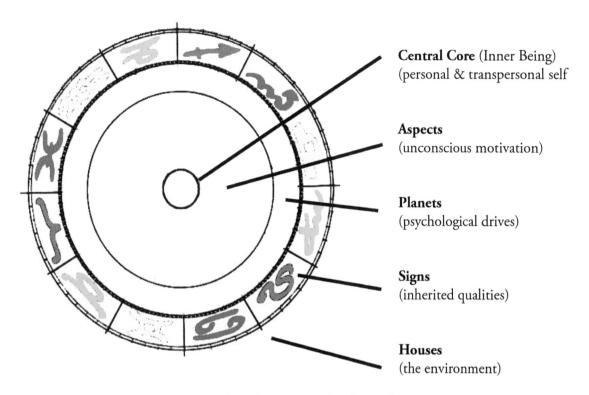

Central Core (Inner Being)
(personal & transpersonal self

Aspects
(unconscious motivation)

Planets
(psychological drives)

Signs
(inherited qualities)

Houses
(the environment)

Figure 1.4.1 The Five Levels of the Chart

The Aspects

The whole aspect configuration makes up a picture which, through its dynamic direction, orientation, coherence, shaping and colour shows a structure of sub-conscious activity. The complete aspect picture can be seen as an individual's inner motivation and energy, having the potential to be focussed on development and self-realisation in certain life areas (houses). The aspects also show the modifying influences at work between one planet and another.

Aspects are selective in that each aspect is capable of selecting a particular type or spectrum of the energy radiating out from the central core and distributing its quality of energy to the planets with which it makes contact.

Central energy contains the full spectrum of human possibilities that exist and the aspects are the 'first selection' that allow for specialisation – or the motivation to have a go at certain things in life. An analogy might be to imagine the centre of the chart as pure white light beaming outwards. White light contains seven colours and each type of aspect line is capable of filtering out one of these and focussing it to a power point (planet) with which it has contact.

An Open Area with no Aspects

If there is an open space in one sector of the chart between the centre and the periphery then energy can flow directly, and unfocussed a) from the centre of the chart out into the world, and b) **from the**

environment into the centre of the chart. This may have the effect of creating a sense of vulnerability, insecurity or inadequacy, depending upon which area of the chart is open.

The Planets

The planets symbolise the potential life forces which represent the ego and the 'tools' with which a person makes contact with the world and establishes vital and functional exchanges with it. The aspect pattern is hidden beneath the surface of human consciousness and it is therefore difficult for the individual to be aware of its structure. The planetary influences are closer to hand and thus their effects can be more clearly established, so we must always be careful not to pay too much attention to the planets and too little to the nature of the aspect structure.

Although we talk of planets as points of energy they are, in fact, more like light bulbs, each with its own special characteristic. Without energy being transmitted into the bulb you are unable, at least in the dark, to see it. The planets pick up particular wavelengths of energy from the aspects and transform and transmit these to the outer world.

The manner in which a planet expresses itself will be defined to a great extent by the nature of the aspects it receives. But the planets are also meeting points of other energies. Not only are they the receptors of inner life forces but they are also the power points where internal and external energies meet and conflict.

A further dimension is added when it is considered that a planet not only receives energy of a particular kind from the sign in which it is placed, it is also the focal point for energy from the environment, or the house in which it is situated. When we look at a birth chart we need to be aware of a multi-directional flow of energy which is ceaselessly stimulating, energising and activating different areas of the chart, or of ourselves, at all times.

Unaspected Planets

If there is no aspect to a planet then it will pick up 'energy' or 'messages' from the environment rather than from the centre, so an inner link has to be forged and consciously maintained for contact to exist between the planet and the core.

Without this link the planet may be 'used' by the outside world, or the individual may unconsciously force its presence on the outside world because its existence can only be felt if it is being reacted to by other people, and to feel that all parts of us exist is important for anyone.

An unaspected Mars may be experienced as very assertive by those people in daily contact with it but, to the person in whose chart it lies, there is not likely to be an understanding of this. "I'm really a very meek person." Recognition of how that Mars (a sub-personality) behaves, and learning how to make contact with it and use it positively is part of the process of psychosynthesis.

Another effect of an unaspected planet may be a divergence of views between the individual and other people about the nature of that planet. For instance, an unaspected Venus in a woman's chart may well mean that her view of herself as a woman will be very different from the way that men see her – with all the possible complications that might result from such a lack of understanding.

The Signs

The signs of the zodiac represent twelve basic archetypes or roles of being human. Since they contain the sum total of human knowledge and experience, they are, as part of the collective unconscious, continually evolving as humanity grows in awareness and understanding. The signs are also indicative of genetic and inherited traits from the immediate family as well as from previous generations.

A planet situated in a sign takes on the flavour or quality of that sign. A simple analogy which might help to explain part of this process is to imagine the planets as actors and actresses in a play, and the signs as the costumes in which each has to dress in order to play the role into which they have been cast.

As an example we might take Venus as a powerful and beautiful female actress. If she is cast in a part which requires her to play the role of Libra she can make the most of her strength and beauty to bring harmony, affection and happiness to those with whom she comes into contact. But in contrast, imagine Venus **inheriting** the costume of Capricorn or Aries. How is she going to feel and behave?

All the Laws of Nature are contained within the signs, and the interaction of planet and sign transmits that particular law to the planet so that it becomes a part of us. The signs reveal what we want or need from life and they clarify and specify the nature of the potential energy contained in the planet.

The Houses

The houses represent the outside world, the environment, the life situations with which a person is confronted from the moment of birth. He either learns to cope with them and find fulfilment, or he bows before them and suffers disappointments

In the areas of life represented by the houses an individual has the opportunity to realise his innate potential but can do this more efficiently if he understands what it is. Through the houses, from the moment of birth the environment starts to form and condition the child to fulfil what it believes its potential to be. But this is often contrary to what exists and the conflict and frustration that ensues as the child passes into adulthood is often the motivation which prompts the young adult to seek the right outlet and environment for self-fulfilment

The houses represent the world into which we are born and in which there already exist certain laws and conventions of society. These may conflict with our own inner energies so we will no doubt have to learn to balance the longings of our inner world with the laws, restrictions and demands of the outer world. To be successful in this requires an understanding of ourselves and a willingness to grow and evolve in a selfless manner – otherwise we may either find ourselves at loggerheads with the world, or we may become just an adapted slave to the demands of others, with all the repression, anger, misery and frustration that will surely ensue.

Colour and Motivation

We have already covered the aspects used in astrological psychology and the use of colour in relation to them. Now we introduce the idea of associating motivation with colour, as well as with the aspects. When we talk about motivation we are referring to strong, basic drives which are attempting to come into consciousness.

Figure 1.4.2 below illustrates the aspects, their motivation and their association with colour, type of energy, and the quality of certain planets.

COLOUR/ASPECT	MOTIVATION	ASSOCIATED WITH THE QUALITY OF:
ORANGE 0°	The seedling talent, the linking together of many components. Inner tension (mostly unconscious)	**SUN** **MOON**
E N E R G Y **RED 90°** **180°**	Release of tension, power, performance and friction to work, stress or aggression. Energy-blocking, impulsive, inflexible, tendency to displacement activity. Suppression – released through lateral aspects.	**MARS** **SATURN**
T H O U G H T **GREEN 30°** **150°**	The 'little step in thinking', reality, disinterest, informative, (perceiving - meditating) The 'big step in thinking', Will-building, challenging, longing, tendency to projection. Decision crisis. Inclination to search.	**MERCURY** **SATURN**
S U B T S T A N C E **BLUE 60°** **120°**	Positively through growth, assimilation, striving for harmony. Fear of conflict, tendency to compromise. Negatively by avoidance. Abundance, harvest, bringing to perfection, sensorial joy, inclination to enjoyment, sense of proportion. Perfectionism, sensorial excess, addiction.	**VENUS** **JUPITER**

Figure 1.4.2 Colour and Motivation

Colour Combinations

When you look at a chart you will usually become aware that there is a certain combination, or mixture of red, blue and green. Consideration of the balance of colours applies not only to the chart as a whole, but also to the colours of the aspects to individual planets. Some examples of colour combinations follow:

red/blue:

Ambivalent, polarity thinking, creative contradiction, over compensation, moving to and fro, striving for harmony and diplomacy.

red/green

Very restless, an argumentative spirit, tendency to exploitation, productive thinking as a result of much fruitless expenditure of energy, energy loss (there's a hole in my bucket), bringing out the highest.

blue/green

Inclined to flight, (an evasive aspect structure), shifting moods and energies, a trail of fantasy, reluctant to produce work but able to perceive what needs to be done.

red/blue/green

Demanding growth, strong evolutionary potential through continuing crisis mechanisms. Conflict, striving to find a solution, bringing into harmony.

The First Step in Chart Interpretation

Chart Picture – Chart Image

Hamlet: "Do you see yonder cloud that's almost in shape and colour of a camel?"

Polonius: "By the mass, and 'tis like a camel indeed"

Hamlet: "Methinks it is a weasel"

Polonius: "It is backed like a weasel"

Hamlet: "Or like a whale?"

Polonius: "Very like a whale"

One of the most important things we can do when starting to look at a chart is to do simply that - to look. Setting aside and perhaps even temporarily "forgetting" any astrology we already **know**, the first way into the chart is via the **senses**, the **eyes** and the **intuition**.

Cast your mind back to the time when you were a small child. Maybe you had a coal fire in the house where you grew up. Can you remember looking into the embers of the fire and seeing pictures or scenes, faces or figures? Similarly, you may have done the same thing when looking at clouds in the sky: "That one looks like a dog... now it's changed and looks more like a dragon...". Using your eyes, your senses and your imagination, you were perhaps able to see pictures and images, based on the shapes you saw in the clouds or the embers of the fire.

Using a similar approach when first looking at a chart, we can train ourselves to look for an intuitive picture or image, and we do this by looking at the overall aspect structure which fills the large central area of the chart. Very often the essence of the person is contained within this area of the chart, and through developing the intuition we can gain a sense of the person simply by looking at this central core of the chart and absorbing and reflecting upon the pictures or images that we see there.

Practical Exercise – Chart Image

- Hold the chart at arm's length, or prop it up and move away from it so you can see the whole chart from a distance.

- Half close your eyes when looking for the chart image – try not to look too "logically"! If you wear spectacles you could try removing them when you look at a chart, to defocus your eyes and allow your senses freer rein.

- Keep the chart upright – don't turn it upside down or on its side. It should be viewed in the normal upright position.

- You may find it useful to make a chart "mask" or template from a sheet of paper or card. This can be used to cover the planets, signs and house cusps, leaving only the aspect structure exposed. This can be made by cutting out and discarding an appropriately sized circle from a sheet of paper.

- Allow yourself to get a sense of what is in the chart. From this a picture or image may emerge. Some of the images people have seen in charts are as diverse as a flower opening, a tent or marquee, a pyramid, a butterfly, a space rocket, an open book, a yacht, a flag – the variety of images is limitless, based upon what has been intuitively seen and perceived from the chart.

- You may not see a picture or image, but you may have a strong sense of a predominant colour in the aspect structure, or a sense that everything in the chart is spread out, or squashed, or clinging to one particular area of the chart.

- If you are unable to see a picture or image, be aware of whether you are picking up something in the chart via your other senses

Jupiterian approach

In astrological psychology, we put a lot of importance upon taking the time to **look** at a chart as a whole before setting off into the realms of deeper and more technical interpretation. This approach is **Jupiterian** – we use our **eyes** and our **intuition** and we **look** at the chart, taking in the **whole picture** before moving on to the finer points and details. This is different from a more conventional Mercurial approach, where facts and detailed information about the chart are considered first and foremost using the logical mind – and the overall picture of the chart is not necessarily taken into consideration.

Looking at and absorbing a chart in this way is the first of a series of foundation stones or building blocks we need to set in place to enable us to find ways into the chart. You are strongly recommended to practice and develop this technique on as many charts of people you know as possible, so that you gain experience and apply your learning to real people and their lives.

> Take the time to look at a chart as a whole before setting off into deeper and more technical interpretation.
>
> This approach is Jupiterian – use your eyes and intuition and look at the chart, taking in the whole picture...

Some Examples

Chart A

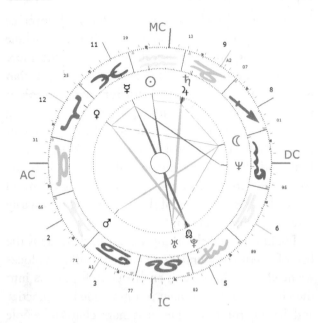

Figure 1.4.3 Chart A – Young woman
9.2.1961, 12.00, Nairobi

This is the chart of a young woman who feels she has to tread very carefully in her everyday life in order not to upset or unbalance the structures in her life which provide her with security. The picture, or image, we can see in her chart is of a tightrope or stilt walker, balanced on a pair of delicately crossed pointed toes, represented by Uranus and Pluto/Node at the bottom of the chart. The stilt walker has a long pole to help her keep her balance, represented by the linear aspect between Moon and Mars which spans the chart. The overall structure appears top-heavy and precariously balanced, relying on the careful placing of the pointed toes at the bottom to keep it upright and steady; a graphic example of how the chart image can reflect the reality of how the person experiences their own life.

Chart B

Chart B (right) has the appearance of a tornado, or "twister". The top of the tornado is open to the sky, formed by the placement of the Sun/Jupiter conjunction and Venus. Unaspected Mars sits prominently in the open funnel at the top, possibly orchestrating the tornado and stirring things up. The Moon is at the base of the tornado, where it touches the ground, and is at the lowest part of the chart. The other planets and aspects seem disorganised and scattered, as though they are being whipped up by the wind which the tornado creates, and are about to be sucked in.

This is the chart of the boxer, Mike Tyson, renowned both in and out of the ring for unpredictable and often violent behaviour.

Chart C

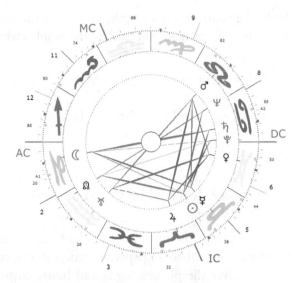

Figure 1.4.5 Chart C – Yehudi Menuhin
22.4.1916, 23.20, New York

If we apply the suggested guidelines to Chart C, we may not get an immediate clear image or picture (although if you do get a picture, this suggests that you have already begun to work successfully with this approach!) Remember that even if no picture emerges, we may still gain a sense of the person through what we can see in the chart.

An intuitive response to Chart C might include noting the intensity and vibrancy of movement which is conveyed by the visual appearance of the aspect structure. The whole structure seems to move and vibrate, and we are reminded of a slow motion film of a humming bird's rapidly beating wings, or of something

Figure 1.4.4 Chart B – Mike Tyson
30.6.1966, 12.00, New York

normally perceived by the eyes as being still, but which is vibrating very fast and at a high frequency.

This is the chart of the violinist, Yehudi Menuhin, and although we may not have seen an image quite so easily with this chart, the overall sense that can be gained relates very much to the vibrating violin strings which were an essential part of his life.

Chart D

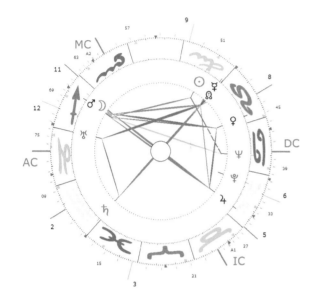

Figure 1.4.6 Chart D – Arthur Koestler
5.9.1905, 15.30, Budapest

Chart D has an immediate visual impact. It seems to come forward towards the viewer and focuses the eye on the circle in the centre, which is flanked by, perhaps, a bow tie? Or wings? Maybe the tail fins of some fast-moving vessel which has just passed by and is now travelling off into the distance? The criss-crossed lines of the aspects give the impression of a "trellis", something which can be folded away flat or opened up large, like it is here.

Sometimes we can find more than one image in a chart, and it is worth bearing this in mind when working with the charts of real people and applying this technique. One image may be more relevant and appropriate to the person than the others that have been seen; the way to find out if this is so is to offer the images and ask if they have meaning for the person. Often, people who have no experience of astrology or of working with a chart in this way will see a picture in their own chart that has meaning for them.

Chart E

Figure 1.4.7 Chart E – Johann Sebastian Bach
31.3.1685, 11.30, Eisenach

Chart E has a large, widely spread appearance, and the image that might come to us when we look and absorb the whole chart is of a tall, straight figure, firmly and centrally placed within the chart, with its "feet" represented by Saturn and Jupiter. The figure wears a large flowing cape or cloak, which is flared out and is being held on either side by Mars and Pluto, as though the person is making a grand entrance with a dramatic grand gesture as if to say "I'm here!"

This is the chart of Johann Sebastian Bach. His *Toccata and Fugue in D Minor* for the organ has the dramatic grandeur of the "grand gesture" seen in this chart picture, as do many of his other magnificent compositions.

Remember

Looking at the chart, using the eyes, the senses and the intuition are always the first steps to take when working with any chart.

Once you have found a picture or image in a chart, do not discard, forget or set it aside as something you have "done" and have no need to refer to again. The chart image can yield up important and relevant information about the person, and is therefore something to hold in mind and refer back to throughout the entire interpretation of the chart.

Summary

It is important to look at the chart as a whole, to see all the layers, because only by doing this is it possible to be aware of the interactions which affect the energies radiating from the inner core. The aspects pick up energies and focus these, through the aspect structure, to the planets (tools). These tools, or functioning organs, are stimulated and modified by the signs and act and react in our daily lives (houses).

As stated at the beginning, this is only an introduction to a major topic but even at this stage you may find it helpful to keep in mind the fact that there will be times in everybody's life when natural opportunities occur to look beneath the outer level of the chart. So, before we conclude this section we are going to introduce an important key which can open up a gateway through which to pass and begin the process of understanding the composition of this five-layered structure.

What goes on beneath the surface of this fundamental structure of personality is not static and dead but vital, living and responsive to the changing energy patterns of our solar system, if not to the universe. We have already mentioned that with the Koch House System it is possible to use the natal chart as a life clock and trace out the progress of the passing years with the Age Point.

This Age Point can be seen as a point of consciousness moving around the chart and, at certain times, illuminating the interior for our examination and better understanding. It can be significant in pinpointing the dates of important psychological growth periods, many of which can be identified with external events in our lives.

Coming From the Centre

Exploration of the existential meaning of the central area of the chart is an important step in your own process of self-discovery. Being able to make contact with it provides the opportunity to stand back from the personality and observe what is going on.

Explore the idea of being able to stand in the centre of your own chart and visualise the planets as seen from this centre. We suggest a practical exercise on the next page, which is not totally dissimilar to becoming the conductor of an orchestra. Your task is to become aware of the way in which each instrument is playing and the ability to do this is likely only to come with practice. Are they in harmony? Is one out of tune? Is every instrument motivated to playing the music which you have chosen?

If you look at a chart which has separated aspect patterns, unaspected planets... you may be able to visualise this as a division in the orchestra, where one group of musicians has decided to play 'their own tune' rather than the one you would like them to. So the conductor's job is to be aware of this 'split' and find how all the musicians can be brought together so the orchestra is able to realise its full potential.

Perhaps your own life experience has included that special and memorable occasion when an orchestra seems to be transported beyond the level of competence of individual musicians and becomes the instrument of some transpersonal energy which enables them to create music of mystical beauty.

Practical Exercise – Dis-identification

This is a simple exercise to practice dis-identification, or the ability to connect with your own centre. It is one step in self-awareness. Remember from section 1.3 that your own centre can be both passive (the observer) and active (the director). In this exercise we invite you to make a connection with the **observer**, and then allow yourself to sink into an even deeper part of the centre – beyond the observer or the director. This is a place where you can become aware of the essence of who you are – ageless and timeless – with a totally peaceful sense of beingness. If you make contact with this part of yourself it is likely that initially it will only be for a brief moment of time. Ideally you will experience a sense of calm, inner peace and joy.

To do this exercise you will find it easiest if you read the instructions once or twice to get a sense of what it is you are doing. Then you can do it in any way that feels right for you. There is no need to remember the exact words.

- Sit down in a comfortable chair. If you want you can have quiet and calming music playing in the background.

- Close your eyes and spend a few moments relaxing your body. Become aware of each part of it and see whether it feels tense. If it does then see if you can allow it to go 'soft'. Begin to sink into the chair and feel at ease in your mind, your feelings and your body.

- Now focus your attention fully on your mind. Become aware of the thoughts which pass through it as they come and go. Your mind is a valuable tool of discovery and expression. Its contents are continually changing, offering new and old thoughts. Sometimes it may even refuse to obey you. It is an instrument of knowledge in regard to both your inner and outer worlds but, since you can observe it, it is NOT you.

(Stop observing your mind, and pause for a moment)

- Now turn your attention to your feelings. Become aware of feelings that emerge from deep down inside you. Recall how they can change from one moment to the next - from calm to anger; from joy to sadness; from love to hate, sometimes in conflict with one another as they attempt to react to the world around you, as well as to your inner needs. Be aware that since you can observe your feelings it is clear that they are not the essence of you.

(Stop observing your feelings and once again pause for a moment)

- Focus your attention on your body. Recognise how it serves you. How it carries you around, obeys your commands, lets you know when it is tired, hungry or unwell. Observe your body sitting in the chair and acknowledge that you value your body as an instrument that serves you well but since you can observe it know that you are not your body.

(Stop observing your body and pause a moment)

- Now be aware that you have a mind but since you can observe it **you** are not your mind;
  Be aware that you have feelings but **you** are not your feelings;
  Be aware that you have a body but **you** are not your body:
  So ask yourself the question '**Who am I**?'.

- Now let yourself become aware that **you** are a centre of pure consciousness. You are a being of self-awareness and of inner balance. Take a few moment to identify with this centre.

- When you feel ready, become aware once again of your body sitting in the chair, of the room around you, and when you feel ready open your eyes, and make some notes about your experience.

Don't be afraid to try this as often as you want – it becomes easier with practice!

Symptoms of Inner Peace

Author Unknown

Be on the lookout for symptoms of Inner Peace. The hearts of a great many have already been exposed to Inner Peace and it is possible that people everywhere could come down with it in epidemic proportions. This could pose a serious threat to what has, up to now, been a fairly stable condition of conflict in the world.

Some signs and symptoms of Inner Peace.

- A tendency to think and act spontaneously rather than on fears based on past experience;

- An unmistakable ability to enjoy every moment;

- A loss of interest in judging other people;

- A loss of interest in interpreting the actions of others;

- A loss of interest in conflict;

- A loss of ability to worry (This is a very serious symptom);

- Frequent, overwhelming episodes of appreciation;

- Contented feelings of connectedness with others, and with nature;

- Frequent attacks of smiling;

- An increasing tendency to let things happen rather than make them happen;

- An increasing susceptibility to the love extended by others as well as the uncontrollable urge to love them back.

It seems appropriate to end this introductory chapter by mentioning that whilst you may not be aware of all the above qualities just by connecting with your own centre, you will begin to experience them more and more as you progress through the process of self-awareness and conscious change.

Study Note

Too many astrologers use a form of technical jargon that implies knowledge and saves them from having to specify what they actually mean. For example: "Ah well, of course he's got Sun opposition Saturn" or "Well, its not surprising with Pluto conjunct Mars". Such statements do not mean much on their own since they are taken out of context. For instance Sun opposition Saturn will have a very different meaning if Saturn rather than Sun is at the top of the chart.

Whilst working through this book, we suggest you avoid making vague astrological comments which assume that someone else understands what you mean. If you want to talk about Sun opposition Saturn then please relate the actual life experience that this aspect gives rise to or, if this is not known, make an interpretation and be specific in explaining what the life experience might be.

Remember that every chart you look at represents a living individual with beliefs, attitudes, behaviour, likes, dislikes, fears, parents, relationships and so on. So, take this learning opportunity to see charts as real people with real lives rather than as pieces of paper on which there are symbols and coloured lines.

Exercise 1.4

1. List each of the aspects used in astrological psychology, the number of degrees, its colour, and the planet with which it is associated.

   Then, working with each aspect in turn, visualise the colour associated with the aspect and make a note of any words that come into your mind which you can associate both with the colour and the aspect. These can be listed under a heading 'Motivation'. See if you can think of at least 6 words for each aspect.

   Example.

   > Aspect – Square
   >
   > Colour – Red.
   >
   > Words which come to mind might be 'Energy', 'Anger', 'Fire', and so on.

2. Reflect on your understanding of each of the Five Levels of a Chart. You may also find it useful to try to summarise each level using no more than 20 words for each.

3. Using the suggestions on how to look for an image, or visual picture in a chart, spend time becoming aware of any images you can see in your chart, and reflect on how these might relate to your personality or behaviour in some way.

4. Practise looking for images in the charts of people you know well and if possible, ask if these have any meaning for them.

Chapter 2. The Aspect Level - Inner Motivation

The coloured aspect lines provide a foundational structure to the chart. This chapter aims to give you insight into the meanings of the colours, shaping, direction and coherence of the chart structure and the patterns made by the aspects. These relate directly to our motivations and inner drives.

Contents:

1. Colour and its Associated Qualities
2. Looking at the Birth Chart
3. Aspect Patterns and their Meanings

2.1 Colour and its Associated Qualities

In this section we cover:

- The significance of the colours used to draw the aspects in the birth chart, i.e. red, green, blue and orange, and the qualities attributed to them.
- The association of these colours with the Cardinal, Fixed and Mutable Crosses of the signs and houses in the chart.
- The psychology of colour

Introduction

When we look at the overall aspect pattern in a birth chart we can discern within it smaller distinct aspect figures. These may be quadrangular or triangular in shape and can be made up of different combinations of red, blue and green aspects.

The combination of shape and colour in these patterns is the key to uncovering and understanding the inner **motivation** of the individual. Motivation differs from temperament in that motivation relates to what is traditionally known in astrology as the quadruplicities, signifying modes of action, e.g. cardinal, fixed, mutable. Temperament relates to the triplicities or elements, i.e. fire, earth, air and water.

Motivation springs from the **causal** level of the human being and represents our unconscious drive to be, act and respond – and very often we have little or no conscious control over the way it expresses itself.

Consideration of these basic life motivations, shown in the aspect figures, will bring about a greater self-awareness, and the ability to understand and make the fullest possible use of the creative potentials embodied in the planets which form these figures. They may be seen as energy configurations within the individual's consciousness, each of which follows its own particular laws and modus operandi.

Each figure has an 'archetypal' meaning or task to perform in the evolution of consciousness and in its relationship to the world. The relative positions of the planets by house and sign specify how and in what direction these motivations can find their full expression in the person's life.

Aspects and Colour

The nature of the energy associated with the three main colours of the aspects corresponds in motivation to the three crosses in the zodiac, i.e. cardinal, fixed and mutable. The following introduces the concept of the three crosses and the way in which motivation is inherent in the houses and signs as well as in the aspects.

Before going any further have another look at Ptolemaic diagram in Figure 2.1.1, which was introduced in Chapter 1.

Figure 2.1.1 Ptolemaic Arrangement

Red – Cardinal

Red aspects correspond to the **cardinal** quality; they embody, pick up and give off energy – energy in potential and energy in process, energy that wants to work and which can be directed towards goals. They are a source of power and can also give rise to conflict, and produce harmony through conflict.

Conflict in this sense is the dynamic energy which provides the drive to achieve something and to strive towards fulfillment. Where there is a lack of red aspects the individual will have little or no get-up-and-go, because there is no conflict experienced in the existing state of affairs, and hence no desire to create better circumstances.

Conflict is the unconscious use, or lack of use, of energy. Conflict is **not** the cause of energy – it is the **result** of energy which is not being properly employed.

The **square** □ has a **Mars** quality (see Figure 2.1.1). It embodies energy that can be put to work. It is the motor function, the joy of action and the joy of effort and achievement. It is masculine libidinal energy which can be used to produce something. At its lowest level it is unconscious will-power in action.

The **opposition** ☍ has a **Saturn** quality. It is energy that is 'blocked off' or suppressed; it is energy in store, awaiting its release through work. The duality embodied in the opposition gives rise to linear thinking and a black and white, either/or view of the world. Other aspects which contact the opposition may provide a resolution to it. Alternatively, the duality of the opposition may drive one inwards towards the centre of the chart, the spiritual centre, from where one may balance and reconcile the opposing forces within one's nature.

The Cardinal Cross

We associate cardinal energy with the zodiac signs of Aries, Cancer, Libra and Capricorn, as well as with their corresponding houses. If we look at these houses and their associated signs we see that they form a cross in the chart. This we call the **Cardinal Cross**.

Aries/Libra

Cancer/Capricorn

Houses 1/7 & 4/10

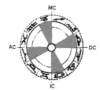

Figure 2.1.2
Cardinal Cross

Blue – Fixed

Blue aspects correspond to the **fixed** quality. They are aspects of **substance** (what you have), of acquisition (what you can get) and **retention** (what you can hold onto). They can be relaxed into and enjoyed. Their motivation is towards **security**.

The sextile ✶ has a **Venus** quality, associated with the smaller rewards and the fruits of your efforts in specific areas. It represents qualities which are being assimilated in order to produce a sense of enrichment, harmony and well-being. It relates to the harmonious relationship of specific factors (planets).

The trine △ has a **Jupiter** quality; the larger rewards and inherent talents; whole qualities which allow for a wider view of life and the containment of substance to the point of saturation; qualities which arise from individual experience, personal observation and insight.

The Fixed Cross

Fixed energy corresponds to the **Fixed Cross** which is associated with the signs of Taurus, Leo, Scorpio and Aquarius and their corresponding houses.

Taurus/Scorpio

Leo/Aquarius

Houses 2/8 & 5/11

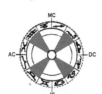

Figure 2.1.3
Fixed Cross

Red and Blue

Where there are only **red** and **blue** aspects, consciousness works on a duality principle, seeing the world in terms of good/bad, black/white, either/or, yes/no... You work to get something and when you have got it you enjoy it, then you work to get more. But consciousness is three-fold and the third pole – the

realm of relativity and evolutionary thinking – brings us to the green aspects. **If there are no green aspects in a chart it is possible for the individual to work consciously towards creating these.**

Green – Mutable

Green aspects correspond to the **mutable** quality, that gives us the ability to learn from experience through thinking or perception and hence to raise our consciousness and awareness. They represent the ability to digest experience and arrive at a new appreciation of life. They provide the motivation to search for 'truth', and to develop the ability to perceive ever deeper truths.

The **semi-sextile** ⊻ has a **Mercury** quality. This is the small step in thinking, concerned with specific factors perceived through the rational intellect. It is collecting information, drawing it in from wherever it may be available. This may happen automatically without one necessarily being conscious of it. It analyses and categorises.

The **quincunx** ⚻ has a **Saturn** quality again. This is the other face of Saturn – the aspect of deep learning which eventually brings real understanding. It is consciousness building – learning, thinking and reflecting; it moulds and tempers. There are three steps involved in realising the potential of the quincunx:

1. A longing for something unknown and not experienced; a divine discontent; the aspiration to reach the whole truth, to encompass everything, to know the essence of something.

2. A decision crisis; making compromises, yet not wanting to restrict oneself to any one thing.

3. Having finally made a decision, the Law of Refusal comes into play. Resolving to go for one thing, committing oneself. This has a will-building quality and involves the sacrifice of everything that does not partake of the nature of that one thing. It is the conscious commitment towards the highest attainable goal.

The Mutable Cross

Mutable energy corresponds to the **Mutable Cross** which is associated with the signs of Gemini, Virgo, Sagittarius and Pisces and their corresponding houses.

Gemini/Sagittarius

Virgo/Pisces

Houses 3/9 & 6/12

Figure 2.1.4
Mutable Cross

Orange – Conjunction

The **conjunction** aspect ☌ moulds and melds together the qualities of the planets involved, to create a **new quality** which is different and greater in potential and energy than the individual planets. It is, or has the ultimate potential to be, a true marriage or *coniunctio*, a union of different planetary characters which can give birth to a new quality within consciousness. The conjunction is a seed potential which depends, for its realisation, upon understanding, careful tending and nurturing.

However, the successful birth of this new quality depends upon each planet first becoming individualized and fully conscious, otherwise the stronger one will tend to dominate and control the weaker, producing a deformed, unbalanced or incomplete quality. With young people it is difficult to separate the energies; success in achieving that can usually only be attained as one grows older.

In essence orange is potential **working energy**, the quality of which will depend upon the planets involved.

Instead of colouring conjunctions in orange (or orange/yellow for one-way) it would in theory make sense for them to be drawn in any mixed shades of red, blue or green depending upon the cardinal, fixed or mutable motivation of the planets. However, this is considered impracticable and you are recommended to keep to orange and/or yellow if you are drawing up charts by hand.

The process of growth is, symbolically, to separate the colours and see each one in its pure state.

Conjunctions: Planetary Energies and Colour

Figure 2.1.5 shows the groupings of planets according to colour and quality.

FIXED Blue	MUTABLE Green	CARDINAL Red
Uranus	Neptune	Pluto
Saturn	Moon	Sun
Venus	Jupiter	Mars
	Mercury	

Figure 2.1.5 Planetary Energies and Colour

A conjunction involving only Sun/Mars/Pluto will be **red**. A conjunction of Mars and, say, Venus will be a mixture of red and blue and will initially behave as a conflict between these two colours and energies. This can only be resolved by recognising and understanding the working of these two focal points of energy in daily life. When this can be achieved it will be possible to use either Mars or Venus, or both together, as appropriate, rather than let them use you in a way which will be either motivated by the environment, or dominated by the strongest planet in the conjunction.

Experience of the techniques used in psychosynthesis may be a valuable aid to understanding the different energies at work within a conjunction. These, together with their aspects to other planets in the chart, may be viewed as sub-personalities which it may be possible to contact and come to recognise through guided imagery work. (Refer to *Psychosynthesis: The Elements and Beyond*, by Will Parfitt.)

It may be more difficult to unravel, recognise and accept the intricacies of a conjunction than of other aspects. The strongest planet tends to dominate and it is possible to lose sight of the weaker ones. And yet these can be of the greatest value. Finally remember that if you have a conjunction of, say, Venus and Saturn (**blue**) this will not be the same as assessing the meaning of a sextile, also blue, of these same planets. The sextile **does not contain working energy**, whereas the conjunction does.

Colour Balance

Counting Aspect Lines

With an understanding of the qualities associated with the three main aspect colours, we can gain information about the person's motivation by assessing the balance of colours in the aspect structure of the chart. We can do this simply by counting the number of aspect lines of each colour.

When counting the number of aspect lines in a chart, where two (or more) aspects to the same planet emanate from a conjunction of planets where the orb is 3 degrees or less, you count these as one aspect line only.

For example: squares to Venus from Moon and Neptune in conjunction with an orb of 2 degrees, would count as one red aspect and not two.

[This rule is not strictly accurate for all semi-sextiles because of their small orb values; however it is recommended that you apply this 3 degree rule to all aspects for simplicity, as this is sufficiently accurate in most cases.]

'Ideal' colour balance

The 'ideal' colour balance of aspects is in the ratio of 6 Blue: 4 Red: 2 Green. It is the **ratio** that is important and 6/4/2 is not necessarily an 'ideal' number of aspect lines.

Significant variation from this ratio will show a preponderance of one or two colours and a corresponding lack of the other colour(s).

Usually a chart with a large number of aspect lines will be one where the planets are spread around the chart, suggesting someone with a wide range of interests. The opposite will suggest someone with a focus on a more specific area of life.

For more information on interpreting the colour balance, see the section on 'Aspect Pattern Colouring' in *Aspect Pattern Astrology*, pages 123-130.

Three-Dimensions of the Aspects

We may experience the energy of aspects at different levels:

1. physical,
2. feeling/emotional
3. mental.

These levels are illustrated in the following.

Conjunction
1. fusion of energies, seed potential
2. sense of power, lack of differentiation
3. source of inspiration, creativity, synthesis

Square
1. 'doing' energy, activity, achievement
2. euphoria, anger, frustration, confrontation
3. conflict, challenge, effort, resistance, assertion

Opposition
1. block, fixation, repression
2. polarisation, vacillation, either/or attitude
3. antagonism, indecision, strength, backbone

Trine
1. lethargy, repletion, need for tranquillity
2. enjoyment, sense of happiness, desire, feeling lucky
3. abundance, superiority, serenity

Sextile
1. love of comforts, beauty, serenity, benevolence
2. striving for harmony, peace-loving, fear of conflict
3. perfectionism, aestheticism, talent potential

Semi-Sextile
1. irritability, nervousness, versatility
2. curiosity, adaptation, insecurity
3. willing to compromise, eager to learn, keen intellect

Quincunx
1. insecurity, easily confused
2. yearning, aspirations, projections, internal friction
3. crises of decision, solution-seeking, potential for awareness

Note
The definitions of aspect colours in this section are not intended to be comprehensive descriptions, but they should foster an understanding of the basic principles and thus help towards gaining a fuller appreciation of the meanings attributed to the aspect figures in section 2.2.

The Psychology of Colour

Cirlot observes that

"every symbol echoes throughout every plane of reality, and... the spiritual ambience of a person is essentially one of these planes... The symbol, then, like water, finds its own level, which is the level of the interpreting mind." (1)

There are many levels of interpretation of the experience and meaning of colour. One or two are outlined below, in order to give you some feel for the range of the subject and to evoke your own intuitive response to this rich field of study.

Physiological Studies

"Colour appears in the picture as an experience deriving from specifically coded patterns in the brain. There is no colour in the outside world."

(Sir John Eccles, Nobel Prize for research on the physiology of the brain).

"The illusion of colour explodes in the mind. It is not colours, odours or sounds which are carried to our brains by nerves, but merely pulses of energy – all of the same kind of electrical potential." (2)

These pulses of energy, like symbols, echo throughout every plane of reality, including the physical body and the emotional nature. Some of the effects have been known intuitively by esoteric teachers and healers. (See below.)

Some have been investigated by experimental psychologists in psychiatric settings; some by Rudolph Steiner in his work with mentally handicapped children; others by Luescher, who correlated colour preferences with human temperament. (Also explored, along with studies of the energies and deeper dimensions of colour, shape and sound, by Hygeia Studios in Gloucestershire, under the direction of Theo Gimbel.)

Findings

Within the visible range, psycho-physiological activation tends to increase with wavelength and with stimulus intensity. This supports the classification:

- warm advancing colours: red, orange, yellow (and by extension, white)
  ....activity, intensity

- cold retreating colours: blue, indigo, violet (and by extension black)
  ....passivity, debilitation

- the transitional colour green spans the two groups.

For example:

There is evidence of an increase in speed and activation of physiological processes on exposure to red light. A precise shade of red has been isolated, which increases the pulse rate, blood pressure, respiration, frequency of eye-blinks and cortical activity; a precise shade of blue reduces them. (3)

It has been established that the quality of certain shades is mysteriously amplified by specific forms; certain combinations of shape and colour have either a destructive or regenerative affect upon living organisms. (2)

Might it be that the interplay of colour and form in the aspect structure is an echo on another plane of these experimental findings?

Esoteric Studies

Any standard textbook of astrology will list the colours, metals, precious stones... associated with the planets. These associations derive from the esoteric theory of correspondences between macrocosm and microcosm: as above, so below. For example, 7 rays, 7 planetary spheres, 7 colours, 7 faculties of the soul, 7 musical notes.

The visions of mystics show from what inner experiences such analogies are formed. For example, Jung records the vision or waking dream of Guillaume de Digulleville, a 14th century Cistercian Prior who had a vision linking the signs of the zodiac with sacred history.

"The angel answers: Now there are 3 principal colours, namely green, red and gold. These 3 colours are seen united in divers works of watered silk and in the feathers of many birds, such as the peacock..."

"Gold, the royal colour, is attributed to God the Father; red to God the Son, because he shed his blood; and to the Holy Ghost green, 'la couleur qui verdoye et réconforte'".

Jung asks why blue is missing and replies:

"We would conjecture that blue, standing for the vertical, means height and depth (the blue sky above, the blue sea below)" (4)

It is when the visions are manifest in form – in liturgy, heraldry, alchemy, art, literature, healing, education – that we begin to see the practical value of these esoteric principles.

Colour in the Waldorf Schools

One of the greatest mystic-scientists, Rudolph Steiner, recognised the integrating and therapeutic value of colour, and a philosophy of colour informs the Waldorf schools, which are based upon his teachings.

They offer:

"a methodical training in the unique language qualities of the different colours;

- they merge and interpenetrate to give known effects;

- how yellow of itself is radiant and expansive, though it can densify to resting gold;

- how blue lends form, how it can hold and also lead into depth;

- how red can be power at rest, can mount to triumph, or turn to anger;

- how colours can be warm or cold;

- how each colour has its range and yet how their effects can multiply like situations on a stage between the actors."

The primary colours reflect primary emotions. They are offered to young children because they are appropriate to them, and preferred by them. At puberty the children cease to work with colour for a while and, instead, turn to black and white.

"This is a medium of sharp contrasts, well suited to the inner struggle of light and darkness, of personal conflict and resolve, into which they must now enter. After a year or two, when greater stability has been acquired, they return to colour, but to a more conscious use of it, and, through the work in black and white, to a clearer appreciation of form." (5)

Colour in the Chart

We hope that in constructing your charts, you will do so in a meditative spirit, so that symbol may find its own true meaning in you.

Colour References

(1) J.E.Cirlot, *A Dictionary of Symbols*, Routledge and Kegan Paul 1971 p.xlvi f.

(2) Lawrence Blair, *Rhythms of Vision*, Paladin 1975 p.125f

(3) Kenneth Bayes, *The Therapeutic effect of Environment on Emotionally Disturbed and Mentally Subnormal Children*, Kaufmann International Design Award Study. 1964-66

(4) C.G.Jung, Psychology and Alchemy: *Vol.12. Collected Works*, Routledge and Kegan Paul 1968 p.212 f

(5) Francis Edmunds, *Rudolph Steiner Education. The Waldorf Schools*, Rudolph Steiner Press London 1979

Exercise 2.1

1. Through the colour in the aspect pattern we are able to gain an insight into whether a person's unconscious motivation is predominantly initiatory, security motivated or motivated towards personal growth. You may find it helpful to look back over what you learned about the colour balance of the aspects in Chapter 1.

2. Look at the aspect pattern in your own chart and list the number of aspects by colour. This will give you a colour ratio.

3. Reflect on what your particular balance of colour suggests about your unconscious motivation.

4. Do the same for any other charts that you may be working with.

2.2 Looking at the Birth Chart

Motivation, Shaping and Direction

In this section we consider

- How we can develop our understanding of a person's motivation by looking at the inner core of the birth chart.

- How this is reflected in the structure created by the aspects in the chart, their shaping, colour, direction and coherence.

Motivation

The structure created by the aspect patterns and lines in a chart has shaping, colour, direction and coherence. Awareness of the meaning of all of these components contributes to a deeper understanding of an individual's inner motivation.

Astrological psychology is not just another astrological approach but rather another branch of psychology. Psychology is a most important science because it encompasses all the levels of experience that human beings can attain.

Astrological principles are represented through symbols. These symbols represent energies which will express themselves in our daily activities in various ways depending upon their relationship to one another, as well as, in the case of planets, their placement by sign and by house.

But there are other important factors which will affect the expression of these energies. One of these is our childhood environment which may have suppressed certain traits which were considered 'undesirable', and omitted to develop others because no-one noticed they were there. Another is a basic life motivation which is an integral part of our personality and which we strive to fulfill, consciously or otherwise, with varying degrees of success or failure.

Understanding of all these factors is essential to chart analysis. Many astrological books tend to define

behaviour as a simple manifestation of planetary placements and aspects, taking little account of motivation and therefore ignoring the relevance, or otherwise, of a particular symbol.

In the same way, many psychologists look for the reasons that cause the behaviour rather than for the underlying motivation. Finding the reasons for a behaviour pattern rarely helps a person to change the pattern, even if she wishes to, but by becoming aware of the motivation behind the behaviour pattern a person is presented with the opportunity to understand and take responsibility for her own actions.

So, in order to help people we first need to understand their motivation. Otherwise any suggestions that we make may only encourage adapted behaviour and be of no long term value, as these will not help them understand what is unconsciously driving them in their life – their life motivation.

Life motivations are basic and remain unconscious to many individuals. To recognise motivation it is important to keep in mind the Five Levels of the Chart and to understand the principles involved at each level, taking care not to mix levels or allow principles from one level to become confused with principles from another. For instance we do not take account of aspects from planets to the ascendant or midheaven because planets and houses function on different levels (see Figure 1.4.1 on page 39).

If we have an understanding of motivation we can then combine our knowledge of astrological principles with our own life experiences and recognise the importance and relevance of the significators that we find in our own chart. However, when we work with the charts of other people, we also need to understand the issue that they present to us and be able, not only to relate it to the principles in the chart, but then to translate our understanding into simple factual language that they can understand and use to solve their problem.

Some astrologers stay with the presenting problem given by the client so their effectiveness is limited. Only through assessing the astrological principles present in the chart, can we recognise and understand the underlying motivation that is causing the problem and help the person move forward. No other human science has this tool.

Looking for Motivation

Our approach might be called Jupiterian astrology, as opposed to more traditional methods which might be referred to as Mercurial astrology, i.e. looking at the chart in a fragmented and analytical manner. We view the chart as a whole and are at first concerned with the initial impression that the chart makes on us. Only later do we analyse the chart in more detail. So the first important factor is 'What visual impact does the chart make on you?' What does it say to you when you first look at it, what sensory impression do you receive, what graphic insight do you gain from that first study?

This initial approach allows you to establish a feeling for colour, shape and movement, all of which will be relevant to that person's motivation. This is the reason why charts are drawn in the way described in Chapter 1.

The reason for this approach is to discover why a person functions in a particular way. We are looking for causes and not symptoms, seeking to establish **true** motivation and to identify a person's inherent creativity so that we will be in a position to help them to become aware of their **real** potential.

Before proceeding further you might find it helpful to refer back to section 1.4, and ensure that you have a thorough understanding of the five levels of human existence and assessment of the intuitive chart image.

The Aspect Structure

The **aspect structure** surrounding the centre is the **key motivational area** in the chart. It represents the inner structure of your consciousness. The planets represent tools in your consciousness and the structure provides the links between these planets. If you do not have some understanding of this inner area your life will be determined by your surroundings – by the environment, by the people around you, influencing you through the houses.

1) Shaping

Is the shaping of the aspect structure linear, triangular or quadrangular?

In other words is the aspect pattern primarily made up of lines or triangles or polygons with 4 or more sides?

1. A **linear** chart consists mainly of aspect lines which make no completed patterns, and is symbolic of someone who never quite gets it together. People with linear charts are always on the go (**cardinal**), searching but perhaps never understanding what it is they are looking for, therefore never finding it. This does not imply that such people cannot achieve worldly success. On the contrary, their continual restlessness may well bring success but whether they can recognise and be happy with their achievements is another matter.

2. A **triangular** chart consists mainly of triangular figures. Triangles are not static but are able to move (red ones more easily than blue ones) and show a motivation that is **mutable**, changeable, adaptable, dynamic and change orientated. Such people live for the present, are happy with a changing world and easily adapt to handling situations of crisis. They can be creative and have the ability to transform their surroundings.

3. A chart with an aspect structure consisting mainly of figures with four or more corners, which we characterize as **quadrangular**, has a **fixed** motivation. These indicate a basic life motivation that looks for stability and security. The more symmetrical the structure the stronger will be the security motivation. An all-red Achievement Square, although consisting entirely of cardinal energy lines, is a fixed structure, and so likely to be the cause of much tension. People with a fixed chart cannot ignore their need for security because it is only when that is met that they can become mentally and emotionally free and healthy.

As you examine the chart in greater detail you will be looking to see how the needs of the inner level contrast with the demands of the outer level, i.e. the environment. For instance, if a person with a fixed chart is constantly being motivated by, say, Uranus on the MC, then they are responding to environmental stimuli and not to their inner motivation.

2) Direction

Does the aspect structure appear to have a vertical or horizontal direction?

Is there a **direction** to the structure? Does it point upwards towards the top of the chart, indicating objectivity and the desire for individuality? Or are all the planets grouped in the lower half of the chart, in the collective area where there is a need to seek security through situations and people that are known and safe?

A chart with all planets at the top and nothing at the bottom (e.g. Figure 2.2.4) suggests someone who is out of touch with the needs and demands of the collective, with no roots there. Such a person, may be outstandingly successful in their career objectives but might still suffer from a suppressed sense of insecurity, of not belonging, perhaps even of rejection.

If the chart has a **vertical** direction (e.g. Figure 2.2.2) there will be a desire to progress upwards, break away from the restrictions of the collective.

If the aspect structure is seen as bridging the left and right sides of the chart, and therefore has more of a **horizontal** direction (e.g. Figure 2.2.1), the motivation will be for human contact rather than for personal success, though this latter will by no means necessarily be denied, e.g. a politician, a salesman, etc. In the latter case one would also have to consider whether the motivation to succeed as an individual would fit the chosen line of business. So bear in mind that, although there may be an emphasis of direction, it is still necessary to take account of all the energies in the chart to ascertain whether or not a person is going to find it easy or difficult to be in harmony with the underlying motivation.

Is the aspect structure lying mainly on the left (I-side) or the right (You-side) of the chart?

If it is on the **I-side** (e.g. Figure 2.2.3), the individual's natural focus will be on self and independence. If it is on the **You-side**, the individual's focus will be on other people with a strong need for contacts and social interaction.

Examples of Direction

Figure 2.2.1
Horizontal direction
Quadrangular shaping/
Fixed mode of action

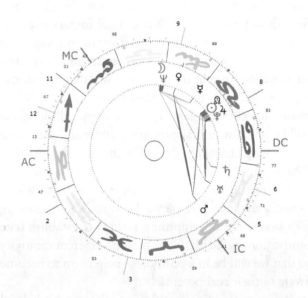

Figure 2.2.2
Vertical direction
Linear shaping/
Cardinal mode of action
You-sided chart

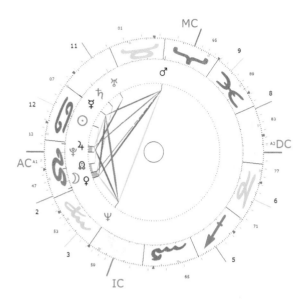

Figure 2.2.3
Vertical direction
Quadrangular shaping/
Fixed mode of action
I-sided chart

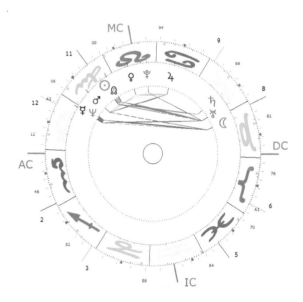

Figure 2.2.4
Vertical emphasis
Mainly Linear shaping

Figure 2.2.4 shows another way of identifying vertical motivation. This time all the planets are at the top of the chart even though the aspects are horizontal. However, with no links into the collective area of the chart at the bottom there will be a distinct sense of insecurity, perhaps a sense of isolation and a lack of understanding as to what the real world needs from this person. They will feel ungrounded and will certainly need to establish links with reality in order to achieve a sense of belonging.

Vertical or horizontal?
When determining whether the direction of the aspect structure is vertical or horizontal you need to remember that the top of the chart is shown by the position of the Midheaven, and not by the top of the page. While the AC/DC axis, which represents the horizon, is always in the same position, the MC/IC axis may be skewed to one side or the other. In these circumstances a chart that may appear on a superficial inspection to be horizontal may in fact be vertical, and vice versa.

It is not unusual to find charts that exhibit the features of both vertical and horizontal direction, and that may indeed indicate mixed motivations. In such cases it may be difficult to decide from the visual impression alone whether one direction is more strongly emphasised than the other.

One way of obtaining clarification is to draw a rectangle in the aspect area of the chart between the centres of the fixed houses 2, 5, 8, 11. Aspects crossing opposite sides of this rectangle may be considered as vertical (if crossing the sides between 2/5 and 8/11) or horizontal (if crossing the sides between 2/11 and 5/8.) A preponderance of such aspects in one direction or the other provides an indication of the overall chart shaping. This technique should be used only as a last resort and in most cases it will be possible to determine the direction of the aspect structure from visual inspection alone.

> **Remember**
> When determining chart direction, the top of the chart is the MC, not the top of the page.

3) Colour

Section 2.1 already looked at the importance of colour balance and the 'ideal' ratio of 2 green aspect lines: 4 red: 6 blue.

Are all three colours present in the aspect structure? Is there one colour that stands out at first glance? Is a colour completely absent? From the answers you can determine the predominant motivation: red=cardinal, blue=fixed, green=mutable.

An excess of red (cardinal) can reduce the ability to enjoy life because red indicates drive, activity, Will and tension. With a shortage of blue to balance red one lacks the capacity to relax, appreciate and enjoy the moment.

Too much blue (fixed) gives a tendency towards a laissez-faire, possibly even lazy attitude. One is comfortable and there does not seem to be much point in making the effort to do anything.

Too much green (mutable) may produce mental and emotional instability through constant doubt and questioning that often results in an inability to make decisions.

Colour to Individual Planets

We also need to consider the likely effect of colour applying to individual planets. For instance all red or all blue aspects to, say, Mars. A red Mars will be very energetic whilst a blue Mars will be lethargic and have difficulty in motivating itself to action.

If Jupiter receives only green aspects this will increase its mutability and it is likely that it will always be searching for the ultimate goal in life. Mercury aspected only by red and green will be constantly stimulated to mental activity, with much nervous tension resulting in disrupted sleep patterns and possibly insomnia.

4) Coherence, Unaspected and Blocked-Off Planets

Is the aspect pattern a complete, integrated structure, or does it consist of a number of individual, separate patterns?

When the aspect structure is not fully integrated people may be driven by different motivations and exhibit behaviour patterns in different contexts. For example, they could be very competitive in the work environment but very laid-back at home.

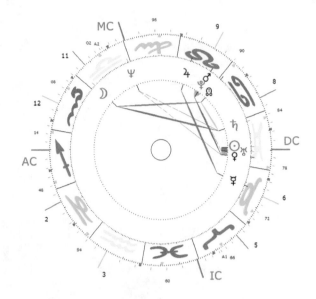

Figure 2.2.5

In Figure 2.2.5 there is a linear aspect between Mercury and Jupiter which is not connected to the rest of the aspect structure. Because that aspect overlaps the other figures, and both focus into the same quadrant, there is greater cohesion and ability to integrate.

Figure 2.2.6

In Figure 2.2.6 the figures are less integrated and emphasise different quadrants. With the Sun and Moon in opposite hemispheres the process of integration may be more difficult.

Unaspected Planets

Are there planets which are unaspected?

If a planet cannot be 'seen' by the psyche then an unconscious action/reaction mechanism comes into play creating a mode of behaviour that will invite a response from the environment, thus bringing reassurance and awareness of the unconnected planet. Depending upon their sign and house position, unaspected planets are more likely therefore to be under the control of the environment. However, when one learns to recognise and take control of unaspected planets these can often be used to greater effect than those limited by aspect lines.

Because Sun, Moon and Saturn represent the major functions of the personality, it is particularly significant if one of them is unaspected.

Unaspected Sun

The Sun represents awareness of the Self. When the Sun is unaspected the person may generate a behaviour for the sole purpose of ensuring a sense of existence, or of 'being'.

Unaspected Moon

With an unaspected Moon, the person's feelings may be at the mercy of others. It could be difficult for them to recognise and understand their own feelings, and there may be an inner sense of emotional loneliness, abandonment or loss.

Unaspected Saturn

With an unaspected Saturn the ego will lack a sense of security so will be motivated to overcompensate and grab all it can get hold of. This might be anything from possessions, to people, food or even knowledge, depending on the house in which natal Saturn is situated. The inner, probably unrecognised, motivation is the need for security.

Blocked-off Planet

All aspect lines can act, to a greater or lesser extent, as energy filters, or in some cases energy blocks. As a guide we would suggest that green aspects have a filtering effect of perhaps 5 to 15%, blue aspects between 20 and 30%, and red aspects up to 50%, though much depends on integration of the chart in other ways.

As a result of this filtering effect the self or centre may, in certain circumstances, find itself with a diminished contact with a planet or area of the chart. An extreme of this would be where a planet was completely blocked off from any useful contact with the centre. Where this happens it may be difficult for that person to recognise, and therefore make effective use of the energy being expressed through that planet.

In Figure 2.2.7 Jupiter is unaspected and strongly blocked-off.

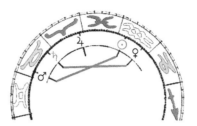

Figure 2.2.7

If such a planet has aspects to other planets outside the block, this gives alternative energy channels to the centre, reducing the effectiveness of the block, depending on number, type and strength of the aspects and planets involved. So the block is only likely to be a major factor for unaspected or weakly aspected planets.

The most difficult case is where the Sun is blocked off, which is similar in effect to an unaspected Sun, i.e. making it difficult for that person to recognise their own Selfhood.

Figure 2.2.8

Figure 2.2.8 shows the chart of a man and illustrates Venus in Pisces cut off behind squares from Sun to Uranus/Saturn. This indicates a partial, but substantial loss of contact.

This man's understanding and acceptance of the feminine side of his personality was severely limited by his childhood upbringing.

5) Shape and Size of Figures

You will see in the following example charts that there is a discernible direction and movement indicated by the aspect pattern. This provides valuable clues about the underlying motivations of a person. This method of entering the chart, through reflection on the colour, shaping, direction and coherence, should always be used.

Aspect figures vary considerably in size. The larger the figure, the more it will dominate life expression and take up more space in the personality. It will have access to more areas of life than smaller structures, which tend to confine their interest and operation to specific and often specialised spheres of life expression which will be defined by the houses which are emphasised.

Linear Figures – Cardinal Motivation

Only **linear**, open-ended figures without enclosure of space, have **cardinal** motivation. There are no complete, closed geometrical figures with such motivation.

A linear pattern indicates restlessness, instability, of someone always on the go, searching, striving, perhaps with a feeling of never quite attaining the goal for which they are searching.

Figure 2.2.9

Figure 2.2.9 is the chart of a man who, in keeping with his Aries Sun, linear pattern and unaspected Uranus in the 10th house, has immense drive, ambition and energy. He is tremendously restless and constantly striving for improvement in his own performance both in his business and in his chosen sport, but he rarely takes time for reflection and considered decision making.

Triangular Figures – Mutable Motivation

Triangular Figures are motivated towards **change, adaptation** and going with the flow – the **mutable** motivation.

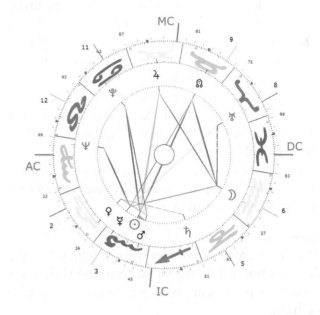

Figure 2.2.10

Figure 2.2.10 is the chart of a woman who raised three children and then branched out and established her own career. With the exception of two small linear extensions this is a triangular/mutable chart, indicating someone who can change and adapt to the circumstances around her. She successfully adapted to a husband with linear motivation and has a wide range of interests. She admits to finding it difficult to concentrate on any one thing for long. She learns best by going out and actively experimenting for herself.

The nature of the individual aspects, and the planets involved in each pattern, show how a person attempts to realise their basic motivations.

Quadrangular Figures – Fixed Motivation

Quadrangular figures are anchored at 4 or more corners and their motivation is the pursuit of **security and stability**.

Figure 2.2.11

Figure 2.2.11 is extremely quadrangular/fixed, spread over a large area of the chart and is also very symmetrical. It is the chart of an extremely talented woman who can successfully turn her hand to anything that interests her. In spite of this her need for stability and security can over-ride everything else. She married a successful and financially secure man 25 years her senior, who was also able to provide the intellectual stimulation that she found lacking in her contemporaries.

Mixed Shaping

It will often be found that there is a combination of patterns in a chart, for example fixed and cardinal, mutable and cardinal... Attention should be paid to what this means in terms of motivation.

For instance a fixed structure intersected by a cardinal pattern may suggest someone whose motivation alternates between the need for security and the need to create something new.

The following two examples show combinations of shaping.

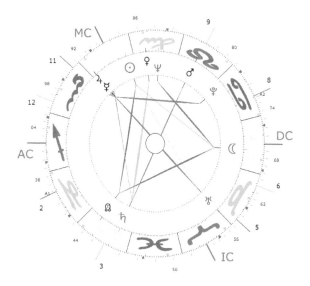

Figure 2.2.12 Brigitte Bardot

The chart in Figure 2.2.12 shows mutable motivation arising from the large blue triangle, but also a strong cardinal motivation through the sequence of oppositions, quincunxes, trines and square which are attached to it. This suggests someone who has a major talent from the triangle, combined with the drive to employ it in attainment of her goals.

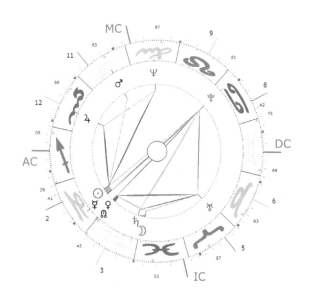

Figure 2.2.13 Elvis Presley

In Figure 2.2.13 there is a combination of fixed motivation shown by the polygonal figure and mutable motivation coming from the small blue triangle. Although the two major figures are integrated through the Sun-Pluto opposition, it does indicate someone whose drive and talent may pull in opposite directions instead of working together.

Technical and Intuitive Approaches to Looking at the Chart

When looking at the shaping of a chart, it is possible to incorporate two approaches. The first approach, which is technical, is covered in this section and is concerned with identifying the actual shaping of the chart (i.e. deciding whether it is predominantly linear/cardinal, triangular/mutable or quadrangular/fixed).

The second is to take a more intuitive, Jupiterian look at the chart, and using the eyes and the senses, gain an initial visual impression. This will enable you to begin to get the feel of the chart, using what you see, together with you already know about aspect structure and shaping.

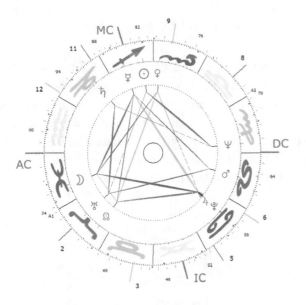

Figure 2.2.14

In Figure 2.2.14 if we were to take the technical approach, we would note that this chart has a mixed structure of fixed and mutable patterns. Using the intuitive approach, we might notice that the visual image of the chart gives an impression of mountain peaks near the top, which might give rise to an impression of movement or mobility so our assessment of this chart's shaping would be mutable.

It is important to remember that the visual appearance of this chart might lead us to say it is mutable whilst our technical understanding would tell us it is both fixed and mutable. Our first impression is of someone whose unconscious motivation is adaptable and flexible, but we would need to be aware that there is also a need for security and stability which may not be at first be apparent.

Further Reading

For further amplification of the material in this section, you are recommended to also read:

Aspect Pattern Astrology, by Bruno & Louise Huber, Chapter 4 'Aspect Pattern Analysis'.

Four Basic Rules to Remember when First Looking at a Chart

1. Use your senses

   Look at the Chart – **the whole chart**, not at individual parts of it.

   Don't think first – get a sense of it.

   What does it say to you?

   Allow an image to emerge.

2. Consider the chart's colour, shaping, direction and coherence.

3. Just work with what you have

   Use what is there, what you can see.

   Do not get side-tracked by using gimmicky calculations, and hopping from one part of the chart to another looking for correlations.

4. Do not mix up the levels

   Do not interpret one planet by house and the next by sign, trying to correlate these.

   For instance, do not start relating the Sun sign to the ascendant. One is sign and the other is house and they represent different functions of the psyche.

Exercise 2.2

1. Looking again at the aspect structure in your chart and bearing in mind what you have learned in section 2.2, make a note of what you now understand about your unconscious motivation and your inner world.

2. Do the same for any other charts that you may be working with.

Appendix – Small Aspect Patterns

Small aspect patterns require special consideration. The following comes from an article written by Louise Huber.

Since 1940 we have often encountered charts featuring small aspect patterns. In the 1940s they extended to the quincunx but not to the opposition. From 1982-85, particularly during the autumn and winter months, these patterns contracted until the sextile was the largest aspect to be found.

Interpretation of these patterns is not easy. It is best to approach the problem by considering the houses which they span. The pattern will also be placed in a specific quadrant or hemisphere of the chart; above or below the horizon, to the left or right of the IC/MC axis (for more on this refer to Chapter 4). From this results a narrow visual perspective, rather like a telescope's field of vision. A subjective way of looking at the life qualities is to be found in the area in which the pattern is placed.

Instead of being able to comprehend the entire complex structure of reality, subjects with these patterns are only able to observe particularised aspects of such a reality. Personal interpretation is coloured by the qualities of whichever horoscope area contains the pattern.

Patterns in the "I" Hemisphere

When the pattern is found in the left hemisphere awareness is focused on self-presentation, One may encounter a state of ego crystallisation where "I" demands are placed before all else. Generally there are clear narcissistic characteristics. However, if the subject is oriented towards spiritual development, then these concentrated ego forces are placed at the service of higher ideals. They can become a dynamic and convincing contact for others. They will not relent their effort until such others have changed their views and come to accept their high ideals. Some effect on others is inevitable and often expectations and perceptions are heightened.

If this concentrated ego structure is able to act as a vehicle for a higher purpose then they act like a transmitting station; a focal point which illuminates the environment. Thus we find teachers, artists, healers, medics, therapists and counsellors who have such a small aspect pattern in this hemisphere. However, this position is somewhat problematical for relationships with the "You", partnerships, etc. Those with this pattern almost invariably have contact problems. The ability to consider other people is lacking because they are predominantly self-centered. They do not really become aware of the "You" as an equal, as their objective in such a relationship is to impose the "I".

Yet in the early part of life there can be identity problems. This manifests as a lack of "I" force, or vitality. Often they build an image of themselves, world events and others that does not correspond to reality at all, but only to their subjective ego viewpoint. There is a continual need to adjust and correct the perceived reality so that such perceptions fit the ego model. This will include the behaviour of others that fit the model, and rejection of those that do not. In this way, some people become falsely valued, whilst others can become defined as enemies.

Empty Areas

Generally, one half of the horoscope is completely empty. This empty area represents the unknown. It is a vacuum into which is sucked unfamiliar phenomena. Again the subject will feel threatened by this invasion of forces alien to personal experience. Thus there is a dialectical situation where reality constantly introduces into the vacuum those elements needed to balance the ego model and yet, at the same time, creates a condition where the subject feels helpless and at the mercy of unfamiliar forces. The defence is a premature crystallisation of the ego model which hurriedly builds higher and higher walls around itself. As in former times, the armies of reality gather outside the ego-castle and lay siege to it. It is not difficult to understand the problems of relationships.

Not only do these forces march to surround the ego-castle but they also march to the unprotected nuclear centre. This is often the reason why subjects with these patterns can suffer deep hurt – even when it is not intended. If such injury has been experienced, it is then hard to form a relationship with anyone again. There is a loss of faith, trust and courage to try again.

The above principle of compensation does not invariably operate with all small aspect patterns. Some subjects search for a parallel in something or someone else. With others, they either acquire new problems or become hampered in their own development. They could then become totally dependent on such a relationship with a resentment and fear of such dependency.

With a degree of self-reflexive consciousness, they often struggle towards a philosophy which promotes a dedication of service to others. Then they find fulfillment in some occupation where they can help others and experience contact. When such contacts are impersonal, they are very sensitive and can react in a positive manner to the needs of others. This is the field of the helping professions. But they can easily become identified with the needs of others, the demands of personal contact and the environment. They can escape from neither a philosophy which has seen the need to admit strange influences from the "You" nor the simultaneous need to offer a true ego-opposition. Thus, in love, they may abandon completely their unique needs and ego model to lose themselves in service to the loved one (or goal). Unconsciously, they look for a strong partner to whom they can submit and delegate responsibility for the missing elements in their ego model.

Small Aspect Patterns in the Lower Hemisphere

If the pattern is in the lower hemisphere, then the upper hemisphere is empty. These people cling closely to the family and relations. They are emotionally dependent on them and generally explore only a limited area of their potential. Their values and judgements are subjectively coloured, distorted by information gaps, personal views, tradition and preferences. Nevertheless, this is not a value judgment. They are unique. For them, the evaluation of an experience or situation is, however one-sided, correct! Owing to the concentration of planets in the evolving or instinctive quadrants, psychic potential is very strong.

With such powers they can, despite commitment to convention, experience a perception of reality and correct the distorted image that limits them. Such powers are creative; an artistic gift is by no means rare. They have the ability to act as a catalyst on the world about them. They do not even have to try very hard. Uniqueness and self-awareness is caused by the 'prism effect' of the small aspect pattern, combined with the instinctive talents found in the lower hemisphere.

Small Aspect Patterns in the Upper Hemisphere

Here all energies are directed towards individuation. For these people, their calling or vocation is a factor which affects all decisions. The central concept is to live a life that is logical, ingenious, efficient, responsible and wise. Only that which serves their goal is grasped, used and retained – generally to the exclusion of other possibilities! They seek perfection in a particular area and become a specialist. Everything subserves to that end. Rather like a radio, they transmit and receive on one frequency only. This frequency is devoted to information that can assist them in obtaining their goal, whether material or spiritual. All opportunities of climbing further up the ladder are made use of immediately.

Their sensitivity is biased towards such possibilities. They are always searching for a unique path to self-expression, often divorced from the norm, and thus open to attack from the 'collective'. Such people need a profession that satisfies them and their ambition to get to the top. In order to achieve this and professional status, they frequently accept onerous duties. In this area one can also find the 'eternal student', always seeking to climb higher and higher.

Esoteric View

We can approach the problems raised by these small patterns from another, more esoteric, viewpoint. To achieve this, we have to extend our considerations into the field of human evolution. According to esoteric doctrines, our plane of existence is interpenetrated by the Devareich (*) which, in the Christian religion can be compared to the angelic dimension. At this time in our evolution, Alice Bailey states that a connection will be made between these two realms of existence. For this purpose a group of egos, normally found in the Devareich, will incarnate themselves. Their mission is to assist in the generation of a new quality of life.

If one now views those with a small aspect pattern as belonging to this group, we can better come to terms with their unique being and motivation in life. We can recognise that they have a special mission and appreciate that they can feel like strangers. This is due to the fact that the very conditions that they have come to promote are not yet part of our fabric of life. We cannot yet speak their language. If one discusses this view with them they immediately show interest and approval. They feel accepted and their mission recognised. There is an immediate response from the centre. To achieve recognition as being a member of a special group, a native of another dimension, is reassuring. Contact with like-minded people, who have the same task, not only increases their self-worth but also indicates that they are not working alone.

Under these circumstances, the "I" problems which are nearly always present and the feelings of inferiority naturally connected with them, achieve some measure of compensation. Recognition of their mission also helps them overcome their narrow view of events, enabling them to enter into new experiences and acquire understanding of a much wider spectrum.

(*) The "Deva" are a feature of Indian mythology. They and the "Asulas" are parts of a complex spectrum of demonology. In the received teaching, Devas are gods and the Asulas are demons. They are generally fighting each other and symbolise the familiar battle between good and evil. Devareich refers to their dimension or plane of existence.

2.3 Aspect Patterns

Working from the inner dimensions of the natal chart, the pattern of the aspects can reveal a wealth of information about our motivation and the ways in which we behave.

In this section you will learn about 30 aspect patterns or figures which may be found in the chart, together with their meanings.

Aspect lines in the chart form a pattern or structure which symbolises unconscious motivation – the basic driving force within us. Understanding the structure is a first important step in chart interpretation.

Aspect Figures

The overall aspect pattern can be broken down into individual aspect figures linking particular planets together. These may be categorised as follows:

1. Figures which are **all red**
2. Figures which are **all blue**
3. Figures which are **red and blue**
4. Figures which are **red and green**
5. Figures which are **blue and green**
6. Figures which are **red, green and blue**

On the following pages you will find diagrams of the most common aspect figures.

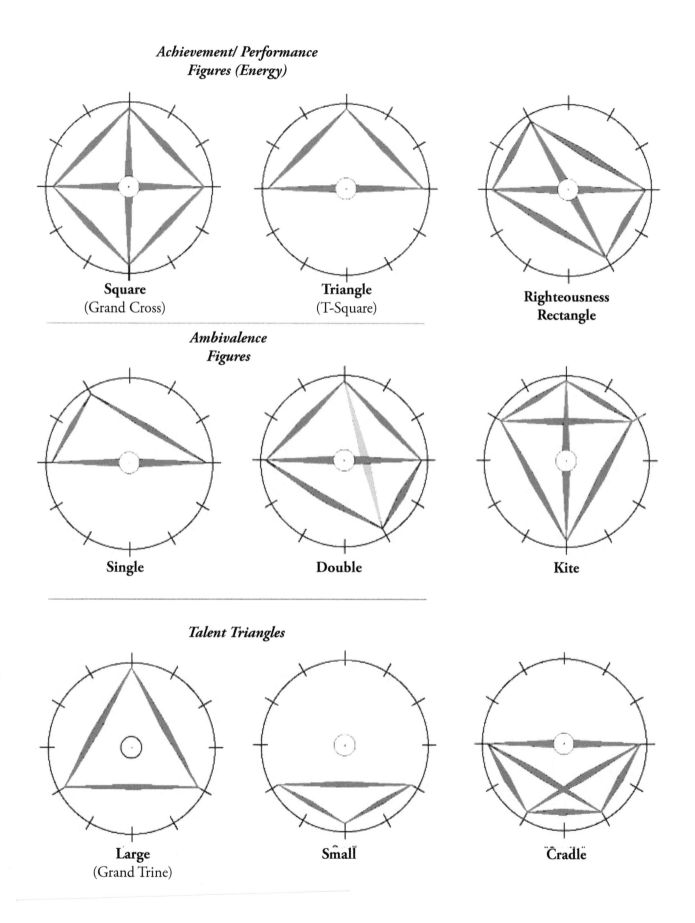

Figure 2.3.1 Common Aspect Figures (a)

Learning Figures

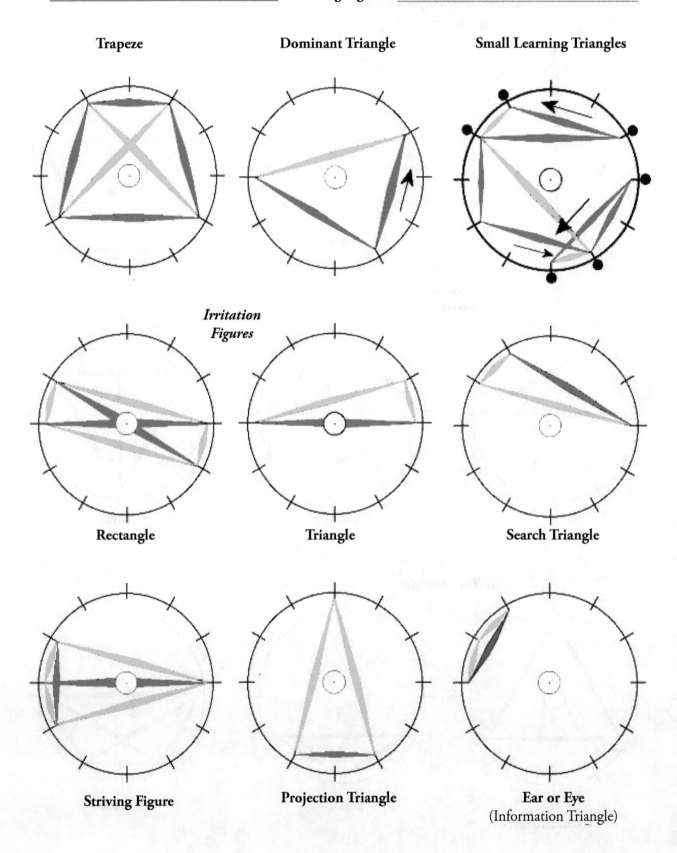

Trapeze

Dominant Triangle

Small Learning Triangles

Irritation Figures

Rectangle

Triangle

Search Triangle

Striving Figure

Projection Triangle

Ear or Eye
(Information Triangle)

Figure 2.3.2 Common Aspect Figures (b)

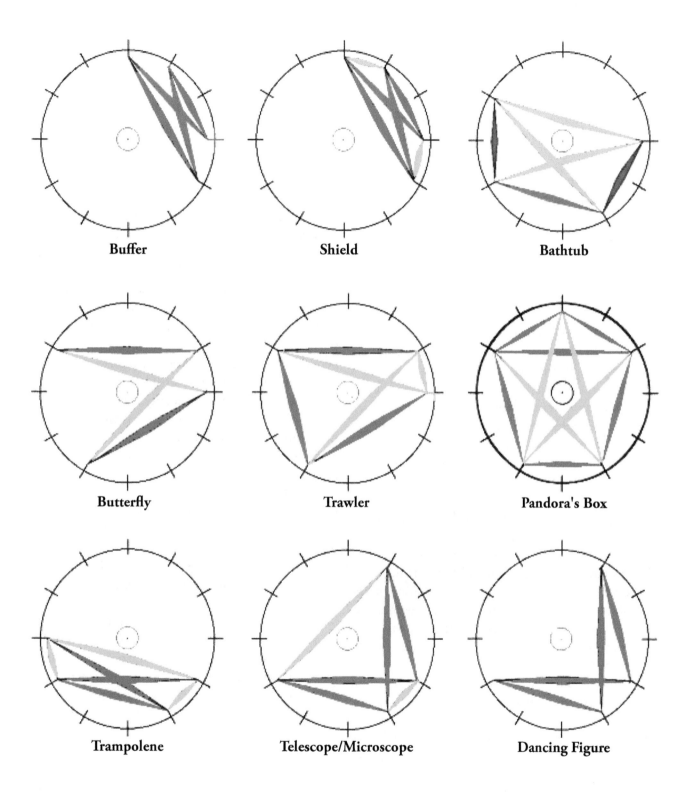

Figure 2.3.3 Common Aspect Figures (c)

Red Figures

To reiterate what was said in section 2.1, red means **energy that needs to be expressed** and directed at something. Red figures are **working figures**, they give the motivation to produce something through the release of energy. If this energy does not find an avenue of release, then it may eventually erupt in a violent manner.

There are two all red figures, called **Achievement** or **Performance** figures, sometimes also called **Efficiency** figures although that is a less accurate description.

The Achievement or Performance Triangle (traditionally the T-Square)

This triangular figure (mutable motivation) comprises an opposition and two squares (cardinal mode of action). It seeks to adapt to changing and conflicting circumstances through energetic activity and movement. The opposition contains energy that is stuck

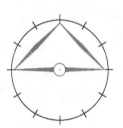

Figure 2.3.4

between two polarities. It acts like a battery, storing up, or holding the energy emanating from the centre, between two poles. It is difficult for this energy to find release since any attempt to release it in one direction will meet with resistance from the opposite pole, causing frustration. The squares, however, act like a machine which can use the energy stored in the battery, through the third planet at the triangle's apex, enabling the energy to be released through work.

This gives extended capacity for intensive periods of work, and people with this figure will often make work for themselves if there is none to be done. The squares can only work in spurts and phases since the mutable quality of the figure demands that time be taken to recoup energy and recharge the battery when it has been exhausted through work.

It is important to recognise this cyclical pattern of work and rest. Since these people consider themselves to be hard workers they may suffer from feelings of guilt or depression when they are not working. These feelings of depression arise from a depletion of energy, so rest must become an integral part of this process. Once this is accepted, this figure can achieve a great deal in a short time, then desist and recover. Certain energetic planets (e.g. Sun, Mars) are better suited to such a working pattern than softer planets such as Moon and Venus. Where softer planets are involved, longer periods of rest will be required and more conscious effort and application needed to work them.

The Achievement or Performance Square (traditionally the Grand Cross)

This square figure (fixed motivation) comprises two oppositions and four squares (cardinal mode of action) and seeks security through persistent hard work and the achievement of goals. The security that arises from such achievement is often more important than the goals

Figure 2.3.5

themselves. This figure is able to work in a more ordered and economical manner than the triangle since there is little or no need for periods of recuperation.

When the energy within one of the oppositions becomes depleted, the focus can be switched to the other battery. In this way there can always be at least one square working. These people are capable of constant, consistent hard work, able to work to fixed schedules and plans, with great efficiency and at a steady pace. However, it is important for them to have periods of free time for relaxation, otherwise they may become workaholics, quite unable to enjoy the fruits of all their efforts and the security for which they have striven so hard. In which case work itself may become the security and they feel insecure when not working.

Because of the tremendous power contained in these figures some people try to suppress their free expression, perhaps through an unconscious fear of the power they possess. This will inevitably result in guilt and frustration, so ways need to be found to master this energy and put it to constructive use without the fear of controlling others. Often there will be a marked ability for organising efficient work schedules for others, such as in a business.

As this is a square figure it is normal to find the planets at the corners all in the same cross (although that may not always be the case due to the possible variation in aspect orbs pertaining to the pinning planets). The nature of the cross in which the Achievement Square is positioned will have an effect on how the figure is expressed. Refer to *Aspect Pattern Astrology* page 145 for descriptions of how this square may function in the cardinal, fixed and mutable crosses.

The output of a burst of tremendous energy from an Achievement Square can sometimes be set in motion by a transit of one of the natal planets involved.

Blue Figures

Blue figures hold **substance** that can be used and also enjoyed. On their own they lack the motivation to act, so it is helpful to have red aspects connected to these figures to provide the impetus to make use of the blue. People with an excess of blue can have a tendency to be somewhat pompous and lazy, expecting others to run around after them and do the work for them. However there are also some very fine qualities embodied in these figures, if handled mindfully.

There are two all-blue figures called **Talent** figures.

The Large Talent Triangle
(traditionally the Grand Trine)

This triangular figure (mutable motivation) comprises three trines (fixed mode of action). People with this figure in their charts can use what they have to adapt to the changing demands of life. They can usually get by quite easily, and may see no need to develop new qualities and

Figure 2.3.6

approaches, putting too much reliance on the obvious talent they already possess. The figure shows a finished quality or inborn talent, capable of encompassing a wide range of experience, permeating and dominating the personality. The planets defining the type of talent usually all fall into one particular element (fire, earth, air, water), suggesting that the talent partakes of the nature of the temperament associated with that element. Obviously an over-reliance on intuition, sensation, thinking or feeling is likely to result in an imbalance with a reluctance to enter into other areas of life which may be rather more problematic. The tendency may be to always seek refuge in the easy blue.

Although such a figure can be enjoyed, blue aspects in general are there to be **used**, so such a talent must **not** be squandered or kept exclusively for oneself but used to give something to the world. Trines, being Jupiter aspects, need to give freely, otherwise those fruits will simply rot and go to waste.

This is the mutable quality of the triangle, to become simply a part of the process of giving. If given freely the talent will grow and develop to even greater depths, continually attracting new substance and experience. The difficulty may lie in the blue fixity, which seeks to hold on to what there already is, thus preventing new levels of experience from flowing into the figure. "To give and not to count the cost" is a particularly relevant motto for this figure because the more it gives the more it receives, and so has even more to give.

The Small Talent Triangle

Being also triangular and blue, this figure has a similar motivation and mode of action to the Large Talent Triangle, but this asymmetrical figure is more dynamic. It indicates a still developing talent in contrast to one that is already complete.

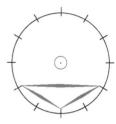

Figure 2.3.7

The sextiles, having a Venus quality, are absorbing and assimilating new experiences and attitudes from the planets and through the signs and houses which they span. These qualities will develop into a talent which is more specific and specialised. It will develop in the course of life, not necessarily through frantic activity or even hard work, but simply through quietly absorbing and digesting experience and being aware that one still has something to learn in the area in which it falls in the chart. Such awareness makes people with this figure more humble than those with the Large Talent Triangle, who may feel they know it all already.

The substance which is absorbed through the sextiles, flows towards the planets at the narrow, or acute, angles of the figure, so that it can be assimilated and stored as part of a growing talent contained in the trine, ready to be called into use when needed. The small Talent figure will often be a part of, or connected to, a larger figure and this will give a clue as to how one goes about the development of this new talent. For example, where it is connected to an Achievement Triangle the talent is likely to become a part of the work done by the Achievement Triangle – an example of energy being turned into substance.

Red and Blue Figures

This brings us to consider the polarity and interplay between red and blue figures in the birth chart.

Red figures embody energy and blue figures embody substance or matter. In a chart where these two colours are predominant they can act in a complementary manner to each other. We know from physics that energy can become matter and matter can become energy, so too in the chart and therefore in the life of the individual. Such a person will go through alternating periods of red and blue, work and enjoyment.

Work will produce more substance, which in turn can be used to provide the material for further work. Where this polarity is present the individual will have to learn to live by this natural alternating rhythm, and to recognise the demands of the red and blue figures as two ends of the same stick, which are complementary rather than antagonistic or conflicting.

The Single Ambivalence Figure (Ambivalence Triangle)

This triangular figure (mutable motivation), comprises an opposition, trine and sextile (cardinal and fixed modes of action.) Hence, people with this figure are seeking to find ways to adapt to the changing demands for energy, for rest and for enjoyment. This is often found as part of a larger structure.

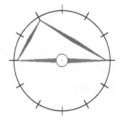

Figure 2.3.8

The ambivalence arises because, from one side you see only the red, and from the other you only see the blue, and these appear to be mutually exclusive states. This gives rise to an oscillation between two conditions of life. Problems arise because the red aspect is not a working aspect (i.e. a square), but is instead producing a strong energy build-up (opposition) with tensions resulting from tasks which have to be fulfilled because life demands this.

These people will tend to spend some time trying to fulfill these tasks, but not enjoying them, and for the rest of the time will retreat into the blue planet and enjoy life, or at least escape from its pressures. Here they can feel at one with themselves and block off the conflict embodied in the opposition, but after a time the demands of the outside world draw them back into duality and the struggles of day-to-day existence start again.

It is important to become aware of this pattern and to develop a manner of working which can be enjoyed, or at least accepted willingly. Otherwise a liking for

the blue condition can develop to such a degree that it will attempt to totally exclude the red, resulting in withdrawal and loss of touch with the environment.

An awareness of the need for both conditions (i.e. work and play) should produce the capacity to deal effectively with any problem presented by the opposition. The blue planet may even be able to provide a detached perspective on how to deal more effectively with the opposition, providing it is not used merely as an escape from the difficulties.

The Double Ambivalence Figure (Ambivalence Quadrangle)

This quadrangular figure (fixed motivation), comprises an opposition, two squares a trine and a sextile, (cardinal and fixed mode of action – more cardinal than fixed). The quadrangular form gives more stability and order than the Single Ambivalence Triangle, with less

Figure 2.3.9

of a tendency towards vacillation and movement.

Here there are three red aspects and two blue, so this figure has more potential working energy. Through the squares it is actually able to work much more easily than the triangle, where the opposition is continually building up energy which it finds difficult to release. In between periods of work, this person can drop into the blue state, but work can be enjoyed and he may even go to the extreme of developing a work philosophy that the only thing important in life is work. This will, of course, produce guilt feelings if he drops into the blue state, but it is important that the blue is lived as well as the red.

We can, perhaps, see the energies of this figure at work within certain areas of our own Western society. Young people are educated to believe that work, performance and achievement are the yardsticks by which success is measured, but with a higher level of conscious awareness many of them are opting out of this and have decided to live in the blue. However, we reap what we sow and we cannot sow in the blue. The figure differs from the Achievement Triangle because the blue can be used as a **conscious** retreat from working activity in order to enjoy the fruits of one's labours. It balances out the red and offers a complete escape from working whereas, with the Achievement Triangle, the lulls in between working periods simply provide the energy for future work, with the focus remaining on work, or on the energy producing conflict (opposition) during these periods.

Finally, mention must be made of the quincunx which, due to its small orb is found in only a small proportion of Ambivalence Quadrangles. Where it is present, the individual does not develop the negative characteristics of this figure because there is the capacity to **think** about the conflicting demands of the red and the blue, to understand and allow for their changing needs.

The Righteousness Rectangle (or Mystic Rectangle)

This quadrangular figure (fixed motivation) comprises blue on the outside (fixed) and red on the inside (cardinal). This person will try to present to the world the perfect image of orderliness, neatness, correctness and consistency – hence the name Righteousness.

Figure 2.3.10

There can be great intolerance towards people who are not righteous, and who do not live up to their strong moral code. But there are problems on the inside (oppositions) which are suppressed and neglected. These people do not accept that others can have problems, and are only too willing to tell them how they should live, making a point of showing them by their own fine example. It is very much the attitude of "I have no problems, so what right have you got to have them – take my advice and your problems will disappear."

However, gradually the inner pressure from the oppositions tends to break them down from the inside, stagnating, rotting and eating away from the core, since it cannot be released. This is one extreme, but sometimes the build-up of inner pressure will eventually produce a breakthrough of realisation, or a conversion experience (Saul becoming Paul). Then they must turn within and face up to the conflicts in their personality. This can result in breaking away from all they have known in the past, nailing themselves to the cross and turning towards religious and mystical concerns – a spiritual rebirth.

Then this figure may legitimately be called a Mystic Rectangle, and there is something of great inner worth which can be given to the world through the blue aspects. It is noteworthy that any other aspects which penetrate the blue from the outside can help towards bringing a realisation of the conflicts within the rectangle. The extreme righteousness and transformation **only occurs** in those figures which are wholly self-contained.

The Kite

This is another quadrangular figure which is blue on the outside. It contains both red and blue on the inside which makes for a more harmonious inner life than the previous figure and brings an awareness of trying to be too blue on the outside. The problem embodied in the

Figure 2.3.11

opposition may be forgotten for a while and projected on to others but eventually, through the experience of failures on the opposition axis, it will have to be confronted again. This will get the blue moving to make use of the energy in a creative manner.

This figure does indeed contain much creativity, since it is made up of both a Large and a Small Talent Triangle; one completed talent and one that is still growing.

The Kite is often found in the horoscopes of artists. So much blue can result in pomposity, but the red opposition, like a sickle, will eventually cut the person down to size again. There is a gradual growing into awareness of the problem presented by the opposition planets; this usually indicates two mutually exclusive extremes. The development of the Small Talent may help towards a solution. The Kite moves towards the Small Talent Triangle and the planet at its apex is an aspiration point. The opposing planet (where the string would be attached) holds it down to earth or holds it back. Hence, the direction of movement of the kite in the horoscope can provide important insights into its meaning and where it seeks to express itself.

The Cradle

This figure has the same proportion of red to blue as with the Kite but now the red is on the outside, shielding the blue from one hemisphere of the chart. This invariably produces some infantile traits and the urge to snuggle up in the blue and shut out the rest of the big bad world.

Figure 2.3.12

There is often the attitude of "don't touch me, I have a right to be here." This person wants to be cared for and cradled or, especially when it is found at the top of the horoscope, will make a career out of caring for others, having an innate understanding of the need for caring which they themselves may have been denied – perhaps they were thrown out of the nest at an early age.

Wherever the Cradle is found, there will be some fear of the opposite hemisphere. Thus a person with a Cradle over on the DC may have a strong need to be looked after and be dependent on others, having a fear of self-confrontation. Conversely, one over on the AC will be very self-contained and afraid of confrontation with others.

By retreating into the blue, one may safely criticise what one fears and even, in a childish manner, manipulate others who come at you from the other hemisphere. Looked at positively, this retreat into the blue can produce something, because of the talents contained there, and such creativity can in turn provide a sense of greater confidence in confronting the empty hemisphere. By producing something which can be presented to others, the sense of self-worth and security is enhanced.

There are in fact two Ambivalence Triangles contained in this figure, but the preponderance of blue does not allow for any real control in getting to grips with the problem in the opposition. Rather, the solution lies in what one can create and give out from the blue corners. Essentially, this figure denotes a contact problem and although contacts may be made, they are rarely deep and genuine, and always have a tendency to hold the other at a distance and to be over-selective.

Red and Green figures

These are rather nervous constructions, being a combination of energy (red) and sensitivity (green) which gives rise to perception and an immediate reaction. There is no blue to soften the blow to one's sensitivity. We see here a continual and somewhat merciless process of perception and reaction, producing **irritation** and **stimulation**. Something irritates you and at the same time stimulates you to react.

Initially, due to the great sensitivity of these figures, one is always on the defensive, ready to fight back and living on one's nerves, unable to relax or open out. Such defensiveness is of little avail and tends only to increase vulnerability.

There are two Irritation figures.

The Irritation Triangle

Being triangular, this figure suggests constant movement and nervous activity. There may be long or short periods of over-stimulation during which it is difficult to adapt to the demands that appear to be made upon it. This may produce sudden explosions of anger as a reaction to outside pressures, but then the matter will be over and forgotten. The ability to move and adapt gives these people a chance to move out of the way and duck the blows which come at them, thus preventing themselves from being too easily manipulated.

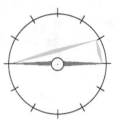

Figure 2.3.13

The Irritation Rectangle

Being rectangular, this figure, in contrast to the Triangle, tends to resist movement. It is less able to bend than the triangle and from the outside a quite different reaction is seen. People with this figure pretend not to perceive and react and will play stiff, whilst hurting intensely on the inside from the oppositions. Of course, they do in fact perceive everything and, in contrast to the Righteousness Rectangle, there is an awareness of the inner conflicts but a reluctance to express them. The Righteousness Rectangle can at least show a solid appearance to the outside world through the blue, but the Irritation Rectangle can only pretend not to react by holding back and remaining tense. There is here a basic insecurity coming from the planets involved, which may manifest in symptoms such as fears, phobias and nervous tics.

Figure 2.3.14

These people often resort to specific repeated reaction patterns and habits in an attempt to govern their situation and produce some kind of stability. It can lead, in some instances, to addictions to drugs, smoking or alcoholism, as ways of seeking to dull the acute sensitivity of this figure. Care and understanding are needed when working with someone with this figure prominent in their chart. Problems are most likely to manifest in the areas of the semi-sextiles, either by house, by sign or by axis.

Looked at in a growth orientated way, the task of these last two figures is to enable a person to perceive and consider factors which their philosophy would otherwise not allow for, and in a way which they simply cannot ignore. These figures can provide the inspiration to look for new solutions (a quality of the quincunx) to problems, and to look towards the blue in the rest of the chart to provide solidity and substance upon which they can draw. This is easier to do when the figures form part of a larger structure which has blue in it.

Despite their extreme sensitivity people with these figures possess incredible reserves of nervous strength – the strength lies in the oppositions – and are usually quite capable of handling levels of stress that others would find intolerable.

Children with these figures may have problems at school but if they are given freedom to explore for themselves, they **may** produce genius, as their sensitivity can open them to ideas and inspirations which are beyond the comprehension of others. The unconscious awareness of the pain involved in these figures may, however, cause them to lie dormant for long periods of time but, sooner or later, something will trigger them and demand that the person rises to meet the challenge they present.

Blue and Green Figures

These figures have an escapist quality about them. There is a tendency to live in fantasy and far-off ideals. They may be a source of inspiration but, of themselves, they lack the energy to realise and manifest that inspiration. Very often they form part of a larger structure, which will provide the red aspects necessary for **doing** something with the inspiration. Otherwise, they have a tendency to float above reality, trying to avoid any kind of hardship or work.

The Projection Triangle
(also Yod, Finger of God/Fate, The Two-Way Mirror)

The apex planet may be seen as a projector throwing a picture on to a screen formed by the sextile between the other two planets. Projection is an important function of the psyche which finds its expression in fantasy, imagination and visualisation. These functions are particularly

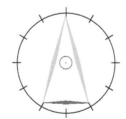

Figure 2.3.15

important for the child, for artistic and scientific creativity and for meditation. The green quality of the apex planet requires one to grow towards a greater understanding and awareness of that particular psychic function. It is not something that can be experienced directly, but one can observe the images which are thrown out on to the screen in order to understand how the planet works.

Bear in mind that the image on the inside of the figure may not coincide with the subjective **reality** seen by others on the outside. So before the creative image on the inside can become reality it will be necessary to find a way of achieving a balance between the two sides of the screen. The two-way mirror can then become pure crystal.

The planets forming the sextile indicate the type of substance and the manner in which this needs to be incorporated into one's experience of the apex planet. So, we could say that the apex planet contains the whole story which gradually unfolds in the form of projections and fantasies. By observing these and the effects they produce in the environment, one can arrive at a greater understanding of what the apex planet means.

It is important to realise that what is seen on the screen is the person's own projection, and not an objective reality, although the screen planets can help one to arrive at a more objective viewpoint and eventually see beyond the projections. Ideally this figure works in three distinct phases:

1. the person projects unconsciously, believing that their projections are real. The discrepancies and conflicts which arise between their projections and reality give rise to the next phase. This is often the stage where individuals become stuck, finding escape easier than facing the reality of self-awareness.

2. the person begins to discriminate between the projections coming from within, and the realities coming from outside, bringing a growing sense of self-awareness and the conscious realisation that they are projecting.

3. lastly they begin to understand the true meaning and potential of the apex planet, and can begin to take conscious control and responsibility for this function of the psyche and can use this mechanism to project their ideas into the world in a constructive and creative manner.

To do this requires some red aspects because, by itself, the Projection Triangle has no powers of manifestation, just ideas. This figure, then, can become a creative mental tool which can produce lasting effects in oneself and/or in the outside world. What has been learned about the apex planet can be offered for the benefit of the whole.

This figure is especially useful for artistic creativity, such as story-telling or postulating new theories. When mastered it can produce in others a spontaneous reaction and enjoyment, something to which they can say "Yes, I can identify with that and understand what he means." It is almost as if someone with this figure has the ability to bring forth some universal quality which lies hidden in many people (the Finger of God quality).

You can gain further insight into this figure by noting where it lies in the chart. When the projection lies across the chart from AC to DC, the person will project strongly their own idea of what others should be like. Conversely, when it projects from DC to AC, they may tend to rely too heavily on other people's ideas of what they are like. From IC to MC, there will be a tendency to project, and try to live up to, an ideal image of themselves as an individual. From MC to IC they may try to impose their conscious ideals onto collective thinking/feeling patterns, when what is required is that they should change their conscious ideals to meet unconscious needs, in both themselves and others.

Figure 2.3.16 Albert Einstein
14.3.1879, 10:50, Ulm, Germany

It is interesting to look at the chart of Albert Einstein in Figure 2.3.16 and note that a period of some 30 years elapsed before Uranus – the apex of the Projection Triangle – could be used in the manner described in 3) above. Since then science has progressed within the framework of the knowledge that Einstein gave to the world.

The Eye – or Ear

This is an information figure. The two semi-sextiles have a mercurial quality, which is constantly gathering information, often unconsciously, from the environment in the area of the houses it spans. It is far from the centre of the chart and works automatically and continually,

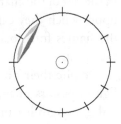

Figure 2.3.17

gathering facts and data from the **outside**, acting like a radar scanner which picks up everything within its range. The information is processed, assimilated and absorbed by the sextile, which stores it for future use. It can gather vast amounts of information. Often the sextile, by itself, is not equal to the task of assimilating and storing it all, so it can be helpful if other figures/aspects are connected to it, i.e. blue to assist in storage and red to make positive use of information acquired.

The accumulated substance can later be called forth, hopefully in an appropriate situation, and often the person will be unaware of exactly how he got hold of the information in the first place. It is difficult to consciously direct this mechanism. It is best to allow it to work automatically, almost like a net which you drag along behind you, picking up a little here, a little there.

Depending upon the size of the house(s) which it spans, it can produce a highly specialised area of interest, especially if it is contained wholly within one house. If it spans two or more houses, then it will act in a more diffuse manner. This figure works in an impersonal and non-selective manner, and the only real difficulty which it may present lies in sorting the wheat from the chaff and in being able to discover, at a later date, what information is useful and what is irrelevant.

As information is gathered in from outside it does not give rise to a clairvoyant ability, although it may appear to do so because people with this figure perceive many factors unconsciously in great detail, and the correct assimilation of these can give deep insight into others' motivations and life patterns. In this context in particular it is important to become conscious of which factors are truly relevant. The Eye, or Ear, works at an unconscious level and it may be difficult to recall the source of the information that has been collected.

The Searching Figure

This figure, often part of a larger structure, is always searching for some distant goal or ideal. There is the feeling "if only I can reach this thing/ideal/ person, then my life will be complete." This may manifest as a search for a great person, or guru whom one may emulate.

Figure 2.3.18

Often this figure will lead to experimentation with different states of consciousness, perhaps through drugs. The semi-sextile makes the person acutely conscious of the deep yearning of the quincunx; in contrast to the Projection figure there is a conscious search to find something which will go beyond and provide deeper meaning to the substance/talent embodied in the trine.

This figure embodies the idea of a 'divine discontent', always looking for something more. It is interesting to note that the German word 'Such' meaning 'search', has the same root as 'Sucht', meaning 'addiction'. One may quite easily become addicted to the type of searching indicated by this figure.

Usually the planet where the trine and quincunx meet poses a question, and the answer is sought at the opposite end of the figure – the all green planet acts as the goal or ideal which leads the person on. At the green and blue planet (where semi-sextile and trine meet) she can absorb, understand and ground her experiences, adding new substance to her life. It will depend on a connection to some red aspects whether she can actually make use of what she discovers, otherwise this may be a purely escapist figure.

Red, Green and Blue Figures

These figures embody **energy (red), awareness (green) and substance (blue).** Having all three colours they offer much potential for growth and self-awareness.

The Striving Figure (Green Kite, Green Dragon)

This is a combination of the Projection figure and the Eye, with an opposition down the centre. With a preponderance of green aspects it is not a particularly balanced expression of the three colours. Seen from the outside the figure appears to be green on all sides, giving the

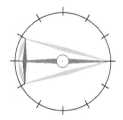

Figure 2.3.19

outward appearance of great sensitivity or exceptional intelligence, which are indeed qualities of this figure.

This is a four-cornered figure but dynamic as there are no rectangles, and it is symmetrical around the opposition only. The outer aspects are all green, like an Irritation Rectangle, but there are two inner aspects, red opposition and blue sextile. Therefore the potential for tension is less than in the Irritation Rectangle.

The sensitive outer aspects give tremendous ability to react to external stimuli. It is chiefly the Eye which facilitates immediate contact with the surroundings; it forms the blunter end of the Dragon, the base or anchor. Effort is mainly concentrated on the sharp ends of the figure. Where there is introjection, when the process of projection is reversed, external stimuli registered through the Eye are turned around and then themselves form the desired goal.

With much toil and trouble we try to reach the sharp point of this figure, try our hardest to function effectively with the planet there, in the sphere of life indicated by its house position. We long to reach the highest standards but it is hard work and there is real danger of failure because we may not have quite enough staying power for the long trek. True, the Eye can show us how to reach the tip of the figure, through looking and listening and general information gathering. But herein lies the problem. The Eye, the detector, merely collects external information. In order to reach the tip we will have to do our own thinking (quincunx), and we must have mastered the technique of coping with the projection (observe, understand, revoke, develop…).

The opposition gives the inner tension and the will to work. But the power of observation given by the green aspects, and the tendency to make sure of our facts and rely on them, can easily trap us in a series of contradictions because it sometimes becomes difficult to see the wood for the trees. The lone blue aspect, the sextile with its harmonising contribution, may not really be quite sufficient to help us reach the high ideals which we have set for ourselves. Therefore people with this figure in their chart often talk about their projects and their good intentions without actually being able to fulfill them. That's why, in spite of the blue aspect, the Green Dragon is still chiefly an uncomfortable figure, a figure embodying challenge.

Learning Figures

There are several types of Learning figures. These all exhibit a much more balanced combination of red, green and blue aspects. They are all concerned with cyclical learning processes, in terms of either the evolution of awareness throughout a lifetime, or learning more specific techniques and attitudes to address specific problems.

Direct or Retrograde

The order of activity in a Learning figure is red, green, blue, so these figures may be either **direct** or **retrograde** (Figures 2.3.20, 2.3.21).

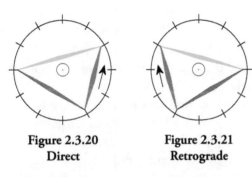

Figure 2.3.20
Direct

Figure 2.3.21
Retrograde

Aspect sequence: red --> green --> blue

Direct moving figures usually work at a deeper level each time the process begins anew.

Retrograde figures have a tendency to resist the changes needed to bring about a new level of understanding and may have to repeat the same lesson over and over again before it is finally understood. However, if we become conscious of the retrograde figure's tendency to resist we can, with some application of will, begin to make them work as though they were direct.

The Dominant Learning Triangle

This is a triangular figure, hence there is a willingness to move with and learn from experience. It is concerned with the gradual development and understanding of life-long lessons, gaining a new perspective on a particular and sometimes recurrent problem, tendency or complex related to

Figure 2.3.22

the nature of the planets, signs and houses involved. As with all the Learning figures, the learning process follows a specific pattern of unfoldment throughout the person's life. This movement begins with a problem presented by the red and blue planet. Something occurs which cannot be ignored. Work needs to be done or one finds oneself in unpleasant or difficult situations.

This initially motivates one to **do** something which activates the red aspect, though very often this does not solve the problem, and it may even get worse.

The next step is then to proceed along the green aspect and to **think** about the problem and really try to understand the deeper issues involved and get the feel of the whole situation. There is a need to see beyond the black and white surface elements to the relative nature of the factors which appear to be causing the problems, and to search for ways of reconciling these.

This stage of the learning process often produces a deep sense of yearning, and a longing for new insights and awareness which will allow one to see the inner relationship between apparently unrelated factors in one's life. Very often something has to be renounced (perhaps a cherished but erroneously held ideal, or a lower expression of the planet involved) in order to be able to arrive at the solution, which can then be applied and enjoyed in the blue part of the figure.

Large, Medium and Small Learning Triangles

These follow the same rules as Dominant Triangles, except that here the person is concerned with learning in more specialised areas, or learning specific techniques which are related to the houses which the figures span. Very often they will be concerned with academic learning, or learning a profession, trade or skill.

Figure 2.3.23
Large

These triangles are frequently found as part of larger structures. For instance, attachment to an Achievement Triangle, suggests that the work involved in the latter requires that one should first learn the technique of how to do it.

The longest aspect in each figure represents the most important stage of the learning process. This may be

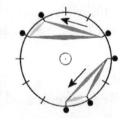

Figure 2.3.24
Medium/Small

- the learning itself (green longest), perhaps just for the sake of understanding

- the work that can be done (red longest) which is the reason for learning

- the end result and enjoyment of what has been learnt (blue longest).

Each of these triangles can have a direct or retrograde movement.

The Trapeze

This is a quadrangular figure, and hence seeks stability, but of a different order to that sought in the Achievement Square or Righteousness Rectangle. It is not so stiff and allows much greater freedom of movement within the basic structure. There are four distinct Learning figures here,

Figure 2.3.25

and very often there will be several learning processes going on at the same time in different areas of life. Also, anything learnt in one area will necessarily have to be reconciled with what is happening in other areas. Consequently, people with a Trapeze often appear not to know exactly where they stand because everything is in a constant process of change and growth. Their squarishness also produces a certain reluctance to continually pick up on the changing conditions both in and around them, and they would usually prefer to have longer periods for digestion and relaxation in between the learning phases.

However, these figures tend to produce eventful, colourful and multi-faceted lives with the potential for encompassing a wide variety of experience. In the final analysis, security for the person with the Trapeze lies in accepting that life is a continual process of change and learning. It is noteworthy that two of the learning triangles in this figure are direct and two are retrograde, which tends to produce a balance between a willingness to move and resistance. This provides the capacity for an overall balanced development.

The Buffer (Incomplete Shock Absorber)

This incomplete linear figure acts like a buffer. The harmonious blue lines act as stiff plates (like a shock absorber). The red aspects are movable, can bend, absorb energy, and go back to their original position. This aspect figure acts like a shield against the environment. Energy (problems, etc.) is absorbed from the outside and then uses the

Figure 2.3.26

structure to push back. The blue aspects will attempt to soften the defensive response though this might be experienced as subliminal aggression. The direction of the pattern is towards the blue sextile.

The open spaces in this figure are a source of fear, representing vulnerable blind spots. There is a fear of things coming from the blind spots where they cannot be seen. There may be a constant fear of being attacked and possibly paranoid traits.

The Shield (Complete Shock Absorber)

This figure is similar to the Buffer, but the two semi-sextiles make this a complete fixed pattern, with the result that there is less flexibility and a consequent defence behaviour that is more stubborn and not so subtle. It is a very fixed structure with strong stability needs and may seek

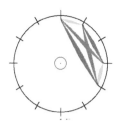

Figure 2.3.26a

expression through expounding moral principles.

This structure can be used as a shield and on the 'You' side may appear nice, but if you invade this person they may hit back strongly. The green aspects give sensitivity. They can accept a great deal, but beware – they can come back strongly.

A shield is a little unwieldy – we put it in front of us but we do not use it to fight with. We attempt to use it to protect us from, or possibly to absorb, the oncoming energies of enemies. The ability to absorb these energies is given through the blue outer aspects. People with this figure can cope with a great deal more than you might give them credit for, as long as they can complain vociferously, as indicated by the semi-sextiles.

If there is only one semi-sextile then the Shield is unstable and develops a list. This can be rather painful and diminishes the ability to absorb the energy harmlessly. People around us are quick enough to see just where we are vulnerable. With the Buffer we can make good use of the knocks life inflicts upon us, but because this figure is not a quadrilateral it is difficult to keep a grip on this progress – the energies can always escape through the open side.

People with the Shield in their chart can protect themselves by moaning a great deal. People with Buffers cannot really do this because, as a linear figure, it has a basically different motivation from a quadrangular figure.

The Dancing Figure – Runner/Jumper

The individual dances (easy), or jumps (hectic), through life depending on whether hard or soft planets are involved. The pattern is continuous – it begins and ends at the same point – it is endless like a figure of 8, coming back on itself again and again. Because the figure has a tendency

Figure 2.3.27

to get used to this circular movement nothing new is achieved in spite of the constant movement; in fact, it can become rather a pointless reflex action. This urge for constant movement plays quite a decisive role because the figure contains only two colours with a ratio of 2:2.

There is a strong polarisation between red and blue, and back again. This can be created internally, or externally through the environment. There is no green so the learning process is slow. There is versatility but a tendency to return to the same themes and problems. With red on the outside life may be experienced as hard, so comfort/relief is sought by hiding in the blue.

The planets involved make a big difference, as does consideration of how dominant the figure is within the overall structure, and its orientation, e.g. I/You.

In order to run we need a great deal of energy and this figure with its two squares has plenty of this. red aspects mean energy with which we can work – for instance to push others. On the other hand we ourselves are sensitive to being pushed around. This figure contains quite an effective flight mechanism, a reflex for flight. If there is pressure from outside, people with this figure react by moving, initially by running or jumping, out of the way. It is not their way to be belligerent as the inside of this figure is blue and they like peace and harmony.

Quite early in childhood people with this figure can develop reflex activities which can become a longing or craving for particular movements or activities. We only need to touch this figure at one of its four corners and we start the activity cycle. Unlike the Butterfly (below) there always seems to be some kind of contradiction involved because of the red/blue polarity.

It is quite possible to use the blue to project something on to the outer world which is really inappropriate. Some people may react by turning into alcoholics, and others may take refuge in an excess of sex. Once activated this mechanism seems to run of its own accord; it is only possible to control it once we understand what is going on. It is easier to be successful if this figure is part of some other aspect picture because that would bring a degree of sensitivity.

The Butterfly

This dynamic linear figure is very similar to the Dancing figure, but since it is only blue and green it may be escapist, ungrounded and difficult to tie down to a task. The quality of movement is beautiful and graceful, rather like a dance. It is not forceful, decisive or purposeful movement.

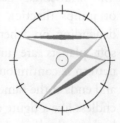

Figure 2.3.28

People with this figure in their chart collect (blue) a lot of information (green) with these dance-like movements, and carry it around with them without knowing what to do with it. There is a strong need to know but knowledge can remain in the realm of ideas and fantasies so as to avoid facing up to harsh realities. They see little need to take sides and prefer to remain neutral, to sit on the fence. The green is eager to experience, the blue looks for calmness and ease.

The figure is interesting and entertaining because whatever we can imbibe depends on information that comes our way from outside. What stimulates us is indicated by the planets involved and perceived on a very personal level.

The blue aspects on the outside of the figure may have the effect of a barrier which keeps things at bay. This can mean that if we do not want to be reached we cannot be reached unless we can be got at from open corners. Within a larger conglomeration of aspects this figure can be extremely useful.

The Telescope/Microscope

This figure contains two possibilities – as a Telescope it will direct its sights into a wide world, and as a Microscope it will view what is near to it. The orientation of this figure within the chart will determine which of these two figures is indicated. The Microscope has the semi-sextile on the 'I' side, whilst the Telescope has the semi-sextile on the 'You' side. Alternatively, if the quincunx aspect is uppermost it is a Microscope, and if it is lower than the semi-sextile then it is a Telescope.

**Figure 2.3.29
Microscope**

**Figure 2.3.30
Telescope**

This is a sensitive figure having red and green external aspects. It can be directed towards a point/ object/place/concept/idea and used to make distant things nearer or small things bigger. As a quadrilateral, it is concerned with security. The red sides give energy and staying power when observing facts. The blue diagonals give the ability to absorb the information and irrespective of the planets involved, this figure conveys a good memory. All figures with blue diagonals follow this pattern (blue collects and contains). We also view this figure as a kind of bucket, albeit with a wobbly base – no firm point of view, no firm position. The red aspects give energy to keep going in difficult situations, but modified and influenced by the planets at the corners.

The colour ratio is 2:2:2; although all 3 colours are involved the ratio shows an emphasis on green that can occasionally cause problems. We do not deal with a protective attitude here for, on the contrary, people with this figure have the courage to actually use the green. The sensitive green aspects are like membranes – they pick things up. The blue digests what is seen, and the red squares are protective in a stabilising/holding way. With the Microscope much detail is observed through the small lens which watches closely, is eager to learn and seeks precise mercurial solutions to problems. The Telescope seeks solutions through a wider picture, which may be difficult to assemble – like having a jigsaw puzzle and not being able to fit all the pieces together.

Actually, it is quite possible to use this figure in either direction but this presupposes a certain amount of self-awareness; we have to realise that we have this possibility within us, and must have learned to handle it wisely. With the semi-sextile we have the power of meticulous observation; with the quincunx we can be aware of interconnections. When we are sufficiently aware we become capable of deducing the greater from the lesser, otherwise we just get stuck in seeing the wider implications but refuse to see the smaller details in the Telescope position, or we only look at the details and don't show any interest in the greater pattern in the microscope position. This kind of one-sidedness is inherent in these figures – we see everything on a narrower scale because one side of the figure is narrower, and we do not consider the other point of view.

It is important to view this figure as a kind of transmission mechanism where the green aspects are lenses which condense the invisible; they are the membranes or sensors – they condense the inaudible. The intangible becomes concrete.

The Trawler or Vacuum Cleaner

This figure is like the Butterfly but with a square aspect which acts as a sucking force, and a semi-sextile which is the selective sucking point with a filter. The two planets forming the square are selective in what they want to suck in – usually psychic/mental stuff, not material things. The green sucks growth stuff and the figure is like a container with an insatiable appetite. It can contain a great deal of knowledge and information which an aware person can make use of in other areas of the chart. This figure can be used to exploit others, especially if the semi-

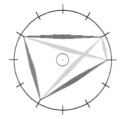

Figure 2.3.31

sextile points downwards towards the IC (collective), or towards the 'You' side of the chart.

The blue aspects form stable walls. The square aspect closes the wider end of the figure and if you stand it on its base it looks rather like a receptacle for catching and collecting things but, because the opening is really rather narrow, not much can fall through it and that is why these people become rather lonely. They can be like hermits. If on the other hand the red side points upwards the figure has the effect of a vacuum cleaner which stirs people up and engulfs them once they have come close, and they cannot escape. It is not so much that they have become imprisoned, but rather that they cannot find their way out anymore.

There is a tendency for people with this figure not to show how they think or feel. The long sides are blue and finely polished so things slip off and cannot get in. The sensitive semi-sextile has the sucking power to take things in, but is too small to allow them out again. They are not secure and will not take a stand on anything. We can never find out what is going on inside. It can be like a black hole, a barrel with no bottom.

Because the green diagonals cross the inside of the figure, these people can work with new ideas and use them consciously and deliberately. They have a good ability to learn selectively what they choose to learn. This figure can produce varied effects ranging from exploitation to creativity, but being predominantly blue/green there is a tendency to want to take the easy way – they do not want to make too much effort. The danger is that a craving for ease and comfort will cause potential wisdom to be left out.

The Trampoline

This structure has 1 red, 2 blue, and 3 green aspects. The red square provides a strong base, the blue trines on the inside form a stable but movable structure, whilst the green semi-sextiles and quincunx are very sensitive and flexible. When confronted with aggression or adversity the whole structure can give and then resume its original shape. Ex-President Gorbachev of the USSR has this structure in his chart. Such people are not aggressive – they use energy to retain stability and keep control of themselves. People with this figure are versatile in their thinking and sensory perception. They are able to 'listen to the grass growing'.

They can accept being pushed around and are able to weather the storm through the flexible green and the

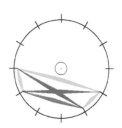

Figure 2.3.32

absorbent blue aspects. However, if pushed too hard the red will push back, and the nature and strength of the response can be gauged by the planets on the square aspect. These people know what they want and can get what they want, but they do so through adjustment to the surrounding world rather than in a direct forceful manner.

On the inside are two blue steel rods jointed at the centre, acting like a hinge. Over the top of them is a green tarpaulin. It is notable that this quadrilateral figure has three green and one red side, therefore these people give the impression of being red/green. They react directly, can be hypersensitive and are easily stirred up. They are always wide awake and are incapable of having any fixed attitudes. Inwardly these people often have an idealistic nature because of the blue colouring.

They are highly sensitive and their ideas have to coincide with their ideals. Often the main theme in their lives is a constant attempt to adapt to new circumstances, to learn to cope with new situations and people. Their inner value system gives the ability to react appropriately. To an outsider it seems as though people with this figure lack staying power because they do not wish to appear in any way fixed. They are like the eternal student; always wanting to collect new experiences. If intellectual planets are involved, then this will happen on an intellectual level. The single square is not quite enough to enable these people to effectively translate their knowledge into deeds. In order to do this other elements of the chart are needed.

The Bathtub

The Bathtub is a large figure encompassing the centre circle, the person's core. It may dominate the chart, and the person's character, even when other aspects are present.

With its fixed shape, the Bathtub's motivation is to hold onto and protect whatever is contained inside. The sturdy blue sides and red base appear to create a strong receptacle. With a long green quincunx covering the top and two more forming the tub's content, there is a great deal of inherent sensitivity which, combined with the red, may result in a defensive or irritable attitude towards other people or situations.

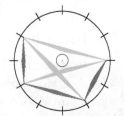

Figure 2.3.33

People with predominantly green aspects, as here, can be extremely sensitive. It can be difficult for them to cope with life, and the outside world may appear to demand more and more adaptive behaviour from them. There may also be the tendency to try and hide away from the realities of life in the tub, or imagine that if they put their house in order, the world will leave them in peace. However the outer quincunx at the top, acts as a permeable membrane and is less able to keep the world out, possibly creating a feeling of vulnerability which in turn provokes the irritability. Although there is usually little aggression shown, people with this figure may live in a state of fear, guilt and suffering, sometimes developing hysteric symptoms. However the red and blue parts of the figure provide the energy and substance to overcome this potential vulnerability.

People with the Bathtub in their chart may also attract trouble through the outer quincunx. They may be very curious about all kinds of things, giving the potential to get into hot water, heated by the red aspect. They may also get into difficulties because they think too simplistically or even perceive the world through rose coloured spectacles and are therefore too trusting.

This figure reacts differently, depending on its orientation in the chart and the planets involved. If, for instance, the outer quincunx faces towards the descendant, then it is possible to develop a strong dependency on the immediate surroundings. Then, like a suction cup, using the energy of the red square, this figure has a tendency to draw energy into itself and bleed other things dry. Conversely it is possible that the person themselves feels devoid of energy, lethargic and may also be quite naïve about the outside world.

Occasionally people with this figure may appear to be reluctant learners because they are not motivated to do much learning and also may protect themselves by concentrating on the simple things of life. However, as life introduces them to new experiences and stimulates their great capacity for sensitivity and awareness, they have the potential to learn through this figure (it includes two learning triangles), even if they do so passively.

Pandora's Box

This figure consists of a container and a lid. Often there will be a gap at one corner of the structure. This creates a need to close the gap and by doing so live in the blue and project even more. The blue is equated with perfection, being perfect. There is a fear of opening the box, which is thought to contain all wickedness, so there are feelings of guilt associated with this. But within the box also lies hope.

Figure 2.3.34

It is unusual to find a Pandora's Box that is absolutely complete. Apart from the possibility of a gap at a corner mentioned above, one or both of the internal quincunxes may be absent due to the smaller orbs for that aspect, especially if a transpersonal planet is involved.

If you remove the Talent triangle you are left with a quadrilateral box with a blue lid. This blue lid closes the box and keeps under wraps, as the saying goes, "all the evil in the world". But, of course, the figure is not really all that black and white because it has many green aspects and, as a 5 cornered figure, it offers even more security than 4 corners. The figure is mostly green inside, and red/blue on the outside, so the person will appear red and blue to those around them, therefore ambivalent. They have many contrasting and conflicting inner energies unconsciously manifesting in their behaviour or the way they express themselves. Many are quite unaware of the turmoil within themselves.

Greek mythology has given us many archetypes and symbols which are portrayed as basically black and white. There was no concept formed of what was inside Pandora's Box, which nowadays we understand to be symbolised by the green aspects – which is consciousness and which could be asleep or awake – the ability to differentiate. Ptolemy, in fact, mentions the green aspects, but he did not really know what to do with them: "they don't convey anything", he said.

Until the present century the green aspects were not really used. To the outer world, people with this figure in their chart make a lot of verbal judgements which make them shine, but they themselves have difficulty with this because their inner world functions on a totally different level. However, in reality, they are capable of differentiating to a high degree, and very consciously.

However, towards the outer world, the person cannot help but make dualistic pronouncements, perhaps because that is just what they feel is expected by the world. These people have to cope with the fact that their value system is one which is vast and generous and finely honed, but which they cannot translate into practical terms. They run with the hounds, which is a great problem for them. Therefore, according to conventional thinking, the so-called evil contained in Pandora's Box is the power of differentiation which will not allow an easy division into good or bad.

A predominance of colours is always difficult to manage, especially if it is, like the green in this case, enclosed. If we open the box just a tiny bit, people around us will usually react negatively – they at once suspect that there is something untoward going on. The person with this configuration will already have experienced in childhood that what he or she says is being rebuffed quite forcibly, and from this the child will have learned to keep his mouth shut! Then, when he grows up, he may no longer know the extent of the treasure he has within. To become conscious of this implies a great deal of personality development work on himself.

Without that, blame will be sought on the outside – all that goes wrong is someone else's fault (projection) – a victim mentality. Whilst it is unusual to find people living on the outside of Pandora's Box, with a fear of what lies inside, it is possible, with awareness of one's own self, to live from the centre and utilise the great wisdom that usually exists in the green. People who live only on the outside are aware only of the red and blue which becomes black and white thinking.

> **Reminder**
> When looking at any aspect figures it is important to consider the nature and strength of the planets involved.

Additional Notes Relating to the Aspect Structure

Incomplete Aspect Figures

Aspect figures which are incomplete can produce greatly exaggerated characteristics where any part is missing.

There are three ways in which an aspect figure may be considered to be incomplete. It may fail to connect up at one corner, it may have one side missing, or in the case of the larger figures an internal aspect may be absent.

In the first example in Figure 2.3.35 two planets are just wide of orb for a conjunction at the apex of an Achievement Triangle, leaving an open gap between them. There will be an energy leak, or loss, making it difficult for the figure to work efficiently and effectively so that

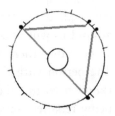

Figure 2.3.35

energy is wasted in trying rather than in achieving. An incomplete figure may also be formed when a corner is incomplete due to an overlapping aspect. In that case there is no gap so there will not be the same sense of vulnerability or energy loss, but the figure will not function as effectively as it should because there can be no continuous flow of energy around the aspects.

In Figure 2.3.36 a side is missing, the natural tendency will be to try to compensate for the missing aspect which will result in additional frustrations and tensions.

Where there is one side missing from an Achievement Square, the person may try to

Figure 2.3.36

act as if he had the complete figure and continually exhaust himself or fail to measure up to self-imposed expectations – it would be much wiser to recognise that here there is not an incomplete Achievement Square, but two interlaced Achievement Triangles; these can then be allowed to work according to their own natural rhythm.

Similarly, where there is one sextile missing from the Righteousness Rectangle, this may produce a greatly exaggerated sense of righteousness in a desperate attempt to construct the sextile. There will always be the danger of falling into the figure and having to confront the oppositions through the open end. But this figure may also be seen as two interlaced Ambivalence Triangles, which will not make the

problems disappear, but may make them somewhat easier to face up to and handle.

This type of incomplete figure can occur only with figures having four or more sides. A triangle with an apparently missing side is simply a linear figure and should be treated as such.

> **Important**
>
> Aspect structures that do not contain complete figures are not necessarily 'incomplete'. Considered judgment should be exercised in assessing whether a figure is incomplete, or whether it is, for instance, linear in shape.
>
> As a rule, if you are unsure it is better to accept the chart as it is rather than assume incomplete figures.

One-Way Aspects

In Chapter 1 you were shown that a one-way aspect could exist between two planets and you were also shown how to draw this on a chart. The aspect exists from the stronger planet to the weaker and indicates that energy is flowing only in one direction. Although it is not uncommon to find people who have unconsciously learned to bridge the gap and complete the aspect structure, account should be taken of the possibility that this hasn't happened and that energy may be being expended on attempting to do this.

Hexagrams

Hexagrams and other large symmetrical multi-sided structures (Diamonds) imply many abilities – almost too many. This can be confusing, and questions such as "Who am I?" may abound. Such figures may be found in the charts of artists – self-discovery is not made with the mind and these charts need living from the centre.

Stars

In some charts you may find three or more aspect lines of the same colour intersecting **at one point**. The aspect lines will be coming from different directions, and in order to form a genuine Star there should be a six-pointed appearance to this configuration.

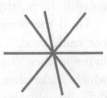

Figure 2.3.37
Red Star

The tighter the intersection of the aspect lines, the more intense the Star.

The planets at the end of the aspects forming a Star will be important factors to consider when interpreting the meaning of this configuration. The consciousness of the planets involved comes together very infrequently but, when they do, it's a most intense moment. It's important to remember that the Star is not always active. When it is on the Star will express its energy through the house to which its energy is directed and affect that area of life. A Star may be activated by transit or age progression over the exit point, which can be found by drawing a line from the centre of the chart through the point of intersection of the aspect lines which form the star and on into the house

Red Star

This is a strong and active energy force – agitated, constantly on the alert, ready to react on demand, easily exhausted and with the potential to implode. In a Star formed by an opposition and two squares, there are tearing energies which are felt inside. Bruno Huber has described a Red Star as a point of constant agitation and consequent exhaustion, of hurting and being hurt as energy is received from the outside.

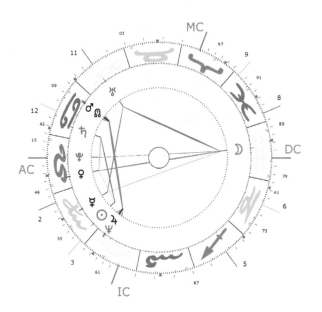

Figure 2.3.38

Note that in the chart shown in Fig. 2.3.38, one of the aspect lines in the Red Star is a one-way aspect. This lessens the effect of the potential implosion, and inner tension, perhaps as well since the nearest planet to the intersection forming the Star is Pluto!

At 6.36 pm on Sunday 4th October 1992, an El Al cargo plane, loaded with aviation fuel and perfume, crashed into a block of flats in a suburb of Amsterdam, engulfing it in flames. Nearly everyone who was in the area of impact was killed. It was a massive and heart-rending disaster. The chart for that moment is shown in Figure 2.3.39.

Figure 2.3.39 El Al Accident

The chart contains a Red Star. In this chart the squares are between Sun and Uranus/Neptune, Mercury and Moon, Venus and Saturn and they form an exact Red Star that exits in the 8th house. In view of the carnage as the plane crashed into a block of flats, the 8th house seems graphic.

Crossing at the Centre

Although no aspect lines are drawn through the circle around the centre of the chart it may be inferred that oppositions pass through the centre. In other words, they have the potential to form channels between the inner being and the outer world. Where 3 or more red oppositions would cross in the centre of the chart, there is no problem. The person has the ability to go into their own centre with less effort, and is able to look at themselves in order to gain more insight and self-knowledge. They will know what to do in the world.

Blue Star

This shows a point of peace, harmony, calmness and quietness. Meditation and esoteric studies come easily, and the urge to connect with eternity. There may also be over-sensibility, stagnation, and the need to give up. However, this is contradictory if Mars, Sun or Pluto are planets on the ends of the aspects making the star.

Green Star

This acts like a membrane, is very sensitive, and with strong vibration at the point of intersection. The person may be lost in their thoughts, or conversely may be unaware of them. With the Green Star there is a vast inner drive, and the person may want to change the world.

Multicoloured Star

There are also other stars with a combination of colours. For example, a red/green star can indicate a very sensitive, and perhaps over-reactive, inner area of the personality, especially if the chart supports this in other ways.

General Approach

When you are assessing a chart's inner motivation, always remember to apply your knowledge of:

- **Colour (inside and out)**
- **Shaping**
- **Cohesion**
- **Direction**
- **Orientation**

Apply these building blocks methodically to all aspect structures in order to understand them fully. This approach cannot be recommended enough when you are trying to remember what the figures mean and make some sense of them. Even when you are more familiar with them, following these simple guidelines will always help you gain a greater understanding and will serve as a useful aide memoire if you cannot readily call to mind the meaning of a particular aspect figure.

Conclusion

This section is not intended to give an exhaustive description of the aspect figures, but should serve to delineate the basic rules and principles involved, so that you may, through practice and insight, develop your own fuller understanding of the many ways and levels in which these figures manifest in real life. These must always be seen in the context of the whole picture, and in terms of how they interconnect with one another.

No two people with the same figure will handle it in quite the same way, quite apart from the subtleties and nuances introduced by the different combinations of planets and their relative sign and house positions. There are no recipes or right interpretations in astrology, only guidelines to help the astrologer and client to work together towards a discovery of the mysteries and hidden potentials of a living individual.

Recommended Reading

Aspect Pattern Astrology by Bruno and Louise Huber, Michael Alexander Huber

> This book goes into the subject of aspect patterns in greater detail than is possible in the current section. It gives insight into the Hubers' thinking and research, and further amplifies many of the aspect figures outlined in this section, plus others besides. They completed this book shortly before Bruno's death in 1999, and regarded it as the most important of the books they have written on astrological psychology.

Aspect Patterns in Colour by Joyce Hopewell

> Provides a valuable reference of all the aspect figures, with examples.

Remember

Fixed charts reflect a builder, earth. The four corners are fixed and not flexible and seek structure.

Triangular charts reflect love, feelings and contact needs.

Linear charts reflect jumpers and seekers – they constantly move from one pattern to another.

Exercise 2.3

1. On copies of Figures 2.3.40-43** on the following four pages, draw each named aspect figure in the blank space provided for it, making sure you use the correct aspect colours.

2. Looking at your own chart, list **all** the aspect figures, naming them correctly and noting the planets involved in each. The easiest way to do this is to identify each pattern separately and draw it with the glyphs of the planets which are involved, included in their appropriate places.

    Also make a note of any unaspected planets and stars.

3. Select an aspect figure in your chart that particularly interests you and look closely at the colours, shape and planets involved. Are these ego, tool or transpersonal planets or a combination of all three? Think about the expression of energies symbolised by these planets. Reflect on whether you are aware of how this aspect figure is expressed in your day to day life.

4. It will help to develop your understanding if you do the same with any other charts that you may be working with.

** You can download a copy of Figures 2.3.40-43 from the Study Resources on the website www.astrologicalpsychology.org.

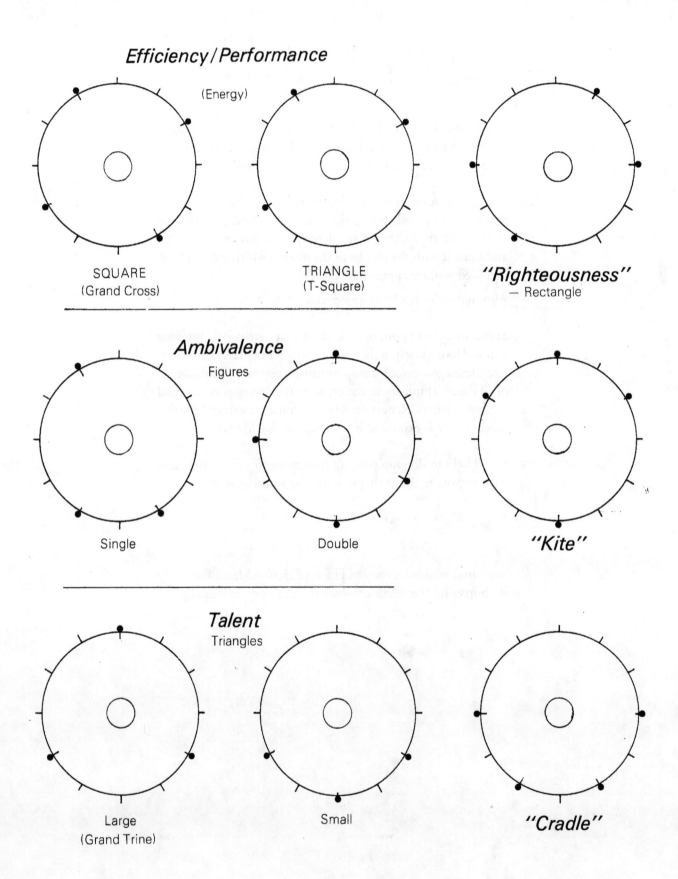

Figure 2.3.40 Aspect Figures (a)

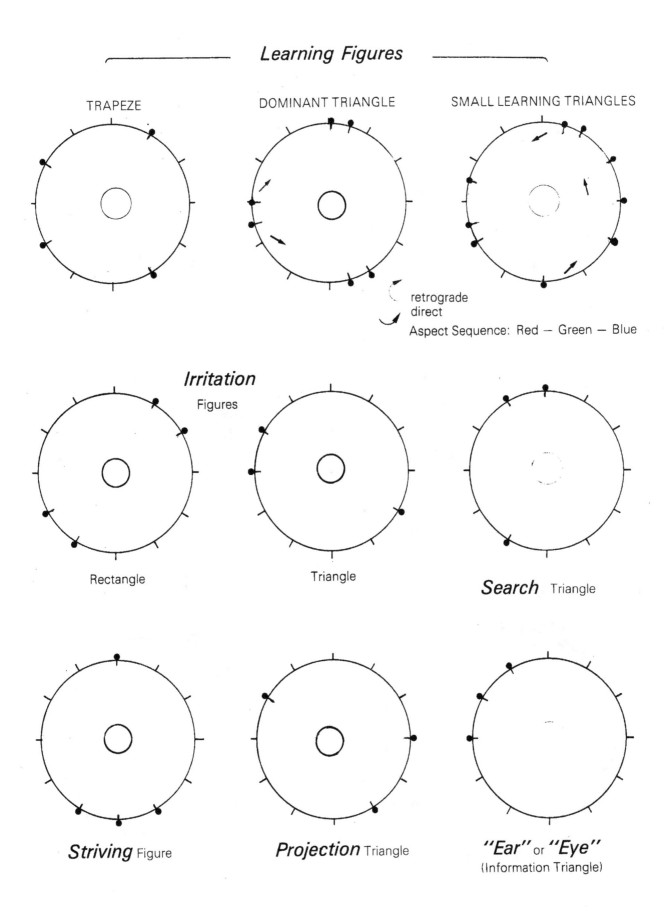

Figure 2.3.41 Aspect Figures (b)

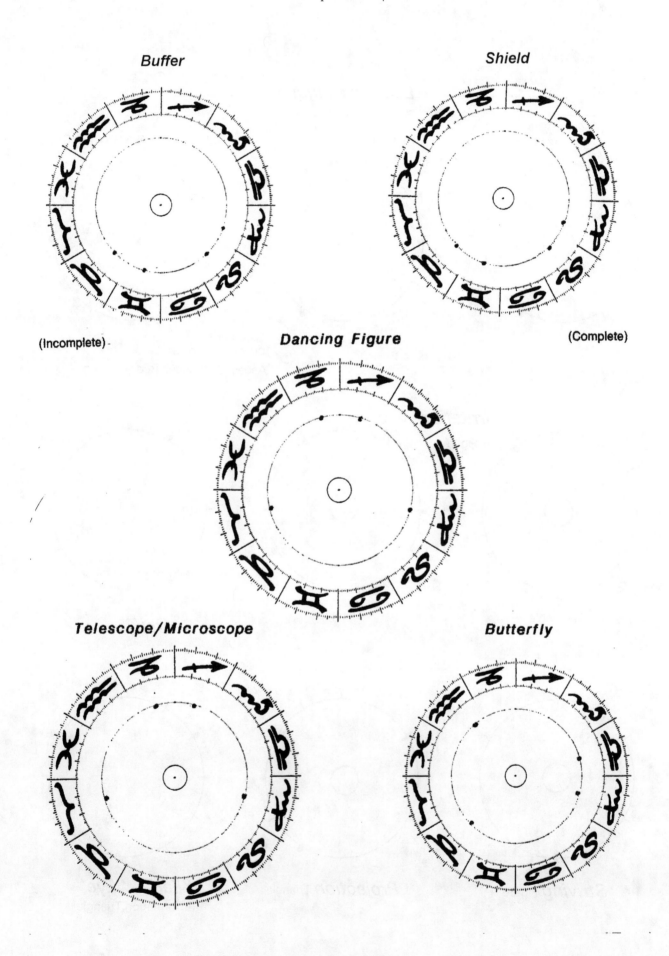

Figure 2.3.42 Aspect Figures (c)

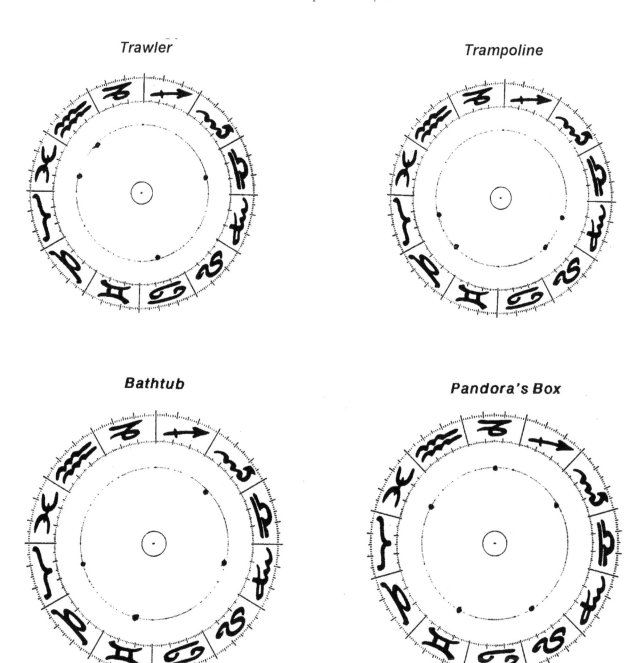

Figure 2.3.43 Aspect Figures (d)

Consolidation Exercise for Chapters 1-2

At the end of every other chapter we include an additional exercise which encourages you to consolidate your learning so far.

1. What is your intuitive response to the chart picture for Sophie in Figure 2.3.44. What initial thoughts does this give you about her?

2. Count the number of aspects for each colour. What does the colour balance imply regarding Sophie's motivation?

3. Identify and name all the aspect figures, including linear figures, observing whether or not they connect with other aspect patterns. Note unaspected planets, if any. Draw sketch diagrams on plain paper, showing the planet glyphs and aspect lines in their correct colours.

4. Choose any three planets, noting the colours of the aspects to each. With your awareness of the quality of aspects, depending on their colour, suggest how the expression of the energy of each of the chosen planets might be affected.

5. Select three named aspect figures, and write a paragraph about each one, showing how each is likely to find expression in Sophie's life. Take into account your present understanding of the planets involved.

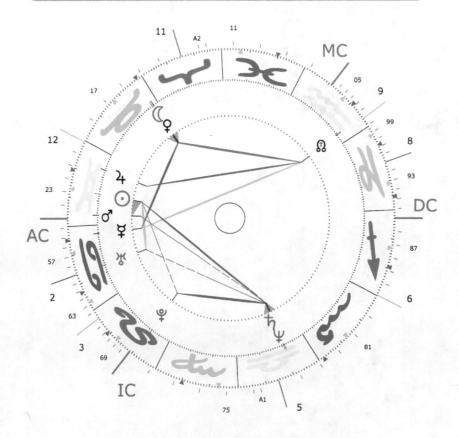

Figure 2.3.44 -Sophie
08.06.1953, 05:30, Mobberley, England

Chapter 3. The Planets – Levels of Consciousness

This chapter covers the planets and how increasing conscious awareness affects the ways in which they function, from early impulsiveness to the wider levels of the transpersonal.

Planets have archetypal qualities and are focal points of energy in the chart. Each planet is influenced by its position in sign and house and by the aspects to it, which affect how these archetypal qualities are expressed.

Contents:

3.1 Tool and Ego Planets

In this section we consider:

- The tool planets, their basic drives, and the role each plays in our lives. By understanding the various influences on each planet we can see how the qualities of that planet may be energised and function in our lives.

- The ego planets and how these relate to body, feelings and mind.

Introduction

We now take a closer look at the third level of human existence and consciousness: the level of the planets. Spiritual and psychic energy, flowing outwards from the centre of the chart, is channeled by the aspect structure to the planets. It is helpful therefore to think of the planets as points where energy is focused and put to work.

Planets have their own archetypal qualities and act as focal points of energy in the chart. Each planet is influenced by its position in sign and house and by the aspects to it, and this affects how the archetypal qualities are expressed.

In Chapter 2 we considered the meaning of specific aspect patterns. For example wherever we find a small blue talent triangle in a chart we know that that person has some gift or talent which will want to express itself as an ease of working in a definite, particular field such as mountain climbing, miniature portrait painting, dressmaking, choral singing...

In order to interpret such an aspect pattern we need to look outwards from the aspects and identify the particular planets linked by the aspect structure. A small Talent triangle focused on the planet Venus may be expressed in an artistic way; focused on the Moon it may be expressed in an inner emotional way. As the energy flowing through the aspect structure reaches the planets it is given form and meaning.

The planets also receive energy from the outside world, from the space outside the chart. They act as our sensors, making sense of our environment and dictating our actions.

Psychologically the planets are a point of balance between our inner and outer worlds. Consciously we live in our planets, through the energy focused into these centres. Organically the planets can be seen as sensory receptors at the outer level, and at the inner level as secretors of the hormones which control bodily reactions.

In recent years many astrological writers have developed the view that the planets correspond to our psychological drives and needs. Here we take this idea one stage further. Each planet can be seen to operate at one of three levels – the conscious level, a lower or subconscious level and a higher or superconscious level. This is set out in Figure 3.1.1 on the next page.

Astrological psychology divides the planets into three distinct groups:

- the **ego planets**: Sun, Moon and Saturn represent our mental, emotional and physical consciousness. They appear in the central row of Figure 3.1.1

- the **tool planets**: Mars, Venus, Mercury, Jupiter act as support to the ego planets and represent instinctive and subconscious functions. They are shown on the bottom row.

- the **transpersonal planets**: Uranus, Neptune and Pluto are connected to the development of a higher consciousness. They are placed on the upper row.

Figure 3.1.1 also divides the ten planets into three columns.

- On the left are the 'feminine' planets Uranus, Saturn and Venus.

- On the right are the 'masculine' planets Pluto, Sun and Mars.

- In the centre are the 'neutral' or androgynous planets Neptune, Moon, Mercury and Jupiter.

Important

Although this planetary model is divided into layers and columns by solid lines for the sake of clarity, we emphasise that psychological energy is not rigidly contained in this way and that it is free to flow in any direction.

The Tool Planets

The tool planets are Venus, Mercury, Mars and Jupiter. Their function is to support our basic existential needs and ensure our survival.

In terms of the millions of years over which the human race has evolved, the achievement of consciousness is very recent. The effort to make conscious what has always been unconscious is the story of human civilisation. It is also a process lived out in each human life and the way in which we play our part in the evolution and development of the human race.

Long before civilisation developed there was a need to survive, a need to fight or run away, a need to relate, to communicate, to explore and to understand. We still carry these earlier needs within us and they remain at the foundation of our lives.

Before we can concentrate our energies on creativity, on our spiritual life, higher imagination or whatever, we must feel sufficiently safe, warm, fed, at ease and cared for. Any threat at this basic fundamental level is automatically given priority as it is a question of survival. When we are in danger creativity must wait. The tool planets are seen as acting instinctively, automatically, largely at a sub-conscious level, safeguarding this basic security.

	CREATIVE INTELLIGENCE	LOVE CAPACITY	MENTAL SELF / WILL
SUPER-CONSCIOUSNESS — Higher Mental Growth	♅ **MEDITATION - METHOD** New Forms – Inventions	♆ **IDENTIFICATION - COMPREHENSION** All Inclusive Healing through Love Will to Help Empathy Osmosis Universal Love	♇ **CONTEMPLATION METAMORPHOSIS**
EGO CONSCIOUSNESS — Personality / Human Level	♄ **PHYSICAL MANIFESTATIONS** Organisation Acquisition Vulnerability Teacher Law of Economy Learning through Experience Practical Thought Processes Need for Protection Security, and Order of Physical Body Preserver, Clear Limits Physical Body & its Awareness Memory Matter Mother Nourishment Centripetal	☽ **YOU-AWARENESS** Radar Wishes, Desires Mirroring Participating Need for Love Perception of Self through Contacts Soul States Astral body Child Sympathy – Antipathy Need for Contacts, Emotional Nature Instinctive Reactions to Stimuli Reflecting Principle Sensitive Adaptations to Life	☉ **SELF-AWARENESS** Quality Choice Judge Creativity Discriminate Centrifugal Individuality Strength Power Goal Orientation Father Control Need for Expansion Personal 'I' Conscious Intelligence Vital Energies – Personal Will Ego – I think therefore I am
SUBCONSCIOUSNESS — Life Supporting Functions	♀ **PERFECTION** Introverted Tool of Selection in any Process Assimilation Striving for Harmony Peace Aesthetics Female Libido Input Relating Organ	☿ **FORMULATION - EVALUATION** Sense Functions Capacity for Perception and Judgement Perspective First Hand Knowledge through observation, Reality Information & Knowledge Gathering Communication Words & Concepts Second Hand Knowledge	♂ **ACHIEVEMENT** Asserting Output Motor Action Energy for Production Work and Self-Assertion Masculine Libido Extroverted Involvement and Motion

Figure 3.1.1 The Threefold Personality

MARS

In both men and women Mars represents outflowing masculine energy. It is best known as the energy to fight or to run away but it is more importantly the energy to work. To initiate is the province of Mars. Masculinity means knowing one's goal and doing whatever is necessary to achieve it.

The roots of Martian energy come from the old tribal needs to fight to defend yourself, to hunt and kill in order to eat, and to compete for possessions. The present equivalents of this energy are the drive to achieve short or long term goals, working to win status and possessions from the world and to defend yourself from attack.

When Mars is over-emphasised these goals are pursued aggressively and forcefully. This will often have the effect of activating Mars in others, making them actively resist what you are trying to achieve which, in turn, demands even more effort on your part, thus depleting your physical body, as well as your mental and emotional resources.

On the other hand, when the expression of Mars is inhibited it leads to a lack of initiative and fighting spirit. This is apparent in someone who is never prepared to commit himself to choosing a goal and achieving it, or perhaps someone who gives up too easily at the first sign of difficulty. Such people find themselves constantly being manipulated by those around them with strong Martian energy until they come to learn how to release their own Mars and act for themselves.

VENUS

Venus represents the equivalent feminine energy in both men and women. Venus and Mars can be seen as joint controllers of our energy household: Venus in charge of input, Mars in charge of output. Venus is the steward of the house watching over the body's energy stocks.

Venus selects the food that is needed to keep our body healthy and oversees the breaking down and assimilation of food, the storing of what is useful and the disposal of what is waste. Minimum levels of vital substances are monitored and when something has to be replenished Martian energy is used to move or work to bring back what is required.

Venus gives us a vital sense of balance, unity and harmony. When this balance is present Venusian energy manifests with an ease that brings perfection. When there is imbalance it expresses itself as acute dissatisfaction or distress and forces us to take action to bring us back to balance again.

One area in which Venus can be seen to operate is in protecting our health. Venus gives us that marvellous feeling of well-being when we are balanced and in good health. It also warns us that we need exercise, that we are straining ourselves through over-work, that we should avoid sugar for a while, lose weight, or even gives us a strong urge to spend a weekend on a purging fast, and so on. If we listen to these instincts then our body protects itself. If we choose to ignore or suppress these messages we can do great damage to our bodies and find ourselves listening to them in more extreme form when our health has broken down.

Another important area in which Venus can be seen to operate is in that of social relationships. Mars energy, in both men and women, is primarily sexual at this level. Mars notices an attractive other person as a sexual target, puts energy into conquering that person sexually and moves on. Venus is the balancing urge of relating to another person, with love. The underlying motivation is security.

Venus is able to give us a precise sense of social harmony. What this involves will differ for each of us, but we will each have an instinctive pattern of the social relationships and environmental beauty that is perfect for us.

When these patterns are present we experience strong feelings of self-worth, of valuing ourselves as individual human beings. For some of us this will centre on the love of a partner; for others it will centre on approval from a social group to which they belong. Others will emphasise family structures such as parents or children, and so on.

When these personal requirements are missing, either for a moment or for a longer period of time, Venus again reports distress and asks that corrective measures are taken. We are lonely, miserable, depressed and seek to resolve the tension by compromising, seeing the other person's point of view or by seeking out new compensatory social contacts. Venus tries to bring us back into social harmony.

Harmony is a particularly important principle in understanding the work of Venus. In the field of medicine, there is an increasing emphasis on harmony and the fact that good health follows naturally where there is harmony in a person's body and life. This is one of the fundamental ideas associated with Venus. The urge to express ideal harmony in physical form leads to the traditional associations of Venus with the arts, such as painting, sculpture and pottery.

Over-emphasis of Venusian energy in either a man or woman can lead to a hedonistic, self-indulgent life in which pleasure is sought before all else. It can also lead to an inability to tolerate disharmony, which can result in anxious behaviour and a desperate need to placate others as soon as they threaten to disturb the emotional peace.

Suppression of the Venus energy, on the other hand, can lead to an emphasis on the Mars male energy to the extent that the individual is so busy achieving, that he or she is unable to form any deep relationships. A marked sense of dissatisfaction with life usually ensues, although the individual is unlikely to admit to the underlying reason for this.

In traditional astrology it is often assumed that a woman's Mars will be projected onto and lived out through her husband, and that a man's Venus will be projected onto and lived out through his wife.

The changes in the social attitudes since the 1960s now make it much easier for people to take back responsibility for their contra-sexual energy and to live out their own Mars or Venus. Typically this can take place in the phase of life between 28 and 36 years when many individuals are thrown into reassessing themselves and their lives because of the breakdown of their health, their marriage, or because of dissatisfaction with their chosen job, career, or some other facet of their life.

MERCURY AND JUPITER

 The two neutral tool planets, Mercury and Jupiter, are both concerned with learning. They involve the processes of learning, understanding and communicating and are therefore neither male nor female but neutral. When we learn we do so in one of two ways. The first is learning from others, the second is learning by observation and experience through our senses.

Mercury allows us to learn what other people already know through language. It acts as a word processor and transmitter. Mercury absorbs an incredible amount of information each day through listening and reading. This gathering of information is largely unselective. What someone has told us, what we read in the papers, hear on the radio, see on television or the internet is taken in and is spoken back to another person as we pass the information on to them. The Mercury function is the type of academic learning that is stressed in our modern Western schools. We listen, read and learn how to reproduce what we have learned as accurately as possible. If we use and develop our Mercury skills efficiently it leads us to knowledge.

The other way to learn, through Jupiter, leads to wisdom. Jupiter is concerned with learning through our own senses. This is a much slower process as the conditions for learning must first be present and we may need to observe again and again before being able to come to any conclusion. What is observed, or appears to be observed, must be weighed and tested through our senses. However, when we eventually reach a conclusion through using our own senses, rather than through hearing or reading about something, we not only know it to be true at a far deeper level, but we also know it to have meaning.

When we sit in an audience listening to a speaker it is quite easy to perceive whether the person to whom we are listening has the flat quality of someone who has gathered up a mass of information through his Mercury function, or has the solid depth of understanding of someone who has experienced what he is describing for himself. Jupiter wisdom carries far more depth than Mercury knowledge.

In Western schools there is relatively little emphasis on the training of Jupiter energy, except in some alternative schools. Even at university level education can still be a continuation of learning through the Mercury function, absorbing and reproducing what is already known. The need to use Jupiter energy may begin to emerge, and students often find themselves struggling if they are asked to find out for themselves, when what they rely on most is the Mercury ability to discover what other people think and know.

As a result of its neglect in our education we often treat our Jupiter energy with suspicion and distrust as we pass through our twenties and thirties. It is only perhaps late in our thirties that we find we are able to detach ourselves sufficiently from the world's values and begin to pay attention and give value to what we have discovered for ourselves, through our own experience. Many people stay with Mercury for the whole of their lives but others wake up to the exciting realisation that their own wisdom may be more valid than any of the worldly principles that they have been following for so long.

Both Mercury and Jupiter have their contributions to make; neither is sufficient without the balance of the other. It is just as unbalanced to overvalue the information brought to us by Mercury and to ignore what our experience shows us to be true, as it is to be so lost in our experience that the world is treated as irrelevant. We do not need to recreate the sum of human knowledge. We simply need to absorb it critically and to use our good senses to develop it further.

Modern city life emphasises our Mercury skills through social communication, phone, e-mail and internet facilities, whilst rural life constantly stimulates the senses and so keeps more of a balance between the Jupiter and Mercury patterns of learning.

Over-emphasis on Mercury can lead to restless, nervy irritability, jumping from subject to subject in search of new stimulation, or it can lead to academic intellectualism where a person presents his store of knowledge **as if it were wisdom**. A lack of Mercury energy on the other hand can lead to slowness in learning through listening and reading, or to difficulties in expressing oneself. This can lead to us being labelled 'unintelligent', and challenge our sense of self-worth.

The position of Jupiter in a birth chart has been traditionally interpreted as an area where one can expand confidently; where good fortune can be expected. The basis for this is the sure touch of those who have learned to trust what their own senses tell them. If you have learned to use your Jupiter skills as well as your Mercury skills you find that your senses accurately lead you to avoid dangerous situations and bring you to what will help you prosper. It is not so much a question of being guided by your sixth sense as learning how to listen to all five senses in order to achieve the sixth.

When Jupiter energy is over-emphasised we can become so over-confident that we refuse to hear objective evidence. Our ideas become exaggerated and we become involved in grandiose schemes or ideals. The ego becomes increasingly identified with grand projects until the success or failure of the projects has been turned into issues of status.

When Jupiter is not given sufficient development, there is normally complete reliance on what Mercury hears from the world, with a sense that what we think or discover for ourselves does not count. This can lead to deep feelings of inadequacy and powerlessness. We feel that we do not matter and cannot have any impact upon the world. A compensatory measure is to over develop Mercury with the resultant distortion already mentioned.

Interpreting the Tool Planets

In practical terms the way in which each of the tool planets expresses itself in a person's life will depend upon the energy reaching that planet through the aspect structure, the sign and the position in the sign, as well as the house and the position in the house. A Mars that receives many red aspects (squares and oppositions) is able to draw on this red energy to work and fight. A Mars that receives mainly blue aspects (trines and sextiles) will be less identifiable since its energy may be used for enjoyment or appreciation.

We also need to take account of which of the three ego planets is the strongest and therefore which one has the greatest influence on each of the tool planets. In other words the planet Venus may be controlled by a person's mind (Sun), his emotions (Moon) or by his need for structure, reality and physical security (Saturn).

When considering the planetary model depicted in Figure 3.1.1, it is important to bear in mind that no boundaries exist between the three levels, neither do they exist between the three columns, i.e. cardinal, mutable and fixed. As we grow older and become more aware of ourselves and our potential there can and should be a free flow of energy in any direction so that all, or any, part of the personality can be activated in the optimum manner as appropriate for any situation.

For example, Jupiter appears in Figure 3.1.1 at the life support level since it is neither an ego planet nor a transpersonal planet. Jupiter is concerned with sense perception and learning and is an integral part of the growth process which any individual embarks upon. Jupiter enlarges our experience of the world through experience itself, an alternative way of contacting our external reality other than by an over-emphasis on Mercury, i.e. words and symbolic communication.

Mars also appears at the life support level. At birth, Mars functions instinctively and unconsciously to attract attention and obtain sustenance, but as we grow older and become aware that we have a will, feelings, and needs for physical activity, we learn to use Mars more skillfully and express its energy in a more positive way. We can work in a more productive, energetic, skillful manner. For instance, we can be caring in intimate sexual relationships, rather than just dominant. Ultimately, if we can become receptive to the transpersonal energies of the planets on the top level, Mars can become a tool for the expression of these energies..

The ego planets are not within the control of a new born baby. In the patriarchal society of the Western world over the past 3,000 years the role of the will (Sun) is initially projected onto the father or father figure, whilst the task of feeding, providing security, protecting, teaching and disciplining is projected onto the mother or mother figure. In a healthy environment the growing child gradually learns to take over these roles from his parents. However, when this does not happen it creates serious problems in adolescence and adulthood. In other words one may remain captive to the unevolved energies of the lower level.

Perhaps it is important to remember that our own will is not able to physically **do** anything on its own. It is only through a combination of planetary energies that we can express ourselves in daily life.

Ego Planets

In the central layer of Figure 3.1.1 we see the three ego or personality planets, the Sun, Moon and Saturn. In the birth chart these are drawn in red to remind us of their importance. We identify ourselves with these three planets; they give us our sense of individuality, how we see ourselves in the world. The Sun gives self-awareness through the mind, the Moon gives self-awareness through the emotions and Saturn gives self-awareness through the body.

Each individual finds his or her own balance between the three ego planets, choosing to live more, or less, in the mind, the emotions or at the physical level. Yet all three of these centres should be allowed to play their part and should be brought into balance and harmony. As our life proceeds we are shown the consequences of over-specialising in, or over-developing, one of these centres. At those crucial times the way forward is to rediscover and befriend whichever of the three ego planets has been neglected, to create a new unity.

In this part we will take a look at Sun, Moon and Saturn and what each requires for its own individual development.

SUN

 The Sun requires the development of self-awareness and the experiencing of **self** through the mind. It requires the expansion of our capacity to control our lives by being able to make mental decisions and know that they are right, by using our will to direct energy in a particular direction, and by trusting the judgments that we have learnt to make at a mental level.

Will is a power within ourselves. It is not a thought or an object or a wish. Will is what can make you succeed when your thoughts tell you that you are defeated. Will is a force that makes you invulnerable. Roberto Assagioli's book *The Act of Will* explores this in detail and is recommended reading.

There are three forms of expression of the will that require development in a co-coordinated manner:

- The **strong will** that enables us to be powerful when it is appropriate for us to be so,

- The **skillful will** that enables us to go about a task in the wisest way,

- The **good will** that gives us the ability to be concerned for the needs of others whilst still being aware of our own needs.

Development of one without the others is a distortion that negates the ability to use our will effectively.

THE MOON

 The Moon requires that we learn to be true to ourselves, to love ourselves and to recognise our **own** emotional needs, and how we can get these met. We have to understand what these are so that we can love other people freely and for the right reasons and receive from them the response that we seek and need so that we can feel emotionally satisfied and secure.

When young we are often taught who to like and make friends with and who to avoid. We are given reasons why we should trust some people and not others. We grow up with an understanding that certain types of people are the ones that we can relate to whilst others are not. We are also set examples as to how we should respond to other things in the world, such as art, literature, music and so on.

We become confused about our emotional needs because we are trying to relate to people and situations with the value judgments of those who educated us. As adults we may form relationships for the wrong reasons, e.g. because of guilt feelings, or perhaps we are afraid to relate because we do not get back the response that we seek from the other. We may also have been discouraged from discovering some of the beauty in life – things that can enrich us at an emotional level.

There is a world of difference between being able to express spontaneous feelings when we see a sad film on TV, or someone suffering, and being able to express our true feelings about situations we encounter every day of our life. We may have learned to hide our true feelings, our ability to love freely, from **ourselves**, let alone from our nearest and dearest for fear of upsetting them. In doing so we hide a part of ourselves and create a distorted situation in which a true relationship cannot survive or flourish.

SATURN

Saturn demands that we concern ourselves with our own physical needs and become responsible for our own bodily well-being and security – not to the exclusion of everything else but in a sensible, caring manner. We can develop Saturn by becoming aware of what it is that keeps us physically healthy, such as exercise, diet, even simple things like cleaning our teeth, having enough fresh air, grooming and dressing ourselves with pride.

Saturn requires us to be aware also of the practicalities of life that demand our attention, and of the material needs that ensure our survival. We may develop the ability to use our will and express our feelings but neither of these will be of great benefit to us if we have not dealt with the practicalities of life, or if we live in a body which is not as healthy as nature intended.

In the development of our personality through the ego planets we must take care that we do not allow one to become so strong as to overrule the others. There is the need for balance. Most of us have a tendency to respond to the needs and demands of one ego planet to the detriment of the other two. In this way we may allow, for instance, our emotions to run our lives so that our decisions are based on emotional reactions rather than reflecting a true act of will. Or we may have become so obsessed with our security needs that we cannot move from the situation in which we find ourselves for fear of the consequences.

Further Reading

This section has provided an introduction to the psychological meaning of the seven classical planets, which are extensively covered in the astrological literature. You are particularly recommended to read the following amplification of the tool and ego planets:

The Planets and their Psychological Meaning
by Bruno & Louise Huber, Chapter 2 'The Seven Classical Planets'.

Note on Chiron

You may already be familiar with the asteroid Chiron. From time to time we are asked why it is not used in astrological psychology.

Bruno Huber suggested that Chiron is a minor asteroid which is in the process of diminishing in size. There are many asteroids and to give significance to just one would give a distorted view of its potential significance. If people want to work with Chiron, they should perhaps include consideration of other significant asteroids and their influences.

Bruno acknowledged the significance that Chiron might have had when discovered in 1977, and felt that in the grand scheme of things, Chiron was probably the herald of alternative therapies and healing. As these alternatives are now much more readily accepted and mainstream, Chiron had now in a sense done its job. His research suggested that Chiron's effect was ephemeral.

Exercise 3.1

Tool planets

Recall some real life situations you have experienced recently and reflect on how these relate to the expression of the tool planetary energies symbolised by your natal chart. Try to think of situations that have involved different tool planets, or combinations of these.

Ego planets

Reflect on how you experience each of your own three ego planets, taking into account their sign and house, the aspect colours they receive, and the relevance of the aspect pattern they are involved in.

3.2 Transpersonal Planets and Levels of Consciousness

In this section we consider personal and spiritual growth, looking at:

- The transpersonal planets and how to interpret them
- The masculine, feminine and neutral planets and how they relate to the threefold personality
- The development of the personality, and transcending material and physical needs, so that we may respond to transpersonal energies trying to express themselves through our lives
- The stages of spiritual growth and how these are reflected on the levels at which the planets operate.

NB The development of a human being is not a simple matter and although you may not fully understand all the material in this section you will find that your understanding will mature as you progress through this book.

Part 1 – The Transpersonal Planets

The three ego planets and the four tool planets together make up the seven planets that were known to man from pre-Babylonian times. All of these planets can be seen with the naked eye. The development of the telescope at the end of the 18th century enabled the discovery of the three outer planets Uranus, Neptune and Pluto.

Even though Pluto was demoted as a planet by astronomers in 2008 on account of its small size, it continues to be treated as a planet in astrology, as the impact of the energy which it symbolizes can be observed at world level as well as experienced personally.

These three higher level planets appear to be connected to the development of a higher consciousness. They are not so much concerned with the individual as with the whole human race. Hence the term transpersonal.

URANUS

The discovery of Uranus in 1781 coincides with the breakdown of the fixed, stable social patterns of an essentially feudal, agricultural society. Revolutionary ideas of individual rights, of "liberty, equality and fraternity" were spread by the French and American revolutions.

All societies were affected by the power of the idea whose time had come and were permanently changed. Democratic ideas, the struggle against slavery, the right to form unions, one man one vote – the effect of these ideas spread far and wide.

At the same time the new sciences and the beginning of the industrial revolution led to great movements of people from the country into towns, to changes in the pattern of wealth away from the old landed aristocracy towards the urban middle classes. Change and upheaval were so obvious that any political or philosophical theory based on natural stable social order, that things should continue as they always had been, inevitably had to give way.

With the security of the religious and social orders, in which man had known his place from birth to death, finally shattered, people were forced to begin the painful and long process of finding their individuality at a level that had previously been impossible. This is still so and seems to herald the Age of Aquarius that Uranus rules.

NEPTUNE

 The first explosion of higher energy associated with the discovery of Uranus operated at a very material level. Where the industrial revolution developed, the "satanic mills" followed. Physical suffering, poverty and starvation increased. The discovery of Neptune can perhaps be seen as a correction to the first revolutionary impulse of Uranus.

Neptune energy is associated with visions of perfection, ideals and compassion. The mid-nineteenth century brought great public concern for the welfare of the sick, the poor and children. Florence Nightingale's work in the Crimea, and Dr. Barnado's in England is reflected on many levels as Victorians became caught up in the impulse to look after the unfortunate.

Neptune energy is also associated with creative inspiration and the mid-nineteenth century saw the artistic exploration of visions of ideal worlds in such fields as the poetry of the Romantics, Gothic revival in architecture and Pre-Raphaelite painting.

The period also brought great interest in the unseen worlds of the occult. Spiritualism became fashionable. Hypnotism was in vogue. The hidden power of gas for lighting and steam for driving machinery was being harnessed. In surgery anesthetics were perfected. There is an overall sense of human consciousness being progressively expanded to take account of the unseen and hidden.

PLUTO

 Pluto, was discovered at the remote edge of the solar system in 1930 at a time when totalitarian regimes were prevalent in Europe. The time of its discovery coincides with the revolution in nuclear physics which has given many benefits, such as X-rays, but has also made humanity confront the possibility of self-destruction. It seems likely that humankind will have to live under the shadow of this threat, constantly at the mercy of individual madness and chance error, until some change that we cannot even imagine takes place in human thinking and feeling.

Pluto forces us to confront our deepest levels of desire and motivation. This theme is reflected in the development of depth psychology and the exploration of the unconscious, also the depths of human nature which is also associated with Pluto. The mass

movements of the 1930s warn us that we can no longer afford to be at the mercy of the dark forces of the collective unconscious. The consequences are now too dangerous. The struggle to accept and meet the darker forces within ourselves must be made by each and every one of us on our own. It is not something that can be left to governments; each of us has to enter into this battle.

We can see therefore that the effect of the energy of the higher planets is to create the conditions in which individuality must be sought and achieved.

Interpreting the Transpersonal Planets

The majority of people live for most of their lives within the patterns set out by the three ego planets and the four tool planets. Energy from the transpersonal planets intrudes into these patterns from time to time, usually with a sense of crisis. This is likely to occur when the Age Point makes a major aspect to one of these planets or where a transit from one of the transpersonal planets falls on one of the angles of a chart or on one of the ego planets.

The energy of **Uranus** brings independence, originality and innovation. When it is over-emphasised in a chart it can indicate a tendency to stubborn nonconformity, being different for its own sake, or holding to the unconventional to the point of extreme. Extremism can manifest on the one hand as the individual who is blinded by his own need for technological or mathematical perfection ("System is all important"), and on the other hand, as the blind tyranny of the terrorist.

Where Uranus is suppressed there is a clinging to the secure old ways with the result that necessary changes are forced upon a reluctant, complaining individual.

The energy of **Neptune** brings a vision of the ideal, compassion and heightened perception. Over-emphasis of this energy in a chart can indicate a person that prefers the ideal to the real and has difficulty in grounding himself. The world outside is seen to be unbearably harsh and is avoided through retreat into inner fantasies, drugs, alcohol or sleep. The more a person tunes himself to the higher energies of Neptune the more sensitive he becomes and the less able he is to deal with practical reality.

When Neptune energy is absent life is made barren by the lack of inner meaning that flows from contact with the inner vision. Love is empty and constantly unsatisfying, becoming a restless search from one person to another until the solution is found within the seeker.

Pluto brings into consciousness what has been hidden or suppressed in the subconscious. With each inner upheaval energy is released and this can give Pluto a sense of compulsive power and ego inflation. Over-emphasis of the Pluto energy leads to concentration on power for its own sake, whether through psychological manipulation or through the fear used in the underworld. Obsession or violence can follow.

When Pluto's energy is suppressed or held back, or even when Pluto is very weak in the chart, there is a sense of brittleness about the person. Others can sense the coming crisis, the tension that is steadily rising. There may be a degeneration of self to the extent that the individual can become caught up in their search for the spiritual father, the guru, the all-powerful replacement for their own weak ego.

When one of the transpersonal planets is found in the natal chart on one of the main angles, or is closely aspecting an ego planet through a conjunction, square or opposition, there is likely to be a lifelong identification with the energy of the transpersonal planet, for example as an artist when the planet is Neptune, or a psychotherapist when the planet is Pluto. Even here caution is necessary when interpreting as the symbols of the transpersonal planets are extremely rich. The energy of Neptune not only inspires the creative artist but also the drug addict, the alcoholic, the priest and the musician.

There is a sense in which we have to learn to allow the energy of the transpersonal planets to act on us and through us, as a healer is taught to act as an open channel. While we are still struggling to solve the problems at the level of our egos any attempt to control or use the higher energy can be disastrous. The ego inflates to the point where it is overthrown by the higher transpersonal energy leaving behind an inhuman terrorist, false guru or dictator.

It must be remembered that the energy of the transpersonal planets will either come into our lives at an unconscious level in the form of "collective correction", i.e. teaching or punishment, or we can evolve to the more conscious and self-aware state where the energy can enter at the transpersonal level and be used for the benefit of the whole.

Further Work on the Transpersonal Planets

Since the energy of the transpersonal planets is relevant to the evolution of the human race more than that of the individual, we can learn to allow this energy to act upon us and through us, as a healer is taught to act as an open channel. We may attune ourselves to this energy as follows.

- **Uranus energy** may be discovered through meditation. Here meditation means the mental process of asking a question in inner quietness and listening for the answer. Each answer takes you nearer your goal.

- **Neptune energy** may be felt through the technique of identification. This means absorbing yourself completely in some other living being, animal or human. Gradually you float into the other creature or person and see the world through their eyes. By experiencing this shift of viewpoint you develop two of Neptune's qualities: compassion and empathy. There are people who can achieve this shift through becoming totally emotionally absorbed in music.

- **Pluto energy** may be understood through the practice of contemplation. Here it is not a question that is asked but a vision that is held in the mind and contemplated. The mind is emptied as far as possible and the attention is gently brought back to the vision whenever it wanders.

It is especially useful to do this before the Age Point or a significant transit makes contact with one of these planets, or when transpersonal planets are due to come into conjunction or opposition with ego planets by transit.

Part 2 – The Planets and the Threefold Personality

Each column in the model of the threefold personality (Figure 3.1.1), can be identified with one of the three astrological qualities. The feminine column of Venus, Saturn and Uranus represents the fixed quality. The motivation of these planets is associated with security. The neutral column of Mercury, Jupiter, Moon and Neptune represents the mutable quality. Their motivation is towards love and contact. The masculine column of Mars, Sun and Pluto represents the cardinal quality and motivation is towards individuation.

The Feminine Planets

The energy of Venus, as we have seen, seeks security by working to maintain harmony and balance, and using discrimination. The action of Saturn is more obviously security-bound. Its focus is on physical safety and body wisdom. Our patterns of driving cars, eating, taking exercise, dealing with threats and so on, are internalised and committed to memory so that they become as automatic as our breathing patterns or the working of our digestive system. This comfortable network of automatic habits protects us and gives us a secure sense of who we are.

With Saturn, we could live ordered lives, such as those lived by medieval monks, from birth to death. However, the energy of Uranus appears to threaten us with change and we often react to it by retreating even further behind the safe walls of Saturnian habits, and refusing to acknowledge the need for change.

In fact the change of Uranus comes to save us from the dangers of stagnation in old routines that have outlived their purpose. Whether we recognize the effect of Uranus as an external wake-up call or we simply see it as an external catastrophe – the break-up of a marriage, a severe accident, sudden redundancy, betrayal or whatever – its contribution is to force us to break out of our protective walls and to go forwards. This may seem frighteningly dangerous as we enter an unknown future, but it leads to individual growth and to a greater sense of security, founded on inner confidence in coping with change.

The crucial and courageous step from the security of Saturn to the adventure of Uranus is the re-enactment of the growing child challenging and leaving the mother. The comfort of the mother/Saturn is infinitely attractive, but it leads to stagnation and death. Away from the mother, into the unknown, is the path to adulthood symbolised by Uranus.

The Masculine Planets

Through action (Mars) and through the use of our mind (Sun) we begin to see our self reflected back to us. We gradually build up an image of who we are, what our role in life is, and how we like to think of ourselves. At the level of Mars we know ourselves through physical actions. At the level of the Sun we know ourselves through our perceptions and through conscious thinking.

Once again, as with the feminine column, this process reaches a point of limitation. Through the Sun we simply act as we are; we do not improve. Pluto, the higher male energy, energises us with images of what the male energy in each of us can be, images of the hero, of god-men, challenging us to not only be the person that we are but to stretch into the best that we could become.

Psychologically this process is the pattern played out between child and father, or the person playing the role of father. Initially the father's influence on the child is vital. The child takes his place in the world as an acceptable member of his society through this initiation by the father. Pluto's energy comes in at the point where the child has outgrown the teachings of his father and needs to pursue his own journey forward. At that point the child may need the influence of higher father figures, heroes of myth or history, to show him a way forward.

The Neutral Planets

We have already seen the role of Mercury and Jupiter in learning from others and in communicating with others. The Moon is the centre of the emotions, the place where the inner child resides within each of us. As such it is constantly reflecting and reacting to everyone else, emotionally sensing the other person, responding instinctively to stimulus. The child has a clear idea of its emotional needs, how it should be loved, and the Moon's energy is used to find this love, to satisfy the child. However when we love at the level of the Moon, we love in a childish way and our ego is too much involved so that we get easily hurt by the emotions and actions of the loved ones.

Neptune helps us transcend our ego and opens us up to the higher form of love that comes from identification with the whole of creation, in the spirit of St Francis. When we feel this level of Neptunian love flowing through us, we give our love to all in a totally selfless way, without any concern for what we will get back. This is essentially a spiritual experience.

Working with all Ten Planets

Further suggestions for developing an understanding of all ten planets include the study of both the mythology of the gods and goddesses associated with the planets and the astronomy of the celestial bodies. It is particularly helpful to develop an inner image of the god or goddess standing for the planet so that the images can be used in guided meditations.

For example, you can develop a series of inner landscapes for each sign and then imagine each of the gods and goddesses entering this landscape to see how they respond. Perhaps a Scorpio landscape of black and silver, dark and powerful, into which Venus or Saturn could be invited so that you can experience how these planets respond.

Similar techniques may be used to understand particular aspect patterns by imagining the appropriate gods and goddesses in those patterns. For example, setting out an Efficiency Triangle of Venus opposed to Saturn, both squared by Mars. You can then view the pattern from each corner in turn, feeling the forces at work on the expression of that planet's energy.

It is important to be able to see how our own psychological and physical 'growth' is reflected in the birth chart and to do this it may be helpful to have an image or analogy of growth. For example, such an image might be as follows:

- Imagine a patch of earth and 10 seeds scattered at random in a circle. Allow yourself to have a clear image of this seed bed, is it fertile or infertile, is it clean, well prepared soil or covered in weeds and stones.

- Next allow your imagination to see each of those 10 seeds go through the stage of germination beneath the soil, see them grow and finally break through the surface into the light of day. Picture the environment which exists for these delicate seedlings as they emerge into the world.

- Perhaps your imagination, and your knowledge of gardening, might allow you to attach a name to each of these plants which relate in some way to the qualities that we associate with the planets.

- Each seedling has the potential to grow into a full size plant, and to flower and fruit before it dies. Imagine everything that might happen to each of these plants as they struggle to become established. Also see each seedling as it starts to grow stronger, as it begins to establish itself, grow taller and send out additional shoots and leaves. This is how we might imagine the development of each planet as it widens its contact with the world around it and develops new skills and talents. But maybe a seedling will get trampled on and remain under-developed and weedy, or another might have an excess of encouragement and spread too quickly so that it smothers an adjacent seedling.

Your own imaginative process is important so it is not the intention here to create too rigid a picture. If it is right for you then give yourself the opportunity to develop your own image of growth. What, for you, is the end result? Is it a garden of beauty where each plant has had the same opportunity to mature into its own fullness so that a garden is created which is beautiful in its colour, its balance and feeling of integration? What is your picture?

Every Day
Every day, in any situation in which you find yourself, it is helpful to become aware of how you express yourself, how you react to what is happening. In this way you begin to develop an understanding of the way your sub-personalities behave in your life.

At the same time you may also become aware of which area of your chart is being energised, and how this influences your attitude or behaviour. To do this it is useful to be able to summon up a mental image of your chart. If you find this difficult it may be helpful to use some blank chart forms and practice drawing your chart from memory until you are able to recall it quite easily.

Part 3 – Development of the Ego and Ways to the Transpersonal

The birth chart reflects a pattern of cosmic energies that were active at the moment of birth, and to which an individual responds in a positive, neutral or negative manner during a life time. The planets are the key factors in the chart that we use to assess how these energies might manifest. However, the process is not simple since the planets have **different levels of activity** and therefore meaning. See Figure 3.2.1.

Life is a continually evolving process from cradle to grave. During the course of it we learn to recognise the path to follow, as well as the need to develop and use our potential abilities to greatest advantage, not just for ourselves but for the benefit of the whole.

In trying to describe concepts such as development and evolving spiritual growth, there is a tendency to become entangled in mental images of a hierarchical kind. Development can be construed as upward, so high is believed to be better than low. Spiritual awareness is equated with being somehow more worthy or laudable than spiritual un-awareness.

Principles in Figure 3.2.1

- Animus is spirit that penetrates and impregnates matter. The animus principle is the creation of life.

- Anima holds the matter and gives it form, thus fixing it. The anima principle is the securing of life.

- The Christ principle is that of relating.

	Fixed	Mutable	Cardinal
SUPER-CONSCIOUS SPHERE	CREATIVE INTELLIGENCE	UNIVERSAL LOVE	UNIVERSAL WILL
Mental & Spiritual Growth	♅ Mother Principle / Anima Principle	♆ Son Principle / Christ Principle	♇ Father Principle / Animus Principle
Aspiration	Meditation METHOD	Identification COMPREHENSION	Contemplation METAMORPHOSIS
CONSCIOUS SPHERE	PHYSICAL MANIFESTATION	EMOTIONAL SENSE OF SELF	SELF-AWARENESS
Personality (Ego)	♄	☽	☉
Role of Self	Mother Practical thought Processes NEED FOR PROTECTION	Child Emotional responses NEED FOR CONTACTS	Father Personal Will NEED FOR EXPANSION
SUB-CONSCIOUS SPHERE	PERFECTION	FORMULATION/ EVALUATION	ACHIEVEMENT
Impulses/ Instincts	♀	☿ ♃	♂
Life Supporting Functions	Balance – Harmony ASSIMILATION	Computing – Sensing LEARNING MECHANISM	Action – Energy MOTOR FUNCTION
THE THREE-FOLD PERSONALITY	FEMALE	NEUTRAL	MALE
	Bio-Chemical Processes CAPACITY	Nervous Function CONSCIOUSNESS	Drive to Achieve POTENCY
	Taste – Touch	Hearing, Seeing, Perceiving	Smell

Figure 3.2.1

Our language and thought forms tend also towards polarity thinking, black or white, good or bad, either/or. We are steeped in thought patterns where each end of a polarity also has a value judgment. Our thought patterns do not readily lend themselves to viewing both ends of a polarity as being two aspects of a single continuum. Thus good and evil are not readily perceived as being two sides of the same coin, the tendency is to treat them as different coins.

As we align our personal self (personality) to our higher transpersonal self (soul), using Assagioli's Egg diagram [Figure 1.1.2, page 12] we become aware of a sense of inclusiveness, acceptance, unconditional love and will. Here everything is included and nothing is excluded.

Our soul has our personality as a vehicle for its expression. So, in this section, when we talk about the 'integration of the personality' and 'spiritual development' we should liken these concepts to the cleaning up, repairing and tuning of a musical instrument in order that it can be used to express the music of the spheres. Our soul will use our personality in whatever form it is to express itself, but through our attempts to integrate the various aspects of our personality we offer the soul a more consciously functioning instrument.

In the process of integrating our personality, we become aware of the various ways in which we think in terms of polarities, and slowly we move towards a synthesis of two apparently contrasting elements within us. Thus the initial thought patterns and ways of hierarchical thinking always give way to perceiving things as they are in a non-judgmental and accepting way.

The Lower, Unconscious, Level.

At birth our only instinct is to survive. We learn quickly the best ways to ensure that our basic needs are met so that we can begin to grow physically, mentally and emotionally. In other words we tap into the lower level of Figure 3.2.1 – the level which initially operates unconsciously and sustains life instinctively and impulsively.

Although at that stage we have little or no control over events we are conscious of what is going on around us and we have a strong, instinctive tendency to adapt. This is necessary for survival, though in later years may be a hindrance to further growth. In these early months of life we are instinctively using Venus, Mercury, Jupiter and Mars without control and with a lack of awareness of their effect other than that their actions keep us alive.

The Middle, Conscious, Level

The middle layer of the threefold personality consists of the Sun, Moon and Saturn. These planets symbolise the ego, or that part of us that can give us choice about our actions and our destiny and allow us to take conscious control over them. However, before we reach that stage in our development the functions of two of these three planets are in the hands of others, namely our parents, or in their absence the people who play the role of mother and father in our life.

The Sun is the archetypal leader or head of the family and fulfils the father role, whilst Saturn, the nurturing teacher, fulfils the role of the mother. This concept of Saturn as the mother conflicts with the traditional astrological symbolism underlying much astrological thinking, which is confused on this point and tends to see the Moon as mother. The Moon is a totally receptive and reflective planet and as such is symbolic of the child in its early receptive state, whereas Saturn's nature is to protect, preserve and ensure that everything is in order and all sources of danger and disruption are avoided. Like a good mother, it provides safety, nourishment and guidance.

As very young children we instinctively understand the need to develop and live for ourselves the ego roles of Sun, Saturn and Moon in order that we might become independent, autonomous human beings.

It is only when we become consciously aware of ourselves that we can use the energies of the planetary tools (Venus, Mercury, Jupiter and Mars) to full advantage and be successful in our efforts to achieve our chosen objectives. Otherwise we will tend to let these energies be used in an instinctive and adaptive manner.

So the middle layer of the personality contains the controlling planets and it is through the balanced development of these that we begin to experience ourselves and our potential. The word balanced is important because it is easy for us to allow our lives to be controlled by our emotions (Moon), our superior opinion of ourselves and our need to dominate situations (Sun) or by our material and security needs (Saturn).

The Transpersonal, Super-Conscious, Level

The Path to Uranus, Neptune and Pluto

It is only when we have achieved the state of balance and control in our lives, as discussed above, that we can begin to explore the spiritual, or transpersonal meanings of the three outer planets. Until that time the energies of Uranus, Neptune and Pluto will tend to affect our lives at a negative level creating instability, self-deception, upheaval, power complexes and so on. Every event and situation that arises in our lives is an opportunity to learn how to manage these energies more positively, even though they may also be perceived initially as external events over which we have no control.

As we progress along the evolutionary path we are likely to experience flashes of inspiration or selfless idealism, or enjoy the occasional peak experience which lights up our life and gives a glimpse of the heights to which we can rise if we can open ourselves up to the spiritual energies of the outer planets.

Reaching new transpersonal dimensions may be a complex process and in the early stages we may well experience a spiritual or even psychological crisis and put up some resistance. In astrological terms progress necessitates working on all three ego planets. However, Saturn forms the bottom rung of the evolutionary ladder and progress is difficult until we are able to realise that true wealth is not represented by the objects and people that we possess, and that ownership of these is not essential for our survival.

Our own energy is finite so if we use it all to acquire material security we are denying ourselves the chance of using it for growth and fulfillment. Saturn is greedy and if we give way to its demands we can get sucked into an endless cycle. The more we have, the more we need.

Evolution of the Personality – Three Stages

Evolution at the level of personality can be described as in three stages:

- The **first stage** is a conscious awareness of the simple fact that body, mind and feelings exist. With Saturn (body), which we may have to tackle first, may come a new awareness of your physical self which prompts a bout of self-nurturing. We become aware of our body and its special needs, we may decide to go on a diet, become vegetarian, take up exercise, give up smoking, or whatever feels necessary.

- The **second stage** is one of conflict, when we begin to realise just how much of our life has been devoted to doing the things that Saturn has suggested are essential to our survival. We become aware of the effect this may have had in restricting our progress in life, on our relationships, and so on.

  A struggle ensues within as to whether or not we have sufficient faith and trust to stop striving for possessions and material security and venture into the unknown in search of the true purpose of our life. Perhaps then we also begin to discover the priceless value of being able to use our own will.

- The **third stage** is reached when we find that we can let go and dissolve the mastery of Saturn and the materialistic world it represents. This frees us for the next step on our journey, which involves getting in touch with our deepest feelings and discovering the freedom to love without conditions. Ultimately the personal will aligns itself in service of universal will.

Progress is not, of course, necessarily in that order or as smooth as the foregoing might suggest. We hop up and down the ladder all the time. When we think we've mastered Saturn along will come a temptation we cannot resist and the process has to be repeated. Yet, at the same time as we are struggling with Saturn, we may be discovering the warmth of feelings and the power of will, and perhaps perceiving the opportunities that are offered through the energies of Uranus as they start to flood through in a blaze of creative new ideas, or the sense of freedom that comes from transcending personal will and surrendering to universal will.

So life can either be a challenging but rewarding struggle in which we consciously seek to break through to new areas of enlightenment and achievement – or we can remain fixed in our belief that Saturn is an all-powerful energy which has to be constantly fed and respected as our lord and master.

The Amphora Model - The Constitution of Man/Woman

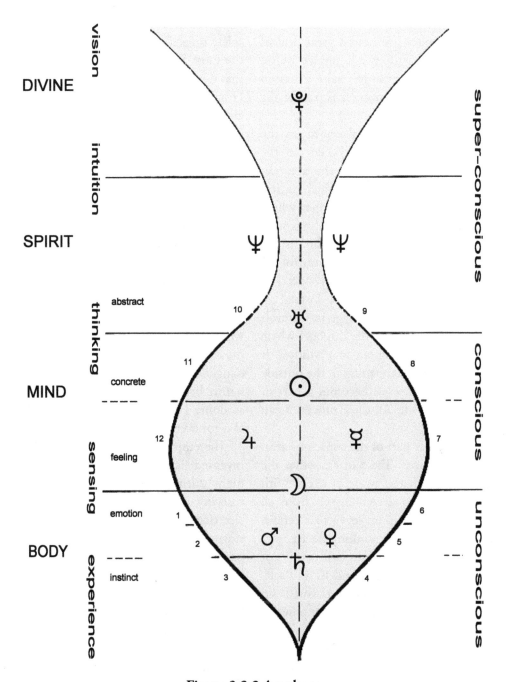

Figure 3.2.2 Amphora

Figure 3.2.2 shows Bruno Huber's Amphora, which is his adaptation of Assagioli's 'Egg' [Figure 1.1.2 page 12]. It can be seen as a means of putting the concept of personality development, as we view it through astrology, into a visual form. The amphora evolved because Bruno Huber wanted to put together into one whole workable principle the concepts surrounding Assagioli's representations of the three states of consciousness, and the threefold personality symbolised by the planets [Figure 3.2.1 page 110].

The amphora incorporates the house system, the planets and the layers of the threefold personality. It may be seen that Saturn, Moon and Sun are not located in the middle area, but rather according to the importance of their role in the structure of the personality. They are shown as the rulers of their respective areas – Saturn of the unconscious, Moon as the bridge to the conscious and Sun as the ruler of the conscious.

Saturn rules memory as well as the body. When working on the mental level, Saturn gives the ability to know a great deal, to be culture-filled. However, this is still a bodily function. Brains and memory are of the body. In the memory we hold a great deal of unconscious knowledge that does not surface unless triggered. It lies dormant until the right situation comes along and suddenly we **know**. It is part of the intuitive mechanism.

The **Moon** governs our emotional centre. In the chart this corresponds to the area adjacent to the AC/DC axis, i.e houses 1, 6, 7 and 12. This area can be divided into two parts: the lower which is less conscious and more emotional and the upper which is more conscious and feeling-oriented. Feelings have their origin in the conscious area, emotion in the unconscious area. Mercury and Jupiter can control the upper part, Mars and Venus control the lower part.

The Moon is especially flexible and instead of staying in the middle as the diagram suggests, it travels up and down, or over to the sides of the amphora where it looks out – rather like looking out of a window. It watches the changing scenes happening in the outside world, identifies with them, even becomes a part of them, and thereby loses itself. All these processes can be seen here.

The **Sun** rules the upper part of the conscious area, rising out of the feeling area. The Sun embodies the conscious mind, the ego that is aware of itself. With the Sun (will) I am able to detach myself from all my attachments and identifications, even to a certain degree from my natural needs. I can think freely.

As I reach towards Uranus, the Sun (will) aims not just to be intelligent but to be independent and self-aware. I think therefore I am, I find out who I am independently of other people. I own my own power. I can do things and I can see that I did them, I also know if what I did is good or bad, I can reflect on what I do and what I know. That knowledge makes me strong, it gives me independent selfhood. That is an important step. The nearer one gets to reaching it the nearer one gets to Uranus.

Uranus is the power of independent selfhood. It is so independent that it can reach beyond the natural limit of thinking in terms that are mundane to those that are universal. I can pierce the eggshell with Uranus and come to insights that are not controlled by my will to survive, or my egotistic need to be bigger or greater.

Uranus seeks insight for its own sake – for the value that insight has rather than for the fact that I have insight. As a super-conscious, or transpersonal planet, that is its function. Here it is important to remember the connection that Uranus has with Saturn.

In the threefold personality model Venus is below Saturn and Uranus above. These are feminine planets whose basic orientation is to secure life. They do it on different levels. Saturn as an ego planet is focused solely on self-protection. 'I want to protect myself' is the most Saturnian sentence one can make. It means that if I can do that I am fine, I am safe and self assured. However, if I encounter danger my first reaction is to close down and secure my world. Saturn's attitude is always defensive.

Uranus functions in the opposite way. It opens the mind by transcending the ego, thus widening the consciousness. If all our energy is geared towards ensuring our safety, we reach a point where the more security we create the more insecure we become. This is a conscious experience of all Saturnians, and we all have Saturn within us.

The only resolution is to look for the **cause** of the danger, which must be greater than our present knowledge, otherwise our security system would have worked. This is a Uranian realisation. I must leave my own fears, and look for the real reason that causes danger. As scientists would say, there must be a law of nature behind this function and I must discover it. In so doing I solve the problem not only for myself but also for everyone in the same situation.

The emphasis is transpersonal. Benjamin Franklin invented lightening conductors. He went out in the night during a bad storm, at great risk to himself, carrying a kite. He had the idea that lightning is electricity and could be led to earth. And so in the storm he flew the kite with a long line to earth to prove his theory. He could himself have been struck by lightning, but he took the risk. Through his experiments we all gained greater understanding and knowledge and so do not have the same need to fear lightning through ignorance.

Uranus demands the overcoming of personal fears in order that a step forward can be taken to find the truth behind that which is bigger than our own concern. We will never take that step as long as our fear is stronger and our ego confined. All scientists and researchers are Uranian 'egg piercers', enabling us to open up to greater knowledge and understanding.

However, knowledge too has its limits. The danger for Uranians is that they believe that knowledge is the only possible way to reach wisdom. They become addicts to knowledge – eggheads. The fact seems to be, however, that the more a person loves knowledge, the less they love people. They become incapable of making good human contacts and developing loving relationships.

This **is the bottleneck** of the amphora. At a point in our development we have to realise that knowledge is not everything. If we persist with a quest for ever greater knowledge then the bottleneck, being unable to contain it all, becomes porous and our essential essence is lost, as well as our own sense of identity. In knowing everything we know nothing. There is no longer a point of orientation. Dr. Faustus is an excellent example of this. The only way of passing the blockage in the bottleneck is to reach out to Neptune.

Neptune stands for Love. It is the power of identification with the **You**, whatever order or quality that the You has, be it a stone on the road, a human being, or anything in between. Knowledge has its limit but love can develop understanding. With love we can understand any object by identifying with it. This identification transcends knowledge. It is not easy to explain to others that, because I understand this object or whatever, I will do it no harm because I see it as a part of the whole – it has its function and its meaning.

The only planet that appears twice, and outside the amphora, is Neptune. To experience Neptune we have to transcend our own sphere, to leave the area where we have been so secure. All the knowledge gained with Uranus does not give us the lasting security we need – that of knowing who we are.

With both Uranus and Saturn there can be a loss of identity, and the way to find ourselves again is to find the You, whatever that may be: another human being, any other form of life (animals, plants, rocks, stars,...), and to understand that being by identification with it.

This identification does not require losing oneself but, by feeling through something other than oneself – feeling all. It is difficult to explain this in words, it needs to be experienced. The bottleneck will then open and we can be within the amphora again, i.e. within our own conscious self-identity.

The next step is **Pluto** and to reach it we must once again use our will. Pluto is a different dimension. It is the upper, transpersonal Sun. It is not driven by the ego, the need for personal identity. Its drive is for perfection of being. It does not matter if it is my being, or any other being. It must be perfected. There is of course a guiding image in Pluto that tells me how perfection looks. That is what I contemplate.

Summary: The Amphora is a Symbol of the Constitution of Man/Woman

At the unconscious/instinctive level Saturn connects us to the physical world and material reality. It symbolises the force of gravity, the drive for security, centripetal force, and it provides the energy for growth.

On the unconscious/emotional level we experience the first planetary drives, of Mars and Venus in particular, to satisfy our needs, wants, libidinal energy and to take us out of the stagnation of Saturn.

At the crossroads between unconscious and conscious is the Moon which reflects inner reality and sensitivity, but with detachment. Unconsciously it expresses our emotional drives, desires and needs. Consciously the Moon symbolises our awareness of feelings and human relationships, our need for love.

On the conscious/feeling level we can become aware of our feeling nature, the part of us that responds to others. We need to become aware that the reality of thought affects the feelings. The Moon teaches lessons of love but may glamorise things. Eventually we realise that we can depend on ourselves rather than on others. Integration with the Moon can give a sense of inner calmness and emotional purification. Jupiter leads us into ourselves and provides 'I' experiences. Through Mercury we gather facts from others and have 'You' experiences. We learn and grow.

As we enter the concrete/thinking level we acquire mental stability. We achieve autonomy and are unaffected by the approval or disapproval of others. Integration with the Sun (will) is the point where we reach independence of life style. It is when we can say we are an individual in our own right. We are in tune with the Law of Refusal, when we have the ability to choose our own experiences. What we think can become a reality and we develop the power of recognition and discrimination, balancing facts with subjective experience.

At the superconscious abstract/thinking level of Uranus we have an intuitive knowing of how the Universe works but we can get stuck at this level.

As we pass through, we have to give up conscious striving for enlightenment and let go of Uranus in order to be drawn up into the neck of the bottle towards Neptune. As we pass through the eye of the needle and open up to the **selfless** love of Neptune we find that through Pluto it is possible to surrender to Universal Will to express Universal Love.

However, our journey is neither linear nor steady. We can find ourselves back at the level of Saturn, with its material security demands, at the same time as we are aware of the power of Uranus, Neptune or Pluto.

Part 4 – Stages of Spiritual Growth

Discrimination between Psychological and Spiritual Crisis

We are living in a space – shown by the Amphora, that has two major forces working on our consciousness:

- the force from below that has the function of keeping us alive (survival). It manifests through the forces of nature and as far as we respond to these we are a part of nature, and are also ruled by the laws of nature.

- the force from above that has the same, or even greater power, but its function is to make us grow and become aware in consciousness of our belonging to the whole. This force applies to the totality of nature, not only our physical nature.

It is not always easy to discriminate as to which force is acting upon us. Are we disturbed by the lower or the higher forces at any given moment, or in any specific problem or situation? The symptoms may be the same. In both cases, our behaviour may show disorders that can be interpreted as complexes, Freudian or other, so it is not possible to tell from the symptoms It needs deeper analysis to find out which is which.

A level worth considering is the level of motivation. Yet again how can we know whether these motivations are the result of the higher force or the lower force working through us or, as is more often the case, a mixture of both?. As a matter of fact the person who starts perceiving higher energies will strongly experience the pull of the two forces and therefore a mixture of motivation. That is inevitable.

Three Stages of Spiritual Growth

Although Assagioli puts forward several more stages here we present only three to keep things more simple but nonetheless pertinent.

First Stage.

The first stage corresponds to the piercing of Assagioli's Egg, the level of Uranus in the Amphora. This is when we have the first insights into greater consciousness and understanding the deeper laws of nature.

This stage can lead to many disorders. At one level we feel fantastic because we have new insights and we are tremendously lifted in our consciousness. At another level we often come into conflict with our surroundings. Our personal relationships are deeply affected by the change in us. A rift occurs as we step out of the mould and start asking different questions and believing in a new code. This may summon up guilt feelings and we may try to return to normal, though it is impossible to do so at this stage, as our new insights when suppressed will break into our dreams, disrupting sleep or affecting our health. Once we have opened that shell it stays opened.

During this phase support and/or therapy can help bring us into harmony with our surroundings. This is not an adaptational process using the rules of society, but is a re-adaptation using spiritual laws as a yardstick. We have to learn to be fully aware of the spiritual dimensions, work with them, live them but at the same time be able to deal with the material world according to its rules.

Many instances of obsession stem from cases like this that have been mishandled. The first stage is often entered with the study of astrology, or any of the occult sciences, but there are other possibilities such as unexpected psychological awakenings of one kind or another. We may start having visions, or experience other psychic phenomena, but it is a happening that sparks off spiritual awareness.

As astrologers we need to have a good understanding of how this stage works and how it feels.

Second Stage

The more we learn to handle spiritual energies the more likely it is that our existing human system, body, psyche, mind, may react because of unsolved problems in the first stage. There are still existing problems in the belly of the Amphora. For example, if we have a strong need for security, we will not like to take risks and we will spend a lot of time in securing our life in all kinds of ways.

At some point in our spiritual development Saturn will feel endangered by these ever changing energies. Our willingness to surrender security in our mind disturbs our psyche and it reacts by trying to make us disbelieve all that stuff.

A typical reaction is to develop philosophies that explain that we must have these problems, and we give them spiritual names. Of course this is illusory because our problems come from below and therefore cannot be spiritual in origin or nature. This approach actually keeps us away from further development.

The answer here is to heed our basic physical, emotional and psychological needs and attend to these. We have these needs and the problems we are experiencing may stem from them, so we need to attend to them. It is important to go through the process of self-discovery and face ourselves honestly. This is the stage of **truth**. The only way is to become more and more true to ourselves. It is sometimes astounding how problems solve themselves, when we truly accept who we are. **No self-delusions**.

Third Stage

The more we become acquainted with the spiritual laws of nature and learn to handle them, the more we have to cope with the tests where the purity of our motivation is tested. Real spiritual work cannot happen with an ego that wants something for itself, be it money, power or something else. These three testings have to do with the three big 'M's:

MIGHT, MATTER & MAGIC.

We have a beautiful description of these three testings in the Bible – Christ went through these testings in the desert. Rarely will they take such a dramatic form as in the Bible. The process is generally much more subtle, less obvious. We know of the attraction in being powerful, in having influence over many people, and it is difficult to know to what degree we have freed ourselves from this enticement.

It is clear that these three stages are quite different: in the first stage the breaking through of the shell brings outrage from others, the second stage produces conflict within our own system, and in the third stage we have to go through the purifying process to get rid of the ego. In the later part of the third stage it becomes important to be able to discriminate between needs that are natural and the fear and greed of the ego.

We have the need to survive as physical human beings and we have to find out how much we need to live in a decent way, but not so much that our focus is given over to providing for the ego. To free ourselves from the ego brings pain.

Pain can take all kinds of forms. It can be emotional, physical or mental. Being a doubting Thomas is a state of mental pain. Not knowing where our real values lie causes both mental and emotional pain. There are unending forms of pain on the three levels on which we live.

These three stages have been presented here in an order and although they do have order, their experience is not necessarily orderly. We may well find ourselves in harmony with the third stage when we suddenly develop problems at the first stage. Funny things happen, one of which could be called the magnifying glass effect. Let us say for instance that in the second stage we start to work on certain distortions, malfunctions and problems of our personality. Now at a certain point in this process we start looking at our these defects as though through a magnifying glass. We see more and more details, and our magnifying glass becomes a zoom lens and we discover little kernels of residual stuff that we do not like. We may have cleared out most of it when we started to work on it sometime ago and now, with the magnifying glass, we become aware of just tiny bits left and we see them out of proportion and we think "I'm not making any progress". We can even think we are going backward. It's one of those things that happens to most people in different stages and areas of the whole process.

Three Levels of Expression of the Transpersonal Planets

We have touched on the stages of personal growth that we need to go through in order to experience the true transpersonal qualities of these planets. Whilst consciously working towards that ultimate stage we may also consider the levels of activity of the transpersonal planets themselves so that we can more easily be aware of the level at which they function in our lives.

The energy of the transpersonal planets is present in our lives at all times, often functioning unconsciously, affecting the way we behave. We may wonder why we always seem to attract aggressive behaviour from other people. The answer may lie in the fact that Pluto is in a strong position in our chart and is functioning independently, out of range of conscious awareness, perhaps attempting to control others. A transit to natal Pluto may bring about a situation that will wake us up to the importance of this energy and how it may be developed and integrated into our consciousness, so that it can begin to function, through us, at a more universal and inclusive level.

The way in which we experience transpersonal energy will be different for each of us and will depend on our own level of conscious awareness, or personal development. But it would also be true to say that we are likely to be more sensitive to the energy of a transpersonal planet if it is conjunct a personal planet, especially an ego planet in our natal chart. Although it does not automatically follow that we will handle this energy in a wiser way, it does mean that it will be more present in our life and perhaps emphasise the need for us to explore its meaning and purpose. Such closeness of the transpersonal planet can be quite uncomfortable until we develop a conscious awareness of its meaning. This is especially so if all three ego planets are conjunct a transpersonal planet.

Through awareness of the way in which the transpersonal planets are active in our lives we can be conscious of the three phases of their unfolding potential (similar to the three levels of Figure 3.2.1).

These phases might be called

1. the **sleeping** state;

2. the **awakening** state, and

3. the **awake** state.

In either of the first two states we may become trapped, in the first as a victim to circumstances and in the second as someone caught in circumstances over which we try to take control, but in a misguided fashion. All unconscious, unawake states tend to produce disaster sooner or later. When we are ready to enter the third state of selfless acceptance we have to be prepared to surrender our ego needs and put our trust in the universe.

URANUS

In the **sleeping state** Uranus may be seen as the ideal vision of a perfect world which contains the right system for achieving universal security. It can be the motivating force not only of astrologers but also of revolutionaries who want to change the world and solve everyone's problems – for the world or on a smaller scale for home and family. The drive to achieve Uranian ideals can produce original, inventive, creative thinking, sudden flashes of intuition which often result from a period of hard preparatory work. Uranus is not concerned with individuals but with the whole and the system, and individuals don't always fit into this. The perfect world is a technically created situation.

The **awakening state** is reached by confronting phenomena that cannot be explained, such as telepathy, or psychic experiences. At the personal level we may have a peak experience that suggests that we have the gift of clairvoyance or channelling. At the collective level, we may welcome new inventions such as nuclear power and the internet. In this state, we become aware of the beneficial qualities of these Uranian discoveries as well as their potential danger and recognize that they should never be used for personal gain.

The scientific age has produced startling technical creations but each contains potential hazards. We have an unconscious belief in what the collective offers but as humans we can recognise our fallibility as being in conflict with collective technology. In this awakening phase we may find nail-benders, crystal ball readers, sword swallowers, hypnotists and suchlike, but we have to recognise that we cannot use new found transpersonal energy for personal gain, for ego reasons.

In the **awake** (transpersonal) **state** Uranus represents the power of **searching**, knowing that any reality is not final, that there is no perfect solution. All knowledge is temporary. Knowing that the only stable thing in life is our own state of conscious awareness. Through Uranus we can be in touch with the pure creativity of the universe.

NEPTUNE

In the **sleeping state** Neptune is not associated with systems in the way that Uranus is, but is concerned with people – the relationships between people. A relationship between two people is the linking of two energy fields (love). Neptune believes in the **ideal** of creating a universal field of love energy, of creating the **perfect** relationship in an unstructured situation, but this can only truly be created when we are free of selfish ego needs and the distortions that these create in any relationship.

In the **awakening state** we may attempt to satisfy Neptunian ideals with things that can be bought. We recognise our need for perfect love but impose our own restrictions from Uranus (laws) and Pluto (perfection). So, in a negative way we may look for pseudo love through such things as TV, drinking, drugs or erotic magazine, whilst a more positive manifestation may be through community groups. We have a sense that we can satisfy our **need for contact** through these. Some mediums and clairvoyants have got stuck in the awakening state of Neptune with the result that they tend to attract people with relationship problems.

In the **awake state**, the Neptunian qualities that we seek may be found through meditation and through active mental processes that enable us to experience a **selfless** love of all beings in the cosmos. We may perceive ourselves at one with the universe. We accept that **everything that is** is right and we are not tempted to make value judgments. Neptune can take us from knowledge to understanding.

PLUTO

In the **sleeping state** Pluto is concerned with the essence of being, with the evolution of the species and the evolution of the human being. We ask ourselves "Who am I/ what is my essence?" Images such as, on the one hand, superman/ God/ guru and on the other hand, pop stars/ football players are Pluto-type images. The negative side of the asleep quality of Pluto is power for transformation used externally instead of internally. The requirements of Pluto are that we let go of what we are, what we have, what we control in a worldly sense and relinquish our image of perfect being.

In the **awakening state** Pluto activates ambitions and power drives which, in men, can be expressed through sexual aggression. We feel limited in our personal growth so we desire to conquer through power, e.g. businessmen who conquer by destroying those in their way. The guru may be an artificial position of power, as may the politician, and sex can be another expression of power. Precognitions, visions, matters to do with the future tend to be Pluto related, as is telekinesis energy, including poltergeist activities, which may be symptomatic of repressed or unexpressed sexual energy.

In the **awake state** Pluto is the power of contemplation and concentration on pneuma (inner space). It is concerned with **growth and transcendence**. This includes the growth of consciousness and our ability to depend upon ourselves and not others. Through Pluto we may find our link with universal will. Pluto is not destructive, only transformative. The only things that get destroyed are man-made creations put in the way of nature.

Recommended Reading
Another perspective on some of the ground covered by this section can be found in:

The Planets and their Psychological Meaning, by Bruno & Louise Huber
Chapter 3 "The Three Spiritual Planets"

Levels of Operation of the Planets

We can apply the idea of levels of operation, introduced above in the context of transpersonal planets, to all of the planets. The following offers insight into the way in which we might experience the energies of each of the planets at each of the three levels

1. Sleeping
2. Awakening
3. Awake.

SUN

1. Egocentricity, vitality, personal impact, vain glory
2. Ambition, self-confidence, pride
3. Self-awareness, autonomy, intelligence, magnitude

MOON

1. Contact needs, emotional dependency, childishness
2. Changeable, moody, wanting to be loved, adaptability, emotional manipulation
3. Harmlessness, openness, receptivity, sensitivity, compassion

SATURN

1. Material security, inertia, habits, resistance to change
2. Security needs, defence mechanisms, fears, basic faith
3. Memory, conscience, tolerance, discipline, maturity, dignity, mentor, benefactor

VENUS

1. Laziness, narcissism, vanity, sluggishness, passivity, pleasure-seeker,
2. Harmony, balance, benevolence, sensuality, yielding, sense of style, relating
3. Aestheticism, love of beauty, appreciation, discrimination, perfectionism

MARS

1. Bellicose, conflict, tearing down barriers, recklessness, aggression
2. Action, powers of achievement, energy, activity, assertion
3. Active devotion, single-mindedness, pioneering spirit, courage, heroism,

MERCURY

1. Literal, information-seeking, speaking, writing
2. Language and Communication, loquaciousness, curiosity, deduction
3. Understanding, clarity, communication channel, meditation, messenger of the gods

JUPITER

1. Enjoyment of the senses, alertness, arrogance, satedness, joie de vivre
2. Joviality, righteousness, boastfulness, optimism, vision, perception
3. Good judgment, sense of values, good perspective, wisdom and ethics, justice, inner knowing

URANUS

1. Striving for security, obsession with technical systems and safety devices, defence mechanisms, strategy
2. Eccentricity, overcoming boundaries/fear, inventive mania, reformatory, revolutionary, magical effect
3. Creative intelligence, originality, explorer spirit, sudden insights, freedom-loving, problem solving

NEPTUNE

1. Idealism, love archetype, romanticism, deceptions, false images
2. Devotion, self-renunciation, social conscience, exaggerated ideologies, irrational, belief in magic
3. Spiritual identification, unity, universal love, mysticism

PLUTO

1. Masks, ego-mania, negative use of power and control, forcing one's will on others, destructive rage
2. Megalomania, being driven, idols, transformations, crises
3. Spiritual will and motivation, goal orientated, power, synthesis

Exercise 3.2

1. In Exercise 3.1 you considered how you experienced the tool planets. Now reflect on your understanding of the level of consciousness at which you are using these planets, and whether they react more to your needs and control, or more to environmental stimuli?

2. Consider the roles Uranus, Neptune and Pluto play in your life at the present time and reflect on whether you see these as positive or negative.

3. In the context of the threefold personality think about how much you are aware of the level the transpersonal planets are functioning at in your life at this stage in your own personal growth.

Chapter 4. The House Level - Meeting the World

This chapter looks at the hemispheres and quadrants of the chart and the astrological houses, their meanings and the positions of the planets within them. It also considers how planetary energies are affected by their placement within a house, and how this can give rise to conflicts within the personality as well as within the environment.

Contents:

4.1 Hemispheres and Quadrants

The orientation of the aspect structure within the chart gives some indication of how inner motivation leads us to react to the outside world consciously or unconsciously, and whether it reflects a drive for individuality or a need for relationships. In this section we introduce:

- The vertical and horizontal hemispheres of the chart
- The four quadrants

Introduction

Now we look at the chart from the viewpoint of a space, as opposed to energy, focusing on the area between the central core and the houses on the outer edge of the chart. Different areas of the chart affect the ease, or otherwise, with which energy can flow to and from the centre of the chart.

Chart Axes and the Cardinal Points

An initial look at the birth chart gives an overall impression of how the planets are distributed within the circle that represents the individual's psychic space. From the general planetary distribution we can discover much about the individual's underlying motivation, and in which areas of life experience his or her interests and aptitudes lie. For instance, if all the planets are concentrated in one half, or perhaps one quarter, of the circle, there will be a particularly strong emphasis and bias towards the theme of that portion of the chart. This is an invaluable starting point for interpretation, as the individual thematic pattern may be grasped at the outset.

To facilitate this approach, we can divide the horoscope by its two main axes – the horizon (from the AC on the left to the DC on the right), and the meridian (from the IC at the bottom to the MC at the top). These two axes define the individual's orientation in time and space, and form the skeleton on which the whole of the structure of the horoscope hangs.

The Four Cardinal Points

The points at the end of each axis (AC, DC, MC, IC) are focal points through which we move out into the world and experience our environment. These four points carry our energies into the world in a direct and dynamic manner. They may be seen as the crests of four energy waves which thrust us into contact with the environment. This is particularly emphasized when a planet is found close to one of these points.

These waves are caused by an outward movement from within ourselves and, at the same time, a pulling out by the environment exerting an attraction similar to the Moon's gravity.

As Figure 4.1.2 shows, there is a gradual build up and outward expansion of energy flow around the cardinal points, followed by a diminution and contraction of energy flow.

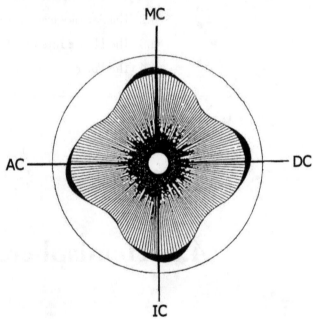

Figure 4.1.2

Each of the energy expansion peaks carries us out into a very different area of experience, whilst in the contraction zones experience is absorbed, assimilated, evaluated and digested. Here, one might say, experience becomes a part of our being.

It is important to gain an overview of this basic energy flow through expansion and contraction zones in the house system, so that when we look at a particular quadrant or hemisphere we are aware that this is a part of a dynamic and organic whole, each part being interdependent with the other parts of the circle. The picture that emerges should be seen as an evolving process, rather than a static condition.

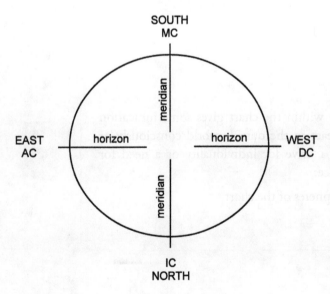

Figure 4.1.1

The Axes

The Horizontal Axis – Encounter Axis

This axis can be seen as the ground upon which we stand, and the axis along which we interact with the world, meet other people and discover our relationship to everything out there in the environment.

On the left the AC relates to the 'I', all that I identify myself with, my sense of self, everything that belongs or pertains to me. On the right, The DC is the 'You', all that is not 'I', and belongs to others, or comes to me through others.

This is the axis along which we go to meet others as fellow human beings, or create barriers to genuine meaningful encounters with others. Here, we must learn to balance our own needs against the needs of others, respect our own rights as well as the rights of others and be mindful of our responsibilities towards them.

Too much emphasis on the 'I' side suggests egocentricity. We may become self-centered and self-absorbed, creating blocks in our relationship with the outside world.

Too much dependence on the 'You', suggest a weak or insecure sense of self. We may be seen to be interfering, over-demanding, and draining of others' energy.

Planets along this axis indicate our possibilities for making contact, and the difficulties which may arise in this area of life.

The AC is how I want to be seen, my chosen self-image. It is the portrait I paint of myself. The DC is how I appear as a social person, and how the world sees and experiences me through my contact behaviour.

A planet close to the AC will strongly influence the quality of the Self portrait that I project, giving my persona, or the mask that I wear, its own distinctive qualities. For instance Mercury conjunct the AC will tend to inject a rational, analytical, talkative quality into the persona, and this is how she will like to come across.

A planet close to the DC indicates what we demand, and what and how we may give to the environment. It indicates the type of people and experiences towards which we are drawn.

The Vertical Axis – Individuality Axis

This axis may be seen as the dimension in which we stand upright in the world and grow into a true individual. Our feet are rooted in the IC, which represents our collective conditioning, the ground from which we sprang and our emotional roots. Our head is at the MC, which has to do with the conscious realisation of our own unique individuality, the growing into our full potential and stature in the world.

True individuality suggests a full integration, both within ourselves, and within the environment in which we live, bringing a deep understanding of our place within the whole. If someone is an 'individual', this means literally that he or she is un-divided. Hence, it is as well to make a clear distinction between individuality, and a false sense of ego that is dependent on power, acclaim and outside support, rather than on inner qualities which show themselves through one's actions.

This axis relates to the process of differentiation, discovering what makes me different from others, and what unique qualities I can bring into the world. Whereas the horizontal axis seeks similarities, points of contact or meeting with others.

Planets close to the IC indicate the characteristics which tend to hold us to collective norms and behaviour patterns. Planets near the MC indicate the qualities we admire in others and aspire to in ourselves.

The Hemispheres

Left Half of the Horoscope –- 'I' Hemisphere

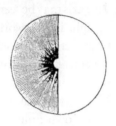

Everything to the left of the meridian falls into the 'I' hemisphere. This relates to my own private space, what interests me and motivates me physically, emotionally and mentally. Here I am on my own. Everything that I experience through planets in this hemisphere affects me personally. This is the subjective area of the chart, where I learn about myself and experience both my unconscious and conscious needs and desires. I encounter others in this space only if I invite them in either consciously or unconsciously. Such unconscious invitations may cause difficulties and result in an over-reaction, perhaps aggression or extreme defensiveness. It is my responsibility to discover what really motivates this self-inflicted abuse of my privacy and to find ways of preventing this. I cannot put the blame on to others, although this is usually the easiest thing to do.

Through the planets in this hemisphere, I can know myself and feel secure in my knowledge, talents, abilities and sense of self, or I can retreat from the world and create barriers that not only keep others out but keep me locked in, unable to make contact, unable to see others as they are, but only coloured by my own subjective experience and projections.

The planets in this realm indicate personal qualities and potentials for which I must accept full responsibility and which I should seek to bring to their fullest and most refined expression. They are the tools with which I can form myself into what I want to be. If I learn to master these tools, I can have something of real value to offer to others. My 'I' can go out full of confidence to meet the 'You'. I will no longer need to hide, or protect myself in a shell, nor be dependent on others for my sense of self.

Right Half of the Horoscope – 'You' Hemisphere

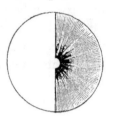

This hemisphere is concerned with how I relate to everything and everyone out there beyond my private realm. Through the planets in this hemisphere, we experience ourselves more objectively, through our contact with, and the feedback we receive from, the 'You'.

Here we encounter ourselves as the world sees us, not as we believe ourselves to be. This hemisphere provides the necessary objectivity to complement the subjectivity of the 'I' hemisphere, so that we may build a total picture of ourselves, our relationship to others and our environment. The planets that we find in this hemisphere are still a dimension of our own psyche, but they function mainly in our interactions with others, and will indicate the qualities that we look for in others, as well as what we learn about ourselves from others.

It is important to realise that what we experience in this hemisphere is, on the one hand, a reflection of another side of ourselves, and on the other hand, the means through which we are able to go out and make contact with others. Clearly, if there is something lacking in our mode of contact behaviour, others will make us aware of this, intentionally or unintentionally so we can take steps to change that.

Through the planets in this space, both a movement outwards to meet others, and a drawing in from the experience and insights of others. This makes a continuous two way flow corresponding to the principles of give and take. Whatever we experience through our 'You' planets, will inevitably affect our sense of 'I' which will in turn affect the way we relate to the 'You' in the future.

If we experience difficulties in the 'You' hemisphere and seek to lay the blame on others, we are merely projecting the short-comings in our own contact behaviour. Here we must accept responsibility towards others; the responsibility to be true to ourselves and to allow others to be themselves.

Lower Half of the Horoscope – Unconscious Hemisphere

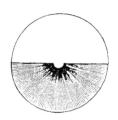

If the horizon represents the ground on which we stand, anything below the horizon is hidden under the earth, hidden from view and beyond our ability to consciously recognise it. This is the realm of the unconscious, where we act and react impulsively and instinctively. In this hemisphere we encounter habitual unconscious patterns of behaviour and behaviour norms which have much in common with the rest of our social group. Here we are in the collective realm of the horoscope where we seek common roots and bonds with the rest of humanity, where we want to belong and to be like everybody else.

Planets in this hemisphere are motivated by collective thought and feeling patterns, education and conditioning. Usually we only become aware of these motivations through observing the results of our actions. What motivated us to act in such and such a way? Very often this question will be asked by others, since we may remain blissfully unaware of the consequences – or choose not to see them.

The planets in this realm act and react reflexively and mechanically, according to our conditioning, to those behaviour patterns which have sunk down into our unconscious. Also they tend to fulfill certain archetypal, collective behavioural norms, sometimes assuming quite mythological proportions as they can tap into the vast store of collective energies available to them in this area of the chart.

Planets in the upper hemisphere can aid the process of becoming more conscious of such behaviour patterns, especially if they aspect the planets in the lower hemisphere.

Upper Half of the Horoscope – Conscious Hemisphere

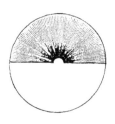

This is the realm of conscious perception, thought processes, planning and achievement. (Although some of these may derive their initial motivation from unconscious processes in the lower half.) In the upper half of the chart we develop self-awareness. We can see the world, and even ourselves, relatively clearly. We can make conscious decisions about ourselves, our lives and how we react to the rest of the world, and we can set about acting on those decisions and attaining our goals.

This is the realm of ideas, ideals and theories about life, that need to find their fulfillment through action in reality (lower hemisphere) An over-emphasis on the upper hemisphere may lead one to live in a world of theories that are totally divorced from reality.

This is the hemisphere where we can become individuals in our own right, where we can formulate and express our uniqueness. But we must be careful not to lose sight of our roots in the collective and the need for humility.

We can develop the real inner authority of an individuated being, one who knows himself. Or, at the other extreme, we can become a demagogue or tyrant if we do not turn consciously and willingly to face ourselves.

The Quadrants

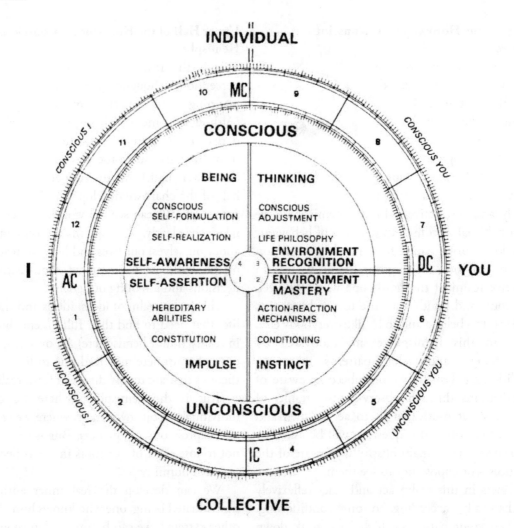

Figure 4.1.3 The Quadrants

Using the two main axes (horizon and meridian), we may further divide the horoscope into four quadrants, allowing for a more clearly defined overall picture to emerge. See Figure 4.1.3.

By observing the distribution of the planets in the quadrants we can see in which areas of expression the person functions most easily and naturally and where the main areas of interest lie. For instance, if all or the majority of the planets are posited in one quadrant, that is where the talents and abilities will lie.

If two adjacent or opposite quadrants contain the concentration of planets, that will give a hemisphere emphasis or a polarity within the horoscope.

If there is an equal distribution in all four quadrants, there will be an interest and an ability to express the self in all areas of life. The difficulty here may be in focusing the energies into a particular course through life, deciding what to do with that life and with the wide range of experience encountered.

If only three quadrants are tenanted, then the remaining quadrant may signify a gap in experience – an area that is not understood and to which the person may be seeking to relate. It may be an area of energy loss, or where energy does not flow so freely, or a part of life that is simply blocked off or ignored. Or it may be an area that simply does not require energy input or development.

First Quadrant – Unconscious 'I' – Impulse – Fire

This is the realm between AC and IC, in which the 'I' plunges into the collective unconscious, seeks impulsive self expression and how to fit into the surroundings into which it is born.

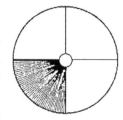

Unmediated by forethought or social conditioning, first quadrant energies have a fiery and impulsive quality. Through them, we react to situations with a swift intuitive appraisal of the environment's apparent challenges to our self-preservation. Until we become aware of these energies by discovering their effects, they remain an unconscious part of our constitution. Over time, we become conscious of their qualities by observing the results of the actions they prompt us to make. What may begin as a primary urge to express our energy and assert survival needs can become an increasingly refined tool for creative spontaneity and intuitive action.

The main theme of this quadrant is **action springing from unconscious impulses within the psyche** – the urge towards self-preservation. It represents the initial processes of self-assertion in the collective environment. Here, there is a challenge for survival and the need to establish a place for ourselves in the sometimes threatening world in which we live. Hence we find here natural defence mechanisms and what we have inherited from our forebears and the collective culture into which we are born.

If we feel overly intimidated by unconscious expectations of the collective, we may react by being especially defensive. On the other hand we may seek to conform to collective patterns of behaviour too readily and lose any sense of our own separateness. In this realm, we encounter the genetic and emotional coding which defines the type of environment, body and mind through which we experience life. We unconsciously seek both a separate identity and conformance with the rules and moral codes of the surrounding culture when we are brought up.

Planets act and react impulsively and reflexively and will tend to play down the patterns of behaviour which will influence us and affect us throughout our lives. They define our basic constitution. Through planets in this quadrant, we may learn about ourselves by retrospectively observing our actions their results. In this way we become aware of unconscious motivations and learn through experience.

The attribution of fire to this quadrant suggests not only the impulsive character of planets found here but also that these may eventually be developed into reliable intuitive tools, once we can break through the

tendency to react in outmoded and inappropriate ways that are merely a product of early experiences. This type of intuition is an active creative process that is able to make a lasting impression in collective consciousness, when the planets are no longer functioning at the level of self-assertion, but as channels for natural and spontaneous creative outflow. This is particularly true where spiritual planets (Uranus, Neptune, Pluto) are in this quadrant.

Second Quadrant – Unconscious 'You' – Instinct – Earth

This is the realm between IC and DC, where we encounter the collective 'You': that part of us which seeks unconsciously to relate to others and accept conditioned social behaviour patterns as the norm. The patterns of behaviour expressed

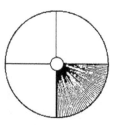

here are those picked up from our home environment: our peer group, first love experiences and the social environment in which we lived – as well as the patterns which we instinctively understand from our contact with collective needs.

Motivated towards contact with the 'You', energies in the second quadrant are no longer concerned with the simple assertion of our own selfhood and space. They are no longer the self-proclaiming shout of ourselves or the accumulation of energy to ourselves for self-extension, sustenance and protection. They are voices seeking to connect with the 'You', attuned to its response. Open to the 'You' at an unconscious level, it is here that we internalise messages about how we should interact with others (social conditioning). Awareness of our conditioning and second quadrant energies comes to us gradually, both by observing others' reactions to us and by learning to understand our own contribution in response. The second quadrant helps to ground and sustain us through instinctive intimacy and participation in the collective.

In this quadrant our unconscious attitudes towards all forms of relationship are imprinted deep within us through parents, teachers, lovers, employers and workmates. We develop certain stereotyped action-reaction mechanisms, without being necessarily conscious of these. We can learn to observe how these work once we become aware of their existence and can adapt them to the changing demands of relationships with the 'You' as we develop and mature.

This is the quadrant in which we acquire the know-how to deal with the outside world. Here we seek to gain some degree of mastery over our environment and find suitable or expedient ways of interacting and relating.

Here we can experiment with different approaches to others. Our responses may come from our collective understanding or we may become fixed with certain behavioural patterns or techniques that have worked, or at have least got us by in the past. When this happens we may find ourselves in later life relating according to immature principles that are no longer appropriate.

In our early years we may have become preoccupied with action and not sought to understand what lies behind our actions. In this quadrant there is a need to develop a certain level of self-awareness through observing the reactions we elicit in others. Also there is a gradual dawning of the inner relationship between mind and body – this is something which arises not from any conscious process, but from the ability to listen and respond to unconscious messages and to be receptive to the deeper significance that lies behind our existential experiences.

If there are discrepancies in our unconscious patterns, then these will lead us into the experiences which eventually force us to look for ways of correcting these discrepancies, recognising that this is our responsibility. This may come about through difficult family relationships, problems in love relationships, illness, work difficulties, etc. These are all situations through which we may learn more about our unconscious patterns of behaviour, if we are willing to seek the faults within ourselves and not seek to lay the blame somewhere out there.

The attribution of earth to this quadrant suggests the need to develop the senses in dealing with the world; to acknowledge the reality of the here and now in the physical world and to master the practicalities of day-to-day existence. It suggests that growth will come about as a result of our coming into contact with outside stimuli from others and the environment.

If we are able to listen to our instinctive understanding of collective needs and life processes then we can apply this knowledge to the world. Counsellors with a strong second quadrant emphasis are able to give to their clients a sense of safety and security

Third Quadrant – Conscious 'You' – Thinking – Air

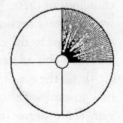

This is the realm of objective thinking, where we engage with the 'You' on a more conscious level. In this quadrant we enter the give and take of partnership in which the exchange of energy is modulated by conscious adjustment or agreement; we share resources and understandings and we journey together, intensely conscious of each other, into deep places of transformation; and we measure our own evolving life views against other philosophies, beliefs and cultures. Our third quadrant transactions help us to develop an objective view of ourselves, our beliefs and values, and our energies in interaction.

In this quadrant we make consciously formulated agreements with others, whether they be partnerships, business agreements or social responsibilities. We learn to gauge our own ideas and experiences against those of others and seek to develop out of this a life philosophy. The main theme of this quadrant is **thinking**, constructively and realistically, exchanging ideas and arriving at certain conclusions about life which encompass all the diversity of our experience.

Planets in this quadrant are concerned with conscious self-expression, action and creativity outward into the world. Here we confront the world head on. We may have to adjust our thinking processes in order to gain social acceptance and a more balanced view of the whole. Planets may be used as tools with which we become aware of our own needs in relating to others and of their needs, requiring attention and respect for the rights of others as individuals. Here we can learn through conscious adaptation and by considering the thoughts and example of others.

The attribution of this quadrant to air places an emphasis on expanding our horizons and thinking concepts and communicating consciously with as many aspects of life as possible. Here we learn to gain a more objective view of ourselves by seeing ourselves as others see us. As with the first and second quadrants, when viewed developmentally this can be seen as a preparation for the quadrant to follow.

Fourth Quadrant – Conscious 'I' – Being – Water

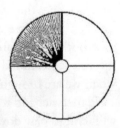

This realm lies between MC and AC. Here we begin to withdraw from the activities of the world and distil our experiences to bring about conscious self-knowledge. We must see ourselves as individuals in our own right and evaluate the world and our life experiences in the light of this individuality. Individuality suggests at one and the same time the need for a clear, consciously formed self-expression and an awareness of our connection with every other living being.

The fourth quadrant returns us to the realm of the 'I' with a more conscious sense of self. Here, a distinct feeling of individuality radiates into being and we have the potential to contact humanity from an awareness of ourselves that enables us to be free of projections and hidden agendas. We may also withdraw towards healing, reflection on life experience and contemplation. As fourth quadrant energies are realised, we can become increasingly centred in a sense of self that is no longer dependent on the environment for confirmation or definition. We can increasingly choose how we express ourselves in the world, open towards creation from a personal place of peace, communing with the **essential** in both ourselves and others.

This is the realm of self integration, where we no longer require experiences out there in order to learn, but can remain true to ourselves and give back to the world just what is required from what we have gleaned from experience. Here we can teach or help others towards their own self-realisation, freed from our own unconscious impulses, demands, projections and expectations.

We can feel safe and self-confident in who we are and what we have achieved and can turn our attention inwards to examine our essential nature. We can be self assured and content or we may try consciously to distance ourselves from the world so that it cannot encroach upon or threaten us.

Planets near the MC will tend to stand out in the world, holding positions of real or assumed authority. Those nearer the AC will tend more towards retreat into the self and isolation.

The attribution of this quadrant to water suggests the need to let go and flow with the inner forces of life, distilling our real self out of our involvement in life. We should seek to let go of everything which is false or egotistical and surrender to our essential nature, the God within.

Essential Reading

The Astrological Houses, by Bruno & Louise Huber
  'Detailed Demonstration of the Houses as Space Structure', pages 45-52

  'The Quadrants', pages 53-59

  'The Linear Structure and Dynamic of the House System', pages 38-41

An Example – Learning to Swim

Here is an example of how behaviour associated with the four quadrants might be expressed in a specific situation:

1st Quadrant:
You are thrown or pushed into a swimming pool as a child. You panic, go under. In this situation you need to survive. Through frantic splashing and shouting, you find yourself staying up in the water and able to reach the life ring someone has thrown to you. You get out of the pool, angry at everyone, especially the one who pushed you in. You discover later that you learnt to swim.

2nd Quadrant:
You try the pool to see what it's like, as all your friends are there doing the same. You splash about, using floats to get around and have a lot of fun with other children there, generally enjoying the new experience. In the shallow end you copy someone else, managing three strokes without help.

3rd Quadrant:
You decide to learn to swim. You buy a book or video, read about it first, and then investigate available swimming lessons. You share your doubts and fears with others in the class and discuss your progress with the teacher. After 10 lessons you have gained increased confidence in yourself by learning to swim, and have made some new friends in the process.

4th Quadrant:
You lie in the sea, floating on your back, relaxed, at one with the water. Looking up at the sky, you feel transported to another world. Putting your head up, you start paddling with your arms to see a different view and to move around. You wonder how anyone could be afraid of the water when it's so easy to float.

Exercise 4.1

1. Take time to reflect on what you have learned about the motivation associated with the four quadrants, bearing in mind that nobody is born conscious, and that each quadrant offers opportunities for our consciousness to develop and evolve.

2. Note the distribution of planets in your chart. With the hemispheres and quadrants in mind, consider how you experience these inner motivating drives and whether or not you are conscious of the way in which they are fulfilled in your life. Take into account everything you have learned about your aspect structure so far.

3. Now look at charts of people you know, and consider what the distribution of planets in the hemispheres and quadrants might tell you about their motivation. Reflect on how this relates to what you know about them or have observed.

4.2 The Astrological Houses

The outer area of the chart symbolises a more precise definition of the world where we live out our lives, fighting for survival and attempting to find security, success, happiness, love etc. This section:

- Introduces the Koch House System and the House Intensity Curve
- Gives underlying meanings of each of the houses, indicating how the placement of planets within them gives a more detailed picture of potential self-expression..

In this section, as in the last, we look at **space** rather than energy. The birth chart gives us a picture of the inherent energies available to the individual and here we will consider how these find expression in space. The nature of energy is dynamic and it moves in a variety of ways. Expressions of energy can be further distinguished as rhythms of **expansion and contraction**.

The chart is a two-dimensional representation of a multi-dimensional process. According to the Laws of Thermodynamics, energy can neither be lost nor gained. There is no beginning and no ending, only change. In the chart the centre represents our inner being, or essence, the source of life energy. We can imagine basic energy radiating outwards through the aspects where it is filtered into specific wavelengths, and focused on specific points, the planets. These inner motivating energies interact with the planetary archetypes, are modified, by them, whilst at the same time receiving inherited qualities or colouring from the signs.

The houses make up the periphery of the chart. They represent the world, the environment, different areas of life experience, the stage on which we perform. On its outward journey from the centre of the chart our energy takes on a pattern of motivation that can be identified from our individual aspect pattern, which results in the way we act and behave in the outside world, i.e. in the houses.

Houses that are occupied by planets show the areas of life that have special significance in our personal development. Empty houses indicate areas of minor or passive interest.

Traditionally the second house is associated with possessions and it is true that planets in this house will be directing energy towards acquisition of security in one form or another. However, the fact that a person doesn't have any planets in the second house does not necessarily mean that they are going to lack security or money, or something else. It means that they will not feel a special need to direct energy in that direction. They may acquire more than someone with many planets in that house, but this will be through the direction of energies into work in the area of life that interests them, where they can be successful.

Koch Houses

In astrological psychology we use the Koch House System. This gives houses of different sizes. In general, small houses are areas of intense life experience, especially if two house cusps fall within one sign, and if the house is occupied by one or more planets.

The larger the house, the more scattered will be the energy coming from the centre, making life experience in that area more diffuse and indirect. See Figures 4.2.1a and 4.2.1b below.

Sign with Two House Cusps

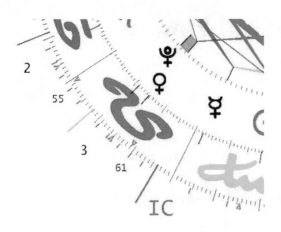

Figure 4.2.1a Leo with two house cusps

Venus and Pluto are in the sign of Leo, which contains both 3rd and 4th house cusps.

Intercepted Signs

Some houses can be large enough to involve three signs, sandwiching one sign in the middle. Such a sign is called an intercepted sign. It has no house cusp and hence no door or outlet to the outside world. The energies within such a sign cannot go out directly. A planet in an intercepted sign is likely to be frustrated to some extent in its expression, and the individual may feel a lack of recognition or response from the environment. See Figure 4.2.1b:

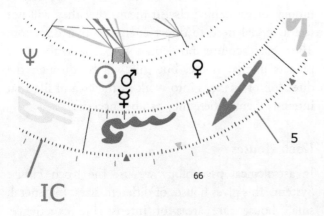

Figure 4.2.1b Intercepted Scorpio

The Sun, Mercury and Mars are in the sign of Scorpio which is intercepted in the 4th house, i.e. Scorpio is contained within the 4th house and has no house cusp that may act as a channel to the outside world for the energies of these planets.

House Intensity Curve

From the foregoing we can see that there is a different energy output depending on the size of the house. Generally the house cusps are areas of intense activity, whilst further into the house the energy flow subsides. Thus in the houses, we can identify movements of energy that follow cycles of rise and fall, or expansion and contraction.

This is called the **House Intensity Curve**. This pattern of energy flow within each house is a reflection of a much deeper, but similar, pattern which exists within the centre of the chart as a whole. Figure 4.2.2 on the next page shows these zones of expansion and contraction.

In Figure 4.2.2 you will see that the houses around the main angles, i.e. AC/DC, IC/MC axes, are areas of particularly high energy output. Those houses falling just after these angles (1, 7, 4, 10) are the strongest. These houses lie on the cardinal axes, forming the cardinal (angular) cross, that results from the basic horizontal and vertical divisions of the circle.

The Latin word 'cardinalis' means 'hinge', hence this is the basic cross upon which the house system hinges. The next division of space gives us the second, or fixed cross, with fixed houses, and the third division gives us the mutable cross with mutable houses.

Cardinal, Fixed and Mutable Houses

- The cardinal houses (1, 4, 7, 10) correspond to the expansion phase. Here the energy impulses are directed towards action. For example, at the AC a burst of energy propels us out into the world as we are born into space and time.

- The fixed houses (2, 5, 8, 11) correspond to the contraction phase. Here, the energy impulse is focused on preservation and our primary concern is dealing with issues of substance, security and maintenance of the status quo.

- In the mutable houses (3, 6, 9, 12) energy is beginning to expand again involving processes of thought and transformation in preparation for another action phase in the subsequent cardinal house.

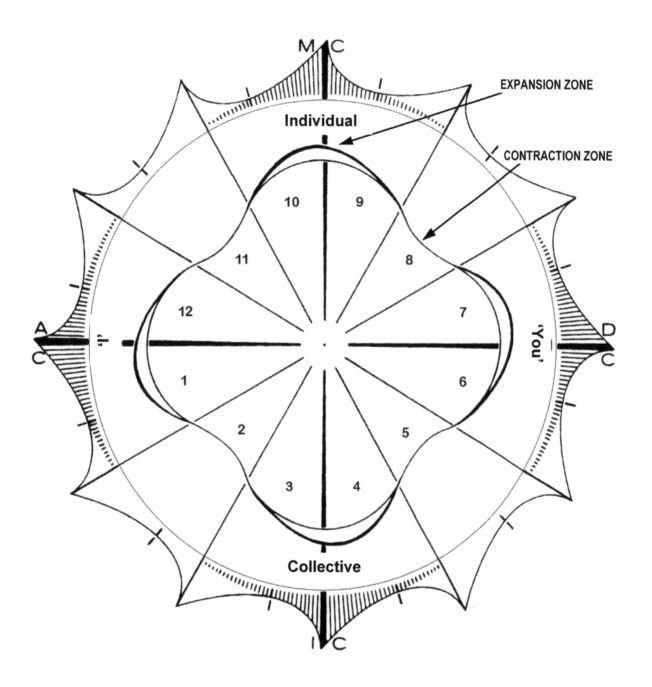

Figure 4.2.2 House Intensity Curve

The Houses

As we look at each house in turn, it is important to keep in mind that the houses represent a sequence of development, and that their individual themes are interlinked, one leading into the next.

The natural house wheel follows the natural horoscope. Therefore the 1st house corresponds to Aries and is a **cardinal fire** house, the 2nd corresponds to Taurus and is a **fixed earth** house and so on.

The **First House** begins at the AC and the action revolves around the 'I'. We are born into the world and we occupy a space in it from which we relate to everything around us. This house tells us how we do this. It describes our personality and how we come across to the environment, through the rising sign and any planets in the house.

A person with the Sun in the First House has a strong sense of self, a forceful presence, because the self-awareness quality of the Sun is fuelled by the high energy output of the cardinal house.

By contrast Saturn in the First House will often inhibit the individual from venturing out into new and untried situations.

Moon in the First House can indicate a certain aloofness: the person wants to make contact through the Moon but because it's on the 'I' side of the chart this may be difficult to do and can create an impression of being stand-offish. Much will depend on the general distribution of planets between the 'I' and 'You' sides.

The **Second House** has the economic principle in common with the other fixed houses. The energies here are used for securing, preserving, conserving or maintaining stability. The orientation is practical (Earth/Taurus). We are concerned with what we have, what use we can make of something concrete around us, or abstract within us. This can include anything from material possessions to our values, talents and sense of self-worth.

People with the Sun in the Second House tend to see themselves in terms of what they have acquired and achieved. Here there are conditions attached to their self-awareness, in contrast to the strong, straightforward self-awareness of a First House Sun. Because their sense of self-worth is linked to what they have, it is important that they hold on to what they possess. The loss of material things, as well as the loss of their capacity to be useful or loving, threatens their self-esteem. Fear of loss can result in a defensive, conservative attitude, which can be particularly pronounced if Saturn is in the Second House.

The 3rd and 4th houses make up the collective sphere of the chart.

The **Third House** is a mutable air house corresponding to Gemini. This house holds the collective, cultural, well-established knowledge that we are taught in school. Collectively, we share more or less the same basic knowledge, or at least we are brought up with the same ideas. The difference lies in how well and how much we absorb individually, and how bound we are to what we are taught.

The Sun in the Third House is indicative of people who are eager to learn through traditional channels: school, textbooks, generally accepted knowledge. They want to be accepted by the environment, the collective, and use their knowledge for this purpose, for example as a teacher, or at the other extreme, the local gossip.

The **Fourth House** is another cardinal house where energy expands out into the world, but it is the world in the form of the collective, the community, the family. It corresponds with the water sign of Cancer. People with the Sun in this house have a strong feeling of belonging to the collective. This could be their country, community, family, or some other group they identify with. Roots, the nest, an emotional sense of security that goes with belonging are all important in this house. When the Moon is in this house, particularly if conjunct the IC, it will often be difficult to get a child to leave the nest.

From the 5th house onward, involvement with the 'You' becomes important, and the 'You' looms larger in relationship to ourselves as we get closer to the DC.

The **Fifth House** is a fixed, fire house, corresponding to Leo. Having left the 'I' side of the chart this is where we begin to experience and express ourselves in relation to the 'You'. It involves taking risks in making contact with the 'You', and being prepared to experiment with life. This is where intimacy and love affairs are found, as well as creativity, eroticism, art and children. But underneath it all is also a fixed house need for security. We may play but we want to win, to impress, to possess someone or something for self-confirmation.

However, losing can also be an important aspect of the Fifth House experience. Disappointments in love may be the result of a possessive attitude towards another, or when we regard someone, perhaps unconsciously, as an extension of ourselves. The notions that 'you belong to me' or that children are little replicas of their parents, are bound to prove wrong. A person with the Sun in the Fifth House may exhibit a certain amount of 'impress behaviour', because of the need to be accepted by the other person.

The Fifth House is the area where we can learn about ourselves through contact and experimentation with other people. A strong Fifth House may make it difficult for a person to concentrate on the more important issues of life because too much time is spent enjoying physical contact with others.

The 6th and 7th houses represent the contact area of the chart.

The **Sixth House** is a mutable earth house corresponding to Virgo. Here the energies have a practical yet adaptable quality. Our everyday working situation, where we have to co-operate with others, illustrates the Sixth House process well. In order to have a good working relationship with others we have to observe their reactions to ourselves. The challenge in this house is to heed what others want from us (in the Fifth House it was more a question of what we want) while at the same time remaining true to ourselves. We have to find a way of doing our job, of earning our daily bread without prostituting ourselves.

Individuals with the Sun in the Sixth House will be looking for ways of serving, helping, working and doing for the 'You', which are also right for them.

The **Seventh House** is a cardinal air house, corresponding to Libra. It is on the horizontal AC/DC, I/YOU axis and in the same way as the first house was the 'I' house, this is the 'You' house, where we are eyeball to eyeball with the other person. Seventh House relationships are meant to be of equal, mutual benefit. Agreements, deals, contracts, commitments are made to define what both parties want out of their partnerships and to maintain fairness. This is where we learn the processes necessary to actively create relationships.

With the Sun in the Seventh House, we experience ourselves most directly through interactions with others. We are looking for our counterpart in the other and put a great deal of energy into our relationships. With Saturn here, on the other hand, we may be very defensive about letting others into our life whereas with the Moon any contacts, good or bad, may be difficult to avoid.

Where there are no planets or aspects on the 'You' side of the chart, leaving the centre exposed to the 'You', there is often as sense of vulnerability or insecurity as one feels the lack of any protection from others.

The **Eighth House** is a fixed water house corresponding to Scorpio. In this area our relationship to the 'You' becomes more impersonal, as we deal here with society, its structures, institutions, roles and laws. This is the adult world of rules and regulations. If we want

a position in society then we have to conform to its dictates and mores. Here it is not unusual to find the professional person, the civil servant.

The Sun in the Eighth House often indicates an inheritance of some sort. This could be anything from money to an ideology, but along with it we inherit responsibility. We have to pay tax, invest the money or live up to the ideology, i.e. fulfill duties, be respectable, be an example. The Eighth House relates to the Law of Give and Take. We have to pay a price in the form of some restriction for whatever we receive here. This applies to both inner and outer worlds. There can be clashes with this law of give and take, on all levels, including deep psychological or spiritual crises, when we refuse to let go of structures which are no longer of benefit to the whole.

The 9th and 10th houses occupy the individuality area of the chart. An individual is someone who stands out from the rest through his own uniqueness which is usually valuable to others in some way. This sets him apart from, for example, an eccentric who may just be different in the sense of being interesting.

In the **Ninth House**, a mutable fire house corresponding to Sagittarius, we distinguish ourselves by our own independent way of thinking. The Ninth House is at the top of the chart, symbolic of a high place, from where we overlook all the other areas and can observe all that is going on. Here we see things in their larger context, see the connections, implication, ramifications, and draw our own conclusions from it all in order to arrive at the meaning behind it.

A person with the Sun in the Ninth House needs to be free to expand his horizons, so that he can find his own truths, which he can then impart to others in the form of advice, opinions, lectures or discussions. With a strong Ninth House there is the risk that an individual can shut himself off from the realities of the world and live in an academic ivory tower, unwilling to communicate his thoughts to lesser mortals.

The **Tenth House**, the cardinal earth house corresponding to Capricorn, is where we put our philosophy, our own ideals into action. Of course this is not easy and individuals with the Sun in the Tenth House set very high standards for themselves. They are conscious of their individuality and have to live up to it, usually in a professional capacity. They can reach a senior role through competency and excellence in their field.

As this is an exposed position, often involving influence and power, personal integrity is an important quality. Provided the overall structure (company, community, country) is sound (e.g. democratic) one cannot get away with deceptions or ruthless schemes which would violate the interests of those one serves. Those who make it to the top under false pretences will find themselves clinging to their position of authority in a very precarious manner.

Saturn is most comfortable at the bottom of the chart where it can feel secure in the collective. When Saturn is at the top of the chart there is invariably a sense of insecurity.

With the Moon at the top of the chart there is a great need for recognition, emotional or practical, from others.

In the **Eleventh House**, the fixed air house corresponding to Aquarius, we return to the 'I' side of the chart and enter a more private sphere of life. Ideals play an important part in this house too, but this being a fixed house, the energies are contracting and the ideals here have a selective, restricting function. This is the house of friends, like-minded people or groups who share the same ideals. The motivation is towards security: we feel safe amongst people who are of the same mindset, with whom we have an affinity.

Friends, the circles in which we move, are very important if we have the Sun in the Eleventh House. These can include larger groups which are actively involved in working towards some humanitarian goal or ideal.

Finally we come to the **Twelfth House**, the mutable water house that corresponds to Pisces. This is our most private sphere ('I' sphere). It is behind the scenes where we withdraw to be alone, to reflect, to meditate, to deal with ontological and teleological questions, to think about life in the deepest sense. People with the Sun in the Twelfth House may need to learn to withdraw from the hurly burly of life and find a deeper meaning to existence. They may appear closed or introverted, for the contemplative aspect of their character is something that others cannot easily share or understand.

Essential Reading

The Astrological Houses, by Bruno & Louise Huber
A Fundamental Look at the Houses, pages 35-38.
Rules for the Analysis of House, page 42.
The Laws of Houses, Zones & Axes, pages 61-79.

Exercise 4.2

1. Bearing in mind what you have learned about Intercepted Signs and the House Intensity Curve in section 4.2, now reflect on any aspects of your personality that might be inhibited in their expression and therefore have particular potential to be developed more fully. Take account of which planets are involved, but focus mainly on your ego and tool planets. In other words don't place too much emphasis on whatever your present understanding of the 3 outer planets might be.

2. Look for these features in any other charts you may be working with. What might this mean for that person?

4.3 The House Intensity Curve

Houses have an energy dynamic of their own which governs the energy output of the planets within them.

In this section we look at:

- The varying strengths of the planets with specific reference to their house positions.
- Two particular areas in each house, the Low Point and the stress zone
- The potential psychological problems caused by planets situated in these areas and how they may be worked on and overcome.

Introduction

In section 4.1 we looked at the space between the centre and the outside of the chart and noted how the placement of planets in particular quadrants affects motivation. We also learnt that the flow of energy is not consistent and that output is governed by the zones of expansion and contraction which correspond with the cardinal, fixed and mutable areas of each quadrant.

Here we will take account of another factor that governs the outward expression of energy. In the same way as each **quadrant** has areas of varying intensity of expression, so each **house** has its own similar areas of expansion and contraction. The particular zone of a house in which a planet is placed will directly influence its expression.

Expansion and Contraction Zones in the Houses

As we progress through childhood we slowly begin to become conscious of ourselves as individual beings, and become aware of our behaviour through our interactions with the world. In astrological terms, we become conscious of the energies in the houses (where our energy flow comes into contact with the environment) before we start to examine the motivations which condition their expression and intensity. Our actions bring forth a reaction.

The houses represent our real world where we battle for survival and achievement. They form a unique, subjective reference system which shows how we react in the outer world, how we struggle to prove ourselves and whether we are successful or not. So an understanding of the houses is fundamental to chart analysis.

You are already familiar with the Figure 4.2.2 on page 135. Energy radiates from the centre of the chart and its ebb and flow corresponds with the cardinal, fixed and mutable sectors of each quadrant.

Cardinal energy is extrovert and expresses itself through activity.

Fixed energy stabilises, preserves, consolidates and maintains order.

Mutable energy experiences, reflects and recognises the need for change.

For instance, I use cardinal energy to build a dwelling, I use fixed energy to live in it and feel secure, and I use mutable energy if I decide that the dwelling is not big enough, or good enough, and that I need to move to another one.

From this you can see that behaviour patterns formed on a fixed axis (2/8, 5/11) are going to be more difficult to change than those on a mutable, or even a cardinal axis, and that the nearer to the main angles planets are situated, the more motivation there is going to be for new beginnings and for achievement.

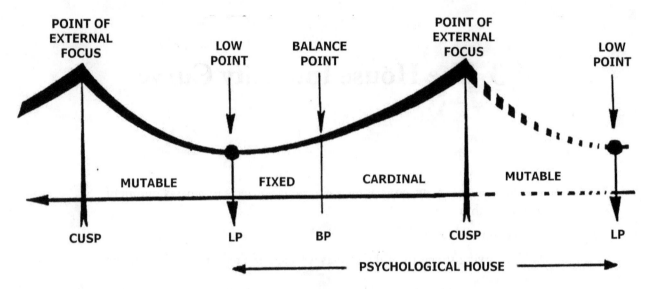

Figure 4.3.1 House Intensity Curve – Detail

Figure 4.3.1 illustrates a part of the House Intensity Curve corresponding to a single house, as seen from the centre of the chart looking outwards.

Within each house are three zones cardinal, fixed and mutable, and three special points cusp, Low Point (LP) and Balance Point (BP).

This pattern of energy corresponds with the Law of the Golden Mean, meaning that the dividing points are in the ratio of the golden section. (See *The Astrological Houses*, chapter 'The Intensity Curve' for a more detailed explanation).

Cardinal Zone

In Figure 4.3.1 you can distinguish a wave-like curve which corresponds with energy output levels. The cardinal zone starts at the cusp of the house, the point of external focus. Output into the world is at its greatest here and a planet positioned on a cusp will express itself with maximum intensity, which might be extreme arrogance, annoyance, emotion, sexuality... In other words output of energy is noisy, spontaneous and not easily controlled, so recognition of this fact may be helpful to a person with one or more planets placed on, or just after a cusp, particularly in a cardinal house (1, 7, 4, 10).

Balance Point

As we progress from the cusp into the house, energy output begins to diminish and become more controlled, until at the point of balance (Balance Point – BP) we have the optimum output of energy. Planets positioned at the Balance Point have the greatest opportunity to show what they can do, without making a fuss. Their energy resources are in balance with the apparent demands of the environment.

Fixed Zone

At the BP we reach the fixed zone of the house and the ability to externalise energy continues to diminish until the Low Point is reached. This area is not motivated towards achievement, but towards stability, maintenance and consolidation. Decisions to make changes, or resolve a difficult behaviour pattern, for example resulting from two planets in fixed house zones in opposition will be hard to make and activate, doubly so if the houses involved are also in the contraction zones of the chart.

Low Point

At the Low Point (LP) it is not only difficult for planets to express energy outwardly in life, but other people find it hard to recognise that these points of energy exist. For this reason, if you force the attentions of an LP planet on to the world such action will meet with disapproval and rejection from others. They just do not want to know about it and the harder you try the more they'll turn away.

It is important therefore for an individual with an LP planet to become aware of the way in which its energy is attempting to be expressed, and to learn to control its output until its potential is fully understood and its energy can be projected outwards, quietly and successfully.

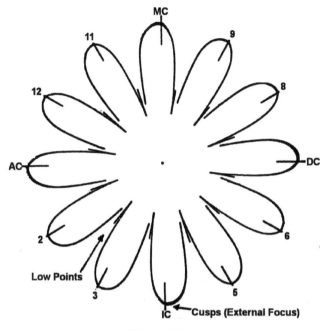

Figure 4.3.2

The 'Flower' in Figure 4.3.2 is a symbolic illustration that gives the feel of the Low Point. It may help you to understand why there can be problems associated with the expression of energy from planets situated at this point in the chart. However, it should also be recognised that, whilst the behaviour that such a planet manifests may initially be rejected by the world, the inner self has a unique channel of communication open to that planet and this can be seen as the pathway for the process of inner understanding that has to take place.

A barrier to assimilation may be encountered should a Low Point planet also be blocked-off by a square aspect. Figure 4.3.2 graphically illustrates that such a placement might make the successful use of that planetary energy difficult.

Analogy

Imagine an island in which the planets are symbolised by 10 lighthouses of varying colours and shapes. Using this image you might imagine an LP planet as being represented by a lighthouse sited at sea level in a small cove always shrouded in a small patch of sea mist. The light cannot fulfill its true function. However, the lighthouse has a loud fog horn that is constantly making a noise because the keeper, unable to see more than a short distance ahead, believes that he must make his position known. Ships sailing by in bright sunshine are irritated by the penetrating siren coming from an unseen source for an unrecognised reason.

The people of the island have to understand what the problem is and find a solution to it – perhaps by raising the height of the light so that it is above the level of the mist. This image has all the limitations of

any analogy but it may help you to gain a sense of the needs and limitations of a Low Point planet.

An Example of a Planet at the Low Point

Let us take Mars as an example. A person with an LP Mars will find it difficult to 'get up and go'. The driving force to be active, to achieve, be enthusiastic, be competitive... will be present but not understood. Attempts will always be made but may be resented by others and seen as pushy, aggressive, misplaced or dominating. That person cannot express Mars energy successfully without first understanding that a problem exists.

When the problem is recognised and Mars energy is experimented with gently, with small tasks being undertaken quietly and behind the scenes, then in due course a real understanding can be built up of what Mars is all about. Success and satisfaction need to be worked on at a personal and humble level so that gradually the individual can progress towards the accomplishment of bigger tasks, ultimately gaining the rewards and respect that are due.

With Mars in a cardinal or mutable house there will be a bigger initial problem to overcome than in a fixed house. If the natural motivation of the house is towards action or change it will exacerbate the frustration felt by an LP planet already striving towards achievement.

Orb for Low Point Planet

The allowable orb for a planet to be considered to be on a Low Point is small and will vary depending on the size of the house. The following is a guide:

- in a small house of around 15° the orb will be as little as ½ degree;

- in a house of average size around 30° the orb will be 1°

- in a large house approaching 60°, the orb may be as much as 2°.

Because the orbs are small it is advisable to be certain of the correct birth time before placing too much emphasis on a Low Point planet.

Recognising and Developing Low Point Planets

It is important to recognise that LP planets, however strong by sign, cannot be used successfully in the outer world until a full understanding of the nature of the energy of that planet has been developed. Because this is a process of discovery it needs to be self-enlightening as well, potentially self-indulgent in the early stages, To make full use of that energy may require many years of study and hard work.

The process can be likened to a flower seed inwardly seeing itself as the fully developed bloom. Nobody else can see this until the growth and development processes have been gone through and there really is a beautiful flower that everyone can accept and admire.

An LP planet is almost always a part of the personality whose development never took place naturally during the early years of childhood. As a consequence it has to be learned about in the way in which a developing child learns about him or herself, through schooling, experiment, experience, action/reaction... It may be difficult for an adult to accept the need to revisit these early developmental stages. However, **awareness**, then **acceptance**, are stages we have to go through before we can bring about change in our life.

Planets on or close to the LP do not make a great noise in the world. They are often not noticed by parents or school teachers at a very critical time in a child's life – a time when they need to be recognised and developed. They may remain dormant – and their potential can be lost. However, when their existence is identified through the birth chart, it is then possible to encourage their self-expression.

For example with an LP Mars, the encouragement should be in the realm of physical activity – not just animal strength but the development of skill – an important part of Mars energy. An LP Mercury would require a more passive activity such as writing a diary or becoming conversational. Venus on the LP would necessitate learning to make friends and become creative. The advice to someone with an LP Sun would be to become aware of themselves and their ability to use their will and take charge of their own life.

Recognising an LP planet does not mean that it will suddenly start performing as though it had been coached and encouraged for years. The process is slow and gentle and can be self-indulgent because the individual has to learn to like what that planet can do for him or her. There would be nothing to be gained from recognising an LP Mercury and suggesting that that person immediately start writing a full length novel whereas starting to keep a diary gives the opportunity for the person to discover that they have a hidden talent, a skill that they can enjoy and develop. In the same way, someone with LP Jupiter in the 9th house cannot become the fount of ideas that can benefit others until that person has developed his own philosophies and understanding of the world – and this takes time. Such people may feel that they have the ability to put their own views to the world but the world **will not listen**, recognise or accept those views until they have been worked on and are ready to be broadcast.

A person with all three ego planets situated at Low Points could suffer from a 'chip on the shoulder' complex and could blame the world for their problems. It is a difficult situation and can only be overcome through self-examination and by learning how to build self-confidence.

If five or more planets are at Low Points, not only could similar problems to those described above be evident, but the person could feel unsafe and misunderstood because the environment finds it virtually impossible to recognise their existence, since it is difficult for others to see a LP planet. Often there is a spiritual quality about such a person and adjustment to life can be made easier if they are made aware of the reason for their insecurity and discomfort.

As with most chart placements there are likely to be other pointers which help to clarify the best way to develop LP planets.

A real life example

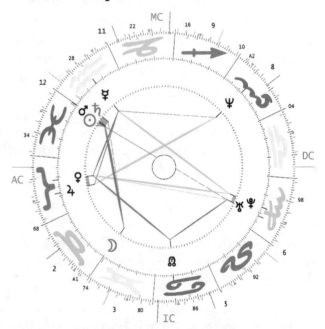

Figure 4.3.3 Sally

Sally, the woman whose chart is shown in Figure 4.3.3 has Mercury on the Low Point. She speaks very softly and quietly so it is often necessary, in a small group of people, to strain to hear what she is saying as her voice is so quiet. However, she also has a very special talent and skill – she is able to communicate with horses and train them using voice and sounds. She uses her LP Mercury in a very specialised way and it is only when she speaks about her work with horses (that means so much to her) that her voice becomes infused with energy and she is really heard.

Mutable Zone

Moving on from the LP we can picture the mutable zone as the side of a hill rising ever more steeply as it nears the summit, the cusp of the next house. The feeling in this area of the house has the character of an uphill journey. The LP is the psychological changing point from one house to the next, so the flavour of the mutable zone is anticipation for what is to come next.

Because it is a mutable area, new ideas abound, there is a sense of excitement about what exists over the other side of the hill. One is gradually becoming involved in the affairs of the next house. A planet placed in the mutable zone of a house will put out energy towards the succeeding house, whilst still being involved in the affairs of the house where it is placed.

This sense of expectation can, however, be stressful because there may be a need to satisfy the urge for change and new beginnings. The problems associated with this mutable area of the house are discussed below.

Stress Zone

In the mutable zone between LP and cusp of the next house there is a growing awareness of the theme of the next house and an increasing sense of urgency to reach it.

We can divide the mutable area of the house into 3 sections: zones A,B and C (Figure 4.3.4 below).

In the first 1/3rd after the LP (A) the ability of a planet to express energy is still weak and any problems are more likely to be associated with the LP itself rather than with the mutable zone.

It is normally sufficient to assess visually whether a planet is in the stress zone.

As Koch houses may be of unequal size, detailed calculations are needed to establish the exact size of the zones in any house:

1. Find the number of degrees from the LP to the next house cusp.

2. Divide this by 3. This is the size of zone B.

3. Find the number of degrees in the house.

4. Divide this by 30. The result is the "house degree", which may be proportionally larger or smaller than the zodiac degree.

5. Size of zone B minus this house degree (1/30th) is the size of zone C. This allows for the gap before the cusp.

6. Size of zone B minus 2 house degrees (2/30th) is the size of zone A. This allows for the gap after the LP.

In the second 1/3rd (B) the stress factor will not yet be so apparent and there is more likely to be a sense of optimism and expectancy.

However, in the last 1/3rd (C) the energy level has built up considerably. This sector is known as the **stress zone**. Any planet in this zone of the house is known as a **stress planet**, with the stress level increasing the closer the planet is to the cusp.

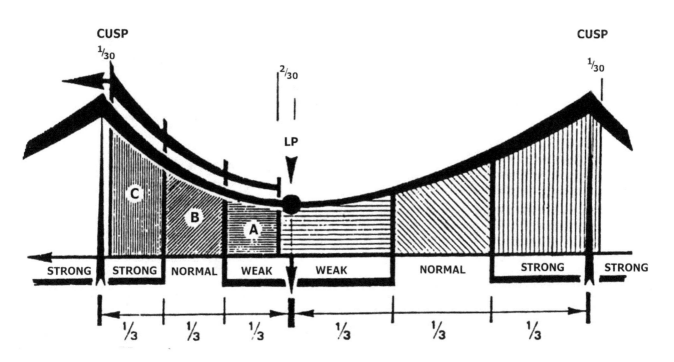

Figure 4.3.4

Stress Planets

A planet situated in the stress zone of the house is referred to as a **stress planet**. It lies in the shadow of the cusp and, as with a mountaineer sensing victory over a peak, it will strive to succeed in its attempts to prove its existence and its success.

The nearer to the peak the greater will be the effort expended in climbing upwards to reach the cusp. Planets in this zone have to serve the demands of the house they are in, but their energy is pulled forward towards the next house. As a result, they expend more energy than they have available. That causes stress and can lead to exploitation and compensation mechanisms in the individual since these planets draw out energy from the other planets which they are aspecting. This is often to the detriment of other areas of the personality which may remain underdeveloped and become a cause for concern when it is no longer possible for the shadow planet to perform because of age or physical condition. This might apply, for instance, to the sportsman who is motivated by a stress planet and neglects everything in life except for sport and the need to prove himself. Many sportsmen do have an early retiring age and if all other areas have been neglected or drained for the sake of success then that person might well find himself on the scrap heap well before his time.

If a planet is just before the cusp by a degree or so (depending on the house size) allowance should be made for the possibility that a discrepancy of only a few minutes in the birth time might actually put it within one house degree of the cusp and therefore out of the stress zone.

The potential effect of the planet's stressed position depends on the house involved.

Stress Planets before the Cardinal Cusps

The cardinal cusps are the main angles in the chart, the gateways to the 1st, 4th, 7th and 10th houses. Planets in the stress zones before these cusps are not only striving towards the cardinal zone of cardinal houses, but are also entering new quadrants. They have a sense of urgency and are strongly motivated.

In the stress zone before the AC, a planet will have a sense of a new beginning, of leaving the hidden realms of the 12th house and coming out into the light. The individual may sense a sub-personality just out of sight, knowing it's there but not quite seeing it. The sub-personality will therefore feel a need to show itself to the world, selfishly, noisily and impulsively.

In the stress zone before the IC a planet will be approaching the 2nd quadrant. In the 2nd quadrant we attempt to break away from all the conditioning of the environment and concentration on self, and begin a new journey where we will learn about

ourselves through interaction with the 'You'. There will be a feeling of excitement at the possibility of new beginnings, making the break from the parental home and perhaps even establishing our own family. We will want to create our own life and build a foundation for ourselves from which we can grow into the future.

In the stress zone before the DC we become aware of the shift between the instinctive relating of the 2nd quadrant to the more conscious relating of the 3rd quadrant. There will again be a feeling of the excitement of new beginnings, but here the focus will be on finding our way in the world, developing new skills and knowledge to establish ourselves in society. To do this we may have to come to terms with the one-to-one relationships which we have already formed in the first half of our lives and assess the relevance of these in the context of the new tasks ahead.

In the stress zone before the MC we are moving from the 3rd to the 4th quadrant, **thinking** to **being**. The 4th quadrant of being is concerned with the building of individuality and status, not only through outer worldly success but also from within. Here there will be a sense of excitement at the prospect of going out into the world and seeking success and recognition for what is achieved. At a deeper level there will also be an awareness that this has to be done in an inclusive manner and not just to satisfy ego needs. Eventually this can bring awareness that a sense of being exists on more than one level of consciousness.

A stress planet in the shadow of a cardinal cusp is competitive and requires the most recognition. However much energy is expended there will always be a sense of under-achievement so a person is motivated to try even harder. The planet will be over-energised and the person with this placing is likely to feel caught up in an alternating manic and depressive type of cycle. A stressed Jupiter may strive for knowledge, attend courses and seminars. The effect of a stressed Mars in a cardinal shadow seems to be borne out by statistical research findings of the Michel Gauquelin (Book *The Influence of the Stars*).

Stress Planets before the Fixed Cusps

Planets in the stress zones before the fixed houses are about to enter the 2nd, 5th, 8th and 11th houses. As these houses are in the contraction zones of the quadrants there will not be the same outer sense of urgency as would be experienced before the cardinal cusps.

Fixed houses are mainly concerned with securing, acquiring, holding and stabilising.

The 2nd house is associated with self-worth and our own sense of security through achieving this. This may be achieved by acquiring any kind of possession, whether it's money in the bank, two cars in the drive, or awards on the mantelpiece. Security is a basic foundation stone for all human beings so planets in the stress zone before the 2nd house cusp will have a sense of urgency to create situations which will meet the needs of the 2nd house.

The 5th house is concerned with relationships and building a sense of belonging in the world by having friends and intimate relationships, and feeling a part of the human race. We discover ourselves and feel secure through situations which involve others. To hold on to friends we may need to impress people by the way we behave. In the stress zone before the 5th house we will seek to do this in any way that we believe will bring us to the notice of others.

In the 8th house we look for our sense of self-worth through being an important part of the society we live in. We can do this by taking on responsibilities within large organisations such as the law, the civil service, medicine, the armed forces or smaller community projects that will get us noticed.

In the 11th house we tend to prefer to distance ourselves from the more physical kind of relationships of the 5th house and are more likely to seek relationships with people who think like us and with whom we can feel safe and secure. In the stress zone before the 11th house we will be more motivated to seek out like-minded people whose company we can enjoy – people through whom we can get a sense of belonging in the world. In this way we feel accepted and secure.

A stress planet in the shadow of a fixed cusp will never quite get the security it needs and this may induce a state of paranoia from fear of losing existing security.

Stress Planets before the Mutable Cusps
The mutable cusps are the doors to the 3rd, 6th, 9th and 12th houses. As in the mutable zone of an individual house, there is a sense of new things to be faced in the next house.

Planets in the stress zones before the mutable cusps will be concerned with relationships. There will be an urge to move away from the safety restrictions of the fixed houses and to learn about ourselves and others through different types of interactions.

In the shadow of the 3rd house, there will be a move from the personal safety of the 2nd house to finding one's place in the collective.

In the shadow of the 6th, the change will involve a shift from personal friendships and relationships to professional interactions with co-workers.

Before the cusp of the 9th house, the inner focus will move from seeking security through social position and status to questioning personal and social values. There will be a strong desire to break free from the shackles of society and to expand horizons, perhaps through study and self-development.

In stress area before the 12th house cusp, there will be an urge to free oneself from attachments and involvements and to retreat from the world.

It is important to remember that stress planets have to manage the affairs of the house they're in as well as the strong pull forward. As a consequence they exert more energy than they have readily available and in the long run this probably gives rise to physical or psychological health problems.

Stress Planets as Keys to Spiritual Growth
As we have seen, stress planets create specific problems that have to be recognised and understood. This understanding is often sparked by a life crisis that causes the individual to completely transform the way he or she has lived their life so that the stressed energy is directed **away** from the self and **towards** others.

The person has to go **consciously** through all the stages of **sublimation** (diversion of energy) and **transformation** (conversion to a higher level) to ensure that the weakness of the stress planet can be turned into creative strength.

Transformation from the personal, small self to the higher self will manifest differently according to the house cross on which the stress planet is placed, and the experiences of the individual concerned.

- The theme of the cardinal cross is **Might and Defeat**. Transformation starts after we "meet our Waterloo".

- The theme of the fixed cross is **Possession and Loss**. Transformation begins after we lose something very dear to us.

- The theme of the mutable cross is **Love and Limitations**. Transformation starts after the desire for freedom has been relinquished.

If we return to sportsmen, consider the man who has been able to take the pressure off himself to be competitively successful in the eyes of the world, and has found a far deeper satisfaction in being able to, say, train youngsters in the skills which made him famous. Contrast this with another who is unable to change course and who, at the end of his public career, is interested only in keeping his name before the public and attempts to do so by running a bar, casino or some equally stressful, and possibly unsuccessful, venture.

Summary

At a house cusp planetary energy will be expressed strongly into the environment – perhaps with a lack of control.

At the Balance Point energy is in a state of equilibrium, is more controlled and can be used with minimum stress to maximum advantage.

At the Low Point energy cannot be expressed outwardly until a learning process has been completed.

From the Low Point the focus moves to the next house theme and there is an increasing urgency to use the energy in a manner that attracts attention.

Note: Earlier translations of the Huber's writings refer to the Balance Point as the Invert Point. This is possibly a misleading term, but there may be occasions when you will come across that translation.

Essential Reading

The Astrological Houses
The House Intensity Curve, pages 94-107.

Recommended Reading

Transformation: Astrology as a Spiritual Path –
Chapter 3 Stress Planets
Chapter 10 Low Point Experiences: Twelve Gates to the Spiritual Life

How to work out the positions of Low Point and Balance Point for any size of House

The table Figure 4.3.5 in the Appendix makes it simple to calculate the positions of the Balance Point and the Low Point within each house. All you have to do is read down the centre column (House Size) and locate the number of degrees which corresponds with the size of each house and then read off to the right. The first column is the Low Point and the second column is the Balance Point. The numbers shown are the degrees, minutes and seconds into the house, from the cusp of entry to the house.

This table can also be used for calculation of the Age Point position (Chapter 6).

As these calculations are performed for you by chart software, this is presented for information only.

Exercise 4.3

1. Consider how planets i) in the cardinal zone, ii) in the fixed zone, and iii) in the mutable zone of a house might express their energy – paying particular attention to the significance of planets at the Low Point and in the stress zone.

2. Look carefully at your chart and identify one planet in each of cardinal, fixed and mutable areas of a house. Try to find at least one of the three either close to a cusp (preferably in the stress zone) or on a Low Point.

3. Now take time to reflect on how you experience these planets in your life, taking into account their aspects and position in the chart.

   NB Where possible be honest with yourself in exploring the way in which you experience a Stress or Low Point planet, and think about whether or how you feel you have been able to develop this planet so far.

4. Look at any charts you may be working with, and identify any Low Point and Stress planets. What might this mean for these individuals, and does it correlate with their real experience?

Appendix AP-LP-BP Table

Per Month	Per Year	House Size	Low Point	Balance Point	Per Month	Per Year	House Size	Low Point	Balance Point
' "	o '	o	o ' "	o ' "	' "	' "	o	o ' "	o ' "
09 10	1 50	11	6 47 54	4 12 06	35 00	7 00	42	25 57 27	16 02 33
10 00	2 00	12	7 24 59	4 35 01	35 50	7 10	43	26 34 32	16 25 28
10 50	2 10	13	8 02 04	4 57 56	36 40	7 20	44	27 11 37	16 48 23
11 40	2 20	14	8 39 09	5 20 51	37 30	7 30	45	27 48 42	17 11 18
12 30	2 30	15	9 16 14	5 43 46	38 20	7 40	46	28 25 46	17 34 14
13 20	2 40	16	9 53 19	6 06 41	39 10	7 50	47	29 02 51	17 57 09
14 10	2 50	17	10 30 24	6 29 36	40 00	8 00	48	29 39 56	18 20 04
15 00	3 00	18	11 07 29	6 52 31	40 50	8 10	49	30 17 01	18 42 59
15 50	3 10	19	11 44 34	7 15 26	41 40	8 20	50	30 54 06	19 05 54
16 40	3 20	20	12 21 38	7 38 22	42 30	8 30	51	31 31 11	19 28 49
17 30	3 30	21	12 58 43	8 01 17	43 20	8 40	52	32 08 16	19 51 44
18 20	3 40	22	13 35 48	8 24 12	44 10	8 50	53	32 45 21	20 14 39
19 10	3 50	23	14 12 53	8 47 07	45 00	9 00	54	33 22 26	20 37 34
20 00	4 00	24	14 49 58	9 10 02	45 50	9 10	55	33 59 31	21 00 29
20 50	4 10	25	15 27 03	9 32 57	46 40	9 20	56	34 36 36	21 23 24
21 40	4 20	26	16 04 08	9 55 52	47 30	9 30	57	35 13 41	21 46 19
22 30	4 30	27	16 41 13	10 18 47	48 20	9 40	58	35 50 45	22 09 15
23 20	4 40	28	17 18 18	10 41 42	49 10	9 50	59	36 27 50	22 32 10
24 10	4 50	29	17 55 23	11 04 37	50 00	10 00	60	37 04 55	22 55 05
25 00	5 00	30	18 32 28	11 27 32	50 50	10 10	61	37 42 00	23 18 00
25 50	5 10	31	19 09 33	11 50 27	51 40	10 20	62	38 19 05	23 40 55
26 40	5 20	32	19 46 38	12 13 22	52 30	10 30	63	38 56 10	24 03 50
27 30	5 30	33	20 23 42	12 36 18	53 20	10 40	64	39 33 15	24 26 45
28 20	5 40	34	21 00 47	12 59 13	54 10	10 50	65	40 10 20	24 49 40
29 10	5 50	35	21 37 52	13 22 08	55 00	11 00	66	40 47 25	25 12 35
30 00	6 00	36	22 14 57	13 45 03	55 50	11 10	67	41 24 30	25 35 30
30 50	6 10	37	22 52 02	14 07 58	56 40	11 20	68	42 01 35	25 58 25
31 40	6 20	38	23 29 07	14 30 53	57 30	11 30	69	42 38 40	26 21 20
32 30	6 30	39	24 06 12	14 53 48	58 20	11 40	70	43 15 45	26 44 15
33 20	6 40	40	24 43 17	15 16 43	59 10	11 50	71	43 52 49	27 07 11
34 10	6 50	41	25 20 22	15 39 38	60 00	12 00	72	44 29 54	27 30 06

Minutes

"	' "	'	' "	' "
08	1 40	10	6 11	03 49
17	3 20	20	12 22	07 38
25	5 00	30	18 32	11 28
33	6 40	40	24 43	15 17
42	8 20	50	30 54	19 06

Age Progression (AP) = 6 years per house

Balance Point (BP) = 2 years 3 months 15 days = 836 days

Low Point (LP) = 3 years 8 months 15 days = 1354 days

      (After passing house cusp)

Number of Golden Mean: 0.381966 + 0.618034 = 1

Figure 4.3.5 AP-LP-BP Table

4.4 The Polarity of Axes

This section considers the meaning of polarities in the chart, identifying potential areas of conflict. Each pair of opposite houses represents an axis of polarity. Planets in opposition, or any imbalance in terms of planetary energies such as a stellium or a strong conjunction on either arm of the axis, create tension in those areas of life represented by the houses on that axis.

The Crosses

When we view the expansion and contraction zones in the birth chart we can see that the areas of maximum expansion mark the main angles (AC/DC, IC/MC) or the cardinal points in the chart, where we are able to achieve maximum thrust into the world. The **contraction** zones correspond with the **fixed** houses, whilst the **expansion** zones encompass the **mutable and cardinal** houses. See Figure 4.2.2 on page 135.

Each zone representing a house, has a similar zone on the opposite side of the chart so that we have 6 pairs of opposing houses: 2 pairs of cardinal houses (1/7 and 4/10), 2 pairs of fixed houses (2/8 and 5/11) and 2 pairs of mutable houses (3/9 and 6/12). Each pair is at right angles to the other and, as can be seen, they form the three crosses: the Cardinal Cross, the Fixed Cross and the Mutable Cross (Figure 4.4.1).

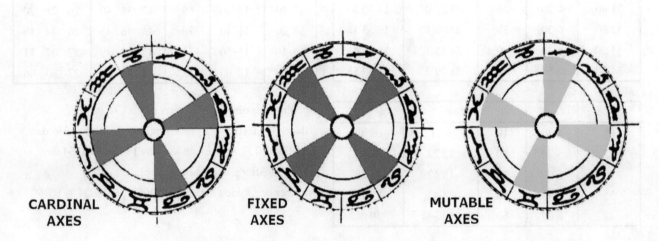

CARDINAL AXES **FIXED AXES** **MUTABLE AXES**

Figure 4.4.1 Axis crosses

Polarity Axes

Each pair of houses represents an **axis of polarity** – so potential conflict. Planets in opposition on one of these axes create tension in those areas of life represented by the houses on that axis. This tension can be reduced by activating the other arm of the cross.

An analogy that may help you to understand this simple process is that of an elastic band stretched tightly across the chart between two opposing planets or groups of planets (Figure 4.4.2). Both centres of energy are working against one another, creating internal stress. If one planet decides to give up the struggle entirely, then the elastic band flies up to the opposite end creating a mass of confused energy which can be overwhelming, difficult to handle and perhaps uncontrollable.

Suppose though, that to relieve the tension you were to take hold of the elastic band in the middle, with one strand in each hand, and you pulled at right angles to the opposition, energising those areas of life on the new axis. This will not only have pulled the two opposing ends towards the centre, thus relieving the tension, but will also have created a completely new pattern around which energy can be encouraged to flow.

Figures 4.4.2 illustrates this principle of conflict resolution.

Because you will have created a square, or fixed aspect pattern, it should be appreciated that there will be variations in the ease with which this new energy **will** flow depending on whether the oppositions are on cardinal, fixed or mutable axes. It will, for instance, be more difficult to change behaviour patterns formed on a fixed axis, particularly if fixed signs are involved as well.

Figure 4.4.3 shows the name assigned to each axis, corresponding to the nature of the houses involved on that axis.

The Axes

Cardinal	House 1/7	Encounter Axis
	House 4/10	Individuality Axis
Fixed	House 2/8	Possession Axis
	House 5/11	Relationship Axis
Mutable	House 3/9	Thought Axis
	House 6/12	Existence Axis

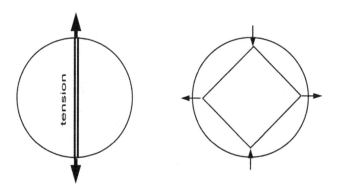

Figure 4.4.2

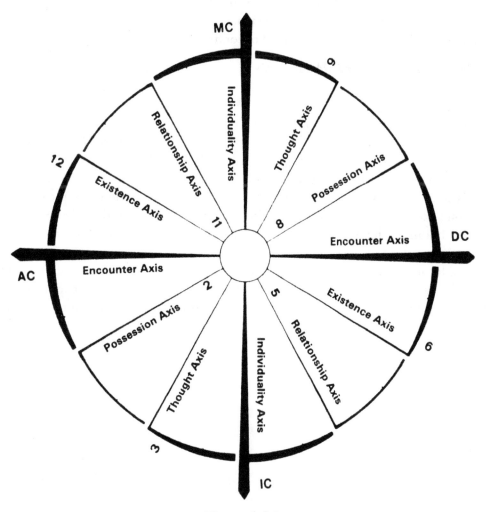

Figure 4.4.3

The Cardinal Cross

Tension on the 1/7 Encounter Axis

Houses 1 and 7 make up the **Encounter Axis**, the 'I' – 'You' axis. These are areas of active, dynamic encounter between the 'I' and the 'You'. With a strong First House emphasis, the encounter revolves around the 'I'. These individuals let others come to them. They attract them with their strong personalities and take from them. Seventh House people, on the other hand, go out to meet, and give to others. They might even lose themselves in the other.

Tensions caused, for example by oppositions, on the Encounter Axis can express themselves as competition, "I want to be better than you".

With tensions on any axis, it is always advisable to look to the other axis on the **same cross** for a possible way out of the conflict. We are already acting from a cardinal motivation, attitude or approach to life, and we can ease the preoccupation of a particular axis by incorporating the complementary axis on the same cross.

Thus, with the problems on the Encounter Axis (1/7), we look to the **Individuality Axis** (4/10) for the solution. By becoming aware of ourselves as individuals, by strengthening our individuality we can rise above the "either me or you" kind of conflicts.

Tension on the 4/10 Individuality Axis

The 4/10 axis contains all the potential of the person growing up from the collective, leaving behind his or her roots, family ties, all the comforts and conditions of this early environment in order to become an individual – someone who is free, autonomous, strong, courageous and unafraid of going it alone.

Tensions on this axis come from a conflict between the expectations of the collective and the individual's need for independence and freedom. The solution lies in the 1/7 axis and the one-to-one encounter which can help bridge the gap between the masses and the individual.

The Fixed Cross

Tension on the 2/8 Possessions Axis

Houses 2 and 8 belong to the **Possessions Axis**. The Second House ('I' Side) is about with our own possessions, material or otherwise, whereas the Eighth House ('You' side) has to do with other people's possessions.

As the energies are in the contracting zone on the Fixed Cross, we look for ways of drawing energy from the outside, from things and people. We want to own and possess something because this will satisfy our need for security. On this axis the more we have the more secure we feel.

Problems on this axis are usually related to loss (Second House) or renunciation (Eighth House), having and not having, which can lead to greed (Second) and envy (Eighth) as extremes. With tension on this axis we need to turn away from our preoccupation with possessions, and soften our object-orientated approach by making space in our lives for the human dimension of the **Relationship Axis**.

Tension on the 5/11 Relationship Axis

The fifth is a fire house. It involves us directly, intimately, possibly sexually with another person. We let our instincts lead us to the 'You'.

As an air house, the Eleventh House is more detached. The contacts we make here are of a more mental nature. We have a more critical approach to others. We choose friends who conform to our ideals and share our mind set.

Tensions on this axis can come out in fixed behaviour – in the Fifth House as "impress behaviour", or in the Eleventh House as rigid, over-selective idealism. Problems related to this can be alleviated by resorting to the 2/8 axis, by turning one's attention to the economic, practical side of things, adopting a more matter-of-fact approach, paying the bills and attending to other down to earth necessities.

Note

There does not have to be an actual opposition of planets for there to be tension on an axis.

If there is a concentration of planets at one end of the axis there will be an over-preoccupation with that particular area of life (house). This one-sidedness causes tension that will respond to the same solution.

The Mutable Cross

Tension on the 3/9 Thinking Axis

Houses 3 and 9 correspond to the **Thinking Axis**. In the Third House we learn from the collective (parents, schools, books, dictionaries, manuals, internet...). The thinking here follows along prescribed paths leading to a specific, definable goal (for example a person studies anatomy to acquire knowledge of the map of the body).

In the Ninth House, the thinking takes on a different form. The goal or end result is more or less unpredictable, and may go against the mainstream of established, collective thinking.

Tensions on the 3/9 axis invariably result in an excessively theoretical approach to life. The **Existence Axis** (6/12) provides the antidote by bringing us back to real life and requiring us to put our theories to practical use for the benefit of others.

Tension on the 6/12 Existence Axis

The Sixth House relates to existence on the mundane level, while the Twelfth House is about existence in the larger sense, the more hidden aspects of it. The Sixth House makes heavy demands on us. Here we have to get involved in the fight for existence, get our hands dirty, fulfil our duties as well as be and remain on good terms with our bosses and colleagues.

The pressure can become so great that we take refuge in the Twelfth House where we isolate ourselves. Illness can serve this purpose as a form of escape, but it can also force us, through isolation, to reflect on what is not right in our daily relationship with the world. This is where the 3/9 axis comes in. We can use our mind constructively to overcome the panic, and the fears of failure which may trouble us on the Existence Axis. Philosophical thinking can help to put things in the right perspective again.

Essential Reading

The Astrological Houses
Page 81 – Chapter: The Polarity of the Axes.

An Example

The man's chart in Figure 4.4.4 illustrates a strong opposition on the 4/10 Individuality Axis which is cardinal by sign as well as by house.

This chart shows a tremendous amount of tension on the Individuality axis. This tension is increased by the placements of the Moon and Saturn both in their own house and sign, by the number of planets in the 10th house, by the fixed nature of the aspect pattern (Cradle) and the lack of green, by the potential resentment engendered by the Moon conjunct Mars and by the fact that houses 4 and 10 are contained within one sign and are therefore areas of hyperactivity and concern.

Life for this man was harmonious until he reached his mid teens. At that point, he became aware of the powerful energy of the tenth house saying to him "You've got to be something special", and the conflicting energy of the fourth house saying "It's easier to stay down here where it is safe".

This man is constantly pulled in two different directions: the responsible adult world of the tenth house and the cosy nest of the fourth. The tenth house energy leads him to build big ideas about himself (Sun/Jupiter in 10th) and make big plans that he is not able to bring to fruition and so he lands back in the fourth house with an increasingly uncomfortable bump. He feels sorry for himself, goes into moods of depression (Capricorn/Cancer axis) and is generally aggressive (Mars conjunct Moon). The resentment of the losing battle increases with each failed attempt to make it in the tenth house so, rather than risk further failures, he finds it easier to say "It's not worth trying" which increases the frustration of the beckoning tenth house and the anger of being a captive of the fourth house. It is important not to underrate the extreme emotional tension, pain and unhappiness that such a situation can create.

How would developing the other arm of the cross, the Encounter Axis (1/7), help to alleviate some of the tension?

On the Individuality Axis, the need to take charge of his own life by using his will (Sun strongest), and making sound judgments and decisions, is indicated. However this is a fixed chart with a blue/ red aspect pattern so this man's attitude is very black and white, right and wrong. There is no green to allow

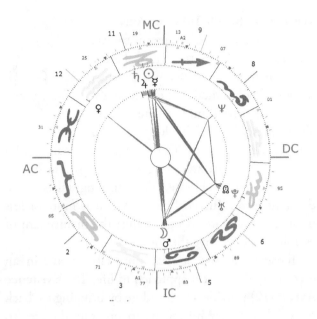

Figure 4.4.4

for compromise and for reflection and learning from experience. In addition there is a Cradle on the 'You' side. This dependency figure tends to aggravate the feeling that the Moon fosters, of wanting to stay put in the fourth house.

Caught up in his own inner conflict, he pays little or no attention to other people, or to the way he presents himself to them from the lofty heights of the Tenth House. It is easy for him to feel superior and believe that no-one else is up to his standard.

If he consciously makes the effort to build up harmonious relationships with people, other than those who filtered in through the blue of the Cradle on the ''You' side of the chart, his sense of self-worth can increase. It will not be easy for him to do this because the first house is virtually cut off behind the wall of the opposition axis and Aries is more concerned about self than others.

Exercise 4.4

1. Look at your chart and see whether a significant polarity exists on an opposition axis. (It is possible that you may have more than one.)

2. Bearing in mind what you have learned in this unit about possible tensions associated with the axis and cross, allow yourself time to reflect on how you express this polarity in your life.

3. Looking at the other axis on the same cross, now reflect on what positive steps you might take to reduce and resolve any inner tensions or conflicts and what this might mean for your overall personal development.

4. In a similar way, consider Jennie's chart (Figure 4.4.5), and any charts you may be working with.

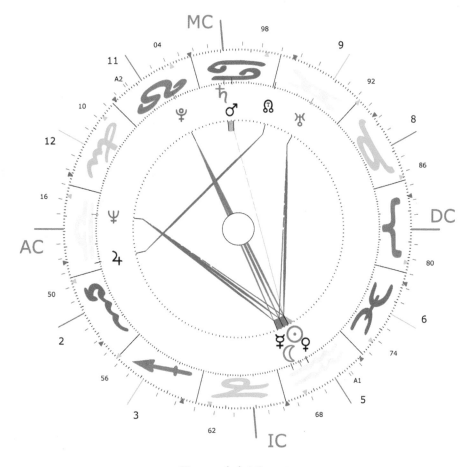

Figure 4.4.5 Jennie
1.2.1946 22:45 Kettlewell, England

Consolidation Exercise for Chapters 1-4

At the end of every other chapter we include an additional exercise which encourages you to consolidate your learning so far.

1. You have already encountered Sophie's chart in the consolidation exercise at the end of Chapter 2. Write a concise summary of Sophie's inner world as symbolised at the aspect level of the chart.

2. Now consider how Sophie might engage with the realities of the outer world by looking at the distribution of planets:-

   a) Through hemispheres and quadrants

   b) Across the house axes.

3. Consider the House Intensity Curve and possible areas of stress, e.g. intercepted or unaspected planets, planets in the stress area or at Low Points.

4. Take 3 planets and with reference to their placement in the chart, i.e. sign, house, quadrant, house axis, aspects etc. speculate on how their energies might be expressed in the context of the three levels of personality (e.g. the sub-conscious, ego-conscious and super-conscious level).

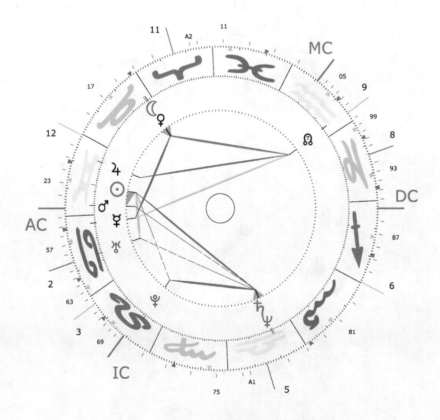

Figure 2.3.44 -Sophie (Repeated)
08.06.1953, 05:30, Mobberley, England

Chapter 5. Nature or Nurture?

Environmental and inherited characteristics are each reflected in the birth charts used in astrological psychology, and are either in conflict or in synergy. This chapter covers a number of areas where clues can be found to the nature of such conflicts or reinforcing energies.

Contents:

5.1 The Family Model

The natal chart can be used to obtain information about the child's subjective view of the relationship which existed between him or her and their parents during the early formative years of life. In many ways the way we think and act as adults is the result of childhood conditioning.

This section describes the Family Model and considers parent/child relationships.

Please note that the term 'parent' is used here to represent the adult that played the role of mother or father to the child. This may not be the 'birth' parent but could be another adult fulfilling that role in the child's life.

There are few hard and fast rules that can be taught about astrological chart interpretation, only guidelines. This particularly applies to understanding the reality of the Family Model, which can only be developed through practical experience.

Introduction

When considering a natal chart we need to bear in mind that the chart can never give us all the information relating to the individual's past, present and future. Each of us is brought up in a family environment which can vary from one extreme of over-nurturing to another extreme of deprivation and even abuse. So even though we might all come into this world with the hope of developing the full positive potential which is suggested by the chart, it doesn't mean that this will happen. If it did, the world would no doubt be a different place.

In astrological psychology we explore with our clients their personal issues, so we need to have acquired skills that enable us to establish trust with them. In this way we are able to learn from them the reality of their life as a child and we can begin to see how the potential in their birth chart is developing. The birth chart gives us pointers, but we have to be able to see how these relate to the reality of the client's life. In this way we can use the chart as a tool to help our clients to resolve current blocks and find ways of moving forward in their life.

In this chapter we are considering ways in which we can develop an understanding of:

- the relationship that existed between the child and parents;

- the relationship that existed between the child's parents;

- the way in which the environment might have perceived the child and how this could have affected the way in which the child developed;

- the conflicts that are likely to exist between inherited traits (signs) and taught or learned behaviour (houses)

- the way in which we can measure this conflict of energies and how it might affect motivation.

When considering the reality of the above it is essential to keep in mind that the way in which a child will see their relationship with a parent, or the relationship which existed between parents, will be totally subjective. The child needs to bring his own chart, or his natal pattern of energies, to life and to do this he needs to create situations around him, real or imaginary, that will allow this to happen.

Part One – The Family Model

Part One was written by Bruno Huber.

One of the problems which, as a psychologist, continued to bother me was the question: how can one make psychologically useful statements from the horoscope about father and mother ties and the complexes that arise? Initially, from the astrological point of view this question seems easy to answer, as according to the opinion of most astrologers, there are sufficient clues to interpretation to be found in astrological literature. However, when one wants to work with this as a practising therapist, one encounters a lack of conceptual clarity.

The comparison of some different sources quickly shows that, in some books the father is identified with the Sun, in others he is identified with, for example Saturn or perhaps also with the tenth house. Even when, as C.G. Jung himself tried, one looks for the anima and animus in the horoscope and one does arrive at a result with astrological rules, then the picture that arises from this does not stand up to careful psychological examination of human reality (tests, analytical discussions, free associations, etc.)

Out of the disappointments which the astrological interpretation material brought me in this area, I undertook a more extensive investigation which finally brought a lot to light. The following are the most important conclusions:

1. Not only the persons who have played the father and mother role for the child are definable in the horoscope, but also the **role of the child**, which the native played in his childhood environment.

2. Inferences about the personality of the father role can be made from the position of the **Sun** (especially in the houses).

3. The **mother figure** or role cannot be deduced from the Moon position, but rather from the position of Saturn in the horoscope.

4. The child is shown by the **Moon position**.

5. The **relationship** of the child to **both parents**, and of the two parents to each other, as the child experienced it subjectively, is shown in the aspects of the three main planets (Sun, Moon, Saturn) to each other.

6. The position of these planets in the house system shows the **hierarchical order** of the family. (Who really had the 'say' in the family?)

Of course I know very well that statement 3 especially is rejected by established astrology. There are two reasons for this. First, in the entire accessible literature back to Greek sources there is not a single author who does not define the Moon as mother.

Second, it goes against the grain for most astrologers to see the 'repulsive malefactor Saturn' identified with the soft and lovely figure of the woman and mother. The latter is understandable, but at least partially an error, because in connection with Saturn we can speak of 'woman' only in qualified terms. The woman as a sexual being is represented in the horoscope by Venus (not the Moon!). Conversely, Saturn has something distinctly asexual about it.

The mother role includes primarily protection, nourishment, care and education of the child. It is easily observable with each woman who becomes a mother that for some time she becomes quite un-erotic. Incidentally, men have complained about this for as long as mankind has existed. It is known to every psychologist how often sexual frustration of new fathers has led to the first 'excursions'. Apparently, many men cannot come to terms with their worshipped Venus suddenly turning into Saturn.

To return once again to the 'malefactor' Saturn: I think that it is about time to strike the concept of 'malefic' from our vocabulary in astrology. From the psychological point of view this is generally insupportable. The fear-mongering about Saturn has existed since the late Greek period. Manilius is, to my knowledge, the first author who formulated things so negatively. Also, we can thank the early Greeks for the Moon as the mother. Prior to that, for example with the Babylonians who are after all the fathers and mothers of our astrology, we find the definition of the mother principle, the archetypal mother, in Saturn. He (or should one now say 'she'?) is also the Earth, the mundane, and the **symbol of fertility** and pregnancy.

The **Moon** on the other hand, is the **receptive soul**, that which is eternally changing, growing and passing. It is rather astonishing that we cannot distinguish in our Moon definition between receptivity and fertility – the Babylonians could do so!

The woman is fertile, the man is potent; and both are receptive – namely for the love which unites them. The Moon is the contact seeking element in us human beings. Its ability is the sensitivity for the you and this receptivity has no gender. In the eroticism of the Moon we do not look for a sexual experience, but rather for the person who loves us and who is willing to give us trust, understanding and tenderness, without conditions. It is precisely that which we, as an infant, experience for the first time through the mother. The Moon is also the mother-seeking part of us, the first love experience with her – but not the mother herself!

Naturally every infant is totally identified with his mother during the first months of his life. He has not yet an individual consciousness, and is totally dependent on his mother in all his life functions. Astrologically, this could be formulated thus: the Moon is in exact conjunction with Saturn. This state does not last – and it shouldn't, according to Nature. The child must develop his own life functions in order to become viable. And here the mother must help him. This is her true function, and this is why it is so difficult to be a good mother, because the tendency to keep the child in some degree of dependency on oneself is a strong human trait, not only in women!

All aspects between the Moon and, either Saturn or the Sun, show such a dependence on the parents (mother tie, father tie), which of course, according to the nature of the aspect, varies in its quality. In addition, a father or mother tie can manifest in very different ways.

All Moon-Saturn aspects for example, make the separation from the parental home difficult, show a lessening of the risk-taking ability in life and bring about an excessive concern with one's own physical security and health. The lack of basic faith is usually compensated by efforts to build a 'whole world' in life.

Conversely Moon-Sun aspects (father tie) seem to have no hindering function in our present-day society, because our patriarchal culture evaluates positively the compulsions towards expansion and achievement coming from the aspects and rewards them with experiences of success. This trust in authority and its forms of compensation, such as success-oriented and competitive thinking and readiness for aggression in order to solve conflicts, often becomes a central drive.

Now I am coming to another important point of view in our theme: the family model has undergone a long history of development. Or, formulated in opposite terms, it has brought about great developments in history through changing societal evaluation. Seen astrologically, the cultural history of mankind to date can be divided into three stages. (Early history we have to exclude here, because we know too little about its societal forms)

1. Nomadic Early Cultures (e.g: Celts and North American Indians)

2. Matriarchal early high cultures (city states) such as the Chaldean - Babylonian, or the Aztecs, Mayas and Incas.

3. Patriarchal empire-building great cultures of antiquity and modern times (such as Rome, Byzantium and present day).

These three cultural forms – they still exist today – can be attributed astrologically to the family model:

Figure 5.1.1

The nomadic culture is the childlike mobile one which can be attributed to the Moon. Specific to it is the unstable roaming. Nomads are not tied by locale, but always go where the possibilities are best for their existence. They are neither building fixed domiciles, nor are they cultivating the soil. Planning ahead and laying up stocks are little developed. Possessions are limited to portable things. Due to these conditions they leave few historical traces and therefore we generally know little about them. Their religious world of images is filled with Nature Spirits (theurgy, voodoo, fetishism...) and transcendental concepts of God are rare.

Folk tales and fairy tales spring from this spiritual realm, therefore they also correspond to the fantasy world of the contemporary child, because every child in his development moves through all the important historical cultural stages of mankind.

Figure 5.1.2

The **matriarchal cultures** originated from the possession of land by collective groups becoming settled. The typical early cultural city states were islands in the nomadic freeland. In order to be able to exist they had to define their boundaries, build hedges, even walls (city walls). They tilled the surrounding land and gathered in the harvests as stores for their barns. Thus they became independent of the changing fortunes of the hunt and climatic variations. Concepts like possessions, order and adaptation assumed utmost importance for the existence of their society. Only the survival of the collective was significant. The individual did not count apart from his function as a part of a caste or a class in the hierarchical order of the state. This even applied to the upper strata (priesthood, monarchy). Everyone, depending on their ancestry, was born into a stratum and thereby into a professional speciality (class and dynasty thinking).

This culture developed writing and thereby group memory and cultural legacy. The gathering place of all striving was the religious life to which everything was subjugated. The polytheistic god-world was a reflection of the hierarchically strictly ordered communal life. In this cultural stage, the basic structure of contemporary astrology came into existence, but in the form of omen astrology which was used for prediction of the collective future.

In the matriarchal (motherly) cultures everything is geared toward delimiting, securing and maintaining, hence Saturn. That is why they often lasted for centuries or millennia (Egypt, China).

Figure 5.1.3

The first **patriarchal cultures** originated around 1000 B.C. Their most typical characteristics are their needs for dynamic expansion and their individualism. This conforms to the **Sun Principle**. 'Carte blanche to those who are competent' is the motto here, or as we like to formulate it today 'God helps those who help themselves' (Oligarchy = rule by the most able).

The king, the leader, the master, the father became the guideline for human striving. The individual effort to distinguish oneself is a masculine trait. We forget too easily that both sexual qualities are present in everyone.

Historically, the patriarchal (then still primitive and small) moved aggressively in on the solidly built matriarchal castles, setting up a masculine-fatherly regime. In human terms, the woman thus became a second-rate being who, only as a companion to man, had any chances of survival. This has also worked its way into astrology.

The motherly-caring and nurturing, albeit static Saturn had to be sacrificed to the sun-like striving for perfection (or monotheistic striving for God). The need for existential security was considered primitive. Finally, it was practically forbidden to pursue fully the pleasures of the body (Saturn turned malefic). The woman had to slip into the role of the child, dependent on its father and never become of age. We can see by our present-day world, where we have a strangely mixed cultural situation with true patriarchy existing side by side with pseudo-patriarchy and many places even having an open matriarchy, that woman did not subjugate herself without protest and that she has retained some special areas of dominance.

When I decided to examine astrologically the father and mother problem, I initially had great difficulties in working out a usable hypothesis. First of all I stumbled over the fixated positions of astrological attributions. According to the old (Ptolemaic) concept, and to this day, Sun and Moon are attributed to Leo and Cancer respectively as so called 'rulers', that is, at the bottom of the Zodiac.

Figure 5.1.4

Opposite these positions, at the top, we find Saturn attributed to Capricorn and Aquarius. I had already succeeded earlier in confirming the 'rulership' (which I would rather call 'participation in the signs') of these and the remaining planets by attempting a different arrangement of rulerships. Therefore I had no reason to have any doubts whatsoever about these attributions.

As in all symbolism, particularly astrological symbolism, above and below are essentially hierarchical values, Saturn being attributed to **above** would be tantamount to **ruling** and the Sun and Moon attributions to **below** would be tantamount to **being ruled**. In a particular culture like ours, this must necessarily mean that Saturn is the ruler, that is, the father. It makes the Moon as the mother comprehensible and may explain why, in the German

language in contrast to the Latin languages, the Sun is feminine.

Here, my examination of test horoscopes revealed something strange: when, in such horoscopes, Saturn stood highest in the house system as compared to the Sun and Moon, then these people had grown up in more or less strongly emphasised matriarchal family situations. Most conspicuous were Saturn positions in the ninth or tenth house. The personality anamnesis for these people showed up a pronounced lack of 'nest warmth' and snugness. They considered their mothers as anything from 'clever' to 'omniscient' (in the ninth house) or from 'dominant' to 'tyrannical' (in the tenth house).

Although these statements initially played havoc with my concepts, they also opened the door to a useful hypothesis:

1. The mother corresponds to Saturn and

2. the hierarchy in the house system is not the same as the one in the zodiac.

Further investigations which included also the fathers showed that so called 'ideal' – and that means of course patriarchal – family situations occurred where the Sun was anywhere from the eighth to the eleventh house, and Saturn anywhere from the second to the fifth house.

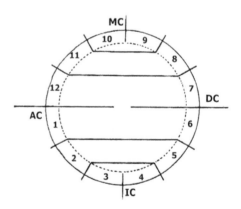

Figure 5.1.5

The higher a main planet is in the House System, the more significance the corresponding personality had in the family.

Thus the Sun shows the father role, Saturn the mother role and the Moon the role that the child played in the collective environment in which he grew up.

It is not the position of the main planets (Sun, Moon, Saturn) in the Zodiac but rather their position in the **house system** that gives information about the true distribution of the roles in the family. And this may awaken a possibly revolutionary insight.

When Saturn is attributed to the highest position in the zodiac, but in contrast to that, the Sun is highest in the house system and when Saturn = mother and Sun = father, then this of necessity means that in terms of historical development an older state (matriarchy) has come through in the zodiac than in the house system (patriarchy). Through a number of further research projects over the years, I have arrived at the conviction that everything which has reached genetic density through long processes of experience, eventually comes through in the system of the Zodiac thereby becoming a fixed component of human standards (archetypal knowledge).

This archetypal knowledge (the total zodiac) from which we receive an individual selection via the genetic pool (the sign position of the planets in the personal horoscope) lies in contrast to the 'cultural knowledge' which comes out of the house system. These ideas of values are the result of more recent history – characteristics of the culture into which we are born and which are passed on to us through life in the community and through education.

So the house system is a more changeable structure in the natal chart than the signs. It expresses the value standards of our own contemporary culture. Therefore it is not surprising that, over the course of the last two thousand years there were more than twenty such different systems of which at least six or more are still in constant use today. In contrast to this there are only two zodiacal systems.

Tips for Use in Practice

It might happen occasionally during the course of your work, when for example telling someone that his mother was dominant in the family because of the high position of Saturn, that he may protest vehemently. This does not necessarily violate the rule set forth in this section, because in a patriarchal society that which is not allowed cannot be. When a mother 'wears the trousers in the family' the life circumstances may have necessitated it but 'officially' this must not be. And so, already in childhood, the true state of affairs gets pushed into the unconscious. Usually the mother will not try to play out her dominance as overtly as men normally do.

The Parental Roles

- as they are subjectively experienced by the child.

These can be understood by a more specific definition of the house and sign position of Sun and Saturn. In terms of the role, the house position is more important and to be given priority. The sign often has a rather more hidden meaning of the existing, but usually only partially lived motivation of the respective parent. This circumstance can most frequently be observed with Sun positions (father) in the lower houses and/or near the Low Point, as well as with Suns positioned on the extreme right (especially near the DC) – fatherless society? The full unfolding of innate abilities is denied such fathers, perhaps due to the surrounding collective (third and fourth house) or roles forced on them by job or career (especially sixth and seventh house) or occasionally by their own impress behaviour (second, fifth, seventh and eighth house).

Similarly, this applies to Saturn positions in the 'I' realm (houses 12 and 1) – both are fear positions (fears of failure which are transmitted to the children) – also frequently to positions from the ninth to eleventh house (fears of responsibility which usually lead to over-compensation). On the Low Point positions Saturn is much less sensitive than the Sun.

These rules are formulated somewhat concisely (re-reading may be worthwhile), so I give a few examples.

Chart A (Figure 5.1.6)

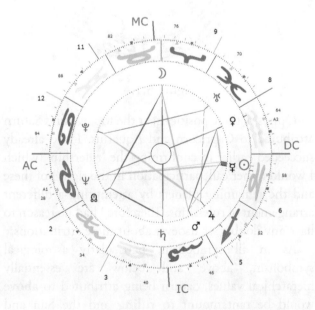

Figure 5.1.6 Chart 'A'

A doctor's daughter. **Father is totally absorbed by his involvement with his patients.** Mother in the household. Both parents had a strong attitude of expectation towards the child (Mother's Saturn opposition Moon 'attitude' and Father Sun square Moon 'attempting to gain the favour of the people'). Attitude and effort still apparent today in maturity. As a child she had the desire to become a singer.

Chart B (Figure 5.1.7)

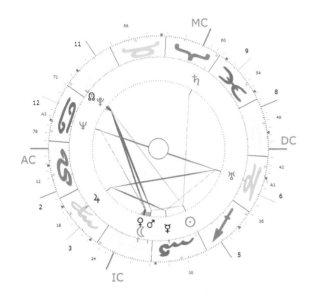

Figure 5.1.7 Chart 'B'

Son of an entrepreneur family in which the **mother surreptitiously dominated** in a subtle way (Saturn LP 9th house). Father was given orders (Sun in intercepted sign = 'low-pointish' and at the bottom of the chart). Son almost clinging in his dependence on the family and inordinately harmony-seeking (Moon conjunct Venus at the IC); somewhat sex-maniacal (conjunct Mars) towards his wife who divorced him at a mature age. The son exhibited a **high-strung mother worship** until his old age.

The Role of the Child (Moon position)

Here we are also dealing with the child's subjective manner of experiencing which, in the adult, is usually distorted in memory. This depends on how much the parents, in their educational efforts, interpreted or explained to the child his situation.

The contact-readiness, contactability and contact satisfaction (eg: strokes/rewards which one rarely receives as an adult) depend on the position of the Moon (again house and sign, in this order).

Qualitatively satisfying contacts are more likely to result from positions near the horizon: houses twelve and one with rather less frequency because the child was left too much to his own devices, houses six and

seven with greater frequency because the child had more contact practice with peers.

The higher the Moon is in the house system, the more the parents or the circumstances urged the child to make itself popular with others. The parents may have been proud of their special child or, with weak positions of the parental planets, they wanted at all cost that 'our child will someday be better off than we are'. Such positions are also the cause of feelings of loneliness 'amongst a crowd of people'. Lowly positioned Moons show strong family or collective ties.

Chart C (Figure 5.1.8)

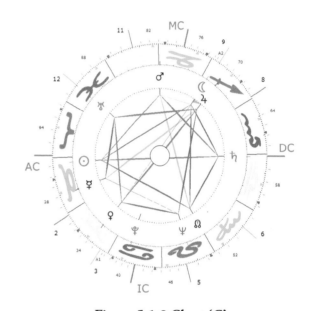

Figure 5.1.8 Chart 'C'

Daughter of a business tycoon. Father inscrutable, stiff, patriarchal figure; very tyrannical and possessive (Sun in Taurus, near Aries AC).

Mother 'grande dame' and patroness of the arts (Saturn on DC in Libra) Both parents had **strong attitudes of expectation toward the child** in terms of intellectual and artistic achievement (trine-sextile aspects to the Moon). Parents mutually fixed in extreme role play, but estranged (Sun opposition Saturn). Extreme nuclear family model. **Strong fulfilment compulsion** of the daughter into maturity.

Aspects in the Family Model

As an expression of the relationships in the family.

Aspects of the Moon to Sun and/or Saturn.

Where such aspects appear, they point to clear ties, even dependencies on the corresponding parent. The type of aspect describes the quality of the relationship. If the Moon is connected to the Sun and Saturn only indirectly via third planets, we have relaxed relationships which were hardly ever experienced as a deficiency (this indirect or functional type of relationship is the statistical norm).

Chart D (Figure 5.1.9)

Figure 5.1.9 Chart 'D'

When there is no connection at all from the Moon to one of the parental planets, the child experienced a substantial deficit in relationship.

Even in these definitions of relationship, the adult's memory of his childhood reality is often totally different. For the same reasons as explained above with Saturn in the high position (parental piety).

Chart E (Figure 5.1.10)

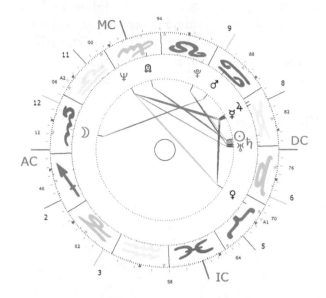

Figure 5.1.10 Chart 'E'

Daughter of a printing press owner and music patron. Family (including mother) were very culturally exposed – 'always people in the house' – (conjunct Sun, Saturn and Uranus on the DC in Gemini). Child in the background and relatively isolated; she was often punitively excluded from the family life (Moon position in the 12th house separate from the aspect picture). As an adult, the daughter separated herself thoroughly from the family in order to start her own family (so that she could do better). Consequently she suffered for a long time from fears of failing as a mother.

As is known from psychology, the parental relationships determine very strongly the selective behaviour of the adult in her search for a partnership.

Aspects between Sun and Saturn.

These reflect the role behaviour of the parents to each other. The child has a tendency, when living in a partnership as an adult, to repeat this parental role play – even when it has fatal consequences. The existent or non-existent aspects are evaluated according to the above pattern.

Chart F (Figure 5.1.11)

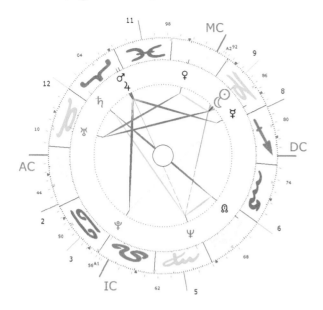

Figure 5.1.11 Chart 'F'

Son of a vicar and craftsman (Sun, Moon, Venus and Uranus). Strong father tie with the son; strong imitation-tendency. Mother; housewife, fears of failure (hardly emancipated), constant existential worries; rigid, moralistic attitude with hysterical note (Saturn just before the twelfth cusp). **Parents totally estranged amongst themselves** (Sun and Saturn without aspect). Child had little affection from the mother (Saturn and Moon without aspect). (see also Chart C).

Aspect Qualities

Finally, a word about the evaluation of the aspect qualities in the context of relationships:

- **Conjunction** = extreme tie.

- **Squares and Oppositions** = tense frictional relationship or achievement demand.

- **Trines and Sextiles** = harmonious, easy-going relationship, but also strong tie. Often a compulsion towards good behaviour.

- **Semi-Sextiles and Quincunxes** = uncertain or longed-for relationship depending on sign and house involvement, or overly mental or pronounced sensual relationship. Here we must look at any third planets which may be in conjunction. They can show up additional needs and conditions.

Part Two – Parent/Child Relationships

Other schools of astrology attempt to identify the mother and father figures in a birth chart and accepts that parental influence may, in some cases, have an effect on subsequent adult behaviour. But there is vagueness and disagreement as to which planet represents which parent and there is no suggestion that the child may be symbolised in the chart – other than as the chart itself. The Hubers clearly identify both the parents and the child in a natal chart and whilst this may at first be difficult to accept, it is likely that after due consideration and **practical assessment** this new view point will become clearer and more meaningful for most astrologers.

An understanding of the **reality** of the Family Model can only be built up by looking at many charts and seeing how they relate to real life situations.

Sun as Father

The Sun is the vital life force within us so, as new arrivals in this world, it is not surprising that **inherited** instinct makes us accept, and expect to find, the father figure in the family as representative of the power over our own life that we shall assume for ourselves as we grow older. He sets an example for us to follow.

Saturn as Mother

During the first few years of a child's life survival normally depends upon the nurturing of the mother. Ideally she feeds us, protects us, teaches us how to care for ourselves, offers us security and disciplines us so that in due course we can survive on our own in the world with a basic understanding of how to handle the problems we will have to face. What a mother offers can be related to the Saturnian principles of **security and structure**.

You may well find that the concept of 'Saturn as mother' is greeted with suspicion by certain fixed thinkers who have learned their astrology in a more conventional school. For this reason it is essential that you not only understand the principle that underlies the concept but also give yourself the opportunity to find out that it works in practice.

What seems vitally important to understand is that the concept of mother as Saturn applies only when we use the chart to examine the child's subjective view of his or her relationship with the person in the family who played the role of mother. In other words the person to whom the child looked for survival.

It is equally important to accept that this concept in no way suggests that the woman who played mother is Saturn. A woman may play the role of mother, wife, lover, artist, sports woman, career person, and so on. In each of these roles she will be expressing herself through a variety of sub-personalities including those we might see symbolised by planets which other astrologers see essentially as the 'mother', e.g. Moon (Free Child), Venus (lover), Neptune (unconditional love).

Moon as Child

As children we are totally dependent on other people. Initially this is usually our parents and we are receptive to everything that comes our way. We hope that this will be food, warmth and love but in the real world this is not always the case. The Moon portrays our receptiveness until we are old enough to express our own feelings.

In a natal chart we always have Sun, Saturn and Moon. How we grow into our own Sun, Saturn and Moon will depend on their position in the chart and the aspects they make to one another. From this we can learn how to use these energies to direct our life, achieve the success we seek and fulfil our destiny.

Growing Up

When we are born we are, physically at least, incapable of doing much for ourselves and we have some basic tools which we use instinctively to express our need to survive. We are small and defenceless and our parents make decisions about us and for us, but from the moment of birth we start to learn about ourselves and our position in life and we gradually begin to take charge. By the time we reach our late teens we have learnt how to run our own life, in other words we have grown into our own Sun and Saturn, and can express our own true feelings through the Moon.

Depending upon the arrangement of Sun, Saturn and Moon in our natal chart, we shall either grow up with the ability to run our own lives and become free individuals, or we shall develop with parental ties which, in some cases, may be strong enough to last throughout a life time and hinder us in the process of becoming self-aware, autonomous human beings.

At this stage it is only fair to point out that we are looking at **our own** Sun, Saturn and Moon and whilst, as adults, we may blame our parents for many things the reality is that, as children, our own psychological energy projected itself in such a way as to attract back the response we were looking for in order to fulfil the pattern of our natal chart. The mother and father in a family may appear, to an outsider, to be the same loving, caring parents to each of their children, but

each child within that family is likely to experience them from a completely different viewpoint.

Each child has a different personality to develop so, sooner or later, will start to behave in a manner that will motivate a particular response from each parent. Sometimes this perceived response will be in conflict with reality but it will be what the child wishes to see and feel. It is important to remember that when we look at the relationship of Sun, Moon and Saturn in the context of the family, we are looking at that individual's **subjective** experience as a child.

Practical Application

When considering the Family Model in individual charts we are looking at the parental roles and how effectively these were carried out, and then at family unity and the enduring ties they left with us. We find the former in the positions of Sun, Moon and Saturn in the chart, by sign, by house and by their strength in each of these, and the latter within the aspects.

In a counselling situation the parent/child model can be a valuable tool. However, there are many variations to the interpretation of the basic theme, and these can only be learned though **practical experience**.

Roles

During childhood, each of us experiences various aspects of 'the mother' and 'the father'. We are dealing here both with individuals and also with archetypal energies. No individual can manifest fully all that is contained within the mother archetype. The same is true for the father archetype. These archetypes have been built up in the collective over thousands of years. Each of us as individuals can make manifest some part of this archetype.

Thus as a child, I come into this world with some links into the collective unconscious which contains, amongst various archetypes, those of the mother and father. I then experience the reality of my own mother and father and however hard they try, it is not possible for them to perfectly portray the vastness and diversity of the archetypal energies. For each of us there is a discrepancy between our experience of our own parents, and our collective archetypal images.

We all had a father and mother, whether or not they were physically present during childhood. From them we learned something of what it is to be a parent. Thus our parents provided us with models of these archetypal energies. When we become parents ourselves, we consciously or otherwise use our own parents as a kind of yardstick against which to fashion our behaviour. In this way various patterns of relating may be passed from one generation to another.

It seems as if, for all of us, there is always some outstanding issue with our parents, however much work we do on the relationship. This can be seen against the background of the archetypes within us and the people out in the world, who in some way put us in touch with these archetypes. Depending on the culture we grow up in, changes in the patterns of parenting may take place relatively rapidly or hardly at all.

For the past three thousand years we have lived in a predominantly patriarchal society. Before that time there was a recorded period in history when a matriarchal society existed, and prior to that a nomadic society. Whilst all three can still be found today, in the Western world we are now in a period when traditional roles are being questioned and we can no longer clearly define behaviours into 'this is something a man does' or 'this is something a woman does'. It is therefore well to remind ourselves that archetypal energies do not have a specific gender. Masculine and feminine expressions of energy are not linked exclusively to one or other sex.

We all have Mars and Venus in our charts as symbols of the masculine and feminine within us. Whilst as a child I may learn from my mother qualities of caring, nurturing, home-making and loving-kindness towards others, it is also possible that from her I may learn determination, self-assertion, and how to focus my energies towards a specific goal. We need to be aware that different individuals will learn different lessons from one particular parent, and we can look to the birth chart to see how the parent was experienced by the child.

In fact, with the ability to deduce from a child's chart how that child sees its relationship with the parents, and if the parents are enlightened and the child's view does not accord with reality, then you can encourage the parents to open a dialogue with the child. Exploring the situation with a child may not appear to alter it immediately, but as the child grows older it will find it easier to resolve it in its own mind.

Sun

In the child's subjective view the planet highest in the chart will have been the ruling member of the family. Whether this was for better or for worse can be ascertained from other factors, as well as from experience. We would expect that the most appropriate figure in this role would be the Father (Sun).

If, for instance, we find the Sun in the Tenth House in Aries, then we might expect to find a strong father who was courageous, energetic and objective, and

perhaps set a good example for the child to follow in his or her own endeavours to be successful.

But what if that Sun was on the Low Point of the Tenth House? The situation might then be dramatically different because the Father was too weak a man to take on the role effectively and successfully and may only have postured and verbalised it. He may have been a pleasant man and, if in a water sign, a sensitive man but he will not have set the required example for the child to follow. He would have been an important father in theory but not in practice.

Another possibility may exist when the Sun is at the top of the chart but the father was so involved in his own role in life that he was not able to play his part as a father at all.

With Sun at the bottom of the chart we may have a weak father, for any number of reasons which could vary from excessive preoccupation with the local community or his own interest, to a disability. Whatever the reason it will have prevented him from fulfilling the role of Father in the way that the child expected. With the Sun low in the chart a person will often respond to the question "What did you expect from your father that you never received?"

A planet conjunct Sun or Saturn may give a clue to the nature of the parent. As an example, in one family Sun conjunct Mercury in the 3rd house was a father who was always hidden behind a newspaper and therefore not involved in setting an example for the son to follow. In another instance Sun conjunct Neptune in the 12th house, on a Low Point, was a weak father who lived in an escapist world of his own. He made loud noises as a father but he was not respected for them.

Sun conjunct Pluto in the 10th house related to a father who was completely involved in running his own business, was at home very seldom and when he was he spoke only of his success as the big boss at work and appeared, to the child, to play the same role at home. So the child grew up with strong ideas of how to use his Sun conjunct Pluto in adult life. Parental messages and behaviour play an important forming function during the child's growing years.

Saturn

In the supportive, nurturing role of mother we might expect Saturn to be strongest at the bottom of the chart. Experience supports the fact that where this is so a child is likely to grow up with an inner sense of security which makes it easier for him/her to weather the storms of life than when, for example, Saturn is found at the top of the chart.

If you picture Saturn as a tree, or even a strong post to which a person can unconsciously cling in times of doubt, then that tree or post can be firmer in the ground if rooted at the bottom of the chart than if it is wobbling around at the top with its roots dangling in the middle: a simple analogy but one which creates an appropriate picture.

When we find Saturn high in the chart then we have a mother who took on a ruling or dominant position in the family. As with the father, whether this was for better or for worse has to be ascertained from other clues. Was she just a strong woman, perhaps with her own career, or was the role necessitated because of the father's inadequacies? Where is the Sun in the chart?

Saturn on the Encounter Axis (AC/DC), whether or not it is the highest planet in the chart, will suggest a mother who played an over-protective role. On the 'You' side, protection from involvement with others and on the 'I' side from situations which might threaten harm to the child. Both these positions carry strong behaviour messages for the individual in adulthood.

The sign in which Saturn is situated can be important. A water sign might suggest a compassionate, or perhaps weak, mother; an earth sign a mother who was firm and effective; an air sign a mother who had her thoughts on other things than being the mother the child expected; a fire sign a very generous or overpowering mother.

Moon

The Moon is most appropriately situated near the AC/DC Encounter axis.

If it is the highest planet then for some reason the child will have seen itself as the most important person in the family – perhaps because it was looked up to by the parents. Or it may have been that the parents sought their own fulfilment through expectations from the child. Or maybe the child felt there was a need, or a feeling of need, to take on a responsible role in the family because of a weak or missing parent.

This placement usually leads to a sense of insecurity or vulnerability. In the adult a Moon at the top often indicates a person who feels they have an important role to play but may not feel secure in this, so needs a constant response from others, such as praise, affection, recognition, acknowledgement.

If we find the Moon at the bottom of the chart the child may have been suppressed or there may have been a surfeit of love that made it difficult for the child to leave the nest (4th house). The Moon low in the chart is most likely to have been influenced by the collective and indicates an individual who may have to recognise much adapted behaviour when they become adult.

A Moon on the ascendant is a private, introverted Moon. In the 12th house this often indicates a lonely or isolated childhood. This may have been forced on the child but is often of the child's own choosing, for example the child who goes straight to their own bedroom on return from school, perhaps to read.

Grouping of Sun, Moon, and Saturn

Next we can look at the grouping of Sun, Moon and Saturn in the chart. Are they grouped together in a comparatively small area of the chart, such as in one quadrant? This is likely to indicate a close family relationship, though closeness must not be taken to mean harmonious as a matter of course. A close grouping at the top of the chart will suggest an outgoing family where the child was given the opportunity to experience life outside the home, whilst at the bottom of a chart a family that stayed close together within the community.

If we find all three planets in close conjunction with one another the child will grow up with difficulties in the area of self-identification.

Are two of the planets on one side of the chart and one on the other side? The MC/IC Axis is the dividing line between the psychological inner and outer worlds.

All the different placings are important and relevant to the child's view of his or her early years.

Aspects between Sun, Moon, and Saturn

In the same way as there is a meaning in the linking together of energies in any aspect between planets, so there is meaning in the aspects between Sun, Moon and Saturn in the context of parent/child relationships.

There are three possibilities: a) a direct link, b) an indirect link, c) no link.

a) Direct Link.

Here there are 4 possibilities: 1) red aspect, 2) blue aspect, 3) green aspect, 4) orange (conjunct) aspect.

In all direct aspects, which imply that an emotional tie of some kind exists, we need to distinguish between one that links the Moon to Sun and/ or Saturn, and one that links Sun and Saturn. The former is a relationship between child and parent(s), whilst the latter is indicative of the child's view of the relationship between the parents themselves.

Aspects between child and parent(s) indicate a learning process of some kind on the part of the child – but it does not automatically suggest whether that process is good or bad.

Red Aspect

Red is cardinal energy that expresses the need to **do** something. Here a red aspect suggests that some kind of effort was needed to build the relationship between the child and the parent. Perhaps the child was expected to prove him or herself in some way in order to be accepted by, and make contact with, the parent. In the opposition there is the tension of polarity with its implication of opposing desires, needs and wishes, whilst in the square aspect open conflict is more likely. However because the conflict is open, it can often be healed more easily with the passing of years.

Blue Aspect

A blue aspect offers little resistance to the learning process. If there is a positive relationship, the child is completely accepting of the parent and the strong loving bond between them. However, the child may often feel compelled, for the sake of harmony, to do as they are told, hence the possibility of adapted behaviour. Whilst there may not be the same feelings of criticism as would be found with the square, the sextile aspect may indicate a sense of expectation that if not fulfilled, may lead to a lasting sense of disappointment and yearning on the part of the child.

Green Aspect

Here green brings ambivalence and doubt. It may have been an easy or a difficult relationship and there may or may not have been a sense of contact. The child would have wondered where he or she stood with the parent, particularly with a quincunx.

Conjunction

Here a strong tie existed between the child and the parent. Whether the relationship was happy or unhappy, the child would have found it difficult to separate from the parent and as an adult may have difficulties in knowing his or her own true feelings. A Saturn/Moon conjunction is indicative of a strong link with the mother, usually with attendant feelings of guilt or obligation.

For instance, in a woman's chart a conjunction between Moon and Saturn near the top of the chart may indicate a mother who had expectations for her daughter and who was trying to get some self-satisfaction from her daughter's ultimate success. Consequently the daughter may experience a constant struggle within herself as to whether or not she is satisfying these expectations. Near the bottom of the chart the message from the mother to the child may have been 'Don't leave me'. As a result the child l will have felt tied to mother's apron strings and this feeling can still be felt in adulthood, impacting on any other worthwhile relationships.

Where a direct link exists between parent and child it is often the case that as the child grows into adulthood the frictions and tensions which existed with the parent in the growing-up stage are resolved and a worthwhile relationship becomes established. This particularly applies where there is a red aspect, but is less likely with a conjunction.

b) Indirect Link

An indirect link exists if it is possible to trace, through the aspect pattern, a connection between Sun, Moon and Saturn where there no direct aspect between them. If such a connection exists, the child is aware of his or her relationship with the parent but without the dependency engendered by direct aspects. The child will experience much more freedom in the growing up process and will be better able to lead his/her own life.

c) No Link

In a chart where there are unaspected planets, or separate aspect patterns, there may be no link at all between the parents, (i.e. between Sun and Saturn) or between the child and the parent(s), (i.e. between Moon and Sun or Saturn). This suggests that the child was not aware that any inner relationship existed between him or herself and one or both parents. It may be that one of the parents left the marriage when the child was very young, or the father was in the army and therefore away from home. Or it could be that one of the parents was out working, late home every night, and the child decided that they didn't exist.

Very often this can leave a sense of loneliness or deprivation. If the Moon is in the same house as Sun or Saturn, but still in a separate aspect pattern, then there was some co-operation or understanding but still no substantial relationship and the child will feel left out.

Where a difficult or unhappy childhood existed the child may well compensate by a change of memory. If situations are too painful to live with then we repress the experience into the lower unconscious and change them in our memory. So there may be a discrepancy between a person's recollection of their childhood and what actually occurred.

You will notice that in the Orb Chart (Figure 1.2.1, page 19) the orb of Saturn is less than that for the Sun and Moon. In the context of the Family Model, this sometimes gives rise to one-way aspects between the Moon and Saturn. Bruno Huber says that the physical reason for the orb to be less is because Saturn is physically further out in the Solar System and is further away from both Sun and Moon. **Psychologically**, and in terms of the Family Model, the child (symbolised by the Moon), may seek to reach out, make contact with and hold on to the mother/security principle (symbolised by Saturn). Here, one-way aspects from

Moon to Saturn show the flow of energy and the need to make and maintain contact flowing more strongly from the Moon/child. Sometimes a one-way aspect between Moon and Saturn may indicate that the child has a feeling it must look after the mother.

Summary

In the natal chart the Sun relates to self-esteem, personal identity and confidence. It symbolises will and our ability to make decisions and direct our life through the use of our will. Saturn symbolises structure, form, stability, security and survival. When a child is born it is neither able to make decisions for itself nor protect itself, and these two aspects of the personality are normally projected on to the two people who can fulfil these roles on behalf of the child until such time as he/she is ready to own them.

A basic motivation in any human being is the need to survive, so a child will normally entrust or project its own Saturn on to Mother, who appears to be the person who is most involved in its survival process. Mother is expected to fulfil all aspects of the child's Saturn, including the provision of food, nurturing, warmth, safety and learning. Love does not enter into this particular equation and is something which the mother will, hopefully, offer from her own Moon, Venus or Neptune.

As the child grows up and reaches an age when she wants to establish her own identity she will normally want to reclaim her own Sun and Saturn from those people in whom these two functions were invested. Needless to say this is not always a straightforward process. So, when interpreting the Family Model it will be important to keep in mind the wisdom of Carl Jung in this respect. When a child projects her own need for survival onto the 'parents' she will re-inherit these aspects of her own personality with all the distortions that have taken place in the intervening years.

This is why it is essential to avoid making assumptions and to be open to the reality of each person, because no two families are the same and even within the same family each child will be likely to have a different experience of the same parents.

> **Remember**
> **Mother is NOT Saturn**, she merely fulfils the temporary role of the child's own Saturn.

One Last Thought

From the time we take our first breath, we receive attention from the world which responds to the part of us that it perceives most clearly. Through this process our birth chart is being stimulated into life and action. Those areas of our chart that are most noticeable, for example cuspal or unaspected planets, receive the most attention and are therefore activated and develop more rapidly than other parts. This may be positive or negative for us. Other parts, like Low Point planets, do not receive the same stimulation and may therefore lie dormant.

Exercise 5.1

1. Have a look at your chart and note the positions of Sun, Moon and Saturn and their relationship in the context of the Family Model.

2. Reflect carefully on, and try to recall, your own childhood as it really was rather than as you may now remember it. Relate this to your chart and summarise your understanding of the roles of Sun and Saturn as the parents in relation to yourself as the Moon.

3. Select another chart of someone you know well and reflect on what you know of the person's childhood experience of their family based on the Family Model.

5.2 The House Chart

> This section covers:
>
> - The House Chart and its use in understanding our formative and environmental influences
> - How the house chart is calculated
> - A number of examples of working with the house chart.

The House Chart can be derived mathematically from the natal chart. Its concept dates back some 2,000 years to the time when charts were made up in the shape of squares and rectangles. In American so-called 'apple-pie' charts, the signs are not shown and there is no insight into where a planet is in the Zodiac, or what aspects are made to it.

Our subjective view, as seen from the point of birth, gives a distorted view of the ecliptic and this worm's eye view of the heavens is reflected in the unequal sizes of the houses in the natal chart. However, we do not subject the signs to the same treatment, at least when using the tropical zodiac, so we end up with signs of equal size, i.e. 30° degrees. But suppose we were to take an objective view of the ecliptic, we would then have houses of equal sizes and the signs would become distorted.

Bruno Huber found that this objective view of the houses in the chart also provides an objective view of the individual, that is, how he or she is seen by the outside world. "This is the way we see this person, so this is the way we will behave towards him." In the natal chart the zodiac is the yardstick but in the house chart the houses become the yardstick.

In analysing a house chart we use the same guidelines that apply in the interpretation of a natal chart but we need to be aware that we are not looking at inherited traits but at learnt ones.

What the world made us.

In most cases, the house chart shows a different motivation from the natal chart, as indicated by the differences in the shaping and colour of the overall aspect patterns.

From the house chart we can therefore see how the environment tried to shape us in our formative years – the effects of the influence of family, schools and surroundings. The natal chart shows inherited potential whilst the house chart shows what we were educated to be. By comparing the two charts we can discriminate between what we were at birth (natal chart) and what the environment tried to make us (house chart).

By the time a person reaches their late teens they may believe that they are what their house chart shows them to be. However, there may also be a growing realisation of what they feel themselves to be – what they were born to be (natal chart) – and in such cases, there will ensue a period in which the growing youngster blindly tries to discover his or her identity, particularly where the divergence between the two charts is very noticeable.

With what appears to be a difficult or demanding natal chart, and where the conditioning can be seen to be beneficial there will still remain a strong inner sense of a need to understand and perhaps experience the pattern of inherited energies as shown in the birth chart. But the way will have been opened to allow that person to see alternative, and perhaps more positive, ways of using or coming to terms with their inheritance.

Sometimes the distortion is minimal but there are also cases where it is extreme and unhelpful, which can present the growing person with considerable problems of readjustment which may take years to unravel.

It should be borne in mind that the influence of the house chart is not necessarily permanent. We can choose what we see and wish to retain, and consciously work at letting go of the rest since it represents something which has been taught and not inherited.

How to Calculate the House Chart

1. Establish the size of each natal house (from the position in sign of each house cusp; 30° signs). Remember that opposite houses have the same size!

   E.g. cusp 1 at 7° Leo and cusp 2 at 19° Virgo gives size of Houses 1 and 7 = 42°.

2. Calculate the House Constant for each house = 30° (i.e. the number of degrees of each house in the house chart) divided by the size of the natal house.

   E.g. for a natal house size of 42° House Constant = 30/42 = 0·71429.

3. Calculate the number of degrees the start of each sign and each planet is from the cusp of the natal house it is in.

   E.g in the above example Virgo is at 42° - 19° = 23° from cusp 1; Mars at 6° Virgo would be at 29° from cusp 1.

4. Multiply these by the appropriate House Constant to give the position of each sign and each planet in the house chart.

   *E.g. in the above example Virgo is at 23° * 0.71429 = 16°26' from cusp 1 in the house chart; Mars is correspondingly at 29° * 0.71429 = 20°43'.*

5. From these planetary positions calculate the aspects for the house chart.

6. Now draw in signs, planets and aspects on a copy of the blank house chart form Figure 5.2.5 on page 172.

Worked Example - Calculations for Drawing a House Chart

The worked example in Figure 5.2.2 illustrates how to work out the sign and planetary positions required to set up a house chart, starting from the natal chart data in Figure 5.2.1. Working with a simple calculator is all that is required.

NB
- To convert minutes to decimal divide by 60.
- To convert decimal to minutes multiply by 60.
- House constant is 30 divided by number of degrees in natal house.
- It is not unusual to find a discrepancy of a few minutes of arc between manual and computer calculations.

Natal Chart Positions

PL	° sign ' "	Koch housecusps		Inv-Point
SO	13 VI 35 29	1	6 LE 38	15 LE 29
MO	23 LE 58 51	2	29 LE 47	8 VI 38
ME	1 VI 7	3	22 VI 58	1 LI 52
VE	28 CN 3	10	16 AR 15	7 TA 4
MA	14 VI 2	11	10 GE 44	22 GE 42
JU	28 SG 42	12	12 CN 4	21 CN 26
SA	19 GE 58			
UR	16 LI 32			Low-Point
NE	2 SG 37			20 LE 56
PL	1 LI 13			14 VI 7
TN	25 CP 9 R			7 LI 21
AS	6 LE 38 29			19 TA 55
MC	16 AR 15 8			0 CN 6
				27 CN 16

Figure 5.2.1 Example Natal Chart Data

Figures 5.2.3 and 5.2.4 show Natal and house charts drawn by computer from the example data (06.09.1972, Newton Abbott, UK).

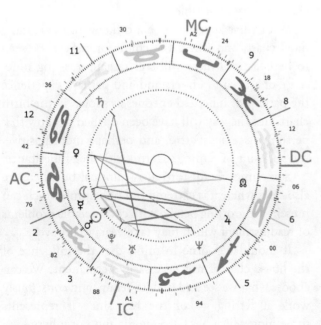

Figure 5.2.3 Natal Chart

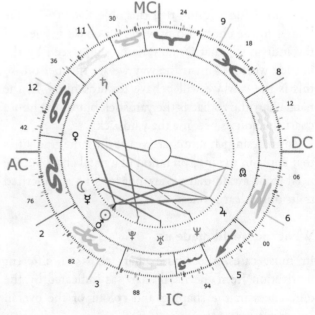

Figure 5.2.4 House Chart

Planet /Sign	House No	House Size Converted to decimal		Degrees from Cusp Converted to decimal (A)		House Constant (B)	House Chart Position (A x B)	
		° '	Decimal	° '	Decimal		Decimal	° '
☽	1	23°09'	23.15	17°21'	17.35	1.30	22.56	22°34'
♍	2	23°11'	23.18	0°13'	0.22	1.29	0.28	0°17'
☿	2			1°20'	1.33		1.72	1°43'
☉	2			13°48'	13.80		17.80	17°48'
♂	2			14°15'	14.25		18.38	18°23'
♎	3	23°17'	23.28	7°02'	7.03	1.29	9.07	9°04'
♇	3			8°15'	8.25		10.64	10°38'
♅	4	54°29'	54.48	0°17'	0.28	0.55	0.15	0°09'
♏	4			13°45'	13.75		7.56	7°34'
♐	4			43°45'	43.75		24.06	24°04'
♆	4			46°22'	46.37		25.50	25°30'
♃	5	31°20'	31.33	17°58'	17.97	0.96	17.25	17°15'
♑	5			19°16'	19.27		18.50	18°30'
☊	6	24°34'	24.57	13°05'	13.08	1.22	15.96	15°58'
♒	6			17°56'	17.93		21.87	21°32'
♄	11	31°20'	31.33	9°14'	9.23	0.96	8.86	8°52'
♀	12	24°34'	24.57	15°59'	15.98	1.22	19.50	19°30'
♌	12			17°56'	17.93		21.87	21°52'

Figure 5.2.2 Calculations for Drawing a House Chart

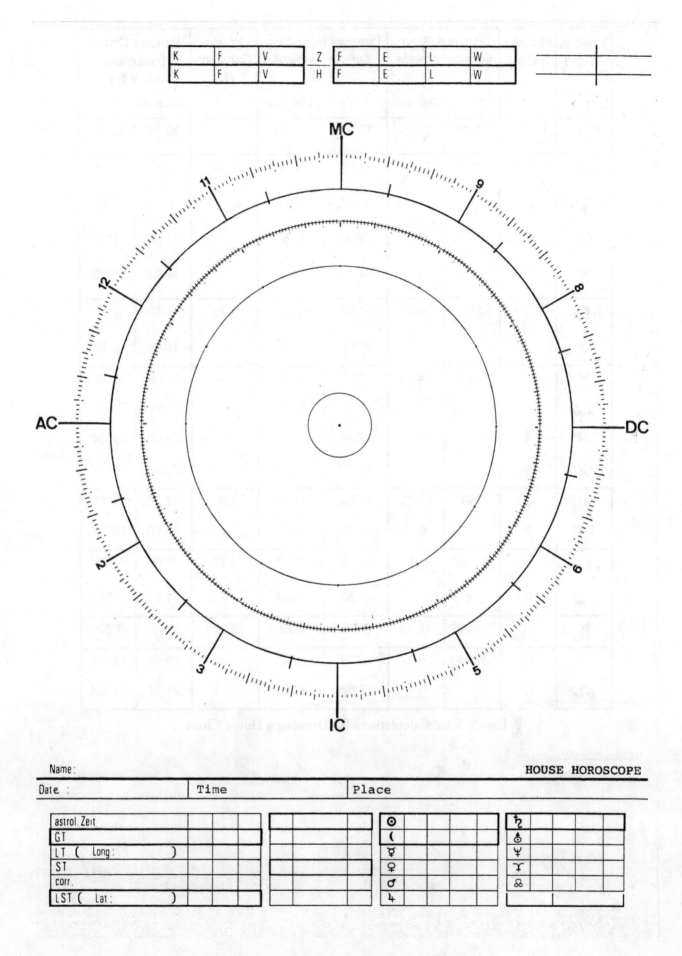

K	F	V	Z	F	E	L	W
K	F	V	H	F	E	L	W

Figure 5.2.5 Blank House Chart Form
Available as a download from Study Resources at www.astrologicalpsychology.org.

Example Hand-Drawn House Chart

Here we show an example of a house chart drawn up
by hand.

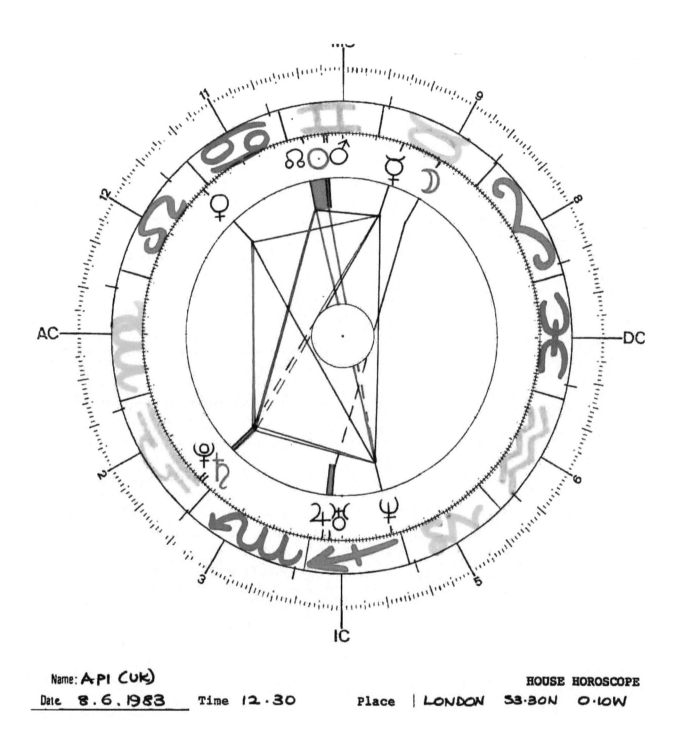

Figure 5.2.5a Example Hand-Drawn House Chart

Working with the House Chart

We are a product of our heredity and environment. A simple formula to remember is:

$$H \times E = I$$

Heredity x Environment = Individual

The house chart therefore provides us with an objective view of the individual. It shows what the world tried to impress on us in our formative years backed up by the conditioning and influences we received from our family, friends, teachers, schools, community, religion and culture, and it incorporates our inherited traits and potential with our taught traits.

The house chart should never be considered on its own but always in conjunction with the natal chart. The value of using both charts is that a comparison can be made between nature (natal chart) and nurture (house chart).

Main points to consider when working with the house chart

As with your natal chart, the first step when studying your house chart, is to look at the overall picture your chart presents and let an intuitive image come up. Is it similar or different from your natal chart? Did the environment see you (and subsequently treat you) in a very different way from that which is indicated in your natal chart?

Look for any changes or discrepancies in colour balance, chart shaping and direction, and any changes in the aspect structure, particularly those involving the Family Model. For instance, if your natal chart has a predominance of red aspects and your house chart a predominance of blue, this would suggest that you have plenty of active, cardinal red energy at your disposal, an inherited tendency, whereas the environment you grew up in expected you, and therefore conditioned you to be more "blue", passive and fixed in your motivation. Consider also any changes in aspect colours involving the Family Model planets.

Most of all, consider if the overall aspect structure that your house chart presents has either been enriched or diminished compared with that of your natal chart: has your natal chart (hence your potential) been enhanced or reduced by the environment and the conditioning you have received?

Working with our own house charts can give us many insights into how our environment shaped us, what it expected from us, and how we felt (and perhaps still feel) about that. This work may not always be easy, and we may connect with both and pain and joy as we explore the messages and expectations we received during childhood. What we need to do is remember that the contents of the house chart are a movable feast and that we can choose from the menu those elements which are the most positive and useful to us. If we can choose consciously, we will gain the most benefit. The amount of freedom we have to move from the house to the natal chart depends on how awake and aware we are, and on our ability to choose.

Practical Exercise

Outlined below are some practical ways of working with the house chart. After reading this through you might like to try some of these out for yourself:

In order to connect with the conditioning you may have received as a child, make a list of messages from your childhood – what were the expectations of your environment for you? Which messages do you still hear or carry in your head? Do you want to hear them? Which do you want to keep/discard?

Include what you consider to be both good and bad. For example, you may have received messages such as "Wash your hands before you eat your dinner", "Don't touch dogs", "Don't make a fuss", "Always try to please others".

Jot down some notes to describe your environment as a child at different ages [you could choose different ages – e.g. 0-6 (home influence), 6-12 (primary and middle school experience), 13+ (secondary/comprehensive)]. Dig into your memories. What was expected of you? You could maybe draw on some of the messages you came up with in the first part of this exercise. What was it like to be in your environment? Use your sensual memories to connect with:

1. the sights and visual memories you have of your environment; your memory may be jogged by looking at old family photographs recording events you were present at; remember any significant experiences you had in childhood that stick in your memory;

2. the sounds/phrases/words and sayings used in your home environment (e.g. did your father have a set phrase he always used?); the music you heard: any songs sung in your environment? Any instruments played, the books, newspapers, TV or radio programmes read, watched, listened to or favoured, the stories told...

3. the smells, tastes of your environment, such as food, comforts, luxuries, things you hated (this could cover the smell of over-boiled cabbage to the smell of baking bread)

4. the activities you took part in (maybe some of these were imposed upon you by the environment), the excursions you went on, the games and sports you played (e.g. were you naturally sporty or did you hate having to play games?), the temper tantrums you might have had – can you remember them, and if so what were they about?

5. the feelings you may have had of safety, security, being OK for who and what you were, feeling good or not, feeling loved and approved of or not. These feelings might have come from being in a special place, like your bedroom, or den, or from being with one, or both parents, or another relative.

Make notes on what was considered important in your environment and what was not. How was this conveyed to you and did it or does it still affect your value system? Are the expectations of your parents, other family members, siblings (if any), neighbours, and other authority figures still with you?

As you do this exercise, remember that the house chart contains **taught** and not **inherited** traits. It does not have to be fixed – the die is not cast once and for ever – we have a choice, and we can choose to extract the positive elements of our own house charts and put them to use for ourselves in ways that are supportive and beneficial.

Real Life Examples from Students

Example 1 Caroline

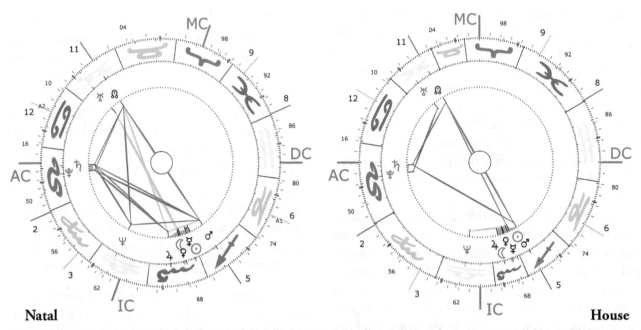

Natal   House

Figure 5.2.6 Caroline 22.11.1946; 2100 GMT; Headley, Nr Bordon, Hants; 51N07 00W50

The differences between the house chart and the natal chart are striking. There are considerably less lines in the house chart, explaining why I have always felt that others have misunderstood me.

When I worked with an image for my natal chart, I came up with a safe harbour, with a train at the dockside driven by Jupiter pulling the carriages out of the LP. In the house chart the harbour is not safe! The cradle is missing, changing the shaping from fixed to dynamic/linear, suggesting that the environment completely overlooked my strong security needs, but also that I have learned to become more adaptable, and to go with the flow rather than resist change. Without the cradle, the environment does not recognise my need to have a safe nest to hide in.

My natal chart shows a green/blue emphasis, which points to my need to escape from time to time. The house chart reflects a perfect ratio of colours – and with the better balance of red I have been taught to be more active.

In the house chart, there is no irritation triangle – true, my irritation is within myself! There is also no learning triangle – my learning and stimulation to grow again has come from within self rather than being provoked by the outside world.

Uranus, as well as the Saturn/Pluto conjunction which has represented major obstacles for me, receive only blue aspects in the house chart, indicating that the outside world does not see them as problematical, nor does it give any impetus to make use of the positive

energies involved. I have been told that I am lucky to be so organised and controlled – and free to do as I wished – whereas I haven't seen it that way at all. I have experienced my extreme self control as inhibiting and restrictive.

There is still a wall blocking off most of the 'You' side of the chart, so my conditioning has not helped me to become less self-sufficient. I find it interesting that most of the aspects in my natal chart tie in with Jupiter and the Moon/Venus part of the stellium, whereas in the house chart it links to Sun and Mars. This is as if the engine of my train has changed ends, having switched from Jupiter to Mars! In addition, the opposition natally links separately to Mars, whereas in the house chart it links to Sun and Mars. I have had to learn, and have been expected to take action, be assertive, and employ conscious, rational decision making. I feel more comfortable operating from an intuitive level, and have placed greater importance on contact, self worth and perceptive understanding. In the house chart, it almost seems that the Moon (and Jupiter) get left out so are not seen as important – and in the natal chart the Moon is on the LP. I certainly felt that my emotional needs were neither understood nor acknowledged.

Looking at the family model, in the natal chart Saturn is challenged by the red aspect to Jupiter, the Moon/Venus are fighting with Uranus, and the Sun is out on a limb. In the house chart Saturn receives only blue aspects – is this why the world saw my mother's influence as beneficial? – whereas I experienced it as inhibiting and felt that it made me inadequate in approaching life. Although I had a good relationship with my father, I always saw him as weak – not taking part in the family. Note that the Moon links to Sun through Venus and Mercury – I loved my father and tried to please him, but he always had his head in a book or a newspaper! However, the world seemed to see him as being a steady, stable and strong influence. In the house chart, it almost seems as if the child is unimportant - and I certainly felt like an outsider most of the time.

In the house chart I have lost the small Talent triangles too! The environment did not recognise my talents – or maybe did not expect me to have any! Maybe this is why I did not discover what I had to offer the world until I was an adult.

To me, my natal Neptune in the third symbolises a talent for intuitive thinking, creative visualisation, and to communicate (counsel) with love and empathy. The house chart shows only a green line to Neptune – and I was certainly conditioned to doubt and question these abilities. In my world, one was taught that such talents were of no particular use – it was preferable to employ concrete skills and practical down to earth methods – Saturn! As a child (and to this day), I believed in the fairies at the bottom of the garden – but my environment vehemently discouraged this.

To sum up, it is obvious that what I was taught was beneficial in some respects – as far as learning to be more adaptable and open was concerned. It also helped me to hone my survival skills to cope in the real world – something that by inclination and temperament (no earth) I have little interest in. However, in other ways it would seem that a lot of my strengths have been developed from within, without any help from the outside world, and almost in spite of my environment.

Example 2 Juliana

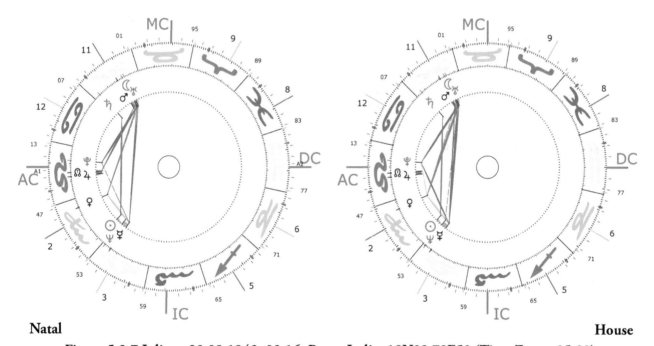

Natal   **House**

Figure 5.2.7 Juliana 20.09.1943; 03.16; Pune, India; 18N32 73E52 (Time Zone –05:30)

My house chart is stronger than the Natal, the pattern is larger. There are two more aspect lines, a red and a green. The semi-sextile creates a four sided figure so instead of a mutable triangle in the natal chart, the pattern is fixed at four points and feels more stable – when I spend a lot of time on my own I can feel as thin as air. The Jupiter/North Node conjunction is no longer integrated.

The second green semi-sextile creates two new forms:

1. a small Learning triangle, retrograde in motion, which seems to facilitate repeating experiences which can be fed into the natal learning triangle – picking up information from outside to further internal growth.

2. an ear or eye formed by semi-sextiles from Pluto and Mercury meeting at Venus in Virgo, which symbolises my love of gathering information – discrimination is essential.

Before examining my house chart, I had thought my Virgo Sun and Mercury in the second house entirely responsible, but this shows clearly the potential to absorb information from the environment – an ear to the ground!

The additional red square, Venus/Mars, adds weight to the Moon/Venus square in the natal chart – so there is a lot more energy available here and I can use the listening ear, watching eye, with purpose. Clues identified, information processed and possible conclusions drawn with the help of Uranus – a process of detection. This is used consciously in my work as a therapist and I love identifying clues with the purpose of establishing the root cause of a problem which has manifested at a level to be recognised and demand attention.

Sun square Saturn is weaker in this chart and the trines linking the third and eleventh houses are stronger, with Mars and Neptune more directly involved, so there is the potential for channelling energy through these planets to express into the environment, and of course that is a two-way process.

The fact that I have good ideas and know exactly what I want to achieve is weakened when challenged by the outer world – nicely expressed by the unaspected Jupiter conjunct North Node in the house chart.

Looking at the family pattern – Sun, Saturn, Moon – in the house chart, the Sun square Saturn is one-way, suggesting my parents relationship was perceived as stronger by me than the environment, and on reflection that is right. It wasn't a comfortable relationship but I hadn't realised until now, that it was obvious to those outside the immediate family.

The Moon has another aspect, with Neptune, seeing the child as not quite there, unreal – which again I can confirm, I was expected to blend with the environment, not express individuality. The Moon is strong towards the top of the chart and it is unnerving to realise now just how important I may have been to my parents. Perhaps I was spoiled but to me it felt more like being overprotected.

The house chart supports earlier conclusions drawn during this course and is helpful in understanding how others see me and react in a particular way. A blue/green figure doesn't appear to have much weight or body and could explain why I can move about and not be seen – which has upset and puzzled me for a long time – a nuisance when one doesn't understand why but admittedly useful at times. This chart explains why I have more energy by sign and quality than the world wants – a resource for inner work.

Information from the environment affects the inner being, there is a reaction, internal change (possible) followed by a response. In the cliché 'no man is an island' I am reminded that there is a two-way permeable membrane through which information passes at many levels, an osmosis which is essential to maintain well-being and growth.

The house chart adds another dimension to the understanding of the personality and interaction with the community and the rest of the world. It confirms the importance of the use of will and how subtle changes in behaviour patterns stimulate different responses.

Example 3 Toni

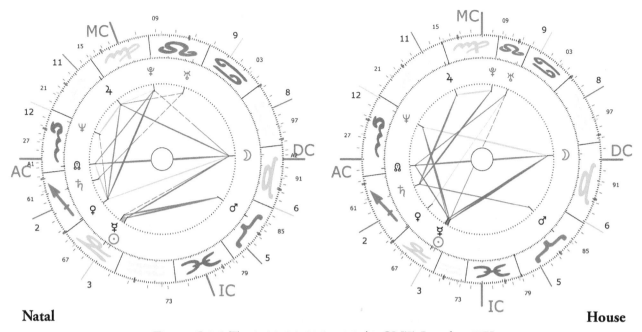

Natal   House

Figure 5.2.8 Toni. 12.01.1957; 03:40 GMT; London UK

My house chart is very different from my natal chart. At the aspect level of motivation my house chart is mutable rather than the fixed. The circumstances of my childhood – parents separating just before my first birthday, living with my mum in a very hand to mouth existence in a series of bedsits – meant that flexibility was essential.

My Moon in the 7th house was already highly relational and became very honed in the skills of being acceptable to others. Relationships ensured survival for both me and my mum who could leave me with any number of people, knowing that I would be good and fit in. My Moon loses its natal quincunx to Venus which is itself out on a limb so that my own sense of harmony and equilibrium in relationships was undeveloped.

Whereas my natal chart is coherent, my house chart contains a completely separate figure - a small retrograde Learning triangle of Saturn, Jupiter and Pluto, with a blue linear extension from Saturn to Mars. My Martian energy changes both ego planet allegiance and its mode of expression. Natally anger and spontaneous creative drive require expression but I learnt to submit in service of survival and co-operation with my mother. The Learning triangle shows a belief that I learnt very early on concerning the nature of life. I decided it was a school for learning hard lessons for the purpose of improvement and the development of character. I was always very aware of the spiritual nature of the task and the imperative to do my best, but it was a heavy load to bear. In fact this configuration formed a sub-personality that continued exerting a powerful

subconscious influence on my behaviour until very recently.

My Sun is better integrated in the house chart and I think my early training served to develop my dutiful and responsible Capricornian will. This resulted in me pushing myself educationally and being ambitious in the pursuit of my career. Whilst living in this chart I was intolerant of my sensitivity which I regarded as a sign of weakness and inadequacy. Conversely my natal chart puts more emphasis on my feeling nature and its evolution. I have had to learn how to understand this aspect of who I am and value the contribution it can make to my life and the life of others. However, without the work I did on my Sun, I believe I would not have been strong enough to function effectively in the world.

I can remember how, in the early days of studying astrological psychology, I struggled to relate to my natal chart. I subsequently realised that I was so caught in my identification with my house chart that I didn't find my natal expression in adolescence as might be expected. When I got to my mid-thirties I suffered a crisis of meaning and could no longer pretend that everything was ok as the incomplete Righteousness rectangle in my house chart might imply. I think that as I approached my Moon by Age Point the square to Pluto kicked in with a vengeance and I could no longer continue my life as before. It was at this time that I went into therapy and started to study astrology. Even then it took me some years of self examination before I could understand and relate fully to my natal chart. But it has been well worth the effort!

Example 4

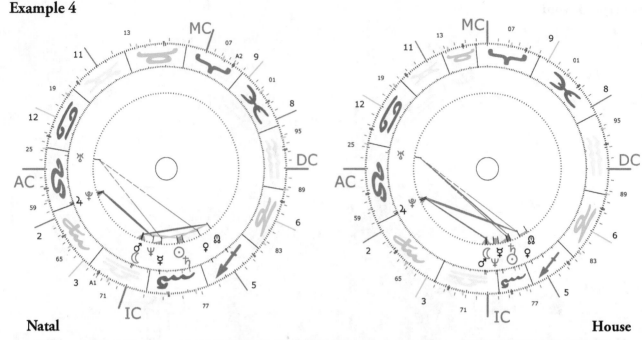

Natal   House

Figure 5.2.9 Pauline: 11/11/1955 22:05 GMT, Weston-super-Mare, UK   (51°N21' 2°W29')

This is the experience of a student where the ego planets are integrated in a Ear or Eye aspect pattern. In the house chart the Ear no longer exists though the ego planets remain linked by conjunctions through ☿ and Ψ.

I was a very wanted baby by my mother as I replaced a baby girl she lost at birth two years earlier. I think my father saw my arrival as making mother happy and helping her recover from her grief of her previous loss.

As a young child my father worked six days a week in a garage and seven nights a week as a drummer in a successful dance band. To maintain my father's lifestyle, my mother was very organized with a strict routine every day in order to meet his needs in the short time he had at home before going out for his evening work. Everything seemed to revolve around mother meeting father's needs and as a child I was encouraged to stay in the background and not make a nuisance of myself or get in the way of their busy lifestyles. I always had to be a good girl by doing as mother said and not getting in father's way.

In retrospect I believe this may have created some deep resentments and anger (☽ ♂ ♂ on the IC) because of my mother always being there for father but not for me and that I was made to stay in the background. I believe the ☽ ♂ ♂ at the IC accurately reflects this as I was certainly at the bottom of the line in order of importance within the family group and I was kept firmly in my place by my mother. I believe ♄ almost unaspected reflects that mother was all consuming and controlling of me.

My relationship with my father was almost non existent and my most vivid memory of him was when we were taken to see him on stage in the dance band. As the drummer he was sat highest on the stage on his own

platform and we would view him from ground level and for his drum solo, the lights would go out except for a single spotlight on him for the several minutes of his solo.

As a small child I saw my father receive a lot of attention from my mother and from the public as a highly regarded musician. I believe resentment set in as I felt denied of this attention and support. But how could I possibly compete with that image of my father? I may well have longed to be as special or as talented as he seemingly was and then maybe I would receive the attention and support that he did. I think I saw my mother as non negotiable, it was pointless trying to compete with her because she would literally not tolerate any interference. I am still to this day aware of some competition between my mother and maybe even with my father also, although this is somewhat fuzzy.

Even though I did feel loved as a child, I still knew my place and somehow there was never any option about whether I did as I was told. My mother was a force that you did not argue with!

Finally I do realize that I do not need my mother's attention or approval any more and the ties are definitely loosening (both my parents are still alive and well). The whole process of separation from them and their conditioning of me however, has certainly prolonged itself well into adulthood and the process of becoming my own person is still going on. But somehow it feels as though the timing of this growth out of parental conditioning into individuality is fixed for me, as though I do not have much control over it other than to try to be aware of the opportunities to develop and change perspective, as they arise within life's mystical way of unfolding.

Exercise 5.2

1. Your computer software/service will calculate and draw the house chart for you. However, you will gain a deeper understanding by drawing up a house chart for yourself.

   Using the method of calculation described in this section, calculate the exact positions of your own planets and sign cusps within the 30 degree houses, and draw up your own house chart on a copy of the blank house chart form Figure 5.2.5 on page 172.

   This will, of course, look like the chart produced by a computer. However, check each aspect and draw in the correct colours.

2. Note any significant variations between your natal and house charts, and also take account of any relationship between Sun, Moon and Saturn which you consider significantly relevant.

3. Compare natal and house charts of people known to you and consider the implications of any key differences.

5.3 Conflicts in Planetary Energy Outputs

This section looks at the varying strengths of energy output from the planets according to their house and sign positions and considers the psychological implications of possible conflicting positions.

Energy Output of Planets in Signs

Planets not only have varying energy output depending upon their house position as taught in section 4.3, they also have varying strengths depending on their longitudinal position within a sign.

Figure 5.3.1 below shows the strongest and the weakest degree positions in a sign.

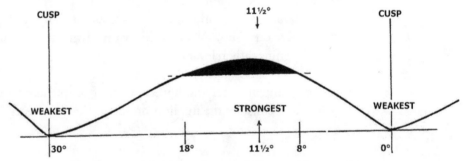

Figure 5.3.1 Sign Position relating to Energy Output

The strongest point in any sign is in the 12th degree. Any planet between 8° and 18° can be considered as being strong in that sign.

The weakest points are between 0° and 3° and between 27° and 30°. A planet very close to the cusp of a sign, i.e. within a degree, may have little strength related to the sign in which it is situated and may be influenced by the adjacent sign, particularly if there are planets in that sign.

Strongest	11½°
Strong	8° – 18°
Average	5° – 8° and 19° – 26°
Weak	0° – 3° and 27° – 30°

Planets Weak by Sign

It is important to understand the manner in which a planet which is weak by sign may influence behaviour. In a sense we might see the beginning of a sign as manifesting behaviour similar to that shown by a planet on a house cusp. This is likely to be energy which is unrefined, uncontrolled and perhaps misdirected: a kind of childish enthusiasm. At the end of a sign the feeling is more likely to be one of lassitude: "I've been through this sign and I really lack the energy to be bothered." This will, of course, express itself differently with each individual, partly depending on the nature of the sign, house position and aspects.

Comparison of Energy Output between Signs and Houses

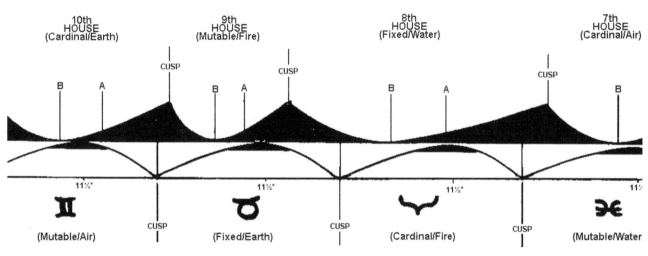

Figure 5.3.2

It is important to remember that the strength of a planet by house can only be ascertained if the birth time is correct. [If you are unsure of this, you should remain open-minded on the validity of any conclusions you might draw, until you come to birth time rectification in Chapter 6.]

Figure 5.3.2 provides an example comparison between points of highest and weakest energy output in signs and houses.

When studying a chart it is important to note the strength of a planet both by sign and by house and to consider the potential conflict between them. For instance, a planet at 2° of Aries on the cusp of the 10th house will be expected to perform strongly by the environment and the individual will attempt to satisfy this. However all these efforts are likely to be without success because the planet is weak by sign. Frustration and compensation will ensue until the weakness is understood and balanced by developing other factors in the chart.

Similarly a planet that is at 12° in a sign, but on the LP of a house, will be unable to express the energy in a successful, outward, worldly manner. It may make a great deal of noise and attract attention but its worth cannot be recognised, or accepted, by the environment. The person with this LP placing will have to understand and accept this fact and be willing to go through a period of inner learning, perhaps over many years, before being able to use this energy successfully in the world. This process of recognition and acceptance has been described in 4.3.

At this stage, a useful exercise using Figure 5.3.2 above would be to pencil in planets in different positions in the signs, note their strength by position

in the sign and then assess how they are likely to be able to express their particular energy through the house.

The energetic quality of planets in signs is inherent in us. But other people, particularly during childhood, sense and respond to the planetary energies in our chart not so much as they express themselves in the signs as in the **houses**, and they react to them accordingly. So it is likely that an imbalance develops during our formative years between **inherited** energy (signs) and **taught**, or adapted energy (houses).

When we are young we are influenced firstly by parents, then by schools, by friends, and others around us. They all react to us in a way that reflects the way they see us (houses) and, because we haven't learnt any means of understanding the process that is going on, we tend to adapt our inherited energy pattern to suit the demands of those who control our life.

As we grow older and start to take control of our own lives we are likely to find that there is an imbalance between what we are expected to be and what we really are. This is by no means necessarily negative, but recognising that imbalance is important in understanding our present behaviour. The creation of an excessive imbalance can be the cause of neuroses and other psychological disturbances.

An imbalance may arise for instance with a planet in a **fixed** sign but a **mutable** house, as this would suggest that the environment saw a mutable trait and attempted to influence and unsettle the natural fixed tendency of the individual towards stability and security.

Another example might be Mars in a **cardinal** sign but in a **fixed** house where the process may have diminished that person's ability to express the cardinal energy in an initiatory way in order to establish a position in the world.

As always, it is necessary to take other factors in the chart into consideration before assessing whether environmental influences are positive or negative. For instance, if the chart shaping is linear it may be important for the child to be taught the need for order and stability.

A chart with a number of planets in water signs might suggest someone who was sensitive, compassionate, emotional. However, if none of these planets are in water houses, the person may have learnt or been taught as a child that a display of emotional feeling (e.g. tears, hugs, loving) was not in keeping with what parents or school felt was appropriate behaviour. The ability to express an important part of their personality will have been suppressed and this may well affect their capacity to form deep and long lasting relationships in adulthood. Knowledge and understanding of the potential which is present in the chart will obviously help in the process of development.

It is well worth remembering that the quality of energy that is inherited (signs) cannot be changed, although its potential can be developed. However, the environment (houses) can be harnessed and used to maximum advantage.

Summary

When studying a chart, always consider the strengths of the planets by sign and by house and assess whether any conflict exists. Take account of motivation and temperament by sign and by house and note whether there are any important differences between inherited and environmental energy values.

Be sure that you are working with the correct birth time before placing undue emphasis on your findings.

Recommended Reading

The Astrological Houses, by Bruno & Louise Huber, pp94 – 107.

Exercise 5.3

1. Using your own chart, list the strength of all except the outer planets by sign and by house. You can devise your own system of valuation of intensity, e.g. Strong/Average/Weak, or 3/2/1, as long as this corresponds with what you have learned.

2. Then comment concisely on your findings. How do you understand and experience these strengths, contrasts and conflicts in your own life?

3. Do the same for one of your working charts and consider how this might manifest in that person's life.

5.4 Dynamic Calculations

Dynamic Calculations are a value system which measures the dynamic between inherited and taught behaviour, using the birth chart. (Dynamic Calculations are readily available from Huber chart software/services.)

This section covers:

- The principles involved in calculating these values
- The use of Dynamic Calculations in interpretation.

Principles and Meaning

In section 5.3 you learned that the exact positions, and therefore strengths, of the planets in the signs and houses are very important factors in determining how these energies are expressed. You also discovered how the conflict between house and sign strengths can affect your understanding and interpretation of a chart.

In order to be able to recognise the implications of this more clearly, Bruno Huber devised a value system which measures the dynamic between inherited and taught planetary energies in respect of both motivation and temperament (inherited character traits). These calculations can be a valuable aid in counselling but they require much time to work out manually, so access to a suitable computer programme is more or less essential for accuracy.

Dynamic Calculations are only valid with an **accurate birth time**.

Figure 5.4.1 [next page] shows extracts from a computer printout for the Dynamic Calculations (here called 'Dynamic Counting').

The table is made up of three main columns:

1. The **Total** or **Stress Total** column relates to the general amount of stress and strain we are likely to experience in life – the demands, the expectations, the squeezing into shape, the needing to meet deadlines...

2. The **Crosses (Motivation)** column has three subsidiary columns marked Card. Fix. Mut., relating to the qualities of cardinal, fixed and mutable. The numbers in these columns show the scores for the planets in each Cross, by Sign and by House.

3. The **Elements (Temperament)** column has four subsidiary columns marked Fire, Earth, Air, Water. These relate to the elements associated with the zodiac signs. The numbers in these columns are the scores for the planets in each of these elements, by Sign and by House.

and three rows:

Row 1) shows the total of planetary scores in their **Signs**.

Row 2) shows the total of planetary scores in their **Houses**.

Row 3) shows the **difference** between these scores.

The difference (Row 3) is obtained by subtracting the Sign score from the House score. A **minus** score is shown when the score in the Sign is higher than the score in the House.

Position

Radix

☉	25°58'12	♋	8
☽	14° 4'44	♒	2
☿	5°59' 1	♋	7
♀	22°54'41	♌	9
♂	0°14'12	♋	7
♃	4°10'31	♎	9
♄	4°32'34	♎	9
♅	26°10'11R	♏	12
♆	22°37'40R	♐	1
♇	21°36'55	♎	10
☊	1°40'14	♌	8
As	13°36'24	♐	1
Mc	13°37'18	♎	10

House Koch

House		Cusp		Invert Point		Low Point	
14°47'11	1	13°36'24	♐	22°56' 6	♐	28°42' 0	♐
29°42'37	2	8° 1'41	♑	21°55'57	♑	0°31'34	♒
27°29'18	3	14°25'49	♒	7° 2'22	♓	21° 0'46	♓
4°17'54	10	13°37'18	♎	21° 8' 2	♎	25°46'36	♎
20°25'43	11	3°17'19	♏	10°48'19	♏	15°27' 3	♏
25°12'44	12	22°58' 3	♏	0°51' 4	♐	5°43'24	♐
25°23'54							
4°39'16							
11° 4'54							
12°11'36							
19°29' 3							
0° 0' 0							
0° 0' 0							

Planet in Sign

Strong	Normal		Weak
☽	☉	♄	
	☿ ♀	♃	♂
	♅ ♆ ♇		

Planet in Hous[e]

Strong	
☽	
☿ ♀	
♅	

D y n a m i c   C o u n t i n g

6 451(421)3

Crosses-Motivation / Elements-Temperament

	Total	CAR	FIX	MUT	Fire	Earth	Air	Water	
Signs	94	51	30	13	20	0	43	31	Row 1
House	124	48	21	55	37	26	31	30	Row 2
Diff.	30	-3	-9	42	17	26	-12	-1	Row 3

Figure 5.4.1 Sample Chart Data
(18/07/81 18:18:30 BST 17:17:30 GMT 003W31 50N43)

How to Interpret the Dynamic Calculations

Consider the example data in Figure 5.4.2.

Chart Dynamics										
	Motivation					Temperament				
Stress Total	Card.	Fixed	Mut.			Fire	Earth	Air	Water	
110	25	48	37	Sign		25	8	15	62	← Row 1
132	56	34	42	House		34	14	32	52	← Row 2
22	31	-14	5			9	6	17	-10	← Row 3

Figure 5.4.2

Row 1 shows, in numerical form, the inherited Sign qualities, traits and characteristics. Those that are highest are likely to predominate.

For example, in Row 1 of Figure 5.4.2 above, we see that under Motivation, the highest score is Fixed (+48) and under Temperament, the highest score is Water (+62). These scores would suggest that this person would have a lot of inherent Fixed characteristics and traits, and a lot of inherent Water characteristics and traits.

Row 2 shows the total or totals relating to the Houses or areas of life experience or expression where expectations for us to perform are at their greatest.

For example, in Row 2 of Figure 5.4.2, the highest score under Motivation, is Cardinal (+56) and the highest score under Temperament is Water (+52). From these, we might expect that there was an emphasis on expectations and conditioning to perform in ways which expressed the qualities of Cardinal and Water.

Row 3 shows the totals obtained after subtracting the **Sign** scores (eg. the inherited traits and characteristics) from the **House** scores (e.g. what the environment demanded).

Using the scores in Row 3 we can begin to interpret the interaction between what the person already has by inheritance (scores by Signs) and what they have been conditioned and expected to express to the world (scores by Houses). For example, the Row 3 score for Figure 5.4.2 shows +31 as the highest score under Cardinal Motivation, and +17 as the highest score under Air Temperament. This suggests that the person was encouraged by the environment to exhibit traits, behaviour and characteristics associated with Cardinality and Air.

If we then look at the lowest (e.g. **minus**) scores on Row 3, we can see that there is a score of –14 under Fixed and –10 under Water, indicating that there is a **surplus** of both Fixed and Water traits, qualities and characteristics that the environment may not have wanted or even recognised. What was favoured and required instead were the traits, behaviour and characteristics of Cardinality and Air.

Plus and Minus Differences in the Motivation and Temperament Columns

A **minus difference** indicates that the energy we have brought with us by inheritance (sign) is more powerful than the world requires. The environment does not make demands on us but neither acknowledges nor wants what we have to offer and the lower the score (high minus), the more our environment will attempt to squash our innate qualities. It is useful to consider the sign and the planet(s) in it and to remember that this is where there is a surplus of energy which can be redirected through the aspect structure to an area of need.

A **plus difference** means that the demands that life is making on us are higher than the inherited qualities we have. We may be expected to perform at a higher level and in a way that is contrary to our natural inclination, hence causing undue stress. Inner adaptation may be necessary to counter the influences which education and conditioning have had in the area(s) of life indicated.

Difference scores of +5 to +25 are considered normal. Scores of over +25 or under +5 will be a source of stress in our lives and we need to understand their implications. With a zero score in Row 3, it is likely that the person will feel that there is no push from the surroundings for this particular quality, and that it is simply accepted. With minus scores, the person may have to teach themselves to develop the relevant quality for its own sake and not for the sake of pleasing others.

A Simple Analogy

In order to understand how to read and interpret the Dynamic Calculation scores, the following analogies may be helpful:

If you were to go shopping, taking 90 pence with you to buy a copy of your daily newspaper, which costs 80 pence, you should end up with 10 pence change.

If we regard the 90 pence you take out with you as your **inherited potential** (Sign score, Row 1) and the 80 pence the newspaper costs as the **environmental demands** (House score, Row 2), it is easy to see how the 10 pence change you have in your pocket is surplus to the requirements of the environment in this particular case. The 10 pence would be shown as a **minus** score (e.g. −10) in Row 3 of the Dynamic Calculations.

Now suppose you go out shopping again, taking 60 pence with you for a pint of milk, (Sign score, Row 1 – **inherited potential**), thinking that this will be enough. When you get to the shop you discover that milk costs 72 pence (House score, Row 2 – **environmental demands**). You will probably be feeling harassed and stressed because you do not have enough money to meet the demands of the environment. This would be shown by a **plus** score (e.g. +12) in Row 3.

Generally speaking, the more the environment makes demands on us for what we do not have (e.g. the higher the **plus** score) the more stress we will experience.

The Stress Total Column

As already mentioned, the Stress Total column relates to the general amount of stress and strain we are likely to experience in life – the demands, the expectations, the squeezing into shape, the needing to meet deadlines and so on. It is generally accepted that we need a certain amount of stress in our lives; too much and we become overloaded, too little and we become passive and inert. The difference score in Row 3 of the Stress Total column tells us about the overall level of stress that we are likely to experience in response to external pressures.

Scores of between +5 and +25 correspond to what we may term 'the comfort range', and indicate a level of stress that is perceived as normal and productive. Note that a score between +5 and +10 indicates little stress on the individual but also limited demand from the environment.

Minus scores

A **minus** score on Row 3 in this column indicates that the energy brought by inheritance is greater than the environment requires, so there is untapped, unused and unrecognised energy to spare – we have something to offer but the world does not want it, or does not see it.

This suggests that we have free space to do whatever we want to as there is an untapped well of wealth within us, that is not recognised by the environment. Outside pressures have little impact on our own inner resources. However, we may feel that the world is not considering our needs and that we do not belong. We may also experience rejection and be the black sheep of the family.

A minus score can also indicate repression or neglect. Discussion with a client will usually elicit which. A score of +5 is already a repression so even a **small minus score** should be considered as potential repression or neglect.

This is called **under forming**. Under forming presents opportunities for growth, and once this has been recognised by the individual the surplus energy maybe understood, harnessed and used.

Plus scores

A **plus** score on Row 3 in this column shows strong external demands our inner resources. It also indicates that we have been conditioned, to a greater or lesser extent by our environment. Plus scores show that the demands life is making are greater than the inherent qualities the individual has to deal with them.

Above +25, the pressures builds up. Generally speaking, the higher the score the more pressure and stress will be experienced. A **high plus score** shows that strong demands were made on our inner resources and that as children, we were strongly conditioned to behave according to the environment's expectations. In our early years and up until our mid-teens we respond by adapting and changing in order to meet the demands made upon us; only later do we start to become aware of our inner needs.

A Stress Total of greater than +35 shows too much conditioning. This can produce success but **is stressful** and the results will show in due course although this may take some years.

This is called **over forming**.

With a score in excess of +65 energy is likely to be channelled into survival of one kind or another. Some may adopt a very materialistic philosophy and have little interest in spiritual growth. They are often driven to succeed and seldom seek the help of psychologists or astrological counsellors. Others may choose to opt out of the world through various means (addictions, trancendental states, religious mania, suicide attempts) as they feel totally unable to meet the demands made upon them. Others, again, may leave society behind and go and live in very remote places like hermits, refusing what the world has to offer.

It is only when these individuals reconnect to who they are and become aware that they have choices that they can peel off some of their conditioning and appreciate what the world can teach them.

Summary

Comfortable:	between +10 and +25
Stressed:	
Underformed	minus score
Overformed	above +35

The zodiac represents our inner, inherited world whilst the house system is the outer world with its demands. Demands are what others expect of us but they are often set in motion by reaction brought about by our own unconscious action – or projection. The Dynamic Calculations highlight the differences.

Some people put out **less** energy than is available to them whilst others have to put out **more** than they have. Where this latter situation is strongly emphasised there is likely to be a specialist interest which demands an excessive energy output and this will be drawn from other planets – which then become a neglected, under-developed part of the personality resulting in problems in certain areas of life.

Those who use **less** energy than they have available put unused energy into the unconscious. Where the imbalance is significant, the result is repression in areas of assertiveness, possibly causing depression or psychosomatic illness as the person becomes eaten up by energy from inside. So the need to become aware of untapped energy, and learn how to develop and use it, is important.

Important Notes

- Dynamic Calculations are a valuable resource in interpretation but they require an **exact birth time**. A few minutes deviation in birth time can dramatically affect the Stress Total.

- Motivation and Temperament should normally be **considered separately**, as they are independently indicated by the analysis. For example, in Figure 5.4.2, the +52 score for the Water temperament represents a significant factor to be considered in its own right. However where there are significant parallel imbalances in both motivation and temperament, it may prove useful to relate these to the corresponding house or sign, as in the student example which follows.

How are Dynamic Calculations calculated?

These complex calculations are best done by computer. If you wish to understand how this is done, you will find a descriptive paper in the Study Resources on the website www.astrologicalpsychology.org.

Appendix Real Life Example from a Student

	Total	Crosses/Motivation			Temperaments/Behaviour			
		Cardinal	Fixed	Mutable	Fire	Earth	Air	Water
Signs	90	35	32	23	35	37	5	13
Houses	114	43	27	44	32	25	48	9
Difference	24	8	-5	21	-3	-12	43	-4

Figure 5.4.3 Toni 12.01.1957 03:40 GMT, London UK (See chart in Section 2, Example 3)

1. Fixed -5, Earth -12

These two totals point to me having more fixed energy and earth energy than the environment requires. Taken together Fixity and Earth relate to the 2nd house. As my age point progresses through it, 2nd house-type environments and the qualities of the sign of Taurus which in my chart lies across the DC and 7th house and contains my angular moon, could expect to be emphasised.

In terms of age progression I did have some very pleasing experiences between the ages of 6 and 12 in relation to my own artistic abilities. I was a very artistic child and loved drawing and painting. I also wrote poetry and stories. During this period I enjoyed a good deal of recognition for these talents at school. I also got my first longed for pet – a guinea pig.

From the point of view of the 2nd house environment, I am very content in my own home and garden where I can combine comfort, practicality and my own aesthetic sense to make a soothing and peaceful home. I also adore animals and love the presence and energy that my dog brings to my home.

In terms of the qualities of the sign, Taurus and my Taurean moon which can act as a vehicle for the expression of the excess energy, I am certainly aware of an abundance of affection and love for others which at times it is not appropriate for me to express. I am a very 'touchy-feely' person and recognise that this type of behaviour is not always welcomed unless the other knows me very well. Even my dog sometimes suffers my affectionate outbursts with resignation rather than enthusiasm!

The other ways I have found to express this energy are through pursuits like being in nature and I love the sensuous experience of walking in the countryside near my home, cooking tasty filling food, eating good food, creating a comfortable and pleasing environment for my home. I also often think that, when I am older and less busy with other things, I will take up drawing and water colours again as a hobby.

2. Mutable +21; Air +43

I have less inherited mutable and air energy than the environment demands of me and so felt most stressed whilst my age point was progressing through the 3rd house, which has Mercury and Sun on its cusp; as well as in 3rd house type environments, and generally in trying to express my own Geminian qualities through the 7th and 8th houses (no planets in Gemini).

From the age of 12 when I entered the 3rd house, school took on a very much more academic tone and I suffered from a sense of constant pressure. I always worked hard and diligently because I regarded education as a very serious business and because I was afraid of failure and of looking foolish (Capricorn). I think that I was protected from the worst stress as my age point progressed through this house by the interception of Aquarius which my age point entered when I was 13 and stayed in until mid-way through my 16th year. I did actually perform relatively well during this time in school work and examinations.

I would further say that I have felt under pressure throughout my life to be quicker, cleverer, sharper and more mentally adaptable. It is particularly in the area of oral expression that I suffer so that however hard I tried through qualifications and courses I could never become what I felt I should be and I always felt less able than those around me.

In terms of where the sign of Gemini lies in my natal chart, I can feel very stressed in social environments which require small talk. Luckily for me I am fascinated by other people and a good listener so that, on the whole, other people do all the talking. I am also easily intimidated by people who are bright and quick mentally and tend to get paralysed by anxiety because I know I can't compete at this level. In the past I was prone to judging myself harshly because of this but now I recognise that I have other things to offer which are equally valuable.

Exercise 5.4

1. First print your radix report, produced by your computer software/service. You will find your dynamic calculations at the bottom of the report.

2. Reflect on your understanding, and life experience, of any house-sign difference score for Motivation or Temperament (Row 3) which is less than +5 or more than +25, or alternatively where there is a marked imbalance in any combination of Motivation and Temperament.

3. If you have a Stress Total difference score (Row 3, extreme left hand column) which is less than +5 or more than +25, reflect on your life experience of this.

4. Look for scores of less than +5 or more than +25 in other charts of people you know, and consider how this relates to what you know of that person.

Chapter 6. The Element of Time

This chapter is concerned with the element of time in the birth chart. The Hubers' powerful method of Age Progression provides a Life Clock of significant influences over a person's lifetime. Traditional astrological approaches such as transits and progressions can provide additional information in the context of Age Progression. Age Progression also provides a valuable tool in the rectification of charts when the birth time is not accurately known.

Contents:

6.1 Age Progression in the Horoscope

Using the birth chart as a Life Clock can help us to identify major psychological growth points in life – past, present and future. These may be positive or negative but each is a potential step on the path to individuation. This section covers:

- The concept of Age Progression and the Age Point, and its relationship to houses, planetary aspects and signs.

- An example of Age Progression as experienced by a student.

Introduction

The concept of Age Progression and its application to the birth chart is both simple and profound. It is a vital part of any chart analysis. Astrology has traditionally linked the movement of the planets to the life of the individual with the 'day for a year' method known as secondary progressions. Age Progression differs markedly from this, in that it deals all the time with the natal chart, and what is reflected symbolically therein.

In some astrological circles there has been a tendency to perceive direct relationships between progressed or transiting planets in a horoscope and specific events in the life of an individual. When taken to extremes, the person may scarcely venture out of doors without having previously consulted an ephemeris to check on the transits for the day. What such a person fails to acknowledge is the complex and intricate relationship between inner and outer events. Just as the microcosm mirrors the macrocosm as described in the universal law 'As above, so below', so this may be seen in similar manner in terms of 'As within, so without'.

In astrological psychology, the individual chart is viewed as a reflection of our inner psychological structure. Through the passage of time, it is possible to indicate variations in our experience and perception of the world. Whilst it may be possible, using age progression, to describe certain qualities that will be associated with a specific experience at a given time in our lives, it does not necessarily follow that there will be any external event linked to this experience.

Since the birth chart reflects an inner psychological structure, inner changes of perception may take place without any specific external triggering event. It can therefore be extremely misleading to enter into the area of event prediction.

The Life Clock:

Man's Relationship to the Cosmic Numbers 72 & 6.

Age Progression involves viewing the birth chart symbolically as a time clock. The AC is the point where time begins for the newborn, and the hand of the clock moves anti-clockwise through the houses. Each house represents a six year period of life. At age 72 the hand of the clock arrives back at the AC and starts another cycle. The hand of the clock is referred to as the Age Point (AP).

Figure 6.1.1 shows the movement of the AP round the chart.

Why 72 years?

Symbolically 72 years can be seen as a 'cosmic day' when viewed against the 'great cosmic year' of 25,920

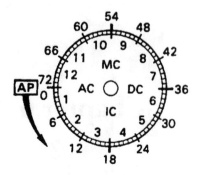

Figure 6.1.1 Life Clock

years. If we divide 25920 by 12 (the number of signs) we arrive at the cosmic month of 2,160 and this divided further by 30 (degrees in a sign) = 72.

Therefore if we divide 25,920 by 72 we arrive at 360°, i.e. the number of degrees in a circle. The number 72 is found in other areas including the time it takes for the precession of the Equinox to move through 1° of the Zodiac. It also approximates to the biblical life span of man – three score years and ten. In these and other ways it is possible to sense a relationship between man and the universe he inhabits. For Pythagoras the number 6 signified the world, and this was represented as a circle. Thus the number 6 has a relationship with the circle, the horoscope and the number 72.

House Systems and Age Progression

Although a relationship can be shown to exist numerically between man and the universe, applying these numbers meaningfully on a time basis to the horoscope took the Hubers many years of research. One of the many factors which required researching in detail was the whole area of House Systems. They investigated three such systems – Campanus, Placidus and Koch. The only system that yielded consistent results with the Age Progression was the Koch House System. All Huber charts are erected using the Koch House System.

The size of individual Koch Houses may show marked variations both within a single chart, and when comparing one chart with another. Sometimes one sign may extend across parts of three houses (and encompass at least one house fully). On other occasions where the house size is large there may be three zodiacal signs within the space of one house.

Whatever the size of the houses, the time taken by the Age Point to travel through a house remains constant at 6 years.

Calculating the Position of the Age Point

It will also be necessary to identify exactly where the Age Point is in the chart. The calculations for this are straightforward and instructions on how to do this are found in *LifeClock* page 24 'Calculation of the Age

Point'. This is usually done by computer, so is not something that you normally need to do.

When looking at a chart in detail it can be helpful to include all the age markers in one or a number of houses. Where there are planets located in a house, or there is a change of sign, these age markers can assist in clarifying the nature and timing of particular experiences or events.

The Intensity Curve in the Houses

As the AP moves through a house we meet another important feature of Age Progression. Within each house there is a focus on a particular theme, but the expression of that theme varies in intensity with the movement of the AP through the house. Just as we observe rhythms and cycles in the world of nature, so we also find cyclical patterns of energy with the movement of the AP. The two poles or extremes between which this energy moves are the house cusp and the Low Point (LP) in the house. See Figure 6.1.2.

The movement towards the period of high intensity begins with the AP moving over the Low Point in the previous house. There is a period of increasing focus which peaks with the AP going over the house cusp and then trails away as the AP travels towards the LP of the house.

You will remember from section 4.3 that the house cusps are zones of high activity, and it is here that energies accumulate most strongly and are intensely directed externally into the environment. Thus as the AP moves over each house cusp we find that our energies are actively engaged in outer work associated with the theme of that house.

In a similar fashion, a planet which is located close to a house cusp is able to express its energies outwards into the world effectively, particularly in relation to the activities associated with that house.

The Low Point is at the opposite end of the spectrum. It is at this point in each house that our outgoing energy is at its lowest. The passage of the AP over a Low Point often signals a period of exhaustion or depression – a time when we become inward-looking and introspective. It is a period of contraction of outer activity. We turn inwards and gather our energies in preparation for a shift in focus from the issues of one house to those of the next. It is a point of change. It may lead to a new awakening in consciousness if we allow the change to happen, or bring about a crisis if we resist.

The Low Point in the house is where we begin to move towards the next stage of our lives. Part of us has a fear of what the unknown may bring and there may be a resistance to the higher energy that is calling us. For at the LP there is a different energy working on

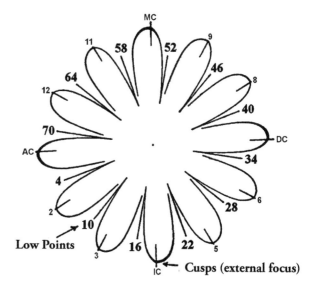

Figure 6.1.2

us. This is the point where we find a channel to our inner self. Planets at this point in our chart are tools we can use to go into the inner realm. At the LP the eternal quality of the Self reaches out to us from the inner circle in our chart. We don't stop our outer work altogether, but this is a time when inner work can be done on the soul. It can be a period of 'coming home' – our soul is always waiting for us.

The Low Point gives an opportunity to re-align ourselves with our inner self. It is the beginning of a new motivation and the energy to move into a new cycle.

The Low Point is reached three years eight months and fifteen days after entering a house. The measurement used for calculating the Low Point was given in section 4.3. In ratio terms this is 0·618034 through the house, slightly less than two thirds of the way through the house (the golden section).

The Balance Point (BP) is less readily identifiable than either the house cusp or the Low Point. Whilst the other two points are found at the extremes of the movement of energy, the BP is where these two extremes are held in balance. There is not the contraction of outer activity found at the LP, nor the intense expression found at the cusp with the possibility of that expression being beyond the control of the person.

At the Balance Point the two extremes are held in balance so that there can be controlled expression of the energies. Energies here can be focussed productively and intelligently. Projects commenced at the Balance Point can be of long duration if they have been undertaken with care and deliberation. The Balance Point is also 0·618034 into the house, but measured backwards from the cusp at the end of the house. We reach the Balance Point two years, three months and fifteen days after entering the house.

Within each house it can be seen that there are three separate areas: (i) house cusp to BP, (ii) BP to LP and (iii) LP to the next house cusp. Each of these areas is associated with one of the three crosses:

- the period from the cusp to the BP belongs to the cardinal cross, and the quality of impulse outward is much in evidence during this phase.

- From BP to LP is a period of consolidation and relates to the fixed cross.

- From the LP to the next house cusp is a period of change associated with the mutable cross.

Further observations on the elements and the crosses are included in the section entitled "The Movement of the Age Point through the Signs" on page 197.

We now move on to consider in turn the following aspects of Age Progression:

- The movement of the Age Point through the houses

- The movement of the Age Point through the signs

- The Age Point and the sign crosses

- The Age Point in aspect to planets

- Planets conjunct the AC

- The movement of the Age Point through occupied and unoccupied houses

- The movement of the Age Point through aspect holes

- The Age Point and counselling.

The Movement of the Age Point through the Houses

The movement of the Age Point through the houses is studied using **dynamic houses**. A dynamic house (or psychological house) stretches from the LP of the previous house to its own LP.

We have seen how there is a waxing and waning of energy through each house with the movement of the AP. As we observe processes both in ourselves and in the world outside we can detect three phases of development taking place. In the first phase (LP to cusp) a thought is conceived. This is followed by the impulse to action in the second phase (cusp to BP). In the third phase (BP to LP) the thought and the action lead to the creation of a form. But the process does not cease at this point. We stand back and look at the form we have created and see ways in which it could be improved, modified or altered completely. We once

again enter the first phase of thought and the process continues.

If we remain at the stage of form, then there is a danger that what we have created becomes fixed and crystallised.

This three-fold process of development can be observed in ourselves as we move through the twelve houses of the birth chart. In each house there is the process of creation taking place and the temptation to hold, in one fixed form or another, that which we have created. This crisis comes at the Low Point in each house, and is followed by the mutable quality of the last third of the house as it dissolves the outward form and leads us towards a new creation.

The Theme of Each House
A Brief Introduction

In the **First House** there is a gradual awakening in the child of the "I". The child initially acquires a sense of himself and his mother as something distinct from the rest of the world. This changes as the child becomes more and more aware of his own sense of identity, separate from his mother, which is highlighted in the 3-4 year age period, the stubborn phase.

In the **Second House** the child begins to create his own life space, and shows possessive behaviour about what he regards as his. This behaviour can lead to various problems or traumas for the child. In this house he is afraid of losing something and may build blocks or defence mechanisms around himself which in time can become crystallised forms.

In the **Third House** the adolescent enters the sphere of learning and education. She pushes out from the influence of the home and relates closely with her peer group. During this period first close friendships and love relationships may be experienced.

In the **Fourth House** the young person crosses over the IC/MC axis, the Individuation Axis. For the first time he enters the "You" side of the chart. He goes out into the world, and may come into conflict with his parents. Just as the first house related to developing a sense of 'I', so the next cardinal house (the fourth) is related to liberating himself as an independent person.

The **Fifth House** is a period related to love, creativity and self-exploration. Being a fixed house, there is an urge to an intimate or private atmosphere, and the person does not want interference from others. Whilst she will defend her privacy at home she can be active and dominant in pursuing professional and family goals.

In the **Sixth House** work and existence are emphasised. The highest value of Virgo has to do with service, and during this time the adult looks to the profession that satisfies him or her at an inner level. If the promptings of the higher Self are ignored at this stage, it may result in a degree of pain or suffering, with some people being thrown into twelfth house areas of behaviour to try and escape.

In the **Seventh House** once again the individual crosses over a major angle (the DC) and enters the conscious hemisphere of the chart. There is a looking across to the "I" on the AC, and some people are shocked at seeing themselves as they really are. When your "I" is right, you are happy with it and can give to the world and receive with reward.

However, if you are not happy with your self image and you project it onto the "You", difficulties will arise in relationships with friends and partners. The seventh house is related to Libra. In trying to achieve a balance whatever you do may be given back to you immediately, both good and bad. During this period decisions may be taken which affect the rest of one's life. This period can be a turning point where opportunities are offered for realising and becoming our true selves.

The **Eighth House** corresponds to a period of transformation, when many of the values of the first half of life are called into question. It is often referred to as the mid-life crisis. Our children become increasingly independent, and our spiritual and intellectual energies are available for other activities. The LP of the eighth house is also the LP of the whole chart, so it is not surprising that many people experience this time either as a crisis, or a period of transformation and rebirth.

The move into the **Ninth House**, and its associations with Sagittarius, Jupiter and wisdom, heralds the development of one's personal philosophy of life, based on the person's experiences. In this house there is a link with what Assagioli described as the super-conscious. From this high position in the chart, if the person has developed discrimination and judgment, they may be able to give advice to others. On the other hand, if a person has not found a reason for life, there may be a crisis of meaning around the Low Point.

As the individual moves into the **Tenth House** he reaches the highest point of the chart (MC). This can be a period of self-realisation and fulfilment. It is like the seed which germinates down on the IC and grows into full bloom on the MC as it rises up the Individuation Axis. The tenth house on the life clock represents the moment of truth insofar as those whose position or success is not based on an alignment with their inner being, but rather as received from others. They may find the collective unconscious operating from the fourth house with a deep shaking of the foundations of their very being. Adolph Hitler's suicide corresponded with Age Point on his Saturn in the tenth house.

It should be made clear that all people with Saturn in the Tenth House do not commit suicide when the AP reaches that planet. Saturn here may however bring some form of crisis related to a person's power. For a fuller description of this placement of Saturn refer to Liz Greene's book *Saturn – A New Look at an Old Devil*, pages 46-52.

In the **Eleventh House** the individual leaves behind the theme of growth along the Axis of Individuation and moves once again into the Relationship Axis. This is the house of freely chosen friendships, where the person can feel secure in him or herself and tolerate the views of others. It is a period when you find your real friends. Around the LP in this house, in the 20th century we approached 'enforced' retirement from work and for some this could be a time of feeling not needed anymore. From this LP up to the twelfth house cusp there appeared to be an increase in deaths, possibly associated with retirement shock.

The **Twelfth House** is a house of reflection and withdrawal from the world – a sense of coming home to the Father's house. Here we feel a sense of belonging to the whole, an inner security and a state of freedom. There is a reduction in personal striving, and the individual withdraws from the outer world into him or herself. The LP is between 69 and 70 years of age. Moving through this period leads to the completion of the path around the zodiac and at 72 we are astrologically re-born. For many this can be experienced as an increased vitality as we move into another spiral and re-experience the first house. It can be a time when the problems of childhood can be seen from a different perspective and more fully understood.

The Movement of the Age Point through the Signs

The speed of movement of the AP through the houses is constant – it takes six years to travel from one house cusp to the next. The size of the houses however can vary greatly. Large houses will contain two or more zodiac signs whilst small houses may only contain part of one sign. This is illustrated on page 61 of *LifeClock* where figure 2.6 shows on the one hand the AP transiting in three years a sign that forms only part of one house and on the other, the AP transiting in ten years a sign that has more than one house contained within it.

Where a house is small the AP moves slowly through it. Planets passed over and aspects formed by the AP make a deeper impression on the individual. Where the house size is large the individual may experience more going on around him and have the impression that time is passing more quickly, as he moves from one sign to another during the course of a six year period.

When the AP enters a sign in which there are planets it can be rather like entering a room and seeing at a glance the people within. It is an instant and important revelation of 'who' is there but, afterwards, it is necessary to meet, talk to and get to know each planet individually in the sign. This will normally happen when the AP becomes conjunct the planet(s).

Sign Changes

With the movement of the AP around the chart, there are a number of interrelated complex changes taking place at various times.

In discussing with a client the implications of the passage of the AP through a sign, the astrologer needs to take into account the relationship between the element of the sign that the AP occupies, the cross it belongs to and how this combines with the cardinal, fixed or mutable quality of the house it is in. Thus when moving through the sign of Pisces with its qualities of mutability and water, the change when Aries is reached will be particularly noticeable as the qualities of cardinality and fire are experienced. If at the same time Pisces occupies the sixth house and Aries the seventh, the mutable quality of the sixth house is very much in harmony with Pisces, and the cardinal quality of the seventh house will blend well with Aries, so the transition from one to the other will be pronounced.

If on the other hand there is not such an easy blending of house quality and sign quality, we need to consider the different energies that are operating to make sense of what was previously experienced as confusing and opposing forces.

The example of a client aged 46 may illustrate this: his AP has reached the LP of the eighth house. It has recently completed its journey through Aries and has been in Taurus for a little while. Already there will have been some unease between the cardinal quality of Aries in the fixed house, but now the fixed qualities of Taurus may try to hold onto things as they are as he enters the mutable zone of the eighth house and will shortly move into the mutable ninth house.

This will not be the first time he has experienced the conflict between sign and house quality and unravelling how he dealt with the conflicts before is likely to give him some insights into how he might respond this time. In making the nature of the discrepancy between sign and house quality conscious the individual is given a choice about how to act.

Moving from Water to Fire Signs
♓ to ♈, ♋ to ♌, ♏ to ♐.

As the AP moves out of the water sign into a fire sign, the marked difference in the nature of the elements is experienced clearly by the individual. The emphasis on feeling and emotion is changed into one of activity and creation. When the AP is going through a fire sign this is generally a time of increased energy and moving towards new goals.

Moving from Fire to Earth Signs
♈ to ♉, ♌ to ♍, ♐ to ♑.

During the fire phase, the individual has become creative, is optimistic in outlook, and there is a sense of moving forward. The move into the earth phase offers an opportunity to adjust and bring the dreams and ideals into some form of concrete expression. This is a time of planning, paying attention to details and working towards long term concrete goals.

Moving from Earth to Air Signs
♉ to ♊, ♍ to ♎, ♑ to ♒.

In the earth phase thinking has been focussed mainly on long term goals and practical realities. The move into air frees your thinking to a much more mental level. It is a good time for further learning or training. It may also be a time when we share knowledge with others, particularly during the AP passage through Gemini. Any rigid thought patterns and attitudes that were built up in the earth phase may now become much more flexible.

Moving from Air to Water Signs
♊ to ♋, ♎ to ♏, ♒ to ♓.

Moving into the water phase, the individual begins to leave behind an emphasis on the mental level and now experiences the emotional sphere and more spiritual dimensions. For those whose usual approach to the world is predominantly through the mind, this can be a strange experience as their patterns of thinking begin to be influenced by their feelings. If the feeling function can be accepted and valued it opens up another important channel of perception for the individual on the path of growth. Where it is resisted it may be experienced through depression or an unaccustomed moodiness, or vulnerability to criticism.

The Age Point and The Sign Crosses

Earlier we mentioned the influence of the crosses on the quality of the house occupied by the AP. We now consider the importance of the cardinal, fixed or mutable quality of the signs.

When the AP traverses the cardinal signs (♈, ♋, ♎, ♑) there is an impulse towards a creative process, a moving forward.

In the fixed signs (♉, ♌, ♏, ♒) attempts are made to bring forth some concrete expression of the creative impulse. Then strenuous efforts are made to defend and preserve what has been created.

With the move into the mutable signs (♊, ♍, ♐, ♓) what has been created is viewed from another perspective, and alternative possibilities present themselves. The old forms may be dissolved. There is no longer any clear goal direction, and the person moves back and forth between various positions. With the coming of the next cardinal sign a new impulse is created and the spiral continues.

The Age Point in Aspect to the Planets

The 72 Year Cycle

The 360° circle, when related to any single planet, can be seen as a cycle of growth. When the AP comes into conjunction with a planet, we usually have a deep experience of that planet and the energy that it symbolises and we become aware of the need for growth in the area of life related to that planet. During the next 36 years each aspect the AP makes to that planet is a time when a challenge is presented in a manner that requires related learning. At the opposition we can confront the challenge from an objective viewpoint so that the next 36 year cycle, from the opposition back to the conjunction, is a time when we can apply what we have learnt. See Figure 6.1.3.

Figure 6.1.3

Over 72 years the AP will form twelve aspects to each planet as it circles the zodiac. Not all of the aspects appear to have the same significance for an individual.

The two **primary aspects** are the conjunction and opposition of the AP to a planet. The semi-sextile, sextile, trine and quincunx are viewed as **secondary aspects** in terms of the Age Progression.

When looking at events or experiences associated with the passage of the AP over a particular planet, it is important to note the natal aspects to that planet and any aspect pattern involving the planet since the position of the AP will activate the aspect pattern or patterns in addition to the planet with which it is conjunct.

The opposition of the AP to a natal planet allows a person a much broader perspective and so it is possible to see the panorama of surrounding conditions associated with the planet.

During a thirty-six year period the individual is given opportunities for learning about the nature and function of the energies symbolised by a particular planet in the chart. The period starts when the AP makes one or other of the primary aspects to the natal planet. There then follow five secondary aspects before meeting the other primary aspect. Life does not expect us to learn everything at one sitting so to speak, but sets a process in motion and then offers additional opportunities to add to one's understanding over a considerable period of time.

Whilst the two primary aspects are usually associated with important experiences and/or events that an individual can recall many years later, due recognition should also be given to the secondary aspects. The two learning aspects, semi-sextile and quincunx, especially the latter, can mark important turning points in a person's life. One example would be the AP quincunx natal Pluto. The square to a planet or to two natal planets in opposition can similarly be an important period.

The nature of individual experience is so varied that it would be misleading to suggest that in a few paragraphs one could encapsulate what each of us experiences as the AP passes a given planet. The few illustrations that follow are not intended to be exhaustive. You will be able to deepen your understanding of this subject as you become aware of your own pattern of growth, listen to the experiences of others and become more familiar with the language of symbolism.

Many people report a sense of awakening, or becoming themselves or contacting their essential nature as the AP passes over the Sun in their chart. The passage over the Moon may be a period of heightened emotion or an intense emotional experience. In the charts of some women it may correspond with the birth of a child. Mercury will usually be found to relate to some theme linked to communication. It can sometimes be a period in which teaching or learning is undertaken. Venus and Mars symbolise the feminine and masculine principles and these will be activated in both men and women. Jupiter can be experienced as a time of expansion, but this will depend on its placing in the chart, and which other planets are aspected to it.

Saturn, the great teacher, often brings important lessons in one form or another. Some people marry on an aspect to Saturn, and the theme of security is likely to be the basis for their marriage. Others may marry on an aspect to Jupiter, signifying that the union is seen as the start of a period of personal growth.

As one would expect, AP passing over Uranus can be accompanied by the unexpected, whilst Neptune can be experienced as being in a fog for a while. It may also activate a spiritual awakening. Pluto for many people is experienced as a time of transformation, although the nature of the transformation may be specific to the person. If one is trying to hold onto old forms when something new is trying to be born, there can be pain associated with the experience. Where there has been a major transforming event or experience in a person's life, the position of Pluto can assist in rectifying the chart. Within the Huber approach, extremely fine gradations of horoscope analysis can be made provided that a birth time has been accurately recorded. With an accurate birth time the experience of the AP conjuncting a planet may cover a six month period, the intensity reaching a peak over a two to four week period somewhere in the middle of this period.

With an approximate birth time the margin for error is wide. It would be ill-advised to be specific about the timing of events or experiences in the future. Age Progression is an extremely useful tool for analysing one's own or another person's chart, but it is essential, with UK births in particular, to constantly bear in mind the uncertainty of birth times.

When discussing a client's birth chart it is easy to relate specific events to individual planets – for example: 'I got married on a sextile to Saturn', or 'My marriage broke up when the Age Point passed over Pluto', and to forget that these events were not just isolated incidents that happened on one day of a year, but rather were part of a process that unfolded over a period of time.

The message is to avoid using Age Progression to forecast specific events on specific days, and to assist a client to perceive the unfolding nature of their experience over time. We may then be able to detect more easily and at an earlier stage our own experiences related to Age Progression in our charts, and thus become more sensitive to the experiences in others.

Planets Conjunct the AC

Planets in the twelfth house within 3° or 4° of the AC may relate to circumstances which affected the mother during pregnancy. Where a planet is within a few minutes of arc of the AC it will relate to the birth process.

Once again however, the importance of accurate birth times cannot be overstressed since it is apparent that a birth time which is five or ten minutes adrift, may invalidate the above interpretation.

Movement of AP through Occupied and Unoccupied Houses

All birth charts have at least one unoccupied house (allowing for the ten planets and the North Node). Some charts have four, five or six unoccupied houses. Is there a different quality of experience when the AP moves through a house with planets in it compared to one where there are no planets?

A tenanted house will generally be more energised than an unoccupied house in the same way that a room full of people is more alive and vibrant than an empty room. Your experience of the passage of the AP through an occupied house will probably therefore be more noticeable and possibly less comfortable than when the AP crosses an unoccupied house. However it is important to be aware that, although a house may be unoccupied by planets, the AP will make aspects to planets in other houses as it moves through, and these aspects may be especially meaningful to us.

Passage of AP over Aspect Holes

The environment has direct access to the core of the individual where one aspect structure ends and there is a hole or an empty space before the beginning of the new aspect structure. See Figure 6.1.4, which shows such a hole between Pluto and Uranus.

The AP crossing such an empty space is usually experienced as a period of vulnerability to the environment. The individual has no direct protection. Leaving one aspect structure and not yet reaching another can be like jumping out into space, and understandably some people resist doing this.

At the **midpoint** between the two aspect structures, the pull of the new structure will be felt, and the intensity of the experience will have passed its peak. This brings awareness of the temporary nature of this experience and give some indication of its duration.

Figure 6.1.4 Aspect Hole

The Age Point and Formative Influences

Although a child is born into this world with a specific pattern of psychological energies it is almost certain that early environmental influences will affect that pattern and, to a greater or lesser extent, determine how the child develops into adulthood. In the same way as a baby learns to behave in ways that will ensure survival, crying to be fed or attracting attention to be loved, so similarly the growing child learns to adapt to and cope with environmental influences and parental messages.

Adapting to, or conforming with, childhood pressures and traumas may be detrimental to natural development and the effects can last well into, if not throughout, adult life. The ability to identify, from the birth chart, the circumstances which might have necessitated adaptation of the natural energy pattern can be a valuable first step in counselling.

The AP in the first quadrant (the first 18 years of life) provides a key to this unravelling process and by looking at its conjunction and opposition aspects to planets in the first and third quadrants, as well as other factors, such as Low Points, an understanding of potentially relevant childhood experiences can be developed.

The nature of the planet(s) aspected, as well as the colour of aspect lines to the planet(s) involved will give clues as to the nature and timing of the childhood experience. For instance conjunctions will indicate experiences in which the child felt a deep personal involvement, whilst oppositions will be more likely to give the feeling of having been caught up with, and carried along by events.

Red aspects will suggest a negative trauma where struggle was involved. Blue aspects may have been an easier experience with a more positive outcome indicated, though it could still have been difficult for the child at the time. Green aspects will signify a learning experience.

The nature of the event suggested by the planet(s) involved will be related to the astrologically accepted meaning of those planets. For example an aspect of the AP to Uranus will imply an upheaval, move or change, i.e. some kind of up-rooting experience which may also result in a psychological break from the mother/caregiver. Whilst a long-lasting disturbance could be created by the event it is not necessarily bad if it can be understood, because the experience might well have provided an opportunity for the child to learn how to stand on its own feet. When looking at childhood experiences in the chart it is, of course, important also to observe the relationships between Sun, Moon and Saturn. (See Chapter 5.)

As a further example, if we look at aspects of the AP to planets in the second and eighth Houses it will be apparent that they will relate to traumas that are going to affect the child's attitude towards security. So, the arrival of a brother or sister might create jealousy and protectionism and trigger-off the build-up of security barriers. The loss of toys, for whatever reason, which were of special significance to the child, may have a similar effect. The loss of a parent through divorce or death can create attitudes which in adult life also reflect the fear of loss and the consequent need to cling to people or possessions.

Barriers built up in the second house can cause problems as the AP moves from the LP of this house and encounters the mutability of the third house. The third house requires flexibility and the ability to adapt to, and mix with, others. Problems carried forward into this area of life can lead to learning difficulties at school.

It is valuable to become aware of our childhood confrontations with life and to reflect on what may have happened at a certain age and how this may have impacted on our adult life.

Essential Reading
LifeClock by Bruno & Louise Huber

Recommended Reading
Saturn – A New Look at an Old Devil by Liz Greene

Real life example of Age Progression

Approach taken

To keep this exercise within bounds I've concentrated on the effects of Age Point (AP) related to house cusps and Low Points (LP), sign changes, and planetary conjunctions (☌) and oppositions (☍). I've tried to relate these to major internal and external events of my life, and indicated the few cases where there doesn't appear to be much correlation.

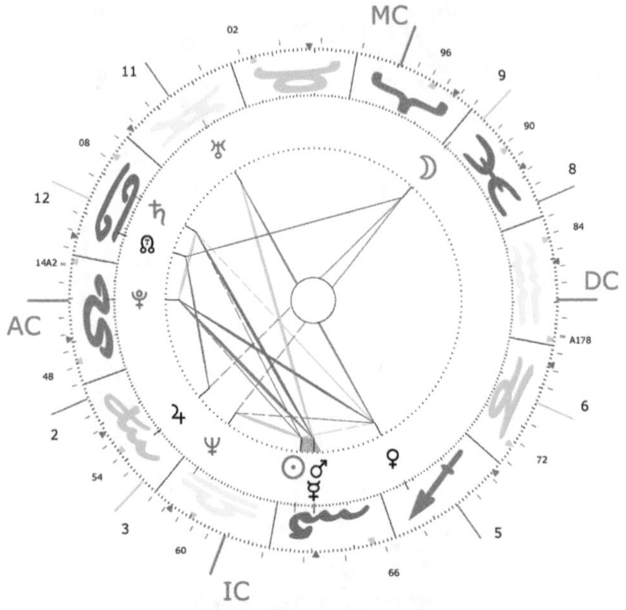

Figure 6.1.5 Peter
28.10.1944, 2245 GMT, 53N14, 0W32

1. Childhood and adolescence – ages 0-17

Bruno and Louise's Life Clock speaks of the emotional traumas that result from conjunctions and oppositions occurring in passing of AP through the first quadrant, i.e. the first 18 years of life. Here is my understanding of how this and the house/sign factors have worked for me.

AP ☌ ♇ in ♌ at birth, at AC

As far as I can remember, I've always had a strong sense of my own powerful and controlled individuality. Perhaps not everyone does?!

After I was born my mother contracted a virus in the maternity hospital and had to stay in for a while. I did not get the virus, but this could have been traumatic from a baby's perspective!

AP into ♍, 11/12/49, age 5, also cusp 2 at age 6

I was a happy young child up to 5, happy to play on my own. Just before AP into Virgo I was appropriately taken into the controlled environment of the infant school, hating it for the first few weeks. After a stressful period (up to cusp?) I adapted and worked hard.

2nd house LP, 9/7/54, age 9¾
AP ☌ ♃☋, 3/2/55, age 10¼

From age 10, around my third year in junior (primary) school, I can identify two significant features embedded in my being, each of which can be fairly obviously related to the qualities of Jupiter:

I was developing a love of learning, which has lasted throughout my life to date. The urge has always been to organise that learning systematically (Virgo).

At primary school I was always near the top of the class, vying with two girls. (This was particularly competitive in the last year or so, as the red aspect to Moon was encountered.) This left a legacy of a feeling of superiority to other people, which only later received its inevitable come-uppance.

♃/♆ midpoint, 5/2/57, age 12¼, also cusp 3, age 12

I remember that my last primary school year was also a time of deep uncertainty. I had fainting fits in assembly, then fear of fainting. I was also afraid of going to secondary school. This can be related to both the stress before the 3rd house cusp and to the gap between Jupiter and Neptune. The cusp is at age 12, just after I went to secondary school. By the midway turning point of the gap, at 12¼, I was comfortably established. The fear of fainting remained hidden, only to emerge in times of stress.

AP ☍☽, 1/6/57, age 12½

My first year in secondary school, soon to be in long trousers(!), before puberty got into full swing. Several significant features emerged around this time, of which I only became self-aware many years later:

I developed a strong fear of authority figures, lasting into adulthood, possibly related to bullies at school – both teachers and boys. Paradoxically I was generally left alone – I was a 'good boy' for the teachers, not bullying-tolerant with Pluto on the AC (and square Mars). Around this time I once hit a boy who tried to bully and ran, regardless of the consequences. This 'cornered response' became apparent again on odd occasions during the other vulnerable 'gap' between Venus and Moon.

I developed a pattern of 'approval seeking', afraid to exert myself and risk the disapproval of others (probably related to my mother and her expectations).

I did not connect fully with my feeling nature at this time (one-way aspects to Moon?), and never really got to understand and own my feelings until AP conjunct Moon.

AP into ♎, 14/10/57, age 13

Later in 1957, near my 13th birthday, AP moved into Libra. Around this time my interest in maths was kindled by a good teacher, and I became very keen on playing chess – both 'airy' enterprises.

AP ☌ ♆, 7/2/59, age 14¼

I developed interests that were to remain and develop further, and are associated with Neptune:

An early interest in science fiction eventually became an interest in strange events, then the occult, and eventually understanding the world of spirit.

There was an essential idealism in my character from around this time that has remained to this day. Fairness and balance (Libra and the 'Ear/Eye' with Sun/Neptune) have always figured strongly here.

Neptune is opposite Moon, and it is perhaps through this 3/9 link that my persistent interest in idealistic philosophy was inspired.

Linking into the green aspect, and the Ear/Eye, for the first time, my enthusiasm for study increased beyond that of my contemporaries at school. I was the one who always finished the maths homework!

3rd house LP, 18/7/60, age 15¾

LP3 perhaps relates to the general uncertainty of adolescence at this time. LP3 is also square Saturn; I remember the relationship with mother being 'on' or 'off' at this stage, reinforcing my approval-seeking pattern.

2. At home in the 4th house – ages 18-23

The 4th is a large house, with lots of planets and signs. There seemed to be a lot going on.

From the cusp – coming under Sun's influence

I worked hard to pass university entry exams, but with less support from the school as my maths teacher had left (now out of third house of learning?). In late 1962 came the impulse, inspired by a school friend, to leave school early and become a holiday camp barman. This provides good evidence of coming under the influence of Sun for the first time, as midpoint Sun-Neptune was passed.

AP into ♏, 13/12/63, age 19

I went to university in October 1963, was soon in an intercepted sign! My first year was hard working, resulting in a scholarship, but correspondingly not very outward-going. The mathematics proved to be not as exciting as I'd anticipated (Libran expectations running aground in Scorpio?).

AP ☌☉, 2/7/64 , age 19¾

In the second year I was much more outgoing, trying out modern pentathlon, joining societies, playing more chess etc. An identity (Sun) was being forged.

There was recognition from the local chess 'family' (4th house) when I was elected president of the university chess club in 1965. [AP was square Pluto on 5/1/65, trine Saturn on 25/1/65 and quincunx Uranus on 1/4/65 – sounds like heavy backup!] The easy-going Trampoline that AP had engaged enabled this presidency to be fulfilled reasonably well.

AP ☌☿/♂, 16/1/65, age 20¼

In this second year I played more chess, and in particular was very excited by 5-minute chess, an archetypal Mercury/Mars sport requiring fast thought and action.

AP into ♐ 10/2/67, age 22¼, also LP 4 at 21¾

I graduated in 1966, immediately followed by uncertainty at the 4th house LP. I did a computing diploma, staying in the safe university environment (still intercepted Scorpio). After this I'd had enough of university and ventured out into the world (now in Sagittarius, not intercepted) getting a job at a computer company.

AP ☌♀, 24/11/67, age 23

I married Jane in December, within a month of the exact conjunction.

I was out in the vulnerable 'gap' accompanied by spiky red aspects rather than the green that had accompanied later school and university years. I **was** more spiky. The incomplete Irritation triangle based on Venus/Uranus erupted a few times as Jane and I adapted to living together, but we still clicked (our Plutos click!)

AP☍♅, 29/5/68, age 23½

In August 1968 we moved up north for work. It was hard work adapting at first – moving through the stress zone to the 5th house cusp.

3. Reaching the horizon – ages 24-35

I was now out in the world and working hard, but the chart was much quieter!

AP □♃ July 1969, age 24¾

We moved into a new house. I had quite a lot of business travel about the country (Sagittarius).

AP into ♑, 18/7/71, age 26¾

I transferred to a 'New Range' project in autumn '71 – more interesting work, involving less travel, a more grounded job (Capricorn – Earth). In 1971 I won the British Correspondence Chess Championship – I'd lived a lot of my 5th house relationships by correspondence!

5th house LP, 8/7/72, age 27¾

Around this time of change I transferred office again, gave up correspondence chess, we decided to have a baby, and had a car crash in the autumn. Harry was born in March just after AP semi-sextile Venus.

6th house cusp 29/10/74, age 30

Late 1974 was very busy workwise, working 12-hour shifts to get a product ready for release. I was very much faced with the realities of life in the 6th house!

Suzanne
In February 1975 our second child Suzanne was born. She died 8 days later due to a problem not understood at the time. We were devastated. There is nothing on the Life Clock, apart from a trine Jupiter coming in August. [In House Chart AP is square Moon – the environment was applying a strong emotional shock.] [Other clues lie in transits, but that's another story.]

AP ☍☊, 19/2/76, age 31¼
I was embedded in the workaday and family world of the South Node at this time. [I had also joined Samaritans as a volunteer in 1975, a very 6th house activity.]

AP into ♒, 13/3/78, age 33¼, also LP6 at 33¾
Aquarius brought new awakenings, and revisiting passions of my teens – when last in an air sign. I joined a tennis club, went to a chess congress, and explored spiritual possibilities.

Midpoint ♀/☽, 18/12/78, age 34¼
Soon after LP6 came the midpoint in the huge gap on the 'you' side of my chart. I emerged from the strong influence of Venus to come increasingly under the Moon. The vulnerabilities that were undoubtedly there began to dissolve. I became more outward going (helped by AP square Sun in 1979).

AP ☍♇, 26/9/80, age 36, also the DC
Coming up to the DC and the Pluto opposition was an exciting time. We became part of a group of friends. There were outings, parties, new experiences. Perhaps inevitably with Pluto there were issues of sex, power and control. It was almost like we were experiencing the 60's, that archetypal Aquarian age, now! I was entering the 7th house of conscious relationships!

4. Third quadrant – ages 36-57

The quiet time for planetary contacts continued as the second part of the Venus/Moon gap was bridged.

7th house LP, 8/7/84, age 39¾
Just before LP7 I left Samaritans, archetypal 6th/7th house activity. Workwise this was a difficult time, being taken over by new management we were struggling to retain influence. This was eventually resolved by change of role and move of job location.

AP into ♓, 11/12/85, age 41¼, also cusp 8 at 42
With the transition to Pisces the Aquarian group of friends had dissolved, and residual relationships were running into the buffers in wells of emotion (Moon/Pisces).

We moved house in the stress zone before the 8th house cusp. Yes it was stressful! The 8th house is about doing things for society and other people's possessions. I was duly first a business manager then a strategic planning manager, responsible for the future of parts of the company's business.

Following AP quincunx Neptune in 1987 I joined a spiritual school early 1988 and was introduced to meditation. (After a couple of years I realised that they were rather cultish, and joined the Arcane School instead.)

AP ☍♃, 3/2/91, age 46¼, also LP 8 at 45¾
Around LP8 it was clear my career was going nowhere – my manager said so. I was uncertain what the future held. However, things changed round about the Jupiter opposition. The management changed. I was offered a more responsible job at the senior management level – a real Jupiterian expansion!

AP ☌☽, 1/6/93, age 48½, also cusp 9 at 48, AP into ♈ 14/10/93, age 49
1992/93 was a period of great activity and new initiatives. At work, I expanded to take on the Quality function, corresponding with my idealism (probably triggered again by the opposition to Jupiter/Neptune midpoint and AP trine North Node).

As AP went into Aries I also led establishing public evening lectures in October 1993, inspired at cusp 9 by Bristol Schumacher Lectures, and by seeing the Dalai Lama just before AP conjunct Moon. These lectures were about the very 9th house pursuit of clarifying philosophies and developing wisdom – someone said I had set them up as my own philosophy course!

Around this time I also started studying astrological psychology.

It was only now, reaching AP☌☽, that the problems/traumas resulting from childhood were clear to me and being reasonably well handled, if not fully resolved. For example, I was no longer scared of senior managers!

Exercise 6.1

1. Study the movement of the Age Point in your own chart and identify individual events or periods of time in your life that coincided with the Age Point making significant aspects to planets, moving into a new house and/or new sign, passing over a Low Point, etc.

   NB If you are unable to find any significant interaction between the journey of the Age Point in your chart and events or periods of time in your life, it may be that your birth time is not accurate. Should this be the case, you may want to come back to this exercise after studying Section 6.3 on Rectification.

2. Once you've identified some important AP transits, allow yourself time to reflect on your experiences of these and the changes that they have had on your understanding and outlook on life.

6.2 Progressions and Transits

This section explores the relationship of two more traditional astrological approaches to time in the birth chart with Age Progression: progressions and transits.

Introduction

Terrestrial time is a human invention based on the movement of the planets in the sky and the movement of the Sun in particular, since it divides day from night and its changing declination also defines the seasons. Our lives are ruled to a great extent by time.

Astronomy, and therefore astrology, is based on time – cycles of time which measure the movements of all heavenly bodies, including the rotation of our own planet on its axis, the movement of all the bodies in our solar system around the Sun and, to a lesser extent, the movement of our solar system around the galactic centre.

A birth chart is a map of the Sun, Moon and planets in our solar system, their relationship to one another, and their relationship to our geographical place of birth. So the birth chart captures not only a moment in time but also the pattern of cosmic energy that existed at that time. As this pattern of energy is in a constant state of movement it follows that if we are linked into a moment in time and the universal energies which existed then, we shall continue to be affected by any subsequent changes in those energies. These changes are cyclical and astronomers can measure them with accuracy.

These cosmic cycles seem to be reflected in our own psychological and spiritual development so it is possible for an astrologer to help a client to become aware of these stages of growth and of their own unfolding personality. In moments of crisis, which can often accompany life changes, it can be reassuring for a client to be told that what is happening in their life corresponds with these cycles and can have a positive outcome.

In the context of time and cycles, every autumn many trees go through a time of crisis as they lose their leaves. But this 'letting go' process needs to happen. New leaves and further growth can come about in the Spring time that will follow. Something similar happens with human beings. It is our ability to understand these cycles and their meaning in terms of an individual life that can make astrology a valuable tool to facilitate this process of personal growth.

However it is important that we do not succumb to the temptation to use this ability to predict the future. Astrology is a powerful tool and predictions can sometimes become self-fulfilling prophecies. Progressions in all their different forms need to be seen as means to bring clarity where confusion exists, and to assist someone to be able to make conscious decisions in taking the next step forward in their life.

There are many books available on the subject of progressions and transits, so in this section we do no more than introduce these topics as being ancillary to the main subject which is the use of the chart as a Life Clock.

The principle underlying progressions and transits is very simple. At the moment of birth the positions of the planets are plotted and the natal chart is drawn. However, the movement of the Moon around the Earth, and of the planets around the Sun, continue and with the passing of time all will make many angular aspects to the natal positions. It has become generally accepted by astrologers that such celestial aspects seem to reflect themselves in the terrestrial environment, at the level of both the individual and the collective.

To have any real understanding of the likely effect of a progressed or transiting planet it is necessary to take account of everything in the natal chart which is relevant to the individual. They can be seen as moments in time when the universe is shining a searchlight on a person's life, highlighting and activating areas of our lives that have special significance at that particular time and need acknowledgement. Our lives are a process of continual growth. In order for this to take place we need to be willing to make changes and let go of some things which are no longer appropriate. In the same way as the leaves on a tree need to die in the Autumn to make room for new growth, so the same process needs to take place in us as human beings.

Transits and progressions, as well as Age Progression, can be used to bring awareness of the areas of life that may demand attention, but **we should be careful not to use them to predict the future**. We have free will and this can always override, for better or for worse, external influences from whatever source.

Progressions

Under this general heading come the different ways of looking at the progressed positions of planets and their relationship to the positions of the planets in the natal chart. Astrologers use various methods to examine the interaction of orbiting planets with the fixed planetary positions of the birth chart. Included amongst these are Primary and Secondary Progressions.

Primary Progressions

These are not in general use, partly because of the complicated calculations necessary and partly because a birth time needs to be known within seconds of time for any degree of accuracy. Calculations are based on the diurnal rotation of the Earth on its axis and an error in the birth time of only 4 minutes would result in an error of a year in the timing of an event.

Secondary Progressions

In more general use, these are based on the concept of a 'day for a year'. In other words the positions of the planets, the AC and the MC on the day after you were born correspond to one year of age. The positions 10 days after you were born correspond to ten years of age, and so on. Needless to say the slower moving outer planets are less significant than the faster moving inner planets, especially the Sun and Moon, as well as the AC & MC. Aspects made by the Moon to natal planets are considered most significant although the interpretation of an aspect made by any progressed planet is taken into account.

Noon Date

Appropriate computer software can give progressed positions on any chosen date. Otherwise, since the positions of planets are only shown for noon and/or midnight in the ephemeris, it is either necessary to interpolate the exact longitude of the planet which corresponds with a particular date in a year, or find the date in any year which corresponds with the noon position of the planet. The position of a planet as shown in a noon ephemeris will always correspond to the same date each year.

This date, known as the noon date, can be calculated quite easily using a 'Calculation of Noon Date' Table published by L.N.Fowler & Co.Ltd.

Transits

The birth chart shows the position of each planet against the zodiac at the time of birth, but we know that planets are in constant motion so their position alters with every moment of passing time.

If, by looking up the positions of the planets in the ephemeris at regular intervals, we plotted the passage of each planet on a chart we would see that eventually each one, **depending upon its speed of movement through the zodiac**, would be at a point in the chart where it was making a significant angular relationship, or aspect, either to its own natal position or to another planet in the chart.

These aspects, known as **transits**, may be times in life when a person can become more aware of both an area of life as well as the nature of the energy symbolised by the planet being aspected in the chart. In view of the fact that the faster moving planets will make very rapid transitory aspects, astrologers tend to pay more attention to the transits of the slower moving planets, those from Jupiter to Pluto.

Transits, Progressions and Age Progression

Why do some transits appear to have a very significant effect in a person's life and others pass with little or no apparent effect?

Most astrologers will have asked themselves why, for example, an important transit of Saturn to its natal position sometimes passes without apparent effect and at other times can be a major turning point in life. So a few words need to be said about transits and secondary progressions and their relationship to Age Progression.

The Age Point is the primary element in studying progressions. Secondary progressions and transits appear to have much more of an effect on the individual when they are thematically related to the AP.

Research suggests that a transit or progression becomes particularly important when the AP is also making an aspect that has a relationship to the planet or life area under consideration. For example if natal Saturn is in the 5th house just before the cusp of the 6th house it will probably be conjoined by the AP at the same time as transiting Saturn is conjunct natal Saturn, i.e. the first 'Saturn Return'. This suggests that this period will be experienced as a significant time by the individual and may well be a time when he or she first consults an astrologer.

Effect of a Transit

It might be worth bearing in mind that a transiting planet is unlikely to have any direct physical effect on an individual. It seems more likely that interacting energies, universal and personal, create psychological disturbances which generate irrational fears or euphoria, triggering behaviour patterns or attitudes which bring about an undesired reaction from the environment, or an effect on our own physical wellbeing.

Transit Orbs

Because of the alternating direct and retrograde motion of a transiting planet it will often happen that it makes a number of contacts with the natal planet. The first will be when its movement is direct, next will be during a retrograde passage, and finally when the transiting planet is moving forward again.

Figure 6.2.1 shows natal Venus at 16° 28' in Pisces with transiting Jupiter making a conjunction on 3 occasions during 1986: direct on 7th May, retrograde on 21st September, direct again on 25th December.

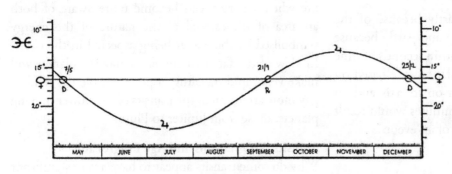

Figure 6.2.1

Experience suggests that when an aspect is repeated because of this retrograde movement each transit of the natal planet will be felt differently.

For instance, the first direct transit may create an awareness of the life situation that is being spotlighted, whilst the retrograde passage will often be felt more strongly and may act as the trigger for action. The third, direct, contact may either be a final nudge or may pass unnoticed depending on what the individual has done during the earlier contacts. Hence, many astrologers believe that the retrograde movement is the one that will be the most significant.

A transit aspect is said to be approaching before the exact point of angular contact with a natal planet, and separating after this point. There is no general agreement on the orb for an aspect from a transiting

planet though it is suggested that 2° of arc might be reasonable during the approach to the exact aspect, and 1° of arc during its separation from being exact.

Recording Transits

We suggest that, initially at least, you take account only of aspects made by the slower moving transiting planets, Pluto, Neptune, Uranus, Saturn and Jupiter, and that you record only the major aspects opposition, trine, square and conjunction. Aspects made by the faster moving planets are more likely to be short term in effect though they could indicate the moment when a more major transit aspect is triggered.

One method used to record transits is as follows. From Figure 6.2.1 you will see that it is important to be aware of whether the transiting planet is moving direct or retrograde. The ephemeris on, say, 4th May 1986, shows that Jupiter was travelling direct and was going to make an exact conjunction with natal Venus in 3 days time. This could be recorded as:

$$\text{♃}_{t} \, \text{☌} \, \text{♀}_{r} \, (A)$$

The 'r' signifies that Venus is the radix, or natal planet, and the 't' that Jupiter is the transiting planet. The (A) indicates that, on the day that you looked up a transit the exact aspect had not yet been made and was approaching. An (S) would indicate that the exact aspect had already been made and that the planets were separating.

Still referring to Figure 6.2.1, if you had looked in the ephemeris on, say, 23rd September 1986 you would note that an exact conjunction of Jupiter with Venus had taken place two days earlier. Therefore the aspect was separating and at the time Jupiter was retrograde. You would have recorded the data thus:

$$\text{♃}_{t\,R} \, \text{☌} \, \text{♀}_{r} \, (S)$$

When looking at transits in relation to a natal chart it is as well to have some method of recording these so that instead of just looking at the transits which are operative on a single day you can become aware of the wider trends at work over a period of time.

The following shows a graphic method of recording planetary transits over a period of time, related to Helen, whose birth chart is in Figure 6.2.2. This method can be adapted to suit the individual astrologer and allows for transiting aspects to be recorded over any period of time.

Figure 6.2.2 Helen's Natal Chart
7th December 1959, 14·25 GMT, London, UK

In Figure 6.2.3 (next page) transits have been calculated and are displayed for the year 2001.

• Planets are listed in numerical order.

• The dates shown are when aspects are exact.

• Only aspects from transiting outer planets have been taken into account.

• Only major aspects have been considered.

• Aspects to AC and MC have not been included.

The display can be made visually more graphic by linking an ongoing aspect with a line of a colour which reflects the nature of the energy of the transit. So an ongoing square aspect of, say, Pluto to natal Sun would be linked with a red line, and an ongoing trine a blue line, and so on. In this way it is possible to get an idea of the overall nature of the aspecting energies for the period under review.

For instance if the dominant colour appeared to be blue, it could be assumed that it would be a period of stability, consolidation, calmness and so on. Whereas if the picture appeared to be predominantly red it is likely that it would be a time of activity, and perhaps conflict.

Secondary Progressions

Figure 6.2.4 shows the secondary progressions for Helen for 2001, the year of her 42nd birthday.

☉	27° 31'	♑	10th House
☽	20° 22'	♍	5th
☿	22° 21'	♑	9th
♀	19° 33'	♒	7th
♂	03° 11'	♑	8th
♃	22° 28'	♒	8th
♄	11° 31'	♑	9th
♅	19° 56'	♌	4th
♆	09° 00'	♒	6th
♇	05° 45'	♍	5th

Figure 6.2.4
Helen's Secondary Progressions for 2001

If you refer to an ephemeris and count 42 days on from the date of birth you can confirm for yourself where these planetary longitudes have been found. Since the birth time was 14:25, you will need to allow for the movement of the Moon between noon and 14:25 on the 18th January.

Interpretation - Secondary Progressions.

In all interpretations of progressed planets, whether secondary progressions or transits, you are considering the effect that one planet is likely to have on another planet which it aspects. Needless to say it is important to consider the interpretation in the context of the natal chart positions. It is also important, when considering secondary progressions, to remember that in the course of one day most planets will make only a maximum progression of 1° or so, other than the Moon which will move approximately 14° in 24 hours.

Looking at Helen's progressed planets we note that progressed Moon will be opposite radix Moon. This would suggest that the early months of 2001 will be a time when Helen will be confronted with emotional issues. In fact progressed Moon will be semi-sextile Uranus so creating an Irritation Triangle. This will be in the 5th house of relationships, perhaps giving a clue to the area of life being affected.

All other planets will also need to be considered in turn.

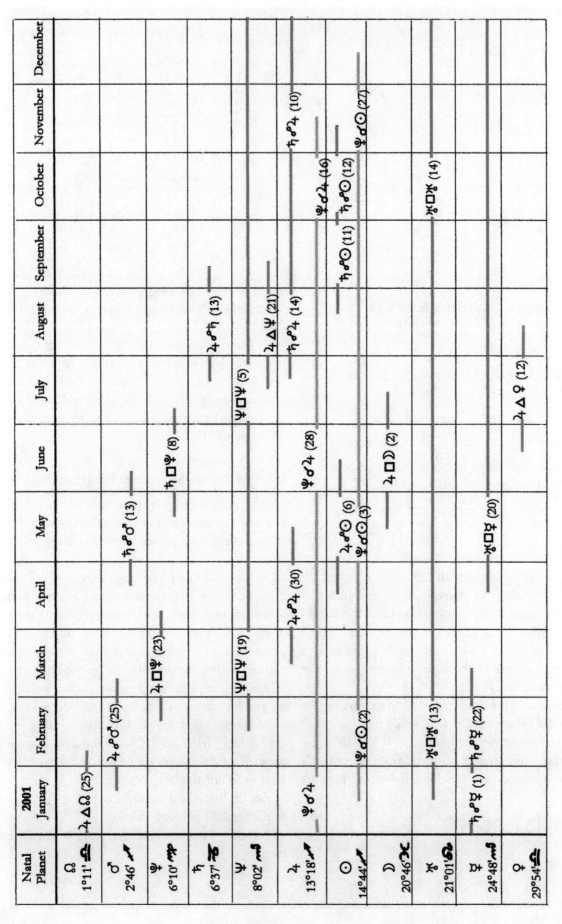

Figure 6.2.3 Helen's Transits for 2001

Interpretation - Transits

The effects of transiting planets are considered in the same way. Helen looks like having a year full of activity and probable changes. It will be noted that the transpersonal planets are all playing a major part in her life during 2001. The ♅t☍♅r is a transit which affects all of us around the age of 38-42 and is sometimes referred to as a time of midlife crisis. It can be a time of rebellion when we consider all that we have accomplished in the first part of life and what we need to change or get rid of in order to progress into the next stage of life, signified by the Age Point entry into the 8th house. Helen's natal Uranus is in her 4th house, so again this might be significant in the context of family and relationships. Perhaps children have flown the nest so it may be a time to move home or embark on a new career.

The ♆t□♆r transit can also indicate a time to question life. The effect of these two transits occurring simultaneously, as well as other major transits of Pluto and Jupiter suggest that 2001 had the potential to be an exciting and transformative year for Helen. Major transits of Pluto often indicate a time when something that has existed in our life for a long time needs to be let go of in order for something new to grow. The transits of Saturn can, positively, allow changes to happen in a structured manner or, negatively, attempt to hold on to the past. For an astrologer to be able to guide Helen through a potentially stressful time could be helpful to her.

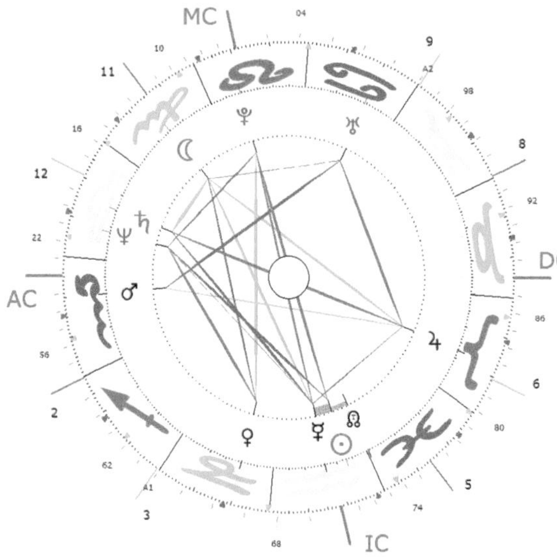

Figure 6.2.5 Lucy
13.02.1952, 00:05 GMT, 53N28 002W18

A Real Life Example – Lucy'sTransits

Lucy was a real life client for astrological psychology consultation. Her chart is shown in Figure 6.2.5. The consultation took place in November 2001. Notes are by the consultant.

Observations:

- This is a fixed chart, and with green as a dominant colour and ☽ in ♍ and high in the chart there will be emotional reaction to any situation which disturbs the equilibrium. Current transits suggest this may be her reason for seeking a session.
- The Age Point entered ♋ at the start of the year. At the present time the Age Point is ☌♅.
- ♅t is ☌☉r and IC, and retrograde ♃t is ☌♅r. ♇t is □☽r and ♃t was □☽r in May. ♃t and ♄t are both □☽r at the present time.

1. ☉P is ☌♃r and you can check other transits for yourself if you wish.

Hypothesis

Lucy is under the influence of major transits which are likely to be affecting her at an emotional level. With ♅t☌ the IC as well as ☉r she probably has a sense of her 'foundations' being undermined. The cause could be a relationship issue, but with AP ☌♅ in the 9th house it may also be affecting her role in life. Certainly I would expect her to be experiencing a traumatic period when many aspects of her life are perhaps needing to change. With a fixed chart shaping this may not be easy.

Reality

In brief, Lucy had a business with her partner, but he walked out and left her with debts. She feels as though she's fallen off her perch and has lost her self-confidence. She says she's feeling low, with money problems. This turned out to be more or less in line with my hypothesis, and I was able to use counselling and therapeutic techniques to help her to look at positive and practical ways to help her to pick herself up, re-climb her ladder and regain her self-respect and self-confidence. Having studied Chapter 5 *Nature or Nurture*, you will be aware that for Lucy to move forward and develop her full potential, there are also early childhood issues to be looked at. Lucy may need to accept and understand her subjective experience of the relationship she had with her mother and father.

Exercise 6.2

1. Take 5 key events in your life and see what, if any, aspects the outer transiting planets (Jupiter to Pluto) were making to your natal planets at the time.

   Consider these in the context of the links you have already established for those events with Age Progression in Exercise 6.1, although you may like to experiment with any significant event where the age point did not seem a particularly strong influence.

   Do the transits help to describe the nature of your experience, and do they amplify what you already understand through Age Progression?

2. Take the past year and plot the transits made by the outer planets (Jupiter to Pluto) to your natal planets over the last 12 months. Also identify significant factors in your age progression over the same period (major aspects to planets, sign or house change, Low Point, etc).

   Can you link the interplay of the transits and age progression with events or phases in your life over the last year?

6.3 Age Point and Rectification of a Birth Time

An understanding of how the Age Progression technique works may provide a means of rectifying a doubtful time of birth. This section explains how this can be achieved.

Introduction

An unknown birth time will undoubtedly make it more difficult to make a valid interpretation of a birth chart. It is possible to use Age Progression to rectify the birth time, but the less that is known about the time of birth the more difficult this is.

For instance, if we are told that the birth happened in the 'early morning', or 'around lunch time', then working with Age Progression will often allow us to come up with a time which is acceptably close to the actual birth time. However, if nothing is known about the time of birth then it will be far more difficult to arrive at a time that can be trusted, though this will to some extent depend upon the placement of the planets in the chart and the depth of understanding the person has of their life experiences – especially those that have a psychological meaning.

Astrologers use different methods of ascertaining an unknown time of birth but it is important to bear in mind that if a birth time is rectified it can never be a 100% certain that the time arrived at is accurate. If asked to rectify a birth time for someone who has an understanding of astrology and the meaning of a birth chart, it is a good idea to suggest that they live with the new time and the new chart for a while and see whether they feel comfortable with it. It can be rather like buying a new suit of clothes. You need to wear this for a while to find out if it really fits you!

In astrological psychology we place a great deal of emphasis on the interpretation of the Moon Node Axis, which is introduced in Chapter 7. It has been found that this house axis can be a helpful tool in rectification when a birth time is completely unknown. Initially it is necessary to work out a number of simple suggestions and scenarios which relate to each moon node axis.

Discussion with the client might elicit whether they respond more positively to one of these than to the others.

For instance, scenarios relating to the 1/7 ('I/You') house axis would aim to explore the client's feelings about self-esteem and meeting their own 'I' needs, as opposed to always giving way and meeting the needs of other people and trying to please them. Discussion of each axis in turn may highlight whether one is more prominent in the client's life than another. If this is so then the initial step would be to set up the chart so that the North Node was placed in the house at the end of the axis which appeared to be the least acceptable end of that polarity, bearing in mind that certain factors might mean that the other end of the axis was more appropriate.

As with all methods of rectification this one has to be used with caution and would probably only be of use when there was no idea at all of a time of birth. Experience suggests that the method discussed in this section is as valid as any other method, especially when the time is known within a couple of hours either way.

The Age Point and Rectification: Significant Life Events

Having studied Section 1 on Age Progression, you will be aware that it is possible to relate significant Age Point aspects to events that have happened in the past. These can be used to help rectify the birth time if it is inaccurate, or work out an approximate birth time if it is unknown. If the person knows how old they were at the time that a significant event occurred in their life then the chart can be adjusted so that the event coincides with an aspect of the AP to an appropriate planet at the specified age.

When using the AP as a means of rectifying the birth time it is important to work with as many significant life events as possible. This number should normally be at least 8.

All the guidelines to interpretation on Age Progression, which were detailed in 6.1, apply to rectification. You can refine the date more accurately by looking in the ephemeris for important and relevant transit aspects which may pinpoint an event exactly.

Important Note

Remember that if you want to alter the birth time by, say, 30 minutes you cannot just work out a new ascendant and move all the house cusps round keeping them in their original positions relative to the ascendant. To be accurate it is necessary to work out the new longitudes of house cusps since the distortion of the zodiac will be changing with every minute of passing time. However, in a **preliminary** examination where there is no great distortion of the houses, it is practical to cut round the signs in the chart, leaving the house cusps where they are, and so be able to revolve the centre of the chart, containing planets and signs, relative to the houses.

Example 1

You are told by the person whose chart you're rectifying that at 6 years of age he was sent away to boarding school and that this had been felt as a traumatic break from home, and from the mother principle. His chart already shows Uranus in the 7th house, in opposition to a point in the first house around the age of four, but the event suggests that it might be significant if it was on the cusp of the 8th house, i.e. in opposition the AP position at age 6. You adjust the chart and check whether other events in his life now fit in with appropriate planetary positions and aspects.

Example 2

You are asked to rectify the chart of a woman who got married when she was 21. You note that Saturn is in this general area at the bottom of the chart so it may be pertinent to re-examine the chart with Saturn conjunct the date of the marriage to see if other life occurrences coincide with appropriate AP aspects. You can check whether there is any awareness of the motivation for marriage and whether this relates to the meaning of Saturn, such as the provision of security in some form.

It is possible to look at a complete scenario extending over a period of years by examining, in addition to the aspects, the progression of the AP through one or more of the signs and houses, noting the relevance of the AP in relation to the different zones of the houses, such as the Low Point or stress area, as well as to the meaning of the sign(s) and house(s). For instance the AP going through Gemini or the 9th house might have coincided with a time when a person decided to take up a new learning project.

This requires practice and may not be easy to do until you have had opportunities to gain experience. It is important to bear in mind that rectification is achieved by identifying events that were **significant from the point of view of psychological growth**, rather that from events which can be remembered only because of their external impact.

Example 3

A child of 8 years of age has an strong attachment to a favourite, but very dilapidated teddy bear. The child goes to school one day and whilst away the mother decides to tidy the child's bedroom. In the process she throws away a great deal of clutter, including the teddy bear, believing it to be past its best! During the day the waste bins are collected by the local council.

The child comes back from school and discovers the bear is missing. He is inconsolable and at a deep unconscious level forms the belief that any possessions need to be held on to securely, otherwise they will be taken away. This child has Saturn in the 2nd house conjunct the age of 8. In later years he is in therapy because he experiences restrictions in his life, which is not developing in the way he desires.

The therapist, who also works with astrological psychology, notes Saturn in the 2nd house but the client has no recollection of anything in his life that happened at the age of 8.

It took some deep exploration to bring back the memory of the teddy bear and, through reconnecting with the experience of the teddy bear and the feelings engendered, begin the process of changing the belief that was formed at that early age.

Approximate and Unknown Birth Times

As with all aspects of astrological psychology and chart interpretation it is essential to blend theory with practical experience. Care should be taken in the initial use of this technique and, until considerable experience has been gained, it is not recommended that it is used in cases where a birth time is completely unknown. In this latter event there is always the **possibility** that rectification may not be accurate.

Where the birth time is very uncertain a further guide may be found through the life experience of an axis cross where one is shown to exist strongly in the chart.

The familiarity of the area of life occupied by the South Node may also prove to be a starting point for rectification.

Note

Figure 4.3.5 on page 147 can be used for assessing the number of degrees and minutes which represent either a month or a year of time, in any house size. These movements are shown in the two columns to the left of the central column headed 'House Size'.

Exercise 6.3

1. Draw up or inspect the chart and data in Figure 6.3.1 (next page). This is the chart for Ann, born on 23rd August 1961. Latitude 18° 58'S, longitude 32° 38'E. The birth time of 07.30 in the morning (05.30 GMT) is based on the fact that she was told she was born "around breakfast time".

2. Taking into account the events in Ann's life outlined below, rectify the birth time and explain your reasons.

   a) Two months before she was born her father left the house to go shopping in the nearest town. He never returned and she has hated her memory of him ever since.

   b) At 6 she went to a new school which she says opened up new horizons for her.

   c) At 14 she says "she rebelled". She fell in love, made love and thought she was pregnant. At 16½ she was expelled from school. This period of rebellion lasted until she was just 17 when life started to calm down.

   d) When she was 21½ she met a man whom she married within a few weeks. This was partly because she had emigrated to another country where she wanted to live but could not get a residence permit. So marriage offered a way to avoid deportation. She says that this time also marked her entry into another rebellious phase and this has been around ever since. She is now 24.

   e) When she was 23 years and 2 months old she left her husband and went off with another man.

	Planets		
Sun	☉:	29°51'	♌ Leo
Moon	☽:	18°55'	♑ Capricorn
Mercury	☿:	8°16'	♍ Virgo
Venus	♀:	22°32'	♋ Cancer
Mars	♂:	3°57'	♎ Libra
Jupiter	♃:	28°52' r	♑ Capricorn
Saturn	♄:	24°13' r	♑ Capricorn
Uranus	♅:	26°23'	♌ Leo
Neptune	♆:	8°50'	♏ Scorpio
Pluto	♇:	7°34'	♍ Virgo
Moon's N.t.	☊:	27°13'	♌ Leo
Moon's Node	☊:	26°56' r	♌ Leo

Houses						
	Cusp		Invert		Low	
AC:	25°27'	♍	8°36'	♎	16°27'	♎
2:	29°37'	♎	11°23'	♏	18°24'	♏
3:	0°10'	♐	10°24'	♐	16°30'	♐
IC:	26°44'	♐	6°40'	♑	12°36'	♑
5:	22°32'	♑	3°51'	♒	10°37'	♒
6:	21°56'	♒	4°50'	♓	12°32'	♓
DC:	25°27'	♓	8°36'	♈	16°27'	♈
8:	29°37'	♈	11°23'	♉	18°24'	♉
9:	0°10'	♊	10°24'	♊	16°30'	♊
MC:	26°44'	♊	6°40'	♋	12°36'	♋
11:	22°32'	♋	3°51'	♌	10°37'	♌
12:	21°56'	♌	4°50'	♍	12°32'	♍

Aspects

	☉	☽	☿	♀	♂	♃	♄	♅	♆	♇	☊
☉	■■■■		9 ☌			2 ⚼ 3		4 ☌ 7		8 ☌	3 ☌ 3
☽		■■■■	4 ☍ 5			6 ☌ 8					
☿			■■■■						2 ⚹ 3	1 ☌ 2	
♀				■■■■		9 ☍ 9	3 ☍ 3				
♂					■■■■	△ 8					
♃						■■■■	6 ☌ 7	6 ⚼		4 ⚼ 4	
♄							■■■■	7 ⚼		9 ⚼ 9	
♅								■■■■		2 ☌ 2	
♆									■■■■	6 ⚹ 6	
♇										■■■■	

Aspect Rating (1-2: strong, 3-7: medium, 8-9: weak)

Figure 6.3.1 Chart Data for Ann

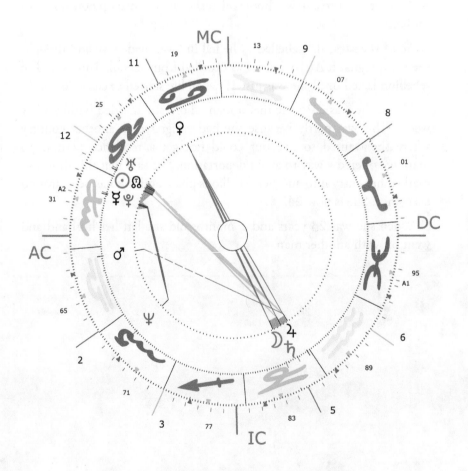

Figure 6.3.2 Ann's chart (set for 0730 birth time)

Consolidation Exercise for Chapters 1-6

At the end of every other chapter we include an additional exercise which encourages you to consolidate your learning so far.

Refer to Sophie's natal chart (already met, Figure 2.3.44 on page 96), house chart (Figure 6.3.3) and chart data (Figure 6.3.4), or draw up/ print this for yourself.

1. Describe Sophie's inner motivations and how they may be lived through, and met by, the outer world.

2. For each Ego Planet consider (a) strength according to house and sign position, and (b) the implications of the aspect colours received and the aspect pattern(s) it is involved in. What are the likely psychological implications.

3. Consider the Family Model and its implications.

4. Identify likely strengths and weaknesses of personality, as indicated by the Tool Planets.

5. Reflect on Sophie's dynamic calculations and what they might mean. What qualities is the environment requiring Sophie to develop in her life? How might this support or challenge her inner motivation.

6. Consider the House Chart alongside the Natal Chart and reflect on the potential (positive and negative) impact on Sophie's inner development.

7. Taking an overall look at what you know of Sophie, what do you feel are the main issues that might hold her back from fulfilling her potential?

8. How do you think awareness of transpersonal energies might help her overcome some of these issues?

9. Reflect on the Age Point progression and how this may support Sophie's individuation process.

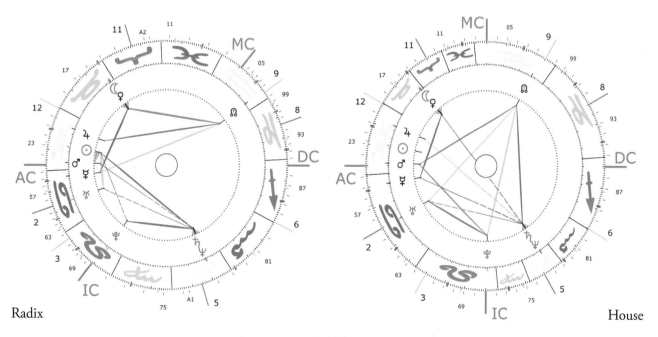

Radix   House

Figure 6.3.3 Sophie Radix and House Charts
08.06.1953, 05:30, Mobberley, England

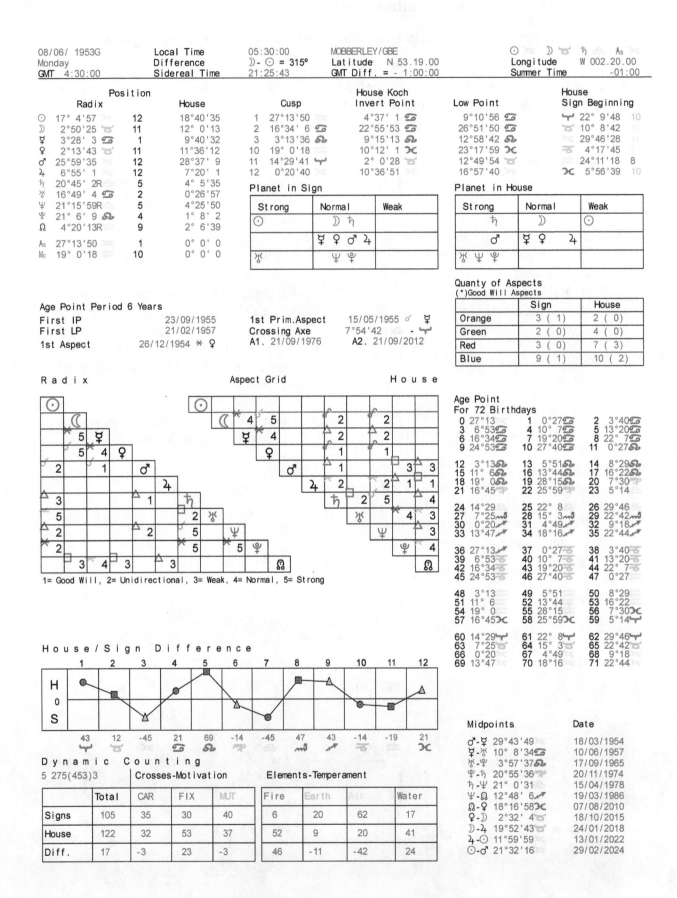

Figure 6.3.4 Chart Data for Sophie

Chapter 7. Personal and Transpersonal Growth

In this chapter we consider how personal development might be achieved through ego integration, and consider the role of the Moon Node and the Moon Node Chart as tools to aid personal and transpersonal growth.

Contents:

7.1 Ego Integration

This section shows how, through the ego planets, we can gain an insight into the process of development of our will and feelings, and the important link with our physical needs and well-being. From this we can become aware of how the ego can be encouraged to function in an integrated, effective and appropriate manner.

Integration of the Ego Planets

In Chapter 3 we stressed the need to work consciously on the development of the energies symbolised by the Sun, Moon and Saturn in order to achieve personal growth and control our lives more effectively. This process requires recognition of the way in which these energies manifest themselves in our own life so that their development and integration can be achieved in a balanced way. In other words we learn to take control over our actions and reactions by using our will, our feelings, and our physical presence.

It is not unusual for someone to be unaware of the existence of one or other of the ego planets, or they may recognise that it is there and be aware that they are not making optimum use of it. An example of this is the person who is not using the Sun energy to its full potential and tells you that they know they should use their will to greater effect, instead of letting other people make decisions and run their life for them.

A look at their birth chart will show you that that the Sun is in a weak position, perhaps at a Low Point, which would explain why it is difficult for that person to use their will effectively. The fact that they know that everything in their life is not as it should be and that other people walk all over them may also mean that they suffer from a feeling of inferiority. To point this out and tell them that they need to work on that particular problem is unlikely to help them to solve it. It is more than likely that they already experience feelings of anger and resentment, although it is unlikely that these will be expressed overtly.

It would be more helpful if you were able to show them, through the chart, that they had an alternative attribute that was strong and that, if developed, would help them overcome their weak Sun – or lack of will. In such a case it is not unusual for the individual to have had so much attention focussed on their 'weakness', both by themselves and others, that they have never had the opportunity to recognise what is strong.

What we are seeking to do in this situation is to identify the strongest of the three ego planets so that its existence can be made known and its meaning and potential explained. If this new-found strength can be recognised (there is often an inner understanding of its existence) and then consciously worked on, the original problem can fade without conscious effort.

In the above case let us suppose that Saturn is found to be the strongest of the ego planets. The advice to a client might be to focus attention on the physical and practical issues of life. This could be something comparatively simple such as taking a pride in dressing, or general outward appearances, or it might mean taking a more down to earth and practical approach to life.

Let's imagine a woman going out to meet a friend and feeling really good in herself, perhaps having been on a diet and lost weight, or maybe with a new hair style, or new clothes. She meets her friend who comments enthusiastically on her new look. The woman gains confidence in her appearance and any feelings of inferiority begin to disperse. This is a simple example but this is the way the process can work.

If, instead of Saturn, the chart shows the Moon to be the strongest of the ego planets, this would suggest that the individual needs to become aware of their own true emotional needs and not be afraid to express them. Only in this way can they receive the love and affection from others that will give them the emotional strength and security needed to overcome any sense of personal inadequacy which may stem from a weak Sun.

It is important that we focus and make use of our strengths as shown in our birth chart. By consciously using our strongest ego planet and meeting its needs, we provide the necessary support to our weaker planets so that they can also find channels of natural expression and come into alignment.

> If you **live** the strongest ego planet
> the weaker ones will integrate themselves

We don't want to over-simplify, or give the impression that the process of encouraging a dormant sub-personality to emerge and be active in our lives is a simple matter. Without professional help or guidance it may not be, but it is nevertheless within our power to accept responsibility for ourselves and to strive consciously to achieve integration and balance.

How do we assess the strength of a planet in this context?

In this context, we are looking at the ease with which a planet can express itself in the outside world. The strength of a planet will therefore be deduced from its house position. The *House Intensity Curve* (Figure 4.3.1 on page 140) shows that a planet is strongest on the cusp of a house and weakest at the Low Point.

A planet in the stress area before a house cusp is also strong but not as strong as a cuspal planet – although it is able to put out a lot of energy to try and satisfy the area of experience required by the next house, it is not 'seen' by the environment (hiding behind the cusp) so the environmental expectations will be less. The stress will mainly come from within.

An intercepted planet is weak in this context since it has no direct outlet for expression. It is dependant on the other planets it is aspecting to voice its message.

If more than one ego planet is cuspal, the first step is to establish which cross they are on. You can see visually in the *House Intensity Curve* that the cardinal cross reaches out much further than the fixed or mutable cross, so the ability of a planet on the cusp of a cardinal house to make an impact will be greater than a planet on any of the other house cusps.

If there is little difference in house strength between the ego planets, other factors need to be considered such as strength by sign, number of aspects and overall position in the chart.

Which is the Strongest Ego Planet?

The strength of a planet is assessed by considering the following quantitative factors in order:

- Its strength by house is the overriding factor and only where there is no difference in house strength are the following factors considered

- Its strength by sign

- The number of aspects to it.

If doubt still exists, the following qualitative factors should be considered:

- Its position in the chart

- The type of aspects it receives: red aspects will energise the Sun while blue aspects will restrict its natural expression.

House and sign strengths have been covered in sections 4.3 "The House Intensity Curve" and 5.3 "Energy Output of Planets in Signs".

The sign position is important **but takes second place to the house position**. For instance, if a planet is at 1º in a sign but situated on the MC, then unless there is another ego planet on an angle **and** stronger by sign, this will be the strongest ego planet, in which case it is likely to have learned ways of compensating for its weak position by sign, and may have associated problems.

Note on Intercepted Planets

As noted above, an intercepted planet is necessarily weaker than its position would indicate by house and sign because it has no direct outlet for expression. However, it is worth bearing in mind that a very well connected intercepted planet, such as the tension ruler of the chart, will potentially still have good energy outlets so may not be too badly affected by its intercepted status. And of course the energies of an intercepted planet can be successfully directed inwards where not dependent on any encouragement from the environment.

Position in the Chart

The **Sun** is at its strongest near the MC. The Family Model (5.1) also shows the upper hemisphere to be the rightful position for the Sun. If the Sun is near the bottom of the chart a person may lack self-confidence in the world outside the collective.

Saturn is strongest at the bottom of the chart. It can be likened to a tree with its roots in the earth, an anchor which provides a sense of grounding.

If Saturn is at the top of the chart the roots of the tree are dangling in space and this placing is nearly always felt as an inner sense of insecurity. On the AC or DC there will probably be a fear of venturing out in to the world or of opening up to other people because this may pose a threat to security.

The **Moon** needs to make contact and this can most easily be achieved on the AC/DC axis. If the Moon is up near the MC it is sensitive but emotionally insecure and requires constant reassurance, probably seeking attention, recognition or love. Near the IC emotional security will be sought within the family or the collective and this may restrict progress in life.

Example

In Figure 7.1.1, Saturn, just over the cusp of the 5th house, is the strongest ego planet. This is true even though it is weak by sign. By contrast the Sun, at 11½ degrees, is very strong by sign, but is in a weaker house position, being further from the cusp, and is intercepted in Libra. These are quantitative strengths and in this instance there is no special need to take account of qualitative values such as the fact that the Sun is at the bottom of the chart. The Moon is weakest by house position, in the fixed zone. It is also intercepted.

Strength by:-

	House	Sign	Aspects	Position	Total
☉	2	3	1	1	7
☽	1	2	2	2	7
♄	3	1	3	3	10

Assessing which is the strongest ego planet in a chart is complex and requires practice. To get more of a feel for this, we suggest that you work with a variety of charts. You can access charts of well-known people through books, your chart software/service or websites such as astrologicalpsychology.org or astro.com.

KOCH		Invert Point		Low Point	
1	25°30'11 ♋	1	3°35' 7 ♌	1	8°34'50 ♌
2	16°39'46 ♌	2	24°34'55 ♌	2	29°28'35 ♌
3	7°23'45 ♍	3	15°22' 2 ♍	3	20°17'38 ♍
4	28°15'56 ♍	4	21°10'12 ♎	4	5°19'32 ♐
5	28°13'48 ♐	5	11° 1'23 ♐	5	18°55'47 ♐
6	1°43'23 ♒	6	10°48'22 ♒	6	16°25'12 ♒
7	25°30'11 ♑	7	3°35' 7 ♒	7	8°34'50 ♒
8	16°39'46 ♒	8	24°34'55 ♒	8	29°28'35 ♒
9	7°23'45 ♓	9	15°22' 2 ♓	9	20°17'38 ♓
10	28°15'56 ♓	10	21°10'12 ♈	10	5°19'32 ♉
11	28°13'48 ♉	11	11° 1'23 ♊	11	18°55'47 ♊
12	1°43'23 ♋	12	10°48'22 ♋	12	16°25'12 ♋

LONGITUDE

SUN	11°41'40 ♎	4
MOON	21°59' 8 ♎	4
MERCURY	27°18'32R ♍	3
VENUS	28°40'50 ♌	2
MARS	13°22'30R ♓	9
JUPITER	18°33'46 ♍	3
SATURN	29°27'45 ♐	5
URANUS	6°19'36 ♌	1
NEPTUNE	29°28'14 ♎	4
PLUTO	29°38'27 ♌	2
TRN T NOD N	29°56' 5R ♐	5

Figure 7.1.1 Example - Saturn Strongest

How to Make Use of the Strongest Ego Planet

If the **Sun** is the strongest planet the integration keyword is **will**. That person has to learn to develop the use of their will. This means recognising they can make decisions they can rely on at a mental level. They can learn to trust their own judgment and generally become aware of their selfhood. The technique of affirmation, which is a comparatively simple method of rewriting life scripts, many of which may originate from childhood, can be helpful for this purpose. Psychosynthesis, Transactional Analysis and NLP are also therapies which can be valuable in the task of developing the use of the will.

Roberto Assagioli's book *The Act of Will* is highly recommended reading.

If the **Moon** is the strongest planet then the integration keyword is **contact**. That person has to learn to recognise their own emotional needs and be true to them. They can learn to differentiate between taught patterns of relating and the real inner longings that exist. When these can be recognised and expressed it is possible to go out into the world without fear of other people and with the ability to reflect back the goodness, love and beauty that is there.

It is a process that requires an understanding of emotional energies, so therapies such as Transpersonal Psychology and Psychosynthesis are likely to be helpful in discovering and learning about Moon energy. If there are few planets on the You side of the chart it may seem a difficult task to go out into the world and begin to have an honest emotional dialogue with others. But this can be made easier if the importance of doing so, and the potential strength to be successful in this, is understood.

When considering feelings we need to be aware of the possible difference between being able to express spontaneous emotions because we see a sad film or become aware of the suffering of humanity in some area of the world, and being able to express our deepest emotional feelings about those things which affect us personally, and which may be easier to suppress for fear of upsetting someone.

If **Saturn** is the strongest planet the emphasis is on the **body**. If you feel physically on top of the world then you can present yourself to the world with assurance. A person can learn to become more body aware and to recognise the need for good health and well-being. This may involve exercise, diet, or may be something as simple as just looking good, taking more care over personal appearance and dress. The Alexander Technique is one therapy aimed at achieving balance of the ego structure by working on the body.

With Saturn strongest it is also possible that attention to life's practicalities and realities may be important. For instance a mystic sub-personality may be very much in evidence which would suggest that in some ways there is a also need to incorporate the down to earth pragmatism of Saturn.

Other Considerations

Ego planets connected

Where a chart shows all three ego planets joined together in one aspect figure you may find that there is already a sense of integration. This could however be a false sense of integration since an understanding of the need to develop and harmonise these energies could be lacking and there may be little motivation for personal growth. Of course, this would be more likely to apply with an all-blue figure such as a Talent Triangle than with a Learning Triangle.

Since parents and child are linked in this pattern it is also possible that family emotional ties have not been broken with the result that there may be difficulty in accepting autonomy and therefore the need to explore and develop a greater consciousness and independence.

An astrological psychology consultant writes:

"Many years ago when I was struggling to understand the Huber's approach, I remember Bruno Huber talking about the way in which the three ego planets might be experienced if they were linked together in a single aspect pattern. As I understood it at the time, his suggestion was that there would be a sense of ego integration which might inhibit further growth."

It will be appreciated that part of our process of development is to achieve an integration of the personality, which includes being able to experience our world through a **balance** of mind, body **and** feelings.

Childhood conditioning and the need for survival often create an imbalance in the way we approach the world through our ego. We are likely to grow into adulthood more identified with one of mind, body or feelings. So we will experience the world, or deal with it, predominantly through only one aspect of the ego. Part of the process of our psychological development is to discover and make fully conscious, whichever aspect of the ego was repressed, or not encouraged to develop in childhood.

Relating this to Figure 7.1.2, imagine that the triangle revolves around a pin in the centre. Integration means that instead of being stuck with one of mind, body, or feelings always leading the personality, the triangle can spin freely so that any one of these can be engaged as appropriate to suit any situation.

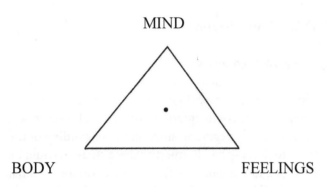

Figure 7.1.2

The consultant continued:

"I understood Bruno's suggestion to mean that, even though the 'triangle' might be stuck, there would be no sense of this and therefore no incentive to change. Working with clients who have this configuration to some extent bore this out but it didn't seem to be the whole story."

To understand what this might be we need to take a look at the Family Model (5.1) and attempt to understand the links which, in the child's objective view, were created to the parents.

It seems possible that whatever these links were, they remain connected at some unconscious level so that **the child grows into adulthood without the same freedom to develop individuality** as would otherwise be the case. For instance a girl brought up in a family where her mother's own upbringing inhibited the development of her own femininity, or sexuality, will not know how to develop confidence in being a woman. Potential partners will be judged by the real, or imaginary, perception of the father.

Sun, Moon and Saturn linked together in the natal chart can inhibit personal development but only because the child grows into adulthood a prisoner to the Family Model. Needless to say the exact interpretation of this will depend upon the relationship of the ego planets to one another, as well as to their position in the natal chart. And it would also be important to consider how the house chart affected the family relationships as the child grew up.

Ego planets not connected

A contrasting arrangement is where all three ego planets exist in separate, unconnected, aspect figures. Here it is not easy for an individual to bring these energies to function together. A compartmentalised feeling may exist with the possibility either that one ego planet will dominate the personality to the exclusion of the other two, or there will be a lack of cohesive control over actions, decisions and feelings. It is helpful for a person with such a chart to understand the problem and thus recognise the need for integration.

Integration

A very small child once had a finger poked in his eye. It really hurt him and his unconscious reaction, in order for it not to happen again, was to keep this eye closed from then on. So he grew into adulthood seeing the world only through one eye. To him, having forgotten the reason for protecting this eye in the first instance, it seemed quite normal. However, he was not aware that there were some things which he was not able to do as well as other people – but he sometimes had a sense, which he did not fully understand, that all was not as it should be.

One day he met a caring and wise person who was able to help him reconnect with what had happened to him as a child, and which had resulted in him growing up with the sight of only one eye. He felt that knowing what had happened would automatically make it possible for him to see with both eyes. But this knowledge on its own did not make this happen. His eye had been closed for so long that it was necessary for him to get help to unseal the eye. As this gradually came about he initially felt disorientated by the brightness of the light and the strangeness of his new vision. He had to learn how to integrate this new faculty into his life, which took time and practice.

As you read this story you would be forgiven for wondering whether it was reality or fantasy. The point being made is that childhood circumstances and conditioning can result in the repression of our connection with either mind, body or feelings.

For instance, take the case of the Aries girl who was the first born to a mother who was quite unable to cope with her high energy level which, to her, seemed inappropriate for a young girl. During the early stages of her development the girl adapted to her mother's pressures and learned that it was wrong to display any show of will, to the extent that she gave up her power and became a victim.

Or the case of the boy who received the opposite treatment from a dominant mother who discouraged any show of emotion. The boy grew into adulthood, emotionally immature and with confused feelings about his sexuality, to the extent that he found it difficult to allow any woman into his life who he felt might dominate him. Although comfortable with casual female relationships, he eventually found it easier to have an emotional relationship with somebody of the same sex.

You may find that the potential for such distortions can be identified from the chart. However, knowing what has happened in childhood may, in itself, not be enough to rectify the situation and it may be that the skills of a professional therapist are required to bring about the process of integration.

Of course, this same theory can be applied to all parts of our personality (our sub-personalities) but when seen in the context of our 'management' structure of Sun, Moon and Saturn it will be apparent that such distortions can affect not only our sense of wholeness but also our ability to achieve real fulfilment.

The Weakest Ego Planet

It is important to recognise that where a significant imbalance exists it is likely to be the planet which is weakest that will create difficulties in life. It may therefore be necessary to pay attention to the area of life most affected by the weakest planet as you work on developing the potential of the strongest planet.

Exercise 7.1

1. Assess which ego planet you consider the weakest and which the strongest in your chart.

2. Consider the following:

   a) How does your strongest ego planet find expression in your life? Is there anything you could do to support its positive expression?

   b) Are you aware of your weakest ego planet? How does it manifest?

   c) Is there a noticeable strength imbalance between your 3 ego planets? What practical steps could you take to help manage it better?

3. Do the same with your other practice charts.

Recommended Reading

Integrating the personality:

The Living Birth Chart, Chapter 3 Integrating the Personality – practical work with the Sun, Moon and Saturn in the chart, pp 63-71

Astrological Psychosynthesis, Part 2 Personality and Integration –Strong and weak positions of the Ego planets, pp 81-84

More general:

The Act of Will, Roberto Assagioli

What We May Be, Piero Ferrucci

7.2 The Moon's Nodes

> The position of the Moon Node Axis in the chart has considerable personal significance, so an understanding of its meaning can give valuable insight into where we may be "stuck" in our lives and what action can be taken in everyday situations in order for us to move on.
>
> This section covers:
>
> - The meaning of the nodes by axis and house position and the significance of aspects to the North Node
>
> - The spiritual significance of the sign on the ascendant
>
> An appendix contains a summary by Bruno and Louise Huber of Moon Node Astrology, as a bridge to section 7.3 on the Moon Node Chart.

The Moon's Nodes and Personal Growth

At the heart of astrological psychology there lies a spiritual perspective. Man does not exist in isolation. He is connected in space and time with the unfolding creative forces of the universe. These energies of the universe manifest in the individual through the central unknowable core of the birth chart.

Through the nodes of the Moon the individual is able to connect with his past and his future whilst standing in the present. Implicit within this spiritual perspective is the concept of reincarnation, with all its ramifications. Thus each of us as seen reflected in our birth chart is not a random happening, but is rather the present stage in the process of the evolution of a soul.

The importance that Bruno and Louise Huber gave to the nodes is signified by the inclusion of the North Node in the aspect structure. You are already familiar with the meaning of the aspect structure as the inner motivation of the individual. The North Node is a pointer towards the future, and as such occupies a significant place within the behaviour patterns of the individual.

It can be identified as a compensatory factor for an imbalance appearing elsewhere in the chart, and it can be seen as the eye of the needle through which we have to pass to grow spiritually. Thus, in order to fully understand the driving forces within the person, as interpreted through the aspect structure, it is essential to include the Node.

When moving towards interpreting the meaning of the nodes in terms of their position in the chart, humility in the face of the ineffable is required. Just as Bruno emphasised the necessity of not confusing different levels in the birth chart, in this area it is particularly important to keep in mind the nature of what is being discussed.

Life can be lived at various levels of awareness. As either astrologers or clients we may find little meaning in the nodes during one phase of our life, whereas at a different time, we begin to glimpse something of the message that is to be perceived.

There is a fundamental difference between the meaning of a planet in a house and the significance of the North Node in the same house. There is a danger that the Node is viewed as if it were another planet, generating energy that we can see at work in our daily life. But this is not so and we can live unconsciously under the influence of our South Node. For this reason it may not be possible to interpret the meaning of the North Node for ourselves, or for another person, beyond the level of awareness that we have reached in our own process of growth.

If we are connected with that part of ourselves which Assagioli called the transpersonal self, we may be able to connect with another person at a deep and meaningful level. If on the other hand, we are caught firmly by one or other of our sub-personalities, our perception of the significance of the nodes will be clouded.

The Moon's Nodes and the Nodal Axis – Physical Perspective

As a student of astrology, you will be familiar with the concept of the ecliptic, the plane indicated by the path of the Earth as it revolves around the Sun. It is also described as the apparent path of the Sun around the Earth.

As the Moon orbits the Earth on its monthly cycle, the path of the Moon cuts through the ecliptic in two places, which are 180 degrees apart. These two meeting points are known as the North Node and the South Node. The point where the Moon rises from the southern hemisphere to the northern one, via the ecliptic, is the North Node. Exactly opposite in the Zodiac lies the South Node. We call the imagined connecting line between these points the Moon-Node line or Nodal Axis. Astronomically, it is important for calculating the eclipses of the Sun and the Moon.

At the physical level, the nodes are just two positions in space. They are therefore different from the planets, which do have a physical reality.

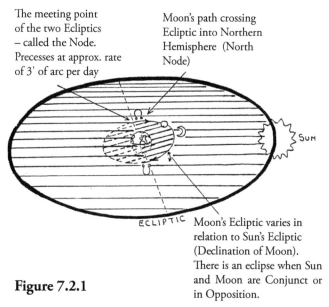

The meeting point of the two Ecliptics – called the Node. Precesses at approx. rate of 3' of arc per day

Moon's path crossing Ecliptic into Northern Hemisphere (North Node)

ECLIPTIC

Moon's Ecliptic varies in relation to Sun's Ecliptic (Declination of Moon). There is an eclipse when Sun and Moon are Conjunct or in Opposition.

Figure 7.2.1

True Node

When consulting the Ephemeris for the position of the Node, one should be conscious of the difference between the True Node and the Mean Node. As the Earth revolves on its axis during the year, there is a slight wobble, and the orbit of the Moon shifts to accommodate this. Thus the rate of motion of the Node is not constant.

It moves approximately three minutes of arc retrograde each day. Some Ephemerides show a constant rate (the Mean Node) but this can be up to 1½° distant from the True Node, which is the actual position of the Node taking into account the shift in the axis of the Earth and the change in the orbit of the Moon. The True Node was not easy to calculate before the introduction computers, and although the Hubers worked with the Mean Node for many years, subsequent re-evaluation suggested greater accuracy in analysis when using the True Node.

North and South Nodes – Symbolic Perspective

It is at the symbolic level that we begin to discern something of the meaning of the nodes. These positions in space represent the points where the paths of two personal planets intersect. The nodal point has a quality of linking or connectedness about it. At the same time it also has the quality of coming together and separating.

With one node being 180° from the other, there is a complete turning around to face in the opposite direction when moving from one node to the other. The nodes connect us with our past and our future. Our South Node has the quality of summarising, in esoteric terms, that which we have accumulated in previous existences, and which we bring with us into our present existence. It includes a range of attitudes and behaviour patterns we feel comfortable with. We slip into these behaviour patterns very easily, and without thinking.

These patterns operate at an unconscious level in the early years of life. Each of us will be able to more readily identify with the meaning of our South Node, and to recognise the ways in which we continue to be aware of its effects.

Louise Huber suggests that the South Node has a Saturnian quality, as it can be a place where we feel safe and secure, where everything is familiar. It is not a place we wish to move from, or that promotes growth. In some astrological texts the South Node is referred to as "the point of a person's undoing". It can be less demanding to stay with the attitudes and behaviour patterns accumulated over many lifetimes than to adopt a new way of being. On the other hand there are matters left over from previous existences that have to be resolved.

This present existence offers us an opportunity to move on from the point where we entered this life. If we choose to stay in the area of our South Node, we fail to take advantage of the opportunities for growth that this lifetime offers, and this can become our undoing.

The North Node is positioned on the opposite side of the chart, and represents qualities we need to develop in order to bring about a balance within ourselves. In moving towards the North Node we have to take this 180° turn and face in the opposite direction from that which is familiar and comfortable. Louise Huber suggests that the North Node has a Jupiterian quality, and as such is a place we can open out and expand from in our lives, and from which we can journey forward into new, and sometimes quite scary and unfamiliar territory.

It is therefore hardly surprising to find that most of us show a marked reluctance to identify with the qualities of our North Node, when we first become aware of some of its meaning in our lives. The North Node is the symbol of our future. It is a permanent point of opportunity for growth.

We gradually learn to recognise that the North Node holds something vital to our lives, and we need to be continuously aware of this in our consciousness. It takes effort and we have to use our will in its various expressions – good will, strong will and skilful will – in moving towards our North Node.

One of the features of the North Node is that however much we may think we understand it, and have achieved its purpose in our daily lives, there is always more to learn, for it represents the continuing journey of the soul back to its source. With this perspective in mind, some meanings of the North Node in the houses are given below. This is not intended to be an exhaustive interpretation. Gradually as we become more aware of our own North Node, we are able to deepen our understanding of its meaning in our lives.

It is worth noting and taking into consideration that not everyone identifies with the comfort and familiarity of the South Node. In some charts there may be a bias of planets in the same hemisphere or quadrant as the North Node, with the South Node isolated in an empty area of the chart. In such cases we should bear in mind that the person may be living in, and identifying with, the North Node rather than the South Node. The task for this person, then, would be to develop the South Node in order to gain some balance in their lives. In such charts it is worth considering that the area of life associated with the South Node is likely to be one of challenge.

Meaning of the North Node by Axis and by House Position

It takes the Node approximately eighteen months to move backwards through one sign. During this time there will be a sizeable group of people born, all of whom will have the North Node in the same sign. The

nodal position of this group of people will be scattered throughout all twelve houses in the chart. Whilst all the group will be coming to learn something of the meaning of that particular sign, what is peculiar to each individual is the house placement of the Node. Thus the emphasis on the meaning of the Node is placed more heavily, though not exclusively, on the house position.

It has already been noted that the Node is a symbol. A symbol is one way in which man makes a representation of one aspect or element of reality. It is **not** the reality.

Where the meanings that follow resonate for you, use them to deepen your own understanding of the purpose and meaning of your life. Be aware of the time it takes for you to make the journey from your South Node towards your North Node. In working with others, allow them time also to become aware of where they have come from, always relating to the divinity within them.

The Six Axes

The meanings of the house positions of the nodes have been grouped along the six house axes, as introduced in Chapter 4, Figure 4.4.3 on page 149.

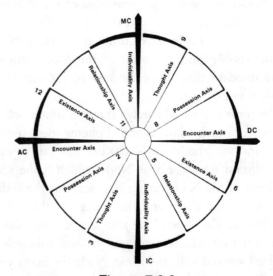

Figure. 7.2.2

The following considers each axis in turn. The meanings of the nodes in the houses are described in the first person singular.

Encounter Axis

This is a cardinal axis, with the qualities of the fire and air elements. Along this axis we go out to meet the world, and the world comes to meet us. The cardinal quality gives this axis the impulse to action, the urge to create, which we focus on our sense of identity.

North Node in the First House

With this placement I enter life with a history of service to others, of having submerged my personality needs to the needs of those around me who are closely related through family, marriage or other partnership ties. There is a distinct lack of evidence in the early part of this life of me putting my needs before those of others. In fact there is a tendency to feel guilty about having any personal wants or desires, with a consequent inhibiting of actions which might lead me to think of performing any act which could be construed as selfish.

I feel more comfortable when trying to make other people happy, and performing all manner of tasks which are thought to be meeting the needs of others. Unfortunately, pleasing others does not seem to bring harmony and peace, but rather only exacerbates other people's selfish requests, and brings frequent arguments between the people I am trying to make happy.

'If only these people would stop putting themselves first and think of others, life would be so much better' thinks my seventh house South Node. 'It is so draining having to be the referee amongst one's nearest and dearest.' I have a hard time making decisions, as it is always much easier to delegate to others. There are so many factors to be taken into account, how can I be sure I am making the correct decision. I am suffering from a weak ego.

The task for me in this life is to develop a strong presentation of my self. I have to learn to own the attitude of being egocentric, of putting myself and my needs above those of other people. My past habits were neither right nor wrong, but they belonged to a different time and place. Now I need to overcome these habits, which retain some of their strength and can still pull me back into my South Node.

I have no self-doubt in the first house. I begin the task of re-building myself in this house. Here I establish my identity, and become conscious of myself as an individual. There is no more delegating of myself to my partner. No more is my first thought that of pleasing others. I now think about pleasing myself. I entered this life with a weak ego, and the task of this life is to build a strong, secure, independent sense of my own identity.

North Node in the Seventh House

Here I am well aware of my own self-identity. I take a pride in being independent of other people. My ego is very demanding and I take much more notice of myself than of others. As you can imagine this presents a conflict in the area of relationships, since the other person is undervalued and comes a poor second, when needs or wants are being considered.

The North Node is calling me to recognise my link with another. To realise that no man is an island, complete unto himself. To acknowledge that I need other people is a hard lesson for me.

Here I have to learn to consider not only my own rights, but also those of other people. I have to learn to give my partner that which I would have for myself. I am seeking the balance of Libra with this placement. In reaching towards it there is much moving back and forth in different directions before I achieve a state of equilibrium. My ego is very demanding, and is in conflict with my partner. I have to learn how to put myself second, and consider the needs of others above my own. If I am unwilling to face away from my South Node, the effects of this are likely to be seen in my important relationships. I may refuse to enter into any binding agreement or partnership because I see it as a threat to my own identity – I might be signing away a part of myself – and this could even apply as far as getting married is concerned. I have to commit myself to others and learn to say 'Yes'.

As I learn how to move towards my North Node, I slowly acquire the quality of the judgment of Libra. I learn about relationships in a deep and powerful way. I no longer need to build up or protect my ego, but now I can help other people develop their self-confidence. My understanding of relationship and partnership problems enables me to be of service to others in a counselling role. Uranus is the esoteric ruler of Libra. In my journey towards my North Node I am able to find new solutions to partnership difficulties.

Possession Axis

Traditionally the second house was associated with money. This is, however, a distortion, and may cloud the deeper meaning of personal ownership. Money can be a means whereby we acquire or own physical objects, but there are other qualities which we can develop and own in ourselves that cannot be purchased. Thus the second house relates to personal possessions, and what we own in relation to our inner selves.

On the other hand the eighth house is more difficult to describe and has meanings at various levels. It signifies the possessions of other people, societies and institutions, as distinct from our own personal possessions. There are links with the processes of regeneration and transformation. Both are fixed houses, and as such take the impulse created in the preceding house and give it form. Along the fixed cross we find the tendency to polarise our thinking is more marked than on the other two axes.

North Node in the Second House

During the first part of my life there is a reliance and a dependency on other people. What I have, comes to me from others, it is not of my own making. There may have been much inner turmoil, involving the breaking down and leaving behind of old ways of living. This may lead me into undermining or destroying, consciously or otherwise, values and belief systems of other people because they are not mine and I am envious.

Now I have to establish a sense of my own self-worth. I have to find out about my own inner evaluation of myself. In order to do this I have to struggle to bring talents out into the open. I have to create something which is my very own, which has the essence of myself. With this North Node I have to show the world what it is that I can create for myself. I cannot rely on, or hang around waiting for, something to be given to me, or for someone to die and leave me something. I have to bring it from within myself.

North Node in the Eighth House

Here I have fully established my self-worth in previous incarnations. The temptation to retain and increase my stockpile of possessions is strong. There is a dislike of the structure and institutions of society. The forces of law and order, both civil and military can be anathema to me. In various ways I may try to undermine these institutions.

The way forward is, to quote the biblical text, 'Render unto Caesar, that which is Caesar's'. I have to become willing to understand the laws of society. I have to accept that policemen and soldiers are the means whereby institutions maintain order in the world. Instead of undermining the establishment, I have to learn how to use the laws. Through a loving identification with these institutions I can use them. Before I can do this, however, many of my pet ideas about the world go through a process of painful change. Many of my old fanatical ideas have to die. In this giving up of what I previously owned and thought necessary I then become open to the world and able to accept a responsibility for it. I can receive from others.

I become open to being able to use the power and talents of other people, although initially I feel too proud to do this. I can use what other people have developed for the benefit of the world. I may even find that I can acquire money that I have not worked for, perhaps by being successful on the stock market, but I have to take a responsible attitude as to how such acquisitions and inheritances are used.

This is not an easy nodal position to work towards. Being a fixed house, the pull to maintain the status quo in the South Node can be particularly strong.

Thought Axis

This is a mutable axis. Whereas on the previous axis there was concern with bringing something of substance into existence, on this dimension there is a breaking down of old forms in preparation for the creation of something new.

North Node in the Third House

Through many lifetimes I have been involved with the higher levels of the mind in the search for wisdom. This is quite distinct from knowledge. In the course of my searching after wisdom, I have developed my *weltanschauung*, my cosmic view of the world and the purpose of life. With this background, I have a deep inner knowing in my youth. I may appear to have a wisdom beyond my years. There can be a sense of separateness from ordinary people.

With this Node I have to become open to the common knowledge of the collective, of the people, the schools, the community, the colleges around me. It becomes necessary to leave the secret places, and join the common man in the market place. Here I have to bring an attitude of humility, as I learn from the man in the street.

There is much to be learned from those around me, but pride from my place in the ninth house can often get in the way. I may think that the common man can teach me nothing. I can give to others from my ninth house wisdom, but it must be done humbly, and at the same time I have to learn to receive from those around me. If I have something to teach, or communicate, I have to learn to do this at the level of ordinary people – I have much to give but it will be of no value if it cannot be understood by those who receive.

North Node in the Ninth House

Here the past experiences of the South Node have focussed my attention in areas of thinking that involve the lower levels of the mind. I relate to collective ideas, or collective knowledge. I am interested in facts and how to do tasks, rather than to the principles and concepts involved. I believe that the only people who have 'the truth' are professors and scholars of various sorts. Truth is beyond the ordinary person like me.

So this nodal position leads me to discover that I can have my own thinking. I can experience my existence on a higher level myself. I begin to find out more about thinking, and the means of wisdom. There is much talk about the exchange of ideas and knowledge. I have to develop the courage to overcome many of the traditional ideas, and stand firm on my own thoughts. It is here that the individuation process starts. Initially I may find it difficult to accept that I have the power of individual thought and I may have to overcome the fear of criticism from others when I voice my own ideas. People can be nasty when someone breaks away from collective thinking.

Individuality Axis

Here we meet the second main axis in the chart. Along the Encounter Axis man meets the world, whilst along this axis man stands with his feet in the nourishing soil of the collective and reaches upwards towards the heavens. This is again a cardinal axis – there is a strong impulse to create something using the theme of individuality. We move to one or other end along this continuum.

North Node in the Fourth House

Here there is a confrontation between the individual and the collective. There is an underlying theme involving hierarchical order. I come into the world from my tenth house position. I am accustomed to being in a position of power. I consider myself to be a ruler. Capricorn is so sure of himself in the tenth house. I see myself above other people, and I struggle hard to retain this position – but in reality I am not superior to my family and those who cared for me when I was young.

To forsake this pinnacle and come down into the fourth house and become one with the family presents a deep emotional challenge. I am asked to enter into feeling relationships, instead of thinking relationships. I struggle with the refusal to come down off my high horse. There may have been battles with one or both of my parents, and part of the learning that I have to do now, is to love and forgive them.

This deals with very deep emotions and I may have to go down on my knees as I do it. I find all this emotional work very hard, but the depth of it brings me into contact with my soul. Neptune is the esoteric ruler of Cancer. I find I am able to be humble, to love and forgive.

North Node in the Tenth House

With this Node I can move toward the peak experience of my own realisation. Early in life I was held firmly and supportively within the security of my family. It was a very comfortable feeling. The family defined goals for me. In leaving my South Node, I have to leave all this behind. I have to release the goals and ambitions which my family gave me. It is necessary for me to find my own goals. In doing this I could well find that I am unsupported, either emotionally or financially by my family. I am standing alone.

Initially I become aware that a particular path, which has been given to me, is not the right one. Yet to turn away requires courage. Dare I face my family with this? If I do I can no longer count on the security of the nest. There are no compromises with this position. When I realise what this means, I find that the ground has gone from under my feet. It can be an intense experience of anxiety.

As I begin to leave my past behind, the rewards are much more than I dared ever dream about. I become a free individual, and am able to move into the higher realms. Before this can fully happen I have to achieve the integration of the threefold personality – my mental (Sun), emotional (Moon) and physical (Saturn) nature. Part of the process of freeing myself from conflicts involves what Alice Bailey describes as going through a stage of initiation. This only becomes clear to me when I am in my self-made state, and I have left behind all my warm nest-like security of family relationships. Love is a great educator. In the tenth house I am free and open to the universe, and as a free individual I can offer my abilities to the universe.

Relationship Axis

The theme changes again to that of the fixed cross. The impulse of individuality in the cardinal cross is changed into something tangible. In the fifth house we seek close physical contact with the other person. It is as if our relationship has a physical quality of existence as well as the closeness of physical skin contact. In the eleventh house our understanding and awareness leads to the creation of ideals.

North Node in the Fifth House

This Node points me towards openness with other people. The learning process in this house involves a deepening understanding of love and sexual relationships. With my eleventh house South Node I will have been highly selective in my choice of friends. I may still find that my South Node calls me to relate to people who in some way are different from the ordinary person.

They may be high up in their own particular hierarchical structure, whether they are professors, well known authors or millionaire businessmen. Formerly I too may have held a high position in hierarchy, maybe as a monk. My close contacts then were with a selected few.

Now I need to come down from my elevated position to the turmoil of ordinary contact. I have to experiment with life in a creative way and be ready to get involved with others, and have close physical contact with them. No longer can I save myself for someone special. I have to learn to become humble, and ordinary. I cannot separate myself. I need to be with others. I learn the lesson that I am nothing without other people. This is part of the high esoteric law of Aquarius.

North Node in the Eleventh House

The direction in which my North Node moves me during my lifetime is towards ideals and values. I learn to become highly selective about the people I relate to. From my South Node position I have experienced a wide variety of close contacts with many people. I have learned much about the games people play around the themes of love and power. At times I am still drawn back to the sense of security I feel in my close contacts with other people.

My North Node calls me to be more discriminating in my relationships. My close friends must prove themselves by their ethical standards and their humanitarianism. Their ideals must reflect the highest potential of the human being. I am aware of the need to demonstrate these ideals and values.

I have to come up to the same level as these new friends and involve myself with them. I gradually deepen my discrimination in relating to others. My knowledge about human relationships from my South Node is used here, and enables me to quickly know about another person's problem in human relationships. I can learn to use my shadow side for the advantage of others.

Up in the clean air of the eleventh house there is a detachment from the calls of the ego. From this position I can look down towards the fifth house and understand that I have to give up my friendship with those to whom I formerly linked myself, and I come to share my knowledge and understanding with others. What is mine I share, but only with a selected group. In being myself, and at the same time being part of a team, I develop an attitude of brotherhood.

Existence Axis

On this, the last of the six axes, in mutable houses we face the existential question of 'to be or not to be', and in doing so we find our 'beingness'.

North Node in the Sixth House

With the South Node in the twelfth house, it feels comfortable to retire into this area of withdrawal from the world. I can easily enter my inner space and avoid contact with other people. The pull of the spiritual dimension towards passive as opposed to active service is strong.

This is what I have to leave behind. I am being called to work on the You side of the chart. The fulfilment of duty involves working my whole life through, joyfully taking on responsibilities, burdens and duties. But I want to resist this as it seems to hold less appeal for me than my twelfth house. To overcome this pull back, I have to discipline myself. I am able to do it when I have grown into a different life motivation, as I move away from my twelfth house.

My North Node is situated in the house of service and love of humanity. I am called to be there all the time, twenty four hours a day. The law of service is the motivation of the soul. The drive of the soul is to serve other people. When I find it happening I know the soul is at work.

In relinquishing the twelfth house attitude of retreat and quiet, I receive joy in the sixth house. I can then reap my harvest from the Virgo house. As each duty comes along I fulfill it cheerfully and happily. In whichever house the Moon's Node is placed, reaching towards it can feel like going through the proverbial eye of the needle.

North Node in the Twelfth House

The call of this Node is to retire from the world, and not to be involved in the myriad of details of daily living. I have to find my own quiet inner space. Here I can recover. My South Node makes it so easy to occupy my time serving others. I do it so easily. I take on other people's burdens. I wonder how other people would manage if I was not there. I cannot begin to imagine how I can give up all these duties and responsibilities. People would not notice that I existed.

Yet it is my task to find this quiet place within. I have to let go of all the feelings of guilt which are attached to not doing my duty to others. I go outside of the everyday world. Through meditation I can begin to train, and move towards peaceful self-realisation. With this nodal placement I have chosen to be linked back with my eternal source. To achieve this requires an effort of will. From that space I can come back peaceful yet full of energy.

It takes courage to retire from worldly preoccupations. I doubt whether it can be achieved. I have daily to make the time to find this quiet inner space. Whilst I remain in my sixth house I am frequently exhausted. The motivation of service and healing can enable me to move towards the twelfth house, and thus overcome the pull of the South Node. Often the twelfth house North Node is found in the chart of healers. I can become a channel through which energies can flow into the world.

Growing Point in the Twelve Houses

The following by Louise Huber provides further thoughts on each of the nodal axes.

The North Node symbolises our growing point. We can see in it an indication of our greatest spiritual and personal potential, and are well-advised to work with it consciously and deliberately. There is great energy and drive in the nodal axis, from South Node to North Node. The North Node is our potential step forward; the South Node is backward-looking. They are the Jupiter and Saturn points. In order to make the best possible progress to achieve our potential, we first have to deal with the effect of the energies of the South Node which is always trying to hold us back. That is why my key phrases are expressed in black and white, dualistically, in an either/or fashion.

To begin with we are not asked to achieve a synthesis of the opposing meanings. We have to acknowledge the pull of the ensuing struggle. In *Moon Node Astrology* we have dealt in detail with the long term aim of effecting a synthesis of these conflicting energies.

Growth Potential of the North Node through the Houses

1st House. The greatest benefit is gained by achieving personal independence and no longer relying on the support of other people.

2nd House. The greatest benefit is gained by a calm acceptance of our own worth and abilities and by relinquishing any need or desire for other people's means and possessions.

3rd House. The greatest benefit is gained by learning from and through other people without proclaiming our own views as being valid ones.

4th House. The greatest benefit is gained by acknowledging the importance of the family, by being content with our origins and putting aside all cravings for power and recognition.

5th House. The greatest benefit is gained by our readiness to take risks and experiment without being unduly anxious about losing out or losing face.

6th House. The greatest benefit is gained through dedication and involvement with our work, through serving all manner of people and concerns and after overcoming any craving for solitude or isolation. The key concept is to get on cheerfully with fulfilling our daily tasks.

7th House. The greatest benefit is gained by being totally absorbed in shared ventures, marriage and other partnerships, after overcoming all tendencies to self-seeking and self-absorption.

8th House. The greatest benefit is gained by breaking our preoccupations with material possessions and certainties, by overcoming all fear of loss and change and when we have learned to "Render unto Caesar what is Caesar's" and to God what is God's.

9th House. The greatest benefit is gained by developing our own thinking, making and standing by our own decisions, travel and study, after learning to abandon any need to follow in other people's footsteps.

10th House. The greatest benefit is gained by realising our own aims, becoming a self-made person, overcoming the restrictions imposed by family traditions and ambitions after renouncing the craving for a quiet life and home comforts.

11th House. The greatest benefit is gained by choosing our own friends, finding groups of like-minded people and working for the effective implementation of ideas after overcoming our urge to 'go it alone' and to indulge our personal whims.

12th House. The greatest benefit is gained by making good use of solitude, to work for inner progress, improve our inner life and spirituality after overcoming the need to always be active and involved because we reckon that the world could not cope without us.

(Translation note – in the original article, the phrase at the start of each of the descriptions of the 12 houses is "Der Aufstieg", meaning literally "up-step". This has been translated so that it reads, "The greatest benefit is gained…" but it could equally well be translated to read, "We make the most progress…" The intention embedded in "Der Aufstieg" is that we should cooperate with the direction of the North Node energies in order to get the most from them.)

North Node in the Stress Area

Experience suggests that when the North Node is found in the stress area before the cusp of a house then there are two tasks to perform. The first task will relate to the axis in which the Nodes are situated in the natal chart, and the second task will relate to the house axis which follows.

The Need for Balance

When we discover our North Node and understand its importance in our lives, we must be careful that we do not isolate ourselves from the South Node. As in any polarity, we need to learn balance. We cannot ignore the South Node but must integrate it into our lives at a new level. For instance, if we discover the joy of inner peace and solitude from a twelfth house North Node we cannot then decide that we will do no more work, that we will opt out of the real world. We must come back into it but the work that we do should be for others, rather than for ourselves or to prove to others that we exist.

Aspects to the North Node

It is common for both the North and South Nodes to be included in astrological charts. However, aspects between the Nodes and the planets are generally not included. In the opening paragraphs of this chapter attention was drawn to the inclusion of the North Node within the aspect structure in a Huber chart.

From the preceding brief descriptions of the meanings of the North Node in each house, it is apparent that the Node is an important directional pointer in each of our charts. The Node operates as a deep motivational level. Until we begin to reach some understanding of its meaning for us, it works at an unconscious level in our lives.

In drawing aspects to the North Node, we see more clearly into our inner make-up. Each of the different aspects has a different quality, which is associated with one of the seven main planets. Thus the quincunx aspect is a deep learning aspect, and is linked with the planet Saturn. We generally find it easier to relate to the energy in an aspect between two planets than we do to the aspect between the Node and a planet.

Aspects from the Node to a planet do not in themselves give energy, but they offer us a means of being consciously, as opposed to unconsciously, aware of our continuing opportunity to grow.

When a planet is conjunct the South Node, we may find we have a great ease with it. The world may well applaud us when we use it, as it operates in areas where we have developed abilities over many lifetimes. Such a planet on the other hand may act as a brake on the balancing we seek to achieve in this life. By remaining with our South Node, we are pulled backwards instead of moving forwards and will need greater encouragement and help in reaching the North Node.

Conversely, a planet conjunct the North Node will feel strangely unfamiliar to us in the early part of life. Alternatively, as this area of the chart is one where we are relatively inexperienced, we may focus on the more negative aspects of that particular planet. The presence of this planet acts as an additional focal point, as it continues to direct our attention to the tasks that we have to accomplish through our North Node.

We can become so in tune with the energies of a planet conjunct the North Node that we should encourage it to become a leading quality in our life so that we can use it successfully in a profession or career which relates to that quality.

Whilst an opposition to the North Node may make it difficult for us to sense its purpose and meaning in our life, a square aspect will tend to make us wilfully ignore the Node, since we will be inclined to see it as a target that is too difficult to achieve.

With blue aspects there will normally be an understanding of the opportunities that exist to reach the Node, but with green aspects ambivalence will cloud the issue and a person may or may not be able to see them. However, there may be less attraction to stay in the South Node, as would be the case with an opposition. The opposition would make it more likely for a person to be too easily persuaded not to bother to try and achieve the objective of the North Node.

A Student's Experience of the North Node

My North Node in the 4th House in Gemini

When our strings are still being pulled by the South Node, it can be very difficult to start our journey towards the North Node. My journey began when I was at an astrological psychology workshop. We were all lying on the floor and the facilitator took us through this visualisation of moving from the South to the North, asking us to be aware of what we saw. My Nodes are on the 4/10 axis with the South in Sagittarius in the 10th and the North in Gemini in the 4th. There I was wearing a tiara, a beautiful gown and to my amazement, when I looked down at my feet I was wearing a pair of very ordinary slippers. I felt as though I was walking down a slope and there was a great reluctance to reach my destination. I began to ponder on this as I could understand it logically but couldn't feel it.

Shortly afterwards, I was invited to Sweden to stay with a student I'd met at the workshop. Her name was Inger. I'd been to Sweden before and loved it but this time it was very special. I cannot read or speak Swedish but even when I was with a group of people all speaking Swedish, I never felt disconnected from the group. I could understand what they were saying but couldn't join in the conversation. There were so many North Node in Gemini in the 4th experiences during my visit – we stayed in a family cabin by the lake with other members of the family who had their own cabins on the family land, we went to a wonderful folk musical event where I was just one of the crowd but able to enjoy the music, dancing and just being connected to the group through eye contact and smiles but what really enabled me to connect with my North Node was my trip back to the airport.

Inger was going to drive me back but she was unwell so I suggested I went by train. The only seat available was in the family carriage. This was unlike any train carriage I'd travelled in before – there was a play area complete with a climbing frame for the children, space for the prams and was filled with Mums, Dads, children and babies. I felt very comfortable to sit there and be part of them and yet not.

Feeling a bit hungry and thirsty, I decided to visit the buffet car but when I went to pay I found I didn't

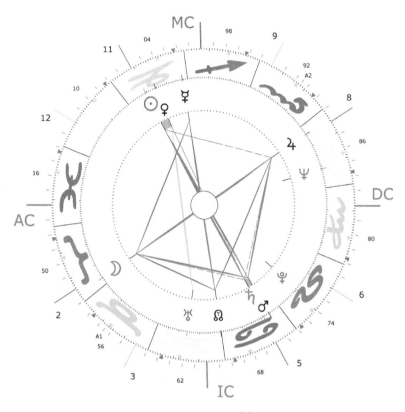

Figure 7.2.3 Geraldine.
11.01.46; 08.00 GMT; Kampala, Uganda; 00N19 32E25

have enough money. Someone else generously offered to pay. I sat down and the lady next to me spoke to me in Swedish and when she found I was English, she was keen to practice her language skills. She asked me what I did and I suddenly felt very uncomfortable and under pressure – now I had to be somebody (house 10)! Thinking quickly, I decided that I wouldn't be forced to be somebody doing something important and decided to say that I was an astrologer. She didn't show much reaction and was much more interested in telling me all about her 10th house family – very clever son and daughter who were in high power jobs that had status and where they earned a lot of money. Both had been to good universities and graduated with excellent degrees. So there we were, house 10 and house 4 sat alongside each other!

When I returned to the family carriage, it felt so good stepping into a space where I didn't have to be anything other than myself. It was very freeing and it became easier and less fearful to take my first steps in my slippers towards my North Node in Gemini in the 4th house.

The Ascendant Sign in the Chart

Just as the Moon's Node is the point of intersection of two spheres in space, so the Ascendant (AC) is also a point of intersection on the Earth level. For each of us our AC has a spiritual significance. Sometimes we find that the Moon's Node house matches the AC.

Until relatively recently in history, the AC was the mask or persona through which a person met the world. The image a person portrayed was considered important. The image was not however the essence of the person. In the wake of transpersonal psychology and other developments, it is now somewhat easier for the self to find expression, without needing a mask. It is important to make the distinction between the essence of a person, as seen through the Sun, and the mask or AC.

The AC is rather like a vaguely discernible signpost, which continues to point us in the direction we need to be going. Some of this direction will have come in our early years from our environment – from our home influences, from school, from many aspects of our surroundings. As we grow older, we gradually develop the qualities of our AC. We should not dismiss the sign on our AC as a mask we do not need. As we grow into the qualities of our AC, we come to understand more of the spiritual significance of that sign.

The ascendant needs to be considered in the context of the spiritual dimension of the chart. It represents, amongst other things, a transcendental dimension from which we come and to which we shall return.

The esoteric seed thought for each sign can, possibly through meditation, give us an indication of how we can develop the spiritual quality of our AC.

Recommended reading
Reflections and Meditations on the Signs of the Zodiac, Louise Huber

Moon Node Astrology, Bruno and Louise Huber – expands upon material presented in this section and 7.3.

Seed Thoughts for each Sign

Aries
I come forth, and from the plane of mind I rule.

Taurus
I see, and when the Eye is opened, all is illumined.

Gemini
I recognise my other Self and in the waning of that Self I grow and glow.

Cancer
I build a lighted house and therein dwell.

Leo
I am That and That am I.

Virgo
I am the Mother and the Child, I God, I matter am.

Libra
I choose the way that leads between the two great lines of force.

Scorpio
Warrior am I, and from the battle I emerge triumphant.

Sagittarius
I see the goal, I reach the goal, then I see another.

Capricorn
Lost am I in light supernal, yet on that light I turn my back.

Aquarius
Water of Life am I, poured forth for thirsty men.

Pisces
I leave the Father's Home and turning back I save.

Exercise 7.2

1. Refer back to section 2.2, which covers motivation, shaping and direction in the chart, and take another look at Figure 2.2.3 on page 61. Consider the position of the North Node in this chart **in relation to the chart as a whole**.

2. Reflect on your own chart, observe the Nodal Axis and aspects to the North Node, and make notes on your answers to the following questions:

   a) Describe in as clear and specific detail as possible how your South Node manifests itself in your life. In other words, stand back from an area of your behaviour where you live easily, automatically and to some extent unconsciously, identify it, make it as visible to yourself as you possibly can. This behaviour will operate in a number of areas in your life so see how broad a spectrum of involvement you can discern.

   b) How do you currently view the meaning and implication of the North Node in your chart? How does this manifest in your everyday life?

   c) Imagine yourself having made the journey from the South to the North Node in your chart. See yourself having fully integrated the spiritual tasks that you placed on your path. In whichever way feels right for you, try to have an image of yourself, living fully in your North Node. You may wish to try this through meditation or visualisation. Describe in as much detail as you can, this image and the quality of your life from this perspective.

   d) What qualities do you need to develop to move from b) to c)? What, in practical terms, can you do to further this development?

Appendix Astrology of the Moon's Nodes - The Inner Guide to our Evolution

As a bridge between studying the Moon Node Axis in this section and the Moon Node Chart in the following section, we offer the following summary by Bruno and Louise Huber of Moon Node Astrology.

The astrology of the Moon's Nodes owes it existence to years of research which was inspired by our need for a holistic approach to horoscope interpretation. It gives answers to questions which have occupied mankind for aeons of time, questions concerning the meaning of our lives. Now it is a basic scientific fact that the type of answer we find is very much determined by the type of question we ask in the first place, and that of course applies to astrology, too. It is obvious that questions concerning psychological and spiritual problems call for a methodology quite different from those which restrict themselves to good luck and material success.

Many more people are now turning to a study of astrology because life no longer makes sense when it is judged by standards acquired in our daily routine at school and at work. We now hope that astrology will widen our horizons and also free us from inner and outer compulsions. A study of astrology does indeed lift our level of consciousness, and helps us to transcend the former limits of our thinking. And the astrology of the Moon's Nodes is an especially fruitful approach; it helps us recognise our roots, gives us new insight into our inner reality and enables us to come to grips with it. It provides recognition of underlying existential, karmic, fated conditions. It offers an overview, synthesis, and clarity. It delivers us, step by step, from the grip of the fear/desire polarity, and gives us the will to work for positive growth. It makes us aware of the interweaving of the inner and outer, the higher and lower, the microcosm and the macrocosm, and encourages us to view the whole of life from a transcendental, a cosmic point of view.

The vexed question of Time

Working with the nodes from an esoteric standpoint can also give us a new slant on the vexed question of Time. By viewing humanity's development over several millennia, by fathoming the purpose and meaning of this process, we gain an enhanced historical long-term perspective. And it is a salutary thought that, as an integral part of humanity, we can look forward to many more centuries of potential growth. The moment we accept the possibility that we do in fact possess an immortal soul which, throughout countless incarnations, has participated in this evolutionary surge, we need no longer be plagued by thoughts of our ephemeral nature. This dissolves some knotty problems, puts them into a wider perspective: a bird's eye view replaces our blinkered vision. It leads straight to a feeling of being involved, to an all-inclusive feeling of love, to the up-to-date attitude of "not-only-but-also". It is the way of thinking of the Aquarian Age which is thus furthered by nodal astrology. It leads us way beyond the restrictions imposed by space/time and the old-fashioned adversarial either/or attitude, which was so divisive in the past. For a holistic understanding of life we have to consider the overriding reality of cosmic laws and at the same time remain aware of the importance of the details, the minutiae of our daily existence.

Esoteric Astrology

The astrology of the Moon's Nodes is an essential part of esoteric astrology. It is an expansive concept which deals with the entire universe, including everything within it, excluding naught. That's why it is such an enormous area of study – we'll never come to the end of it. The astrology of the future will have to build more and more on an ever-deepening understanding of cosmic laws if it wants to convey an all-inclusive picture of nature, of mankind, our world, of the whole universe. It can be thought of as being the ABC of the cosmos, as providing the key to all-encompassing, limitless knowledge. A skilful interpretation of astrological charts teaches us to work with symbolism and it leads us to appreciate our interconnectedness. Our lives are interwoven with other dimensions that go way beyond our everyday consciousness. More than any other philosophical system, esoteric astrology leads us to the fundamental principles underlying all existence. It asks the fundamental question of all philosophies: What makes the world tick? And its answers speak not merely to our reasoning faculties. Therefore this type of astrology gives us vastly more than a mere cook-book approach to the fate and condition of individual people.

New Needs

The last few decades have seen an enormous surge in our need to see ourselves as a small but integral part of the entire cosmos. Traditional astrology tended to consist of a series of detailed pronouncements. But now we more and more look for a holistic approach. We are looking for an esoteric content and context. In fact many people study astrology specifically to gain added insight into their spiritual potential. They want to find out about their karma, and about the direction which they have to follow in this life. They want to work for inner growth, and to remove misconceptions and avoid blind alleys. As long as they feel they are on the right track, they gladly accept the need for periods of sacrifice, cleansing, crisis and transformation. That's where nodal astrology is such a help. Clearly only an integrative method of chart interpretation could provide answers to the questions posed by depth psychology: "Who am I? Where do I come from? Where am I going?"

In the past astrological expertise consisted of an enumeration of outward symptoms. We tried to prove everything by referring to a set of rules which were combined and recombined according to our hopes and fears. But modern astrology asks the question "Why?" It checks its veracity against the reality of our actual lives and points to principles which reflect our true nature. Such astrology is for grown-ups only, for people who dare to form their own opinions and go their own way. It gives us increased knowledge, so that we can detect root causes of inappropriate behaviour, so that we can stop making the same mistakes over and over again, and learn instead to do better in the future. A comparison of the nodal and natal horoscopes highlights the deeper meaning of apparent tragedy, and shows just what we might learn through it. It also helps us to understand other people better, and to offer them constructive help in their hour of need.

Nodal Horoscope

By working with both the nodal and the natal horoscope we can sense the potential of synthesis which facilitates the integration of the personality, and this applies equally to the client and the therapist. By examining the nodal chart in a therapeutic setting, it is, for instance, very easy to have a good look at our shadow personality. Using only the ordinary psychological tools at our disposal this could be a long-winded and wearying process. With astrology it is much easier, quicker and less aggravating. In the nodal chart, trained and enlightened counsellors can point to meaningful connections and deeper causes way beyond the concepts of analytical astrology. Based on the theory of reincarnation, we can probe questions of the person's growth potential and thus throw some light on the purpose of life in general, and this life in particular.

Integration of the Shadow

In our long years as teachers and counsellors, our students have assured us over and over again that it gave them great comfort and help to examine their nodal position and their nodal chart. It enabled them to accept themselves in their entirety, and to widen and deepen their level of consciousness. Those that were familiar with esoteric thinking could now detect the roots of their present problems in previous lifetimes, which made sense of many situations that had previously appeared quite meaningless. Their understanding increased by leaps and bounds, and they achieved a degree of transformation and individuation which was far more lasting and far-reaching than could have been achieved by a mere character delineation based on examining their innate strengths and weaknesses.

7.3 The Moon Node Chart

The Moon Node Chart, or nodal chart, can be interpreted as revealing the shadow side of our personality, or as providing a summary of our past/karmic experiences.

This section teaches:

- How to erect the Moon Node Chart
- Its role as a resource to better understand the shadow personality
- Its use with Age Progression to provide insight into the unconscious drives that create inexplicable, but significant occurrences in life.

The Shadow Function of the Moon Node Chart

The Moon Node chart gives information about our desire nature. In esoteric terms, it symbolises the astral body. It is the so-called mirror-sphere where our motivations, wishes and actions from the past (our karma) are projected into the present.

Expressed in terms of depth psychology, the Moon Node chart makes visible the shadow of our personality. We all have an invisible part of our nature containing drives, wishes and projections. Since these are not accessible to our waking consciousness, we usually suppress them, as they are unusable or even seem dangerous in everyday life. Thus, this shadow in us is usually designated as negative or 'black'.

However, we also unconsciously suppress personal qualities and character traits that are positive simply because they may not fit into the dogmatism of our thinking or are not welcome by our environment. It is important to realise that they are nonetheless parts of ourselves which do not find outward expression and that we use up considerable energy in keeping them hidden from consciousness.

C.G. Jung speaks of "man's shadow", considering it a part of the unconscious which is particularly difficult to reach and which is explored by depth psychology. We are hardly conscious of the motivations, secret wishes or split parts of our self in this shadow sphere, much less so do we admit to them. At best, they may appear in our dreams. Nevertheless, they affect us, only we do not relate them to ourselves; they appear as reactions of our unconscious projections. They come out of the blue, entering our lives from the outside as situations, as objects or people. With magnetic force, they seem to bring us precisely that which we suppress or fear.

Many a chaotic external situation is a reflection which can easily fool us. We cannot handle it consciously as long as we regard it as external – not belonging to us. This is why the after-effects of the shadow functions are usually beyond our control. In a sense, they represent determinative tendencies or automatic response mechanisms. We first have to go through them as inevitable experience before we relate them to ourselves.

Age Progression in the Moon Node Chart

There is a time dimension or age progression to the Moon Node chart. We use the same time span, of 72 years, for the progression of the Moon Node Age Point through the whole circle, just as with the Age Point in the Natal Chart. As the Moon Node houses are all of size 30°, each year of life corresponds to 5°.

Through the progression of the Moon Node AP, the shadow qualities already described can come into our consciousness in various forms or they can result in behavioural patterns which are not recognised. They can also trigger regression to former modes of behaviour.

The Moon Node AP is often associated with karmic experiences, which, in reality, are nothing but automatisms of the psyche. Coming from the deepest layers of the unconscious, from the suppressed or unlived shadow-sphere of our psyche, they can appear as 'fate' or 'karma' during the AP transit over a planet.

The combined effect of the two Age Points (natal and nodal) can be observed. With the transit of natal AP we experience rationally comprehensible psychological processes which can either bring about events or be triggered by events. With the Moon Node AP, we can recognise the real motives for doing the things we do and behaving the way we do. Thus, we uncover a deeper layer of motivation that can explain things that seemed incomprehensible before. If our consciousness is strong enough and our intelligent powers of discrimination are working, we can consciously carry out a part of this, liberating ourselves step by step from wrong attitudes.

How to Erect the Moon Node Chart

Just as we divide the apparent path of the Sun into 12 zodiacal signs, we can also, starting from the North Node, divide the Moon's path into 12 houses, the Moon houses. Technically this is quite simple.

The essential differences between the Natal chart and the Moon Node chart are:

- The natal position of the North Node becomes the AC.
- The natal position of the AC becomes the new North Node.

Using the natal chart positions:

1. Draw the chart with the new AC position (the longitude of the natal North Node) and draw in the remaining signs in the normal way but clockwise instead of anti-clockwise. (See your own Moon Node chart computer printout if in doubt).

2. Use the equal house system of house division, so that each house is 30°. The first house will as usual be the one just below the AC.

3. Draw in the remaining planets in their correct positions within the signs.

4. Draw in the North Node in its new position (at the longitude of the natal AC)

5. The aspects between planets will remain the same except for the aspects to the natal North Node that has now become the AC.

6. Calculate new aspects to the nodal North Node.

Notes

- Most software that will produce natal charts also has the option to produce the Moon Node chart.
- Remember that in the Moon Node chart, the signs rotate in a clockwise direction but that the Age Point moves in an anti-clockwise direction through the houses and enters a new house every 6 years (as in the natal chart). See also section 6.1 Age Progression.

Example Moon Node and Natal Charts

Figure 7.3.1 shows the example of Jane's natal and nodal charts.

The natal Moon North Node has become the nodal chart AC and the natal AC has become the nodal Moon North Node and aspects have been calculated and drawn to this point.

Note that the longitudes of the nodal cusps correspond to the position of the node chart AC which is the same as the longitude of the natal North Node. The houses are of equal size, 30°, and therefore will always be the same number of degrees and minutes as the AC.

Age Point in Nodal Chart

In the nodal chart the signs go **clockwise,** but we still trace the Age Point **anti-clockwise** in the same way as in the natal chart.

	Position						House Koch			
	Radix		House		Cusp		Invert Point		Low Point	
☉	8° 8'18 ♓	2	28°25'32	1	14°21'13 ♋		24°44' 0 ♋		1° 8'53	
☽	9° 2'23	1	27°15'12	2	11°31'39 ♌		22°15'18 ♌		28°53' 6	
☿	21° 2'13	2	10° 9'28	3	9°36'44 ♓		20°40'10 ♓		27°30'10 ♓	
♀	26°25'49	2	15°55' 8	10	8°33'35		22°28'59		1° 5'18 ♍	
♂	18° 9'33 ♉	5	3° 0'23	11	15° 0'41 ♍		27° 0'33 ♍		4°25'27 ♐	
♃	29°12'55R ♈	9	20°18'56	12	16°25'18 ♐		27° 5'27 ♐		3°41' 5 ♋	
♄	13°47'16 ♐	11	27°29' 3							
♅	3°37'21R ♌	7	21°16'22							
♆	2°26'13R ♏	10	19°39' 4							
♇	28°59'26R ♌	8	18°39'14							
☊	23° 2'19R ♏	11	7°40' 0							
As	14°21'13 ♋	1	0° 0' 0							
Mc	8°33'35 ♌	10	0° 0' 0							

Chart data extract

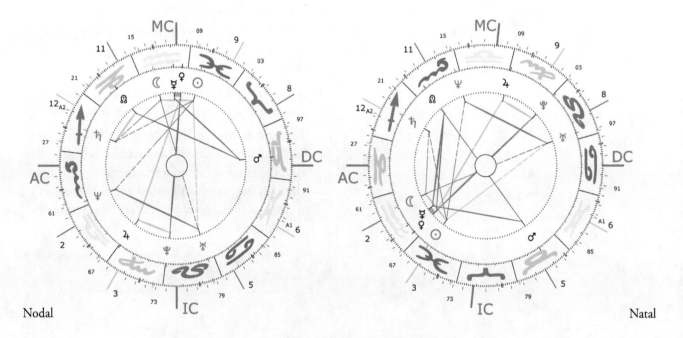

Nodal   Natal

Figure 7.3.1 Example – Jane's Nodal and Natal Charts

The Intersection of the Two Age Points or Shadow Axis

There are two points of intersection between the natal chart and the Moon Node chart. Twice in 72 years, the natal AP and the nodal AP fall on the **same degree of the same sign**. These **crossing points** or intersection points can be experienced as marked turning-points in life. Even if they are not immediately recognised as such, in retrospect they can almost always be observed.

Finding the Crossing Points

Referring to Figure 7.3.1, the following shows how the two points are calculated.

If we track the Age Point anti-clockwise in both charts we can see that at 6 years of age it is at 11° 31' in Aquarius in the natal chart, and at 23° 05' in Libra in the nodal chart. If we tabulate the movement of the two Age Points the result is as follows:

Age	AP in Natal Chart	AP in Nodal Chart
0	14° 20' Capricorn	23° 05' Scorpio
6	11° 31' Aquarius	23° 05' Libra
12	9° 35' Pisces	23° 05' Virgo
18	8° 32 ' Aries	23° 05' Leo
24	14° 59' Taurus	23° 05' Cancer
30	16° 25' Gemini	23° 05' Gemini

At this point we can see that the Age Points in both charts are close together so we can start to calculate in yearly and 3 monthly intervals as necessary:

Age	AP in Natal Chart	AP in Nodal Chart
30¼	17° 35' Gemini	21° 50' Gemini
30½	18° 45' Gemini	20° 35' Gemini
30¾	19° 55' Gemini	19° 20' Gemini
31	21° 05' Gemini	18° 05' Gemini
36	14° 20' Cancer	23° 05' Taurus

From the above we can see that the Age Points are at the same longitude around the age of 30¾. In practical terms a week or so before she reaches age 30 years and 9 months will be close enough.

The next meeting point will be 36 years later, i.e. at 66¾.

Significance of Crossing Points and Shadow Axis

These two points of intersection are shadow-points which can be defined according to the house or axis theme. For example, if the shadow axis falls in the Encounter Axis (houses 1/7), 'I-You' issues will be prominent throughout the individual's life. If the two crossing points are on the Possession Axis (houses 2/8), material security and personal responsibility will be the life issues, and on the Thought Axis (houses 3/9) learning and communication will be the main focus.

In Figure 7.3.1 we can see that the crossing points in Jane's natal chart fall on the Existence Axis (6/12). This suggests that the underlying issue in Jane's life will ultimately be the right to exist that manifests through the need to keep busy, work hard and serve others. At age 30, Jane had so far in her life driven herself in work situations, always complaining that she had no time for anything else. She had just started a relationship and because her partner complained that he never saw her she was faced with the need to find a balance between work and time for herself with her partner.

[Jane is now a very active, involved, sociable but unmarried, successful private medical practitioner, which allows her to encompass 5th house (Mars conjunct South Node) human contacts in a safe professional environment whilst also embracing the 11th house North Node and Saturn, from which area she can feel in control of relationships. So, whilst she has achieved some kind of balance on this axis it does not appear to get to the root of relationship issues, which she is now recognising as something she needs to give serious attention to.

It is worth noting that the other fixed axis (2/8) is also accentuated in the chart and that the fixed cross (by house as well as by sign) becomes an important life issue for her. So although she went through a very stressful time when the Age Points intersected at 30/31 years of age, her own professional success and resultant self-worth on the 2/8 axis continued to create an imbalance. An opportunity for her to take a deeper look at what the 5/11 relationship axis meant in her life was avoided. It is worth noting how very strong inner motivation can be, and the extent to which it can inhibit positive change. However, in the case of Jane it would be important to also take account of other factors such as the Family Model (Chapter 5). It seems that it is only now, with the Age Point on the 2/8 axis, is she beginning to come to terms with balancing her own security needs with the ability to allow a partner into her a life in a free and fearless manner. Only when this happens is she likely to be able to connect with the emotional needs of a Pisces Sun.]

The first crossing of the two APs occurs between 0 and 36 years of age and the second between 36 and 72 years. With each person it occurs at a different time in life according to the position of the Moon Node in the chart. If the intersection of the APs falls into the 2/8 axis, the first crossing point will be experienced in the 2nd house, between the ages of 6 and 12 depending on the exact degree within the house, and the second crossing point in the 8th house between the ages of 42 and 48.

Effects of Crossing Point

In general we observe that if, up to the first crossing point, our life has been rather passive and strongly influenced and shaped by the environment, afterwards we become increasingly dominant with a more active approach to life. On the other hand, a dominant, extroverted approach usually becomes calmer, more passive and defensive after the crossing point. The first crossing point is generally striking. If the person then integrates the learning related to the first crossing point, the second crossing is hardly noticeable. The stronger the effect of the second crossing point, the less we have learned in the previous 36 years.

It is also possible that drastic, incisive events take place at the crossing points, incidents that change the reality of our lives, sudden blows of fate coming out of the blue. Often we find that the crossing point relates to a phase in life rather than to a single event. This phase may extend in time up to a year or so either side of the age signified by the exact degree of intersection.

Everyone is more or less subject to fateful life-changing incidents that can hardly be explained in rational terms. Many an astrologer has tried in vain to find an explanation with traditional prognostic techniques. Often the only astrological explanation can be found in the intersection of the two Age Points.

If you have had such an inexplicable experience, perhaps you can check whether it occurred at one of your crossing points.

Recommended Reading
The Living Birth Chart, Joyce Hopewell, Chapter 5

Note
It is important not to confuse the **Crossing Axis** with the **Moon Node Axis** in the natal chart that is indicated by the placement of the North Node.

Exercise 7.3

1. Compare your natal and nodal charts and get a feel for the similarities and differences.

   If you want to get a real understanding of this, you are recommended to manually draw out your Moon Node chart using an ordinary natal chart form. Use computer data generated by your chart software/service.

2. Look at the progress of the Moon Node AP (working anti-clockwise from the AC and dividing each house into 6 years) and comment on life experiences that relate to conjunction and opposition aspects made by the AP to planets in your Moon Node chart.

3. Compare the positions of the crossing points on your natal and nodal charts.

   If you manually calculate the position of the crossing points, this will help your understanding.

4. If you have already reached a crossing point in your chart, reflect on the importance of this/these period(s) in your own life, bearing in mind that the significance of the period in question may extend for a year or even two either side of the date of the exact crossing point.

   If you have not reached your first crossing point, work out the crossing point on one of your practice charts, preferably that of a friend you can talk to – discuss with him/her what this may have meant in the context of their life and chart.

Chapter 8. Applied Astrological Psychology

This final chapter aims to consolidate the method of chart interpretation as presented in this book, and give practical guidance in its use with clients' charts.

Contents:

        8.1 Working as an Astrological Consultant

        8.2 Working with the Three Charts

        8.3 Practical Chart Interpretation

8.1 Working as an Astrological Consultant

In this section we look at the implications of working with others as an astrological consultant. We consider:

- basic communication and listening skills required,
- pitfalls to avoid
- practical points to bear in mind when setting up an astrological consultation.
- the benefits of an astrological consultation

Working with Others

This section provides an introduction to the use of astrology in the field of human relationships. Every situation find ourselves in involves other people in some way, so understanding how we relate to others, as well as to ourselves, is important. It becomes essential if we plan to work with people in a professional capacity.

The Growth Cycle

Let's take an analogy with nature. If we plant a seed in a garden, it will in due time, if all goes well, emerge through the soil first as a single leaf, then as it continues to grow it will produce more and bigger leaves and ultimately flowers that will provide colour, scent and beauty.

However what can we do if all does not go well? If the emerging seedling is overrun by weeds or crowded out by other plants? If it becomes diseased, or is growing where there is insufficient light or moisture to enable it to achieve its full potential?

A number of possibilities are open to us – we can read the instructions on the seed packet, study a book on gardening, go to classes or, if there is no improvement, call in an expert to advise us.

How does this relate to astrological psychology?

If we substitute a human being for the seed in the garden we can see that our own environment for growth can be as varied and sometimes as hostile as that in the average garden. As a consequence many individuals go through life without ever understanding what their potential is and how they might achieve it. Some are conscious of frustrations, anxieties, worries and problems that they would like to overcome.

It is in this area that the experienced astrologer, who chooses to work with people, can play an important role by helping those who seek to become more consciously aware. He or she may use the birth chart in much the same way as the gardener will use the instructions on a seed packet. For instance it is possible to identify potential skills which the childhood environment may have left underdeveloped, offer suggestions on careers, relationships, and so on.

It is wise however to recognise your limits as an astrologer and to refer clients to fully qualified counsellors or therapists if they show psychological or emotional problems which you are not trained to deal with.

How do your want to work as an astrologer?

The applications of astrology are almost limitless so at some stage you will need to take a conscious decision regarding the way you want to use astrology in your work. If working with people is your prime objective, then you need to decide on your level of participation.

Most astrologers interested in helping people develop their potential will gain experience initially by testing out their knowledge and skills at a fairly superficial level. They will find out what works for them and what doesn't, and begin to gain a perspective of the relationship between a natal chart and the individual person.

At some stage, astrologers can easily find themselves working at a level of emotional complexity that they are not prepared for. It then becomes necessary to decide whether their knowledge and experience as an astrologer needs to be widened to encompass the skills of the counsellor or the therapist.

Since there is no one method of counselling or therapy that is necessarily better than another, you need to be aware that formal training in a particular therapeutic discipline may prove to be a limitation to the potential value of the tools that you have at your disposal, i.e. the three astrological charts. So it is wise to be clear on your personal needs and motivation before making a decision on the additional skills that you would like to acquire and the type of formal training that will help you gain these skills.

> It is wise to recognise your limits as an astrologer and to refer clients to fully qualified counsellors or therapists if they show psychological or emotional problems that you are not trained to deal with.

Basic Skills Required of the Astrological Consultant

Even if you don't feel the need for additional training in counselling, here are some basic skills that you will need in order to communicate effectively with clients.

Establishing Rapport

Rapport between two people is the most important foundation stone for positive and successful communication.

Communication happens at several levels and we can pick up many important clues from body language and voice tone in addition to what is being said. In order to establish rapport, we need to pay close attention to the other person, their breathing, movement, language, pace of delivery, posture... We can match and mirror these to create a space in which the other person unconsciously feels comfortable and can develop trust.

Matching and mirroring

Matching language is very powerful and creates a deep understanding between two people. Particularly important is the use of a similar register or style of communication, to avoid using terms that are unknown or whose meaning is unclear to the other. Using the same or similar words and expressions will help convey our message in a way that is easily understood.

Mirroring focuses more on non-verbal clues, for instance sitting in a similar way so that we appear to be reflecting the image that we receive, as a mirror would. Paying attention to movement and eye patterns will greatly help us knowing how our client is feeling and what is going on inside them: are they anxious, confused, calm and in control, testing us? It can also tell us how they access their information and how they make sense of what we say.

Pacing

Pacing helps create a feeling of time and space in which communication can happen unhurriedly. This means helping the other person relax using unconscious signals such as sitting back, lowering our tone of voice, slowing our delivery.

If good rapport has been established through matching and mirroring, then pacing follows naturally when you initiate it.

Active Listening

When we actively listen to another person they feel heard and valued. We are present in the moment for them. We are both listener and observer and in the space created, we hear the meaning behind the words and pick up many clues that will suggest the psychological stage the other person is at and how we might best help them.

Being Genuine and Congruent

Self-awareness of the non-verbal messages we are giving is also essential. Are we really present? Is what we say and do congruent with what we convey to our client? Do we hide behind a 'professional façade'?

Genuiness requires transparency. We need to be real and honest with our clients. This includes feeling comfortable in ourselves as professional astrologers and in our abilities to interpret charts. We also need to be clear about our limitations and be able to share these if and when appropriate. It's about being truly authentic as a person.

Showing Unconditional Acceptance

This is very important if we are to avoid assumptions and prejudices. Accepting our clients and their charts without judgment is what's most valuable in our work as astrologers. There are charts that may bring out strong positive or negative responses in us, and it is essential that we learn to set these aside before the consultation and work consciously with what is. Our work is not to make friends or alliances but to genuinely help those who come to us, whatever their background and experiences.

Responding with Empathy

This means being able to convey with authenticity our clear and genuine understanding of what our client's feelings and experiences are as well as the meanings they give to these.

It also means being able to sensitively reflect aspects of our client's experience to help them understand aspects of themselves or patterns of behaviour that they have not been aware of.

The Astrological Consultation

Preparing for the Consultation

Contract

Most consultation requests will come to you by telephone or email. Make sure that your prospective client knows about your terms before agreeing to a consultation. These include: the astrological approach that you take, the length of the consultation, the type of consultation (e.g. face-to-face, Skype), your fee and how you want to be paid, arrangements/charges if the consultation is cancelled with less than 24/48 hours in advance, confidentiality issues.

You may also wish to take down details such as the address and telephone number of your contact.

You will need their birth details to draw their charts prior to meeting them. It is always desirable to ask for these in writing so that the onus is on your client to make sure they are correct.

Finally you need to agree a suitable date and time and confirm the venue for the consultation if face-to-face.

Setting the Scene for a Face-to-Face Consultation

Paying attention to the room where you will meet is important. You will want to create an environment that is conducive to the work you do. Ensure that the temperature of the room is adequate, that the chairs are comfortable and positioned in a way that you can make eye contact and that both of you can see the chart(s) clearly. Have glasses of fresh water available, pens, paper and tissues.

During the consultation

Give Space and Responsibility

Giving your client time to define what it is they want from the session (even if you think you already know) will give them an important stake in the work you will be doing together and some responsibility for the process.

Allow for silences. Your own comfort with silence can be used sensitively to help speakers express what they wish to express.

Seek information

Asking a series of questions is not the only way to gain information. Appropriate questions include open questions, which allow for a wide variety of response, e.g. 'How did you get on? How do you feel? What will you do next?' Questions also vary in their difficulty, e.g. the difference between Why? as a question and What? How? Who? Where? and When?

Do not interrupt unless you need clarification. The most appropriate way is to ask for a concrete example of what is meant by a more general point, such as 'Can you be more specific?'

Questions about the process of what occurs as well as the content are often just as important.

Summarise

Summarising and paraphrasing specific points of fact and feeling as well as broader issues or trends will enable you to check your understanding of what was said.

Summarising skills do help in memorising, as does the ability to cope with anxiety about forgetting.

Practices to avoid

1. Psychologising

This implies that you know better than your client what the issues are and you impose your insights and know-how rather than sensitively helping them to make sense of what's happening in their lives.

2. Using Astrological Jargon

As much as possible use simple words for clarity and ease of understanding.

3. Making Assumptions

Assuming that you know what's happening for your client because you have the same aspect pattern in your chart, or you have experienced a similar Pluto transit to the one that the person seeking your help is currently in the midst of.

4. Inappropriate Reassuring

For example, offering reassurances such as 'Everything will be alright', 'Don't you worry about it', 'Everybody goes through a stage like this' that may be dismissive of your client's concern.

5. Moralising and/or Judging

Allowing your words, attitude and/or behaviour to limit the exploration of an issue by expressing a biased position.

6. Over-Eagerness

Trying too hard, concerned to be really good, trying all your tricks and techniques as opposed to simply being there with your client.

The Benefits of an Astrological Consultation

As astrologers, we have a very significant advantage above all others in the helping professions.

"... in cases of difficult diagnosis, I usually get a horoscope in order to have a further point of view from an entirely new angle. I must say that I have found that the astrological data elucidated certain points which I otherwise would have been unable to understand"

Carl Jung, 1947

The aspect pattern, colour, direction and orientation of our clients' birth charts tell us of their unconscious life motivation. At the time of the consultation, the birth chart can also indicate the motivational stage that they're at. The position of the AP by sign, house and aspect is a good indicator. For instance if the AP is transiting over Saturn in Taurus in the 5th house, you might look for and recognise traits associated with fixed motivation in your client's expression and attitude.

Cardinal, Fixed and Mutable Motivational Stages

Clients in the fixed stage may feel blocked, helpless, inactive and passive. Things happen to them. They cannot control fate, their environment or themselves. They feel stuck and powerless to alter the situation they're in. Their feelings may alternate between anger and depression.

Clients in the mutable stage will have some awareness of the part they play in their difficulties. They may already be looking at their conditioning and be questioning how they have arrived in their present situation. They are psychologically uncomfortable and wish to know more of themselves, others and the reasons why. They seek awareness.

Clients in the cardinal phase are ready to take responsibility for what they feel, believe and do. They are ready to make decisions and take control of their lives. They tend to be looking for guidance as to how, when and where to act and though aware of existential fears of life, death, isolation, meaninglessness they accept that they have freedom to take charge of their lives. They can look insightfully at their present circumstances.

Motivation and Locus of Control

Cardinal, fixed and mutable responses can sometimes be seen in people's reactions to problems and life crises. These energies can be expressed appropriately or inappropriately and this seems to correspond to the way people experience their own locus of control, internally or externally respectively.

The locus of control represents the place where a person feels their power centre to be and is a key factor here. If **internal** the person usually feels effective and is effective in their own life. When **external** a person may feel ineffective and helpless, 'their life is not their own', and at the same time they assign their power to something external, like their job, parents, spouse, society.

Cardinality associated with an external locus of control may be seen in such behaviour as immediately looking for something to do to try and change the situation without stopping to look deeper. This urge to act may be an attempt to escape from the situation and the uncomfortable emotions triggered by it. Help is needed to explore the emotions.

A cardinal response associated with an internal locus of control may be one of taking responsibility for decision making and initiating action whilst understanding the deeper need for this change. Here this is the most appropriate response and the client is not running away.

Fixity in association with an external locus of control may produce such behaviour as doing nothing; capitulation. Blocks may be put up and a stubborn inactive stance taken against any transformative agent. A person here may feel stuck and have a fear of losing control.

A fixed response in association with an internal locus of control may be seen in a person who has a commitment to seeing a situation through. They have accepted the situation for the immediate future and know why this is the best approach for them; they are prepared to stick with it. They may learn to accept themselves as they are – "I love myself as I am, there is no need to change." Fixity can deepen understanding, it does not have to block it.

Mutability in association with an external locus of control may result in such behaviour as 'moving around in circles' and 'sitting on the fence'; in short – indecision. This can be a form of non-commitment and again unconscious fears and emotions are often being triggered by the situation.

Mutability in association with an internal locus of control may be seen in a person who has realised that it is they themselves who need to change and not the apparent problem. The way through is on a different level beyond action (cardinality), or acceptance (fixity). With a change in consciousness the situation can be viewed under a new light which may clarify it for the client, or even change it to the point where it is transformed into an opportunity. This internal change can be a point of personal breakthrough.

The process from fixed through mutable to cardinal is often circular and can form an upward spiral. It may flow consistently forward, turn retrograde or be at different phases with different problems.

People often feel they come to us out of necessity. Our role is to show them the possibilities and potentials inherent in their birth charts and to give them choices.

During a consultation, the astrologer takes on board the client's fixed, mutable or cardinal attitude and allocates time accordingly. Clients in the fixed stage will need time to vent their feelings before being receptive to the possibilities and potential shown in their charts.

The astrologer has further specialist knowledge that concerns the quality and quantity of time. Aspects, transits, stress planets and planetary tensions are interpreted as opportunities for transformation and change. We know what type of experiences are available to our clients, their intensity and duration. By sharing with them our understanding of their life's theme and its process, we give them the opportunity to learn about themselves, their qualities, skills, limitations and potential.

What can an Astrological Consultation Offer?

1. Explores client's experience of the chart without making assumptions

2. Uses the chart as a diagnostic tool

3. Identifies problems/issues

4. Gives information relevant to the issue

5. Helps the client to achieve more self-awareness and understanding

6. Explores potential growth. Sensitively done, this can lead to insights.

Some Check Points for Yourself

We hope that by now you will have had considerable experience of working with charts of real people – family, friends etc. We strongly recommend that you observe how you work and develop your own awareness of how you interact with your 'clients'. Note if you:

1. Tolerate silence

2. Interrupt

3. Demonstrate empathy

4. Give advice or solve problems

5. Make assumptions

6. Talk in astrological "jargon"

7. Demonstrate acceptance of your client and their issue

8. Make appropriate use of the chart

9. Listen attentively

10. Inappropriately show off astrological knowledge

Personal Checklist of Preoccupations and Prejudices

Possible preoccupations	Experience	Present in you?
ATTRACTION	You find your client either attractive or unattractive, so you may pay more attention to your own feelings than to what is being said.	
PHYSICAL CONDITION	You may be tired or sick. You may "tune out" some of the things your client is saying.	
CONCERNS	You may be preoccupied with your own problems or worries.	
OVER-EAGERNESS	You are so eager to respond to something that you stop listening.	
SIMILARITY OF PROBLEMS	The client's problem is so similar to one of your own that you start thinking about your own situation.	
PREJUDICE	You may have a prejudice against your client because of: sexual attitude/orientation race/colour religion politics social status, so you pigeon-hole or make unwarranted assumptions.	
DIFFERENCES	The client's experience or life style is so different from your own that communication is impaired, and this is a distraction.	

My Perspective on the Astrological Consultation

by Ghislaine Adams Dip.API

We know that the most important ingredient in any one-to-one interaction is the relationship between the two people involved. Where there is a good rapport between them, the interaction is positive and successful outcomes can be achieved.

Good rapport creates an environment where trust can develop. It is first established through matching and mirroring the other person's body language and voice tone. As an astrologer, I have an early advantage here as I know instantly by looking at the balance of elements in the birth chart whether my client is an intuitive person (fire) who has a sense of what is possible and how things could be; a sensation person (earth) who deals in facts and needs detailed frameworks; a thinking person (air) who can analyse and theorise but shies away from close interactions; or a feeling person (water) who gets tied down by emotions.

This allows me to choose appropriate language to convey my deep understanding of the client's world. As a result, a connection happens between us that allows us to start our journey of exploration from a position of familiarity with the territory. If I only had a client's story to go on, it would not be so easy. Two different clients may express confusion and a loss of direction, but one may be lost at sea without any buoys in sight, while the other may be caught in the middle of a forest, unable to fathom the way out.

The first client (earth) needs a detailed chart and close reference points so that she can work out each tack in turn whilst the other (fire) wants a larger scale map so that she can visualise her position with reference to the whole and work out the best way to proceed. If we believe that we all have our own internal maps and that our world gets disturbed when our map is suddenly altered, then this initial information from the chart already provides the astrologer with a valuable insight into what the problem might be and how to go about rectifying it.

The birth chart is a visual metaphor of a person's psychological make-up. The picture that is created by the aspect structure often reveals the underlying life theme and acts as a stimulus for clients to talk about the world that they inhabit and their experience of it. Their chart's direction and colour give a clue to their general motivation and uncover inner tensions and struggles. At a glance, I can know whether my client's deepest need is to learn about herself and find her own individuality or whether it is to learn about relationships and closeness. Difficulties always arise when we do not face up to life's lessons and ignore our intrinsic needs.

I am also able to predict the type of energy that is prevalent in the chart, i.e. dynamic, fixed or mutable, and whether, with my support, the client will take a proactive approach towards resolving her difficulties or whether she will have a tendency to remain passive and dependent on others to do it for her. I am then better able to select the most appropriate way to help her.

I can also get a sense of what the person is going to bring to the session by looking at the position of the Age Point and the current transits and progressions at the time of the initial contact. I can then reflect on her experience over the years by studying the progression of the Age Point through each house, the conjunctions and oppositions that it has made and the triggering effect it would have had according to the area of life that it touched and the planets to which it applied.

More insights and background information can be gained from the positions of the ego planets, Saturn, Sun and Moon, and the aspects that they may make to each other and to other planets. These positions will show which is the strongest ego planet and tell the client's family model (mother, father, child) and the Transactional Analysis model (parent, adult, child). Other sources of information are provided by the Dynamic Calculations which point out under- or over-forming; the House Chart which gives an indication of the imprint that the environment has had on the individual and the Moon Node Chart to which the roots of the presenting problem can often be traced.

The chart shows a unique imprint of the person's signature. It does not, however, reveal the person's experience. Two people may have a similar chart configuration but their life experience may be very dissimilar. The Age Point transiting Moon opposite Sun may suggest tension between father/parent and child, but it does not tell how this tension manifests.

The chart gives pointers that can be used to gather information and lead the client to explore issues that may otherwise remain overlooked or hidden. The chart also shows potentialities but it does not reveal at what level of awareness the client is functioning at the present time. It is therefore of the utmost importance for me as an astrologer to remind myself that I do not know and to be sensitive and attentive to my client's experience.

Astrology is a wonderful tool to help us see things in a new light and look upon problems and anxieties as potential challenges and opportunities. The use of the natal chart allows us to help clients to get in touch with their own resources, make choices and take responsibility for their own lives. We cannot change our birth chart but we can decide how we want to experience it.

I conclude by quoting Ralph Metzner, a psychologist and psychotherapist who uses astrology in his practice and writes in *Maps of Consciousness*:

> *"Unlike any other personality assessment device, the astrological pattern has an inherent dynamic: the horoscope interpreted by a skilled and practiced astrologer not only provides a synthetic picture of the person's hereditary inclinations and tendencies, but points to latent potentials, suggests directions of needed growth — in short, gives a symbolic map of the process of self-realization."*

(Metzner, 1970).

Recommended Reading

On Becoming a Counsellor—The Basic Guide for Non-Professional Counsellors
Eugene Kennedy and Sara C. Charles
Published by The Crossroad Publishing Company, Newleaf Books 2000

Psychosynthesis: The Elements and Beyond Will Parfitt

What We May Be	Piero Ferrucci
Inevitable Grace	Piero Ferrucci
Inner World of Childhood	Frances G. Wickes
Inner World of Choice	Frances G. Wickes
Transpersonal Psychotherapy	Nigel Wellings &
	Eliz. Wilde McCormick (Eds)
The Gift of Therapy	Irvin D. Yalom
Relating	Liz Greene
Astrological Counselling	Christine Rose
Astrotherapy	Gregory Szanto

Exercise 8.1

1. Consider your present understanding and/or experience of using the birth chart to help others and the benefits that can be gained from this. What might be your limitations in attempting this?

2. What further training or practical experience might you need in order to effectively help people in a consultation?

8.2 Working with the Three Charts

In this section we look at the meaning of the nodal, natal and house charts in astrological psychology and how to use them together to enhance interpretation. We include examples of case studies using the three charts to give an experiential flavour of the process.

Nodal Chart

The nodal chart represents the sum total of past experiences, behaviour patterns and belief systems which we are deeply familiar with. We carry the essence of them within us at the unconscious level. For instance, if we have spent many years, or life times, in positions of authority then this will be deeply ingrained in our unconscious and will form part of our shadow personality. The nodal chart does not specifically identify with any one experience from any previous incarnation.

Natal Chart

The natal chart is the chart that we have been given to work with in this lifetime. It shows a pattern of possibilities that we need to recognise and, to the best of our ability, develop in order to fulfil the potential it symbolises. It has been suggested that we could see it as a link in a chain which joins us both to the past, the nodal chart, and to the future that the environment is drawing us towards, the house chart.

House Chart

The house chart represents the environment that we are born into (family, social class, culture) and shows the opportunities, constraints and challenges that this environment provides us with in order to grow and fulfil our potential (natal chart). It reflects the conditioning we receive as children when we absorb everything the environment presents, without awareness or discrimination. As we get older and learn to use our free will to manage the influence of others, the house chart can be experienced as a resource for us to tap into in order to develop the qualities and abilities that we need to function most effectively and express our highest potential. It can show us aspects of our personality we can work on, which will help in this process of development.

The Ascendant

In the same way as the ascendant in the natal chart is a link with the nodal chart and the past, so also is it a pointer towards the future. Quoting Bruno Huber:

"The AC is a destination board – spelling out the goal of my inner life. We may be unaware of the goal but we struggle towards it – automatically following the path laid down – like a tourist in a National Park – without awareness."

"The AC is both a goal and the Way. It shows the qualities we need to develop if the goal is to be reached."

"As our life develops we tend to develop the qualities of the Rising Sign [sign at the AC] – but it is hard for us to know how to proceed as there are no clues! But the North Node supplies the clues for taking the next step."

The qualities that Bruno refers to are those associated with the esoteric meaning of the ascending sign (see 7.2).

Recommended Reading

The Living Birth Chart, Joyce Hopewell, Chapter 7 "Working with the Three Charts"

Moon Node Astrology, Bruno & Louise Huber, Chapter 5 " Consultation Work Using the Three Horoscopes"

Example 1 – Jenny

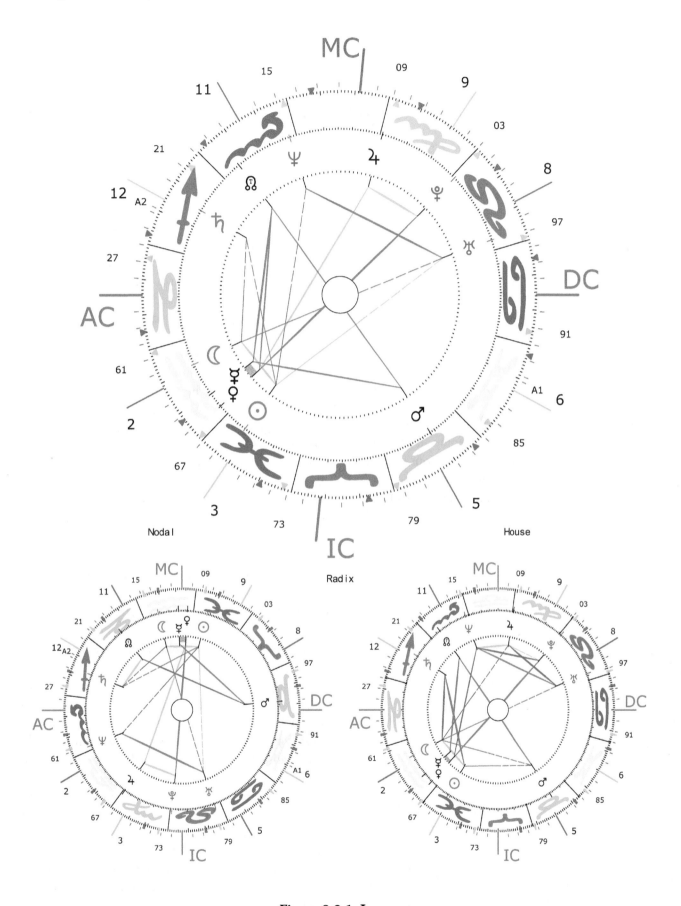

Figure 8.2.1 Jenny
27.02.1957, 02:01, Harare, Zimbabwe

Example 1 - Jenny

This is the chart of a woman who, on the surface, is outward going and active, with a wide range of friends, and sporting, social, artistic interests. As might be expected with a Pisces Sun and a predominantly red/green chart there is a level of sensitivity which can create an over-reaction in a situation if she feels she is being criticised or under-valued.

She is qualified and works as a physiotherapist, cranial sacral therapist, teacher and psychotherapist. She is skilled and respected by her patients, as well as by other medical practitioners in each of these disciplines .

She has her own practice, employs a partner, and now works 3 days a week. You might expect therefore that all would be well but in some ways it is not. If we look beneath the surface and explore a little more deeply we might find that underlying everything there is a feeling of inner insecurity which drives her on to acquire more knowledge, more skills, become even more proficient in what she does. She is always driving herself and says she has no time even though she has now chosen to work a shorter week. Security appears to be a big issue and this probably contributes to her being unable to relax and enjoy all that she has achieved in her life. Dynamic Calculations give a total count of 40, which is a difficult stress number.

If we look at the **natal chart** we see a strong focus on the 2nd house, fixed house and fixed sign. If we look for an intuitive image we might imagine an airplane plunging in a nose dive to earth. Both these pointers might well contribute to her feelings of a need for security and self-protection.

The three ego planets are linked in a small Learning Triangle in both natal and house charts. The Family Model suggests that, at some unconscious level, the child will have grown into adulthood with these links unbroken and therefore without the same freedom to develop her own individuality as would otherwise be the case, because of the fears and guilt which will be associated with breaking this link. Brought up in a family where the mother's own upbringing inhibited the development of her femininity and sexuality, the developing girl child would not have had the role model, or the freedom, which would have allowed her to develop her ability to express herself as a woman. Potential male partners will be judged by the real, or imaginary, perception of the father. An unconscious compensation could drive her to achieve individuality through work and the acquisition of possessions and status.

The nodal axis is in houses 5/11 and relevant to the overall picture. With Mars in Taurus in the 5th house conjunct the South Node you would expect that she would have been comfortable in the intimate relations of the 5th house. But the opposite has been the case and she has tended to live the North Node being content to find physical contact in a safe professional role.

So, what are the origins of these insecurities? What drives her at a deep unconscious level? Reference to the **moon node chart** most significantly shows the Sun and Moon at the top of the chart, and the focus of energy moving from the 2nd to the 9th house. This suggests that Jenny has been familiar with a role as a leader, an individual with authority and, with Saturn in the 12th house, somebody who has been used to having their orders obeyed. Here Mars is in the 7th house and this suggests that authority could have been used in an aggressive way, and this might explain any reluctance or fears experienced with natal Mars in the 5th house.

In the present incarnation, the emphasis of the ego planets changes completely, with the exception of Saturn which, seen in the role of the dominant mother, perhaps contains messages which help to generate the feelings of fear and guilt. Now in the shadow personality there will be a sense of being deposed, or dispossessed, and of having lost everything. Lurking deep in the unconscious such feelings could easily trigger the drive for security in this life, and the need to compensate for the feeling of lost authority and status, through the acquisition of skills and possessions.

Bruno Huber (*Moon Node Astrology*) suggests that where there is a significant shift of house positions between the nodal and natal charts, as in this case, it could take several incarnations before an adjustment can be made.

If we look to the **house chart** can we seek a solution, or at least guidance as to a way forward in this life? The one thing which really stands out is the way in which aspects to 9th house Jupiter have changed, and the way in which this planet has assumed greater significance. Jupiter, at the apex of a little Ear or Eye, is linked to the three transpersonal planets through this and a learning triangle. The intuitive image now suggests something rising out of the plummeting plane and creating a pull away from the 2nd house. All these planets are on low points so integrating these energies will be an inner process.

In addition, the opposition on the 5/11 nodal axis in both natal and house charts suggest the need to reach an understanding of the conflict between morals and ethics which lies on this axis.

Finally we can look at the esoteric meaning of the ascendant, in this case Capricorn. 'Lost am I in Light Supernal, yet on that Light I turn my back'. This suggests a need to balance spiritual isolation, or exclusiveness, with the reality of human existence. Very much a theme of the nodal axis.

Footnote

When Age Point in the natal chart was conjunct Mars, Jenny broke a relationship which she felt was hindering the setting up of her first physiotherapy practice. After that potential partners were rejected on the grounds that they did not fit with Jenny's developing spirituality. It was not until the AP was conjunct Uranus that things began to change. She began to see life from the other side of the 2/8 axis and she started to become more relaxed and more content with what she had. Another relationship started and with AP about to conjunct Pluto as 2002 drew to a close. This signalled a possible further transformation. Jenny got married in 2005 and has at last been able to find a happy balance in her life which has taken away the over-sensitivity of the natal chart and achieved a more balanced and integrated personality

Certainly Jenny has spent many years in self-development and has made enormous progress in her journey from the top of the nodal chart to the bottom of the natal chart.

Example 2 – Jay

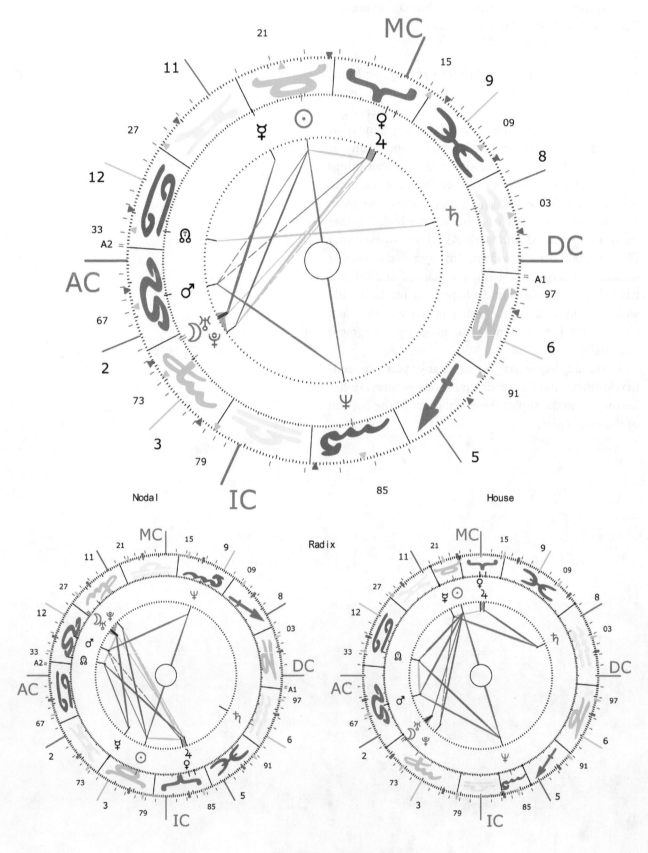

Figure 8.2.2 Jay
02.05.1963, 11:05, Birkenhead, UK

An initial glance at Jay's **natal chart** shows a vertical chart with a ratio of more green and red to blue suggesting an active achiever. The image is of someone reaching upwards but the Saturn/Node quincunx gives the impression that Jay is somehow painfully pierced through, perhaps feeling punctured or pinned down. Although the Sun is intercepted in the 10th house there is an aspect to the Venus/Jupiter conjunction strongly positioned by house and sign on the MC. Mars is the apex of an Efficiency Triangle in the fixed area of the first house and its aspects to the Sun and Jupiter/Venus suggests that it might be a dominant feature in the personality.

When Jay asked for a consultation she said there was no special reason for it but the astrologer noted that her AP was conjunct the first crossing of the two Age Points, just before the DC. She said she had a very humdrum job and felt no special motivation to change this situation.

Jay said she had few memories of her childhood but thought it was 'happy'. Exploring these early years Jay said her mother used to be an infant school teacher and she remembered that she had been very strict. Eventually Jay got in touch with an early memory of being smacked and in her mind's eye she could still see the imprint of her mother's hand on her legs.

These memories stemmed from about the age of 3, when the natal AP was conjunct Mars. Since adaptation and survival are the name of the game at that age an hypothesis was formed that perhaps Jay unconsciously made the decision to shut down this part of her personality at that time. Since Mars might have become the outlet for the energy contained in the intercepted Sun/Neptune opposition was it possible that this accounted for Jay's apparent lack of motivation to do anything with her life?

In conforming to her mother's authority had she retreated to her second house (where her Moon lies) and more or less remained there ever since? She is security orientated, has a strongly protected comfort zone, and in fact is still living at home with her mother. It's almost as though she is still pinned down by that Saturn 'spear'.

If we look at the **moon node chart** is there anything that might suggest that the origins of this inertia lie deep in the unconscious? We notice that the Sun has dramatically changed position from the 3rd house where it was a part of the collective, rising up to the 10th house. This new position will require a huge shift in consciousness that will be hard to handle in one go. The Moon also moved from 11th house to the 2nd house and nodal Saturn, unaspected, is on the cusp of the 6th house.

Saturn in the moon node chart shows where we looked for security. In Jay's case it looks as though she might have become used to a 'nose to the grindstone' kind of existence – perhaps working in the same job that probably stopped her from ever exploring her own potential abilities. So she may have been cut off from having fun and knowing how to enjoy life.

With the Sun in 3rd house, on the mutable cross, it is possible that Jay has a history of working for others, perhaps for her own family with Jupiter/Venus in the 4th house. With Moon and its attendant transpersonal planets in the 11th house there is the suggestion that she might have come from a good family background so is it possible that she was abused in some way? This might explain her fear of using Mars. There are, of course, other possibilities shown in the nodal chart and we can only speculate.

Whatever the 'truth' it will be important for the Moon to make the shift from the heights of the relationship axis to the practicalities of the 2nd house and the possession axis – involved with self-worth, and so on. There seems to be a lesson there somewhere.

So, Jay enters this life with a low sense of self-esteem, self-worth and self-confidence, and a limited view of what she can achieve for herself. We could ask ourselves whether somebody with such a background would find it easy make the most of the energy pattern with which she arrives in this world? And, of course, her mother has, unwittingly, played an important role in reinforcing this unconscious sense of who she is.

Could we use the **house chart** to show a way forward? Here there is quite a strong change in the energy pattern. The chart has a more robust feeling to it, and it has lost some of the sensitivity of the natal chart (more blue, less green).

- Mars becomes a stronger release point for the intercepted Sun/Neptune having lost the one-way aspect from the Sun.

- Saturn is now well integrated into a Learning Triangle with Sun, and with Jupiter/Venus

- The intensity of Pluto is separated from the Moon

- The South Node is, of course still in the 6th house, with its potential burden of taking on the responsibilities of the world, but now the North Node is integrated and more accessible.

So, in practice what does Jay need to do? Leaving any comfort zone needs courage but the house chart says this can be done. Probably the first thing she needs to do is to make an assessment of her strengths and start developing a better sense of self-worth, and this would assist with the development of the Moon in the natal second house.

Jupiter/Venus is a wonderful combination. Alan Oken calls it a 'gift from heaven'. It is aspected to Saturn and, by house position Saturn is the strongest ego planet. So, if she starts to take a pride in herself at a physical level, for example in the way she looks and presents herself to the world, she stands a good chance of lighting up the Jupiter/Venus and making it work for her. Her sense of self-esteem can grow and since self-esteem brings in the Sun it will help in the development of another part of the personality. This could start a process of integration that the house chart suggests is the way forward.

Also integrated in the house chart is the North Node. The nodal axis symbolises a path to follow. In this case the 6/12 existence axis requires Jay to achieve a balance between serving the community in order to have a sense of ego existence, and being able to do this from the soul with an inner sense of self-knowing. At the time of the consultation it seemed possible that Jay has unconsciously chosen to live in isolation in the 12th house and in doing so avoid facing up to the realities of life in the 6th house.

Finally, we can look at the esoteric seed thought of the rising sign, Leo: 'I am That, and That am I', which implies a need for self-knowing, and the ability to be oneself and live life with an inner sense of 'beingness' rather than seek, and satisfy, ego needs from acts performed in the community.

Exercise 8.2

Choosing the charts of someone you know well, write a case study of working with the three charts similar to the examples provided in this section.

8.3 Practical Chart Interpretation

Applying the astrological techniques learned in this book and synthesising them into a chart interpretation is a skill that can be acquired and learned. You have been honing this skill as you worked through the exercises following each section. We hope that you will, by this stage, have been practising your interpretation skills on the charts of people known to you.

In this section we offer:

- Guidelines and suggestions on how to approach chart interpretation and prepare for an astrological consultation
- A detailed example of preparation for a session
- A number of further examples of chart interpretation.

Part 1 – The Approach

Chart interpretation is a skill that can be learned and acquired. The more experience you gain from working with the charts of as many people as possible over a period of time, the more confident and competent you will become.

Working through this book, you have learned many techniques of interpretation. However it is advisable to keep some basic 'first steps' in mind, and to remember the importance of the various stages and ways into the chart.

When interpreting a chart you are looking for a **theme** that will emerge as you apply the techniques that you've learned. Sometimes more than one theme may emerge. When this happens, the emerging themes are likely to relate to, cross refer with, or possibly even conflict with, each other. Human beings are, after all, prone to contradictions!

As the theme or themes unfold, a picture of the **whole person** will start to appear, and you will begin to get a tangible sense of what the person might be like.

Ways into the Chart

The Four Basic Rules

You encountered these in 2.2 and we repeat them here, because of their importance. When first looking at a chart:

1. Use your Senses.

Look at the chart – the whole chart, not at individual parts of it. Get a sense of it. What does it say to you? Allow an image to emerge. This is the first step before moving on to more detailed considerations.

2. Just work with what you have.

Use what is there, what you can see. Don't get side-tracked by using gimmicky calculations, and hopping from one part of the chart to another looking for correlations.

3. Do not confuse Qualities and Quantities.

Qualities relate to planets and the signs.
Quantities relate to the houses, the environment.

For instance Mars is a strong planet qualitatively but also very often quantitatively so far as its effect on the outside world is concerned. Venus is strong also, but in a different way. It has a different quality of strength. However, it rarely has the same quantitative strength as Mars in terms of its effect on the environment.

4. Do not mix up the Levels.

Do not interpret one planet by house and the next by sign, trying to correlate these. For instance do not start relating the Sun sign to the ascendant. One is a sign and the other is a house and they represent different functions of the psyche.

At this stage, we recommend that you re-read Chapter 2.

Checklist of Topics Covered in this Book

The following should be taken into consideration when starting to interpret a chart:

1. Intuitive chart picture/image

2. Chart shaping, motivation, colour balance, direction, coherence, gaps in aspect structure, aspect pattern(s)

3. I/You sidedness, upper/lower hemisphere emphasis, quadrant emphasis, expansion/contraction zone in houses, house intensity curve, axis crosses and polarity

4. Planets: unaspected, blocked-off, intercepted, low point, stress zone, cuspal, strength by sign and house

5. The threefold personality: development and integration of the ego planets, strength of ego planets, aspects from the transpersonal planets, conflict resolution

6. The Family Model

7. Age Progression, current transits of Outer Planets

8. The Moon's nodes and moon node axis, the moon node chart, the crossing points and crossing axis, the ascendant sign

9. The house chart

10. Dynamic Calculations

Dos and Don'ts

- **Do** look for, and work with, themes in the chart as you explore it. A theme or themes may show up in the house and node chart as well, and will relate to what is significant in the natal chart. Use these themes – they are the clues and threads that will help you pull the interpretation together.

- **Don't** describe or list features of the chart without interpreting them. For example, there is little point in stating that someone has a Small Talent Triangle in their chart, that it is an all-blue figure with a dynamic motivation, and is pinned by Moon, Neptune and Saturn without saying what this might suggest, in practical, tangible terms for the person.

- **Do** form hypotheses on how this particular aspect pattern might operate in real life. Speculate and take risks. Play with various ideas of how an aspect pattern, or any other feature of the chart, might be expressed by the person concerned. This is part of the process of interpretation.

- **Do** work with all three charts. They will add important additional dimensions, and will give a rounded and holistic view of the person. Bruno Huber described the node chart as relating to the person's past, the natal chart as relating to their present life situation, and the house chart as relating to the future, in the sense that it contains conditioning that was deemed essential to help us realise our own potential.

- **Do** check that the time of birth is correct before proceeding with your interpretation!

Astrological Consultation in Practice

Preparation

Before an astrological consultation you need to have studied your client's chart so that you can be aware of the issues that might come up during the session. For this it is useful to have a checklist of what to look for, reading the client's chart from the centre outwards and studying what occurs within each of the five concentric circles.

It is helpful to make notes as an *aide memoire* for the first consultation and any subsequent ones. More detailed notes might raise issues of confidentiality, and you would need to seek permission from your client to keep these.

What to look for (initially – this is not a complete list)

1. **The chart image.** This can give an important insights into the person's motivation and psychological make-up. You would, of course, discuss with your client the image or images that you have identified in order to ascertain their relevance.

   Important: Keep your image in mind as you proceed with your notes on the chart. Check its relevance. It may give you some important clues to the overall theme of the chart.

2. **The colours of the aspects.** Are they all present? Is there a preponderance or lack of a colour or colours?

3. **The overall aspect pattern.** Where does it lie? How much of the chart does it cover? How 'busy' is it? Is it mainly linear, triangular or quadrangular? Are patterns complete or fragmented? Are there gaps in the structure?

4. **The distribution of the planets in the hemispheres and quadrants.** Is there a general spread or are some areas of the chart more populated than others?

From these four stages it is possible to see the basic energies involved and the client's type of motivation. Often the same message, or theme, is repeated in a chart and communicated in various ways.

5. **The AC, DC, IC and MC.** These show the individual's orientation to self, others, collective ties and life aspirations. Where is the client coming from? What is her focus? She may be unaware of these tendencies or blocked in some way. Awareness will bring some understanding of the issue(s) as well as clarity as to what can be done and in which area change can take place.

6. **The Age Point.** Its position at the time of the consultation is of prime importance as it will highlight the particular problems that are bringing the client to the session.

   - What is the focus of the house the AP is transiting? Are there obvious issues in this area? Consider the house/sign relationship. Is the AP on the house cusp, balance point, low point or in the stress area of the next house?

   - What planets are involved? These are the pressures of which the client will be most conscious and where the astrologer's knowledge of the time span required towards an abating or resolution of the problem may prove invaluable.

   - Look back on previous aspects made by the Age Point. What is being reactivated? What other aspects, planets, houses, signs were involved?

7. **The Planets.** Unaspected, blocked-off, intercepted, low point, stress zone, cuspal.

8. **The Personality Planets.** Which is the strongest? Is there a serious imbalance in the strengths? are any of them unaspected or blocked-off? How do they relate by aspects? What support do they get from the tool planets? What influence do they get, if any, from the transpersonal planets?

9. **The Family Model.** Who was linked or not, important, distant?

10. **Aspect Figures.** What distinct figures can you identify? Are they connected or disjoint? This could be useful information in contacting the client's various sub-personalities.

11. **The Moon's Nodes.** Study their house position and linkages into the rest of the chart. What are the implications of these for the client's life journey?

This extensive list may appear generalised but the considered study of the individual points will reveal personality potentials that are actualised or dormant.

As we have mentioned before, certain themes or issues will run through the chart and be interlinked. It may be that these interlinkings are the problems as they may relate to conflicts, frictions and tensions.

As well as looking for areas of imbalance and stress it is useful to note the positive attributes of both tensions and harmonies. It is very easy for clients to focus on their problems and our role as astrologers is to be able, when necessary, to reframe how they are experiencing their chart.

Working with the Client

This preparation helps us to have a psychological impression of the person we are about to meet. You have now gathered a huge amount of information from the chart, so take care not to let the consultation simply be an exchange of information or advice.

Start the process by asking sensitive and focused questions that will allow your client to examine the crux of his or her problems and get in touch with their deeper needs.

Follow these with an interpretation of relevant chart features. If your client is acting in accordance with their chart it can be comforting for them to know that they possess these inner conflicts and tensions, and that what they are experiencing is indeed appropriate and correlates to the movement of the age point. This starts to make the client's experience objective and to give them the opportunity to view their problems apart from, and not a part of, themselves. They can begin to perceive their share of the responsibility and the innate tendencies that have shaped their behaviour.

Some clients may live out their early conditioning and be out-of-touch with their natal chart. Others may be stuck in their moon node chart and continue to manifest past patterns that do not match the requirements of this lifetime. Finding out alternative ways of being may be a challenge for them or it may confirm what they already knew unconsciously – that they were out of synch with their true self.

It may be that this is all that your client can cope with in one session. Self-examination can be both tiring and painful and understanding the astrologer's interpretation may also take up a lot of mental and emotional energy. Nevertheless some learning will have taken place and some re-evaluation of themselves, their situation and the significance of their present predicament will be set in train. Frequently clients have no ability to go any further.

Before bringing the session to a close, it is important to ensure that your client feels that their issues have been fully acknowledged and given appropriate focus and that he or she satisfied with the outcomes of the session, whatever these may be. It is also useful to consider what other elements of the birth chart could be looked at in future sessions in order to continue the process of self-discovery and empowerment. If appropriate, another session may be booked.

Reflections on the Consultation Process

After a consultation, it is helpful to spend a few moments reflecting on the process.

Check Points

You may wish to go back to the list of check points we provide in 8.1 and identify the areas you could improve on.

Chart Information

- What information was valuable?

- What was superfluous?

- How far was what you had identified the same as that identified by your client?

- What had you not seen or overlooked?

- What personal challenges did you meet?

- Were you aware of the synastry of your two charts and did it affect the session?

Personal Reactions

- Were you comfortable with how the session proceeded?

- Are you pleased with the way you managed the time available?

- Do you feel that you fully supported your client in his explorations by staying in focus?

- In retrospect, is there anything you would have liked to do differently?

- What did you learn about yourself?.

Part 2 – Practical Examples

In this first example, we reproduce an astrologer's preparatory observations on a chart before seeing a client. The chart and computer data are shown on this and the following page.

Anna

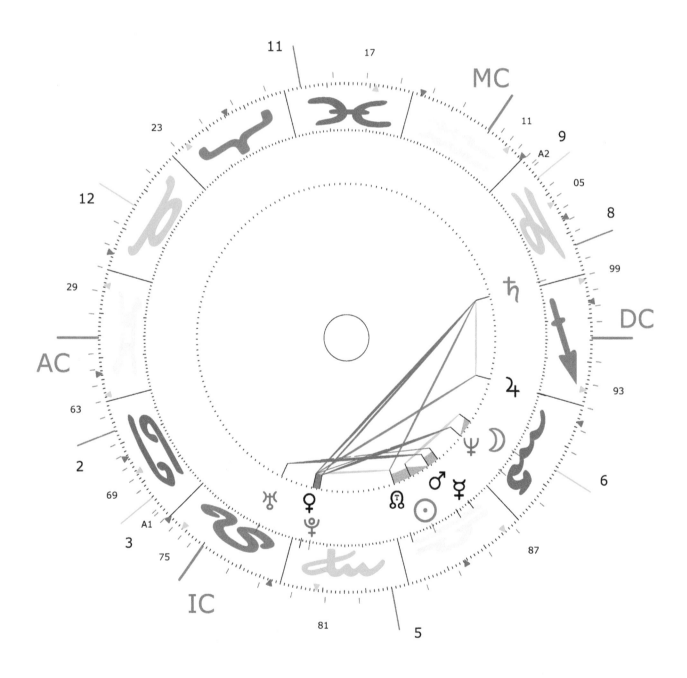

Figure 8.3.1 Anna's Natal Chart

8.3.1 Anna,

04/10/ 1959G	Local Time	20:00:00	LONDON/GBE		☉ ♎ ☽ ♏ ♄ ♑ As ♊
Sunday	Difference	☽- ☉ = 31°	Latitude N 51.30.00	Longitude	W 000.10.00
GMT 20:00:00	Sidereal Time	20:50:22	GMT Diff. = + 0:00:00	Summer Time	00:00

Position

	Radix		House
☉	10°50'28 ♎	5	9°11'36
☽	12°18'21 ♏	5	28°47'56
☿	23°14'48 ♎	5	16°55'23
♀	2°32'10 ♍	4	14°37'17
♂	18°54' 6 ♎	5	14°12'57
♃	29°51'33 ♏	6	15° 0'11
♄	1°10'26 ♑	7	22° 3'50
♅	19°49' 9 ♌	4	6°19' 3
♆	5°44'45 ♏	5	24°42'41
♇	5° 8'50 ♍	4	16°19'35
☊	4° 0'38R ♎	5	4°56'14
As	15°28'42 ♊	1	0° 0' 0
Mc	10° 8'40 ♒	10	0° 0' 0

House Koch

	Cusp	Invert Point	Low Point	House Sign Beginning	
1	15°28'42 ♊	23°37'48 ♊	28°40' 4 ♊	♈ 2°26'17	11
2	6°49' 9 ♋	13°28' 1 ♋	17°34'32 ♋	♉ 21° 7'51	11
3	24°13'23 ♋	0°18'17 ♌	4° 3'47 ♌	♊ 15° 8'17	12
10	10° 8'40 ♒	27°41'35 ♒	8°32'18 ♓	♑ 20°24'48	7
11	26° 5'12 ♓	14°28'38 ♈	25°50'35 ♈	♒ 10°53' 5	9
12	14°14' 0 ♉	26°10' 5 ♉	3°32'38 ♊	♓ 12°57'55	10

Planet in Sign

Strong	Normal	Weak
☉ ☽		♄
	☿ ♀ ♂	♃
	♅ ♆ ♇	

Planet in House

Strong	Normal	Weak
☽	☉	♄
		☿ ♀ ♂ ♃
	♅ ♆	♇

Quanty of Aspects
(*)Good Will Aspects

	Sign	House
Orange	5 (0)	6 (0)
Green	3 (0)	5 (0)
Red	2 (1)	0 (0)
Blue	6 (1)	3 (0)

Age Point Period 6 Years

First IP	18/01/1962	1st Prim.Aspect	02/03/1964 ☍ ♄
First LP	19/06/1963	Crossing Axe	27°36'58 ♋ - ♑
1st Aspect	19/09/1960 △ ♂	A1. 13/01/1973	A2. 12/01/2009

Radix Aspect Grid House

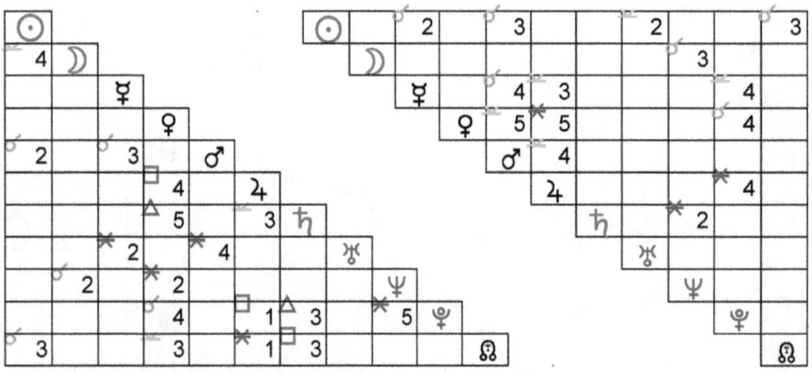

1= Good Will, 2= Unidirectional, 3= Weak, 4= Normal, 5= Strong

Age Point
For 72 Birthdays

0	15°28 ♊	1	19° 2 ♊	2	22°35 ♊
3	26° 8 ♊	4	29°42 ♊	5	3°15 ♋
6	6°49 ♋	7	9°43 ♋	8	12°37 ♋
9	15°31 ♋	10	18°25 ♋	11	21°19 ♋
12	24°13 ♋	13	26°52 ♋	14	29°31 ♋
15	2°11 ♌	16	4°50 ♌	17	7°29 ♌
18	10° 8 ♌	19	17°48 ♌	20	25°27 ♌
21	3° 6 ♍	22	10°46 ♍	23	18°25 ♍
24	26° 5 ♍	25	4° 6 ♎	26	12° 8 ♎
27	20° 9 ♎	28	28°11 ♎	29	6°12 ♏
30	14°14 ♏	31	19°26 ♏	32	24°38 ♏
33	29°51 ♏	34	5° 3 ♐	35	10°16 ♐
36	15°28 ♐	37	19° 2 ♐	38	22°35 ♐
39	26° 8 ♐	40	29°42 ♐	41	3°15 ♑
42	6°49 ♑	43	9°43 ♑	44	12°37 ♑
45	15°31 ♑	46	18°25 ♑	47	21°19 ♑
48	24°13 ♑	49	26°52 ♑	50	29°31 ♑
51	2°11 ♒	52	4°50 ♒	53	7°29 ♒
54	10° 8 ♒	55	17°48 ♒	56	25°27 ♒
57	3° 6 ♓	58	10°46 ♓	59	18°25 ♓
60	26° 5 ♓	61	4° 6 ♈	62	12° 8 ♈
63	20° 9 ♈	64	28°11 ♈	65	6°12 ♉
66	14°14 ♉	67	19°26 ♉	68	24°38 ♉
69	29°51 ♉	70	5° 3 ♊	71	10°16 ♊

House / Sign Difference

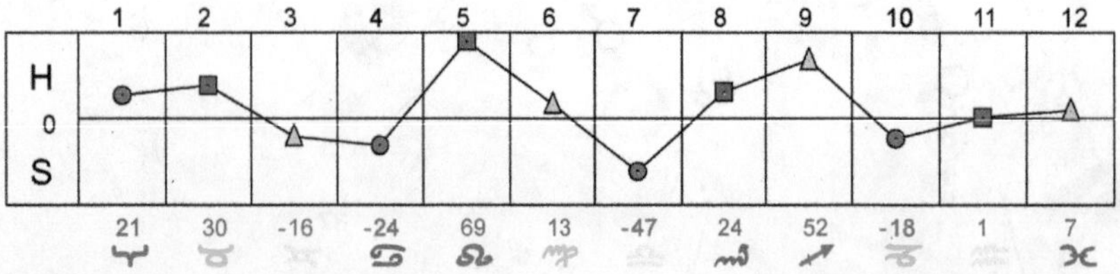
1 2 3 4 5 6 7 8 9 10 11 12
H
0
S
21 30 -16 -24 69 13 -47 24 52 -18 1 7
♈ ♉ ♊ ♋ ♌ ♍ ♎ ♏ ♐ ♑ ♒ ♓

Dynamic Counting

5 547(347)1

	Total	CAR	FIX	MUT	Fire	Earth	Air	Water
		Crosses-Motivation			Elements-Temperament			
Signs	92	44	32	16	8	23	35	26
House	108	23	59	26	50	26	9	23
Diff.	16	-21	27	10	42	3	-26	-3

Midpoints		Date
♅-♀	26°10'40 ♌	07/11/1979
♀-♇	3°50'30 ♍	06/11/1980
♇-☊	19°34'44 ♍	27/11/1982
☊-☉	7°25'33 ♎	03/03/1985
☉-♂	14°52'17 ♎	05/02/1986
♂-☿	21° 4'27 ♎	14/11/1986
☿-♆	29°29'47 ♎	02/12/1987
♆-☽	9° 1'33 ♏	08/02/1989
☽-♃	21° 4'57 ♏	26/01/1991
♃-♄	15°31' 0 ♐	07/10/1995
♄-♅	25°29'48 ♈	03/06/2023

Figure 8.3.2 Chart Data for Anna

Observations on Anna's chart

Before I meet a client I like to set up the birth chart myself so that I can see, and reflect upon, every energy and sub-personality as I draw it in. I feel that I am already establishing a relationship with the person I shall be seeing. Having erected the chart I will study it and then list all the features within it which seem important, regardless of whether or not I am aware of the reason why the person is coming to see me.

I consider that anyone who comes to see me does so for a very specific reason which may be anything from an awakening sense of self to an immediate crisis in their life. The latter is more easily identified from the chart first of all by age progression and then transits, and my aim, should it prove necessary, is to be able to guide the client into talking about what is important to **them**. I consider that a client is not coming to listen to me talking for an hour or so about things of which they are probably already aware – even if only subconsciously. So, for the most part, it is I who listens and the client who talks.

Listening is perhaps the most difficult skill to learn since it is so easy to let the mind pick up the client's words and, whilst you're daydreaming about them, he or she goes on talking and perhaps voices the one vital clue which relates to the heart of the reason for their presence.

Anna's chart is visually striking. The aspect structure is concentrated into the 2nd quadrant of the chart, leaving the central core of the chart, and other areas, very open and potentially vulnerable. The chart image that comes to mind is that of a stick insect, or maybe a praying mantis, poised and sensitive towards the "You" side of the chart. Another image that can be seen is that of a windsurfer – there is wind in the sail so the board has the potential to move very fast. However, it is held down by heavy weights (the conjunctions) attached to the board. I take note of this as these images may well have meaning for Anna, and could give me some additional clues about her life.

In looking at Anna's chart I note that her chart shaping indicates a dynamic motivation, there being triangular figures involved, and that there are two linear extensions only connected to the main structure through conjunctions, so I would expect her to be a flexible person with perhaps the occasional impulse to change direction or do something new. Motivation, as shown by the aspects, has a colour ratio of 2 red: 3 green: 4 blue giving a predominantly fixed mode of action. I note that she lacks red, and has quite a high ratio of green. There is a strong emphasis into the 2nd quadrant – 5th house, instinct, unconscious 'You'. This suggests that relationships of a social nature

may be important to her, particularly since there is more of a horizontal than vertical direction, and **all** planets are on the 'You' side of the chart and, apart from Saturn, below the horizon. I also note that she has two intersecting Small Learning Triangles, which may operate as an incomplete Shield. I would have to check this out with her in our discussion of her chart, to ascertain how she experiences these figures. In addition to this, there is an Ear/Eye figure, but this is not quite complete at the Moon/Neptune conjunction; this makes me aware that she may not always be able to use the figure successfully, and that the information gathered through it might be confused in some way.

Looking further into this I note that the Dynamic Calculations suggest that childhood conditioning (houses) has apparently encouraged cardinal and air energy to be suppressed in favour of fixed and fire energy associated with the 5th house. The North Node is also in the 5th house conjunct the Sun so I feel that the attraction of the 5th house may be a dominant feature of Anna's life.

However, the sign of Libra, including the Sun which is strong by sign, is intercepted in the 5th house and this would make it likely that its Libran energy had not been able to develop and perhaps achieve the sense of balance in relationships which may be sought. This may well bear closer exploration, particularly in the context of the "weighted windsurfer" image I saw, and which may have a direct bearing upon relationships in her life.

The intercepted Sun suggests a weak sense of self esteem and perhaps poor control over life events. With little recognition of 5th house response she may push out into 5th house experiences in a strong, extrovert way – seeking feedback from the environment about herself but probably not getting this – or maybe just not hearing it. This once again picks up a possible theme around relationships.

There is a strong polarity (though one-sided) on the 5/11 axis and I would anticipate that at the age of 23 Anna's life was linked into the pleasures of the social scene, parties and boy friends, perhaps to the exclusion of the development of other more fulfilling interests.

There is a great deal of awareness (green) in the chart and the aspect patterns show a predominance of learning triangles, one direct and one retrograde. However, with the Sun at the bottom, Saturn as the dominant planet in the Family Model, and the only planet above the horizon, it would seem likely that Anna has been brought up as a rather self-indulgent child with little or no understanding, or example set, of how she can develop her life.

Saturn in the 7th house is just past the low point and is not very strong so, whilst Anna's mother may have made attempts to control the 'boy friend scene' these were probably not very successful. Jupiter in square aspect (Mars) to Venus/Pluto would not have been easy to contest and I would also anticipate that Anna is an attractive girl with a great deal of charm and sensitivity, but perhaps willing to be too easily influenced by anyone with whom she has contact.

With a conflict of 5th house versus Libran energy she is probably still in a rather uncertain state of mind about her true role in life and it is possible that Saturn, rather than acting as a protective filter against the 'You' may actually be attracting the wrong kind of person into her life. With strong, perhaps untapped Libran energy, and an intercepted Sun, she may find it difficult to say 'No' to demands made on her by others. She may well be feeling that, not only is she unable to find the 100% ideal relationship for which she is looking, but that her relationships are not providing the security and stability that she seeks at this moment in her life.

Why is she seeking advice from an astrologer? Anna requested this astrological consultation in when she was 23, and if the birth time is correct the Age Point is in the stress area of the 5th house and is in the sign of Virgo. It would seem that not only is she becoming acutely aware of the 5th house conflicts which exist in the field of relationships but that she is also aware that there are likely to be upcoming issues to deal with this in this area, when she enters the 5th house by age progression and makes direct contact with the large number of planets there, including those which are intercepted.

With regard to whether or not her birth time was correct it would be valuable to find out her feelings when the AP was at the LP of the 4th house, and also when it conjoined Uranus at 19 and Venus/Pluto trine Saturn at around 21.

If my assessment of Anna's present situation is correct it is likely to prove helpful, initially, to get her talking about her life in the context of childhood and family, as well as about present relationships. I would seek to find out how well she understands herself and her motivations so far as relationships are concerned and whether work and security are an issue and if so, whether she has found a **creative** way of using the 5th house energy.

She may not recognise that the 'I' side of the chart exists so it may be helpful for her to find out about the intercepted energies of Sun, Mars and Venus and see how these can be developed creatively through inner reflection, rather than defensively – which may be the case at the moment. Exploration of relationships in the context of the 5/11 axis nodes would also be important. Equally relevant might be the fact that the Moon is

the strongest of the ego planets – which are not well balanced in the chart – and it is possible that the use of this energy is being neglected because of over-concern about Saturn issues. It is possible that she has to learn to recognise, and express, her own emotional needs.

There seems to be a big emphasis on relationships and security and that these will be the most likely areas which will prove helpful for Anna to talk about. But I still have to listen to what she is telling me and see how the reality of **her** life fits in with what the birth chart clearly suggests to be the case. I have to be able to talk in the same language as she does.

Summary

I feel that there may be a strong concentration of surface energy on false (fun) values. Inwardly though, Saturn in the 7th house suggests that Anna has, or feels, a need to grow through a more serious approach to life and relationships. Saturn may be attracting the wrong sort of partners so that she can blame them for her own avoidance of the need to understand herself and grow at a deep, serious, inner level. The dangers of dependency (concentration in the 5th house) and awareness of the vulnerability indicated by the open nature of the chart are avoided by not having to face up to them.

So the chart suggests that there is a need to understand herself and to consciously look at the way she is currently living her life. Then have the courage to develop relationships which are founded on her own emotional needs rather than on those of others (Moon), and thus open the way to inner integration. This is my assessment of the chart and of the stage which Anna may have reached at the moment. However, I have to be careful not to be dogmatic or judgmental or pronounce solutions. All that I can do is to give her the opportunity to talk without presuming that the wisdom is in me because, in fact, wisdom exists in each and every individual.

Further Examples of Chart Interpretation

The following charts and interpretations belong to real people who sought the help of astrological consultants who, in these interpretations, are sharing their experiences of working with astrological psychology.

Susannah

Sun	27.48 VI
Moon	13.57 GE
Mercury	13.49 VI
Venus	12.00 SC
Mars	11.26 VI
Jupiter	6.07 SC
MC	17.50 GE
Saturn	22.22 TA
Uranus	8.27 LI
Neptune	28.36 SC
Pluto	27.14 VI
T. Node	2.32 PI
AC	20.32.VI
2	19.16 LI
3	17.48 SC
5	22.55 CP
6	21.58 AQ

Figure 8.3.3 Chart Data for Susannah

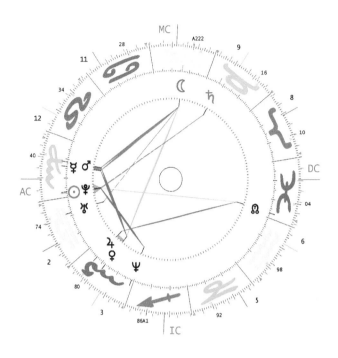

Figure 8.3.4 Susannah's Natal Chart

Specific significators have not been stressed in this interpretation as these are quite easily found and are, in this example, best left to the student to use his or her own knowledge and skill.

The astrologer who wrote this says, "When I set up Susannah's chart my initial look at it showed up the following points of interest:

Aspects

1. Either too much blue, or too little red, suggesting blue/green motivation;

2. A dynamic and linear aspect structure with only one complete learning pattern;

3. An emphasis on the 'I' side of the chart with an open, and potentially vulnerable area on the 'You' side.

4. An emphasis on the first quadrant;

5. My symbolic image is of an open mouth which is passively receptive rather than active.

I made no specific interpretation of the above other than to hypothesise that Susannah might be somewhat placid, perhaps withdrawn, though with bursts of impulsive energy.

Planets

6. Moon highest in the chart and the only planet integrated into an aspect pattern;

7. Saturn also high in the chart and the only planet truly on the 'You' side;

8. Three interesting conjunctions, two of which (Sun/Pluto & Mars/Mercury) are potentially assertive;

9. Three planets not very integrated;

10. South Node in the 12th house.

Taking account of all the above I began to envisage two possibilities. The first was that here was someone who could be quite demanding and assertive in getting what she wanted, making use of the two conjunctions near the AC, and the impulsive energies of the first quadrant planets, thus creating her own defence against any vulnerability experienced through the open area on the 'You' side, or through the Moon and Saturn alone at the top of the chart.

However, if I paid attention to my symbolic image and took account of other factors such as the Moon in a separate aspect pattern from Sun and Saturn, and the placing of the south Node in the 12th house I began to wonder whether Susannah had had a disturbed childhood and was really quite shy and unassertive, with a great deal of repressed energy. There appears to be no great difference in the strengths of the ego planets. Saturn seems to be strongest by house and could have acted as some kind of defence mechanism for her. I felt that the Moon might be a strong influence and, since this is both the child in the family model as well as the inner child in the adult, it might mean that she has seen, or does still see herself as a child in need of nurturing and protection. The Sun is potentially very strong but tucked away in the recesses of the 'I' side.

Learning Triangle

The hypothesis would suggest that she was living principally in the learning triangle, responding via the Moon/Venus quincunx, and occasionally showing outbursts of feelings. I viewed the dynamic calculations and low points with caution because I didn't know how accurate the birth time might be. However, I noted that Jupiter might be on a low point and that both cardinal motivation and fire temperament had a low value by sign but high by house giving a high plus total and suggesting considerable environmental expectations in the context of action. I also noted that the reverse was the case as far as fixed motivation and earth temperament were concerned suggesting qualities of practicality and doggedness which she might have felt were not really appreciated. The overall stress total is a low 4 and this might emphasise the possibility of a rather withdrawn individual with no great incentive to 'perform', other than to meet the needs of the Moon at the top of the chart.

Susannah is 23 years of age and I didn't know why she was coming to see me. Her chart showed the age point in Capricorn, beginning its upward climb to the 5th house cusp and it could therefore be imagined that perhaps she was sensing the departure from the security of the home environment and childhood, and the inevitable progress into that area of life when it becomes necessary to find oneself in the outside world. This could be creating either conscious or unconscious stress if my second hypothesis was correct. In any case, her age point at 15° Capricorn is making approximate blue or green aspects to all the planets in the learning triangle – perhaps focussing attention on these parts of herself – and maybe on their limitations

When I met Susannah she was neatly dressed, good looking and somewhat reserved. I talked a while about the meaning of the birth chart and how it can be used in a positive way. She told me that she had graduated from university and that on completion she was offered a job in the personnel department which she's enjoyed but, with a limited budget, the university had only been able to employ her for 6 months and she was now wondering what to do next. There were various choices open to her but she had so far not been able to make any decision. She was visiting home briefly before returning to her university town where she had been living for the past 4 years.

Her parents separated when she was 13 and her father had left home. As a young child she experienced her father as being a powerful man and says she was quite afraid of him. She isn't any longer and is able to talk with him about the breakdown of the family. Whilst she finds she cannot yet forgive him, she is able to accept what happened. The Moon remains in a separate aspect pattern from the Sun in the house chart.

Fear of self-assertion

I noticed that Susannah blushes very easily and she said that whilst she wants to know what decision to make about her future, she feels that one of her main difficulties is her lack of self-confidence. She said that she allows herself to be taken advantage of, and she tends to respond to the demands of others rather than meeting her own needs, though she does very occasionally lose her temper. She wasn't sure what she got out of this behaviour but it was easier to live life like this than to assert herself. Her fear of asserting herself, or expressing her own ideas, was because she felt it might result in an argument and she would probably lose. She said that her ex-boyfriend had found it hard to cope with her passivity in dealing with others. We briefly explored how she might experience the South Node in the 12th house and the way in which it is more comfortable and secure to live in this area of life than face up to the nitty-gritties of life.

We talked about her emotional needs and how she attempted to get these met – for instance she says she still sees herself as a girl rather than a young woman – and by continuing this role of child whether it makes it easier for her to get emotional support, or not to have to take responsibility for herself. When I work through a chart with a client I have no fixed way of doing this, going along with the client's needs rather than dictating them. In this case we looked at each of the planets in turn, seeing them as though they were sub-personalities, each one symbolising a powerful inner drive and each wanting to realise its full potential. I sometimes use analogies with a client to help them understand the process of growth more easily, for instance talking about a small acorn as containing all that is required to create an immense oak tree. For me, astrology is all to do with self-awareness and growth.

We looked at the potential strengths of the 4 planets in Virgo, especially the Sun/Pluto conjunction, and we discussed various exercises which she might do to help develop will and to achieve conscious clarity which would make choices and decisions easier. We also examined ways of helping the energies of the Mercury/Mars conjunction grow, ideas such as keeping a journal in which she can record experiences, how she felt about them and how she resolved them. This might also help her to see more clearly how she was developing the power of her will. We talked about the benefits which she might get from joining in with some kind of growth or self awareness group.

I was aware that I would be unlikely to see Susannah again, or if I did, it would not be for months, so I felt it was important to spend our time together talking principally about areas of her life which might benefit from having a spotlight shone on them. We reached these areas gradually and sensitively, and only after exploring how life is for Susannah at this moment in time. For instance, although I had formed hypotheses before meeting her it was she who told me about her lack of self-confidence and about her difficulties in relating to others. And I always search for, and stress, positive resolutions to any life experiences that might be experienced as creating difficulties."

Sandra

"There has to be more to life than this… I want to give something back – the time has come when I want to put something back in return for all I've gained so far."

The astrological consultant who saw Sandra as a client writes, "These words were spoken by Sandra, who came to see me for a consultation. A pleasant, friendly woman, Sandra told me on the phone prior to our meeting that she was seeking help, guidance and a deeper understanding of her current situation. She told me that she had been off work for four months, and was recovering from an operation on her feet. The following comments are based upon the notes I made prior to seeing Sandra.

When I drew up her chart the first thing that struck me was the image I could see. Poised in the centre of the chart was what looked like a trapeze artist in full flight, with arms and legs outstretched and cape flying out behind. This made me think also of Superman – in Sandra's case Superwoman – and I wondered if she flew through life, as if through the air, appearing to cope with everything admirably, or being expected to?

I noticed, too, the excessive amount of red in her chart (she has 8 red, 3 green and 5 blue aspects) and wondered if she was super-active, always on the go. Taking into consideration the 'You' sided emphasis of the chart and the heavily tenanted 3rd quadrant, together with the Sun/Uranus conjunction on the DC at the apex of the Efficiency Triangle plus the chart's dynamic shaping, I began to build up a picture of someone who was likely to devote a lot of time and energy to the needs of others, yet was regarded by many who met her as someone who might be 'different', maybe erratic or slightly eccentric even, in the way she made or maintained contact with the 'You'.

I was aware of unaspected Venus on the 5th house cusp and expected that something about the way she related to people, using the energies of this planet, would come up in our discussion. I wondered if we might find that her own image and sense of herself as a woman had been shaped and moulded by external expectations and social pressures of what she, as a woman, should be like, rather than her already having a sense of her own womanliness which came from inside. If this was so, and I was right, this could be an issue that might come up during the session.

Her Moon, I noticed, was weak by sign in Leo, intercepted, and just after the 8th house low point. In terms of ego planet strength, it rated as weakest, with

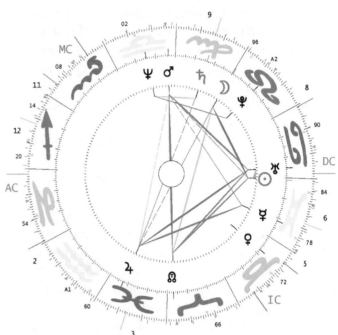

Figure 8.3.5 Sandra's Natal Chart

Sun strongest. I expected that there might be an inner conflict at work for Sandra as she sought to balance out the need to have her feeling/emotional needs recognised, and to begin to acknowledge the existence of her inner child against the potential strength of her Sun, which would assist her in being strong and coping with her life with comparative confidence, and perhaps pushiness as her Sun is in the shadow of the DC.

Considering what she had already told me about her operation and period of recuperation which had sparked off an urge to understand what was going on in her life, I looked at her Age Point (AP). At the time of our meeting, she was 45, with her AP in the 8th house, approaching the low point (LP). LP 8 is regarded as the turning point of the whole chart, the real 'big' LP experience where we may be offered life changing opportunities.

As well as her AP approaching LP8, it had made a recent conjunction with Pluto, and was approaching conjunction with Moon. Approaching the LP, and between Pluto and Moon, suggested to me that there was likely to be something much deeper going on here for Sandra, and my hypothesis included major life changes in the area of how she expressed her feelings, and asked for what she wanted and needed emotionally. I wondered if, up to now, she was able to ask for a hug either to comfort her when she needed this or when she needed to be recognised as a woman.

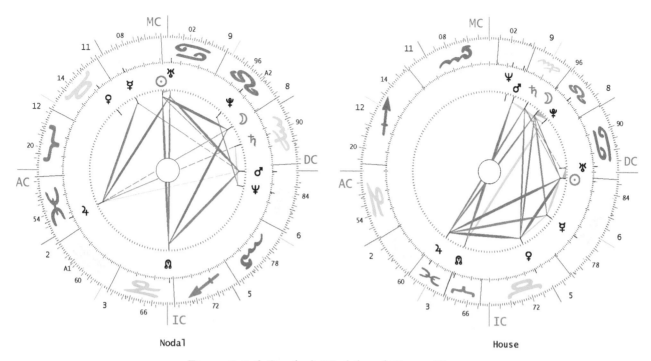

Nodal

House

Figure 8.3.6 Sandra's Nodal and House Charts

As I had also drawn up her moon node and house charts, I looked first at the nodal chart, and discovered that the AP on both natal and nodal charts was crossing for the second time. The first time had been between the ages of 8 and 9 years, when her natal AP was opposite Pluto. Now, in her nodal chart, her AP was conjunct Pluto, echoing the conjunction of this planet in the natal chart some 4 months previously, when she had her operation. This, together with the second intersection of the AP, added strength and depth to what she was likely to be experiencing in her life right now.

Her house chart showed quite a dramatic change in shaping; gone was the dynamic motivation of the natal chart, as the house chart yielded a firm, fixed structure, complete with a Cradle formation oriented towards the 2nd quadrant. The message here, I thought, might well have been "Stay where you're safe", and I expected that there would be some conflict between what she was feeling and experiencing right now, and how she felt she ought to behave and respond.

The Session

What follows is an account of our session together. When Sandra came to see me, she confessed to having little or no knowledge of astrology, but said she was very interested. I therefore began our session by explaining to her the component parts of her chart, as this was recorded, along with the rest of the session. Sandra will be able to play this back and listen to what

was said. Although unfamiliar with astrology, she noticed straight away how red her chart appeared, and this was a good starting point from which to open up our discussion.

Sandra is indeed a very active lady – or would like to be – her period of recuperation has stunted her activities and she is feeling tied down, frustrated, and unable to relax and 'be' in the blue in her chart. She told me that she enjoyed running and active sporting activities. Since she has been off sick she has used her red energy to clean the house, even when this is not really needed, and now simply cannot see the point of excessive cleaning. She is currently using workout videos at home to keep fit and work off excessive energy, but cannot do any standing exercises because of her feet. Early on in the session she questioned the futility of housework, cleaning and doing what she had always done (keeping the home smart for her family). At this stage, she was giving out clues and hints about her underlying reasons for coming to see me.

Our discussion covered her dynamic motivation, the Efficiency Triangle with its apex on the DC, the Sun/Uranus conjunction there and her strongly 'You' sided chart, and she told me that other people did find her ideas a bit strange. The example she gave was at work, where she has devised some games which involve everyone in her department and include scoring points via the movement of pictures and photographs of work colleagues from her notice board to another, rival notice board. She has devised these games to avoid dissent amongst fellow workers and talking about the boss behind backs. She said that people working together, both in work and in the world, is very important to her.

She told me she has a lot of energy and doesn't know what to do with it, and spoke the words quoted earlier. Being at home, unable to be physically active in the way she is used to, had precipitated her current crisis. She is strongly aware of changes taking place within herself – she is no longer satisfied with being who and what she has been for the past 25 years, yet is uncertain of what it is that she wants. This urge to change began when her feet were operated upon and shortly after her AP was conjunct Pluto. She said that her husband has told her she is not the person she used to be.

We moved on to her intercepted Moon. The issues with this revolve around feeling dissatisfied about how her emotional needs go unrecognised within her family, who assume she will be able to cope, mainly because she never asks for help or support, or if, on a rare occasion she does, she is not heard. Her Capricorn AC may encourage her to keep everything under control, whilst her Leo Moon is hungry for the care, nurturing and attention which she finds so difficult to ask for. I did not explore her Family Model in great depth, although I learned from Sandra that she was closest to her father (Moon sextile Sun) and that her mother disciplined her and her four sisters quite firmly (Saturn at top of chart). What was interesting was her response when I referred to her upbringing and conditioning. She said she felt "reined in" by her upbringing and was encouraged never to break out, but to stay safe. So another potential area of conflict emerged in her current situation as she lives close to her family and sees them often.

Next Step

I asked Sandra to close her eyes and find an image which would express how she thought other people saw her and would expect her to be. Her response was that the person she got an image for was so familiar, and yet there was something about her that people didn't really know at all. I then asked her to allow another image to emerge which was of herself as she would like to be. She found herself walking alone on a beach with the wind blowing in her face and on her hair – the essence of this, for her, was freedom, and this is what she feels she wants right now.

In the time we had together, Sandra covered a lot of ground and found confirmation for what she is currently feeling inside, as reflected in her chart. I have no doubt that Sandra is at a crossroads, and am reminded of the Chinese proverb, "Crisis is danger and opportunity". Sandra said she will come and see me again, but in the meantime, she has decided that her "next step" (on her painful but recovering feet) will be to take a trip to the coast for that walk along the beach on her own, experiencing some of the freedom she seeks as she moves through this period of her life which for her is about danger and opportunity, transformation and change.

Alf

(19/4/1930 23:20 [-1 hour] 53N08 0E14)

This was written by an astrologer as a chart study. It is included to gives additional insights into the process of applying the astrological techniques covered in this book. You are encouraged to set up the chart for yourself to refer to as you read this.

Alf was born in 1930, the son of a Lincolnshire couple, and grew up against the background of the bleak fenland landscape and the depression. When Alf was nearly three, his father died, leaving mother and child to support and nurture each other through the hard times of the 1930's on a pension of fifteen shillings (75 pence) a week.

The Moon/Saturn conjunction in the 2nd house, from which the whole chart appears to spring, is a graphic example of the close and binding relationship which developed between mother and son. They were close and supportive through necessity: on fifteen shillings a week in the thirties the main aim in life was to survive.

Saturn is strong by both sign and house. In cautious but reliable Capricorn, it is placed on the balance point of the 2nd house, making the most of resources available and turning them to best advantage. The opposition from Pluto to Moon/Saturn on the 2/8 possession axis indicates tension in this area of life, together with an extreme need to hold one's head up high and be respectable in the eyes of society. Speaking of his early childhood, Alf describes life as "possible because income financed only a part of the cost of living". They lived in "a partial money economy –

the rest was self-help, charity, making do and doing without", a sharply remembered experience of this Moon/Saturn opposition Pluto on 2/8.

Although survival and making ends meet were all-important during childhood, with a strong 2nd quadrant emphasis, Alf grew up with a keen awareness of how to behave and fit into his world. Much of this awareness will have stemmed again from his mother, herself a devout Salvationist. Despite the lack of money to go out and literally broaden horizons further than the surrounding fens (hard on a DC Jupiter!), and a dearth of reading material more stimulating than old copies of the *War Cry*, Alf's high proportion of green aspects, together with the Search figure and Learning Triangle, were drawn upon to ensure his place at the local grammar school. A look at his house chart, full of learning triangles, confirms the encouragement he received from the environment to learn, absorb knowledge, skills and information.

The dynamic/linear motivation of his natal chart contrasts sharply with the fixed shaping of the house chart; mother wanted him to be an officer in the Salvation Army (as solid and reliable as her, the 2nd house Saturn in Capricorn). Alf had other ideas and went to university to study economics, continuing the 2/8 theme. It is interesting to note the Sun conjunct the North Node in a separate linear aspect structure. Weak by sign, and lacking red aspects, it appears to be thrust out into the world through the 5th house of creativity and often impress behaviour with the

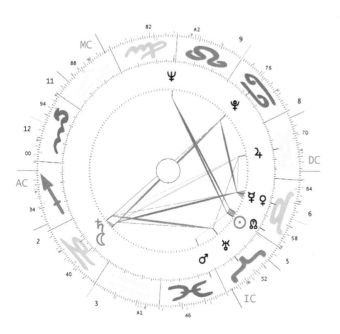

Figure 8.3.7 Alf's Natal Chart

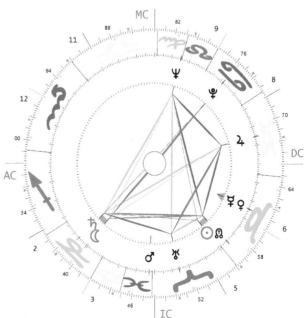

Figure 8.3.8 Alf's House Chart

"You". Intercepted Neptune, the highest planet in the chart, finds expression for its creative imagination through the Sun and, in terms of the Family Model, its detachment from the main aspect structure symbolises the father who was "lost" when Alf was three.

Alf had no male role model as he grew up; his mother was a respectable widow, and did not remarry. Yet gifts of food from men who served in the Great War with his father were sometimes donated to alleviate need. Alf has no memory of his father; he is a figure both unfamiliar and unknown, indicated on one level by the Sun conjunct the North Node. In recent years Alf has tried to discover more about his father and the part he played in the 1914-18 war. As an employee of the BBC, Alf came across some old film footage taken in the trenches, and believes that one of the soldiers filmed was his father. A still of this shot is framed and on display in his home.

Meet Alf and you will find a warm, friendly, easy going person who likes to chat and strike up new friendships, manifesting his Jupiter in Gemini in 7th, and close to the DC in this very "You" sided chart. Alf enjoys swapping travel stories and experiences. In the course of his employment with the BBC he travelled extensively, meeting people of many different nationalities. On a personal level he is a seasoned caravan camper abroad, and his Venus (sense of taste) in Taurus takes great delight in eating and drinking the dishes and wines of the countries he visits, collecting the recipes and trying them out when he gets back home.

Since taking early retirement he has been activating his Mercury conjunct Venus by writing a series of articles on dishes he has tasted abroad, and through this is connecting with the essential creativity of his 5th house Sun. Integrating that Sun, the sense of "I" and will, is something that Alf continues to work on. A rough version of an article he is writing will be slipped through my door with "What do you think of this?" scrawled on it. The Sun needs feedback, and to know that it's as OK as the safe and secure Moon/Saturn in 2nd.

Now in the 11th house by Age Progression, Alf is approaching the balance point, a change of sign, and his AP opposite the Sun. Following a period of readjustment after his early retirement, he is writing articles for various magazines, and sometimes having them published. Rather than be discouraged when he receives a rejection, he is able to bounce back with Aries Sun energy and enthusiasm, and keep going. He recently recorded an item, written by himself, for Radio 4, on his experiences of childhood life in the Fens in the thirties. As an astrologer using the techniques I've learned in the Huber School, I am fascinated to see how his chart reflects this early experience so accurately.

At 25 his AP was conjunct his Sun, and it was then that he left university, started his first job in teaching, and married – a period of settling down as the AP entered Taurus. As his AP moves round to oppose his Sun perhaps he will experience a greater sense of himself now that he has found hitherto undiscovered ways of expressing his creativity in a manner that he truly enjoys.

Conclusion

Exercise 8.3 and the Consolidation Exercise on the following pages encourage you to reflect on what you have learned while going through the process offered by this book. You now know a fair bit about astrological psychology and should have a fair idea of how it can help both yourself and others. This is really the starting point for you to become fully proficient, which can only come with further practice and real experience.

Certainly, if you intend to work with others, you should consider carefully whether you have the necessary training in counselling skills and working with people.

If you do choose to follow a consulting or counselling route, it is particularly important that you bear in mind the following key points from the Code of Ethics originated by Bruno Huber, which all practitioners of astrological psychology consider to be of the utmost importance.

Code of Ethics

- We identify ourselves with the general declaration of human rights: "All human beings are to be allowed equal rights and liberties, are born equal in rights and dignity, are endowed with reason and conscience and should meet each other in the spirit of brotherhood…"

- We regard astrology exclusively as a diagnostic tool, with which we can recognise differences in character, problems of the human psyche and of psychological-spiritual development. Thus, astrological knowledge should above all be used to gain self-knowledge and as therapeutic help, as well as a means for solving conflicts – and not for a prediction of the future.

- Astrological psychology combines the astrological knowledge of the past with modern psychological insights. It is capable of explaining a person's subjective attitude and its cause by revealing his/her inherent motivations and the conditioning affecting them. As astrological-psychological counsellor or teacher must have solid psychological knowledge in order to be able to fully grasp the problems of another person.

- The basic concept of astrological psychology is based on the understanding of man as a whole; he has a psyche which is linked with the environment, but he is also a spiritual entity (individuality) who can be responsible for itself. With this basic concept it is impossible to consider or treat man as predetermined or like a computer.

- We take as a precept the originality of the human individual and therefore regard uniform thinking only valid within the context of the subjective, single being.

- The only acceptable goal of the astrological-psychological consultant must be to increase the freedom of their clients.

We wish you well in your further use of this gilt edged method! Do stay in touch via the Astrological Psychology Association and the website www.astrologicalpsychology.org.

Exercise 8.3

1. Please refer back to the checklist of topics covered in this book, provided in "Astrological Consultation in Practice" on page 265. Make notes on each of the topics as it applies to your own charts.

2. Give yourself plenty of time to consider what your findings mean for you and write your thoughts down. The following questions aim to help your focus:

   • What are your main strengths? How much do you really value and admire these?

   • How comfortable are you about your natural mode of operation?

   • What do you need to do to achieve your optimum well-being? What is holding you back?

   • Are there any current issues arising that need your attention? Make a list if necessary.

   • Are you aware of any patterns of behaviour learned from your early environment (family/schooling/community etc) that do not serve you well? Any personal resources/strengths/skills that you gained from that same environment?

   • Can you identify a specific quality that, if developed, would improve your life?

3. One of the aims of Astrological Psychology is to increase self-awareness and thus facilitate personal growth. What have you learned from studying this course which you feel is going to be of most help to you in furthering your own personal development?

Final Consolidation Exercise

This is the last of the additional exercises at the end of alternate chapters, encouraging you to consolidate your learning.

1. You have already considered Sophie's natal and house charts in earlier Consolidation Exercises, most recently on page 217. Now draw up/ print Sophie's three charts for yourself.

2. Bearing in mind what has been covered in Chapters 7-8, reflect on what further understanding you have gained about her inner and outer worlds.

3. Assess the relative strengths of Sophie's Sun, Moon and Saturn. What practical suggestions might you give her to help her begin to develop and appropriately integrate these Ego planets?

4. Imagine that Sophie is coming to you for a consultation. Consider how you might prepare the physical space and yourself psychologically for this encounter. Take time to reflect on what her current needs or concerns may be and how you might respond, and also think about what general issues, conflicts or difficulties she could bring to the session.

5. Taking into account what you have learned about the Nodal Axis, Ascending Sign and Moon Node chart, think about how you might help Sophie gain a greater understanding of herself in the context of her ongoing personal development and life path.

Bibliography

The following covers recommended books and complementary reading.

Astrological Psychology

The following books will be found most helpful at various stages of your study, as indicated:

Chapter 1

The Cosmic Egg Timer by Joyce Hopewell & Richard Llewellyn *(introductory overview - strongly recommended)*

Chapter 2

Aspect Pattern Astrology by Bruno, Louise & Michael Huber *(vital book)*

Aspect Patterns in Colour by Joyce Hopewell *(valuable reference)*

Chapter 2 and all following Chapters

The Living Birth Chart by Joyce Hopewell (strongly recommended as a companion workbook)

Chapter 3

The Planets and their Psychological Meaning by Bruno & Louise Huber

Chapter 4

The Astrological Houses by Bruno & Louise Huber *(vital book)*

Chapter 5

Astrological Psychosynthesis by Bruno Huber

Chapter 6

LifeClock by Bruno & Louise Huber

Chapter 7

Moon Node Astrology by Bruno & Louise Huber

Transformation: Astrology as a Spiritual Path by Bruno & Louise Huber

Reflections and Meditations on the Signs of the Zodiac by Louise Huber

Astrology/Psychology

You are encouraged to read as widely as possible. The following titles are particularly recommended:

Astrology, Psychology and the Four Elements by Stephen Arroyo

Astrology, Karma & Transformation by Stephen Arroyo

Archetypes of the Zodiac by Kathleen Burt

The Astrology of Fate by Liz Greene

Saturn: A New Look at an Old Devil by Liz Greene

Barriers & Boundaries by Liz Greene

The Art of Stealing Fire by Liz Greene

Dynamics of the Unconscious by Liz Greene & Howard Sasportas

The Development of the Personality by Liz Greene & Howard Sasportas

Astrotherapy by Gregory Szanto

The Marriage of Heaven and Earth by Gregory Szanto

The Astrological Houses by Dane Rudhyar

The Elements of House Division by Ralph William Holden

The Astrology of Transformation by Dane Rudhyar

An Astrological Tryptich—the Illumined Road by Dane Rudhyar

Wisdom in the Stars by Joan Hodgson

Psychosynthesis

Good introductions:

Psychosynthesis: The Elements and Beyond by Will Parfitt

What We May Be by Piero Ferrucci

Other general psychosynthesis titles:

Psychosynthesis – A Psychology of the Spirit by John Firman & Ann Gila

A Psychology with a Soul by Jean Hardy

Discover your Subpersonalities by John Rowan

Our Inner Actors – the Theory and Application of Subpersonality Work in Psychosynthesis by Dr Margaret Rueffler

Esoteric

The Seven Rays Made Visual by Helen S. Burmester

Transpersonal Astrology by Errol Weiner

Astrology, the Sacred Science by Joan Hodgson

Astrology and the Seven Rays by Bruno & Louise Huber

Index

CPSIA information can be obtained
at www.ICGtesting.com
Printed in the USA
LVHW022135210723
753108LV00010B/307